ENCYCLOPEDIA OF MICROCOMPUTERS

VOLUME 6

ENCYCLOPEDIA OF MICROCOMPUTERS

EXECUTIVE EDITORS

Allen Kent   *James G. Williams*

UNIVERSITY OF PITTSBURGH
PITTSBURGH, PENNSYLVANIA

ADMINISTRATIVE EDITORS

Rosalind Kent   *Carolyn M. Hall*

PITTSBURGH, PENNSYLVANIA

VOLUME 6

Electronic Dictionaries in Machine Translation to Evaluation of Software: Microsoft Word Version 4.0

CRC Press
Taylor & Francis Group
Boca Raton London New York

CRC Press is an imprint of the
Taylor & Francis Group, an **informa** business

CRC Press
Taylor & Francis Group
6000 Broken Sound Parkway NW, Suite 300
Boca Raton, FL 33487-2742

© 1990 by Taylor & Francis Group, LLC
CRC Press is an imprint of Taylor & Francis Group, an Informa business

First issued in paperback 2019

No claim to original U.S. Government works

ISBN 13: 978-0-367-45601-6 (pbk)
ISBN 13: 978-0-8247-2705-5 (hbk)

Visit the Taylor & Francis Web site at
http://www.taylorandfrancis.com

and the CRC Press Web site at
http://www.crcpress.com

CONTENTS OF VOLUME 6

CONTRIBUTORS TO VOLUME 6

STUART R. BALL,   Principal Engineer, BTI Systems, Inc. Oklahoma City, Oklahoma: *EPROM*

MICHAEL J. BENNETT,   Management Engineer, DALFI, Inc., San Diego, California: *Equipment Life Cycle Management Through Microcomputers*

ANDREW G. DEAN,   Epidemiology Program Office, Centers for Disease Control, Altlanta, Georgia: *Epidemiology and Microcomputers*

ROGER R. FLYNN,   Associate Professor, Department of Information Science, University of Pittsburgh, Pittsburgh, Pennsylvania: *Error Detection and Correction*

ADRIAN V. GHEORGHE, Ph.D.,   Professor, Department of Management Science, Faculty of Electrotechnics and Power Engineering, Bucharest Polytechnic Institute, Bucharest, Romania: *Energy Management*

CURT GISTRUP,   Research Scientist, Novo Nordisk, Bagsvaerd, Denmark: *Enhanced Graphics: Molecular Modeling*

MICHAEL G. GONZALES,   Assistant Professor and Chairman, Computer and Information Sciences, Gwynedd-Mercy College, Gwynedd Valley, Pennsylvania: *The Electronic Timesheet*

EBEN LEE KENT,   Standard Rate & Data Service, Inc., Wilmette, Illinois: *Electronic Mail*

DOUGLAS KLINE,   Ketchum/Boyle Public Relations, Los Angeles, California: *Epson Corporation*

DONALD O. KNIGHT, Ph.D., P.E.,   Professor, Arizona State University, College of Engineering and Applied Science, Tempe, Arizona: *The Engineering Workstation and the Engineering Support System*

BENNET P. LIENTZ,   Professor, Graduate School of Management, University of California, Los Angeles, California: *Equipment and Software Maintenance*

NOREEN MAC MORROW,   Lecturer, Department of Information Science, University of Strathclyde, Glasgow, Scotland: *Ergonomic Aspects of Computer Use*

LEIF NØRSKOV-LAURITSEN,   Research Scientist, Novo Nordisk, Bagsvaerd, Denmark: *Enhanced Graphics: Molecular Modeling*

STEFFEN B. PETERSEN,   Senior Research Scientist and Department Head, Biostructure, Novo Nordisk, Bagsvaerd, Denmark and Adjunct Professor of Biostructure, Arhus University, Denmark: *Enhanced Graphics: Molecular Modeling*

MALCOLM C. RUBEL,   President, Performance Dynamics Associates, New York, New York: *Evaluation of Software: Microsoft Version 4.0*

PIETRO SCHICKER, Ph.D.,   Zellweger Telecommunications AG, Hombrechtikon, Switzerland: *Electronic Mail Message Handling Systems x.400*

MICHAEL B. SPRING, Ph.D.,   Assistant Professor, Department of Information Science, University of Pittsburgh, Pittsburgh, Pennsylvania: *Electronic Publishing*

J. NEIL STONE,   Chief Engineer, Esco Engineering, Kingsville, Ontario: *Engineering Applications*

RALPH SWALM,   International Management Center, Cazenovia, New York: *Engineering Economy Software*

VICTOR SHOU-CHUAN YANG,   University of Pittsburgh, School of Library and Information Science, Department of Information Science, Pittsburgh, Pennsylvania: *Electronic Dictionaries in Machine Translation*

ENCYCLOPEDIA OF MICROCOMPUTERS

VOLUME 6

ELECTRONIC DICTIONARIES IN MACHINE TRANSLATION

INTRODUCTION

With the rapid advancement in electronic and computer technology, traditional dictionaries of various types are now becoming available in different electronic media. The complete set of the world-famous *Oxford English Dictionary* has been available since 1987 on CD-ROM (Compact Disc-Read Only Memory). Another CD-ROM, the CD-WORD, containing thirteen bilingual and multilingual dictionaries in eight languages has also been on the market since last year.

Furthermore, electronic dictionaries in the form of reusable computer storage devices such as magnetic tapes and discs have been in existence since the birth of machine translation in the late 1940s [1—8]. These were bilingual dictionary database systems created exclusively for their respective machine translation systems. The complexity of these dictionaries varies according to the designated needs of the translation designs. In other words, each dictionary system could be used for only one particular machine translation system. However, in recent years, monolingual dictionary systems have also been available on floppy discs for spelling corrections in word processors such as WORD-PERFECT. In a sophisticated system such as IBM's EPISTLE, not only can the spelling of the word be checked, but also the syntax of the sentence including subject—verb agreement and misuse of pronouns and articles.

A dictionary entry in a bilingual or multilingual dictionary may contain simply the keyword or headword in the source language, along with one or more of its equivalent words in the target language or languages. However, most of these dictionaries have included a combination of linguistic information such as word classes, various forms of prefixes and suffixes, other grammatical markers, compound words, and even some examples of usage in order to facilitate translation needs.

During the first generation of machine translation from the late 1940s to the mid-1960s, the electronic or machine-readable dictionary was the heart of all machine translation systems [8—10]. These systems were classified as the Direct Model of machine translation. Their major component was the direct replacement of source language words with equivalent target language words. The operations were called dictionary or table lookup procedures and were used for searching through the electronic dictionary to match and retrieve the translation equivalents. The engineering approach

is also known as word-for-word translation although some local word reordering may also be performed.

For the second generation of machine translation from the mid-1960s
to the 1980s, the transfer module was introduced as the centerpiece of the
system. These systems were grouped under the Transfer Model with three
major components: analysis, transfer, and synthesis. In the analysis
module, heuristic as well as algorithmic procedures have been applied to
the parsing of the source language sentence. The resulting syntactic structure of the sentence along with its constituents and their linguistic information is then transferred into the syntactic structure of the target language
in the transfer module. Finally, the synthesis module is given the responsibility to replace constituents in the source language with their target
language equivalents. The specially designed bilingual dictionary is searched
in the analysis module to match the input sentence and may be consulted
again in the synthesis module for final output generation. Alternatively,
since the transfer module serves as an intermediary between each language
pair, two independent monolingual dictionaries may be used for multilingual
translations as suggested in the Eurotra project [8, 11—17].

From the late 1970s to the present, the third-generation systems under
development focus on the semantics and pragmatics rather than the syntax
for machine translation. Some sort of universal knowledge representation
scheme has been sought to be an interlingua or intermediate language between all natural languages [8, 18, 19]. Thus only the analysis and synthesis modules are needed to perform a meaning-based translation. The syntactic information is integrated into semantic and pragmatic requirements in
the analysis module for the source language input and in the synthesis
module for the target language output [20]. For each language, one or two
monolingual dictionaries are used for input/output either jointly or separately.

Due to the current shifting of emphasis from syntactic grammar to
semantic meaning, relationships between words, concepts, and messages are
being re-examined closely in light of the intended information content [8, 21,
22]. Since concepts are the basic unit of information and are usually represented in keywords and phrases, a return of the dictionary to its primary
importance as in the first-generation systems is only natural [20, 23—27].

Early in 1988, Systran Japan obtained major contracts from the U.S.
Department of Defense and the European Economic Commission for machine
translation between Japanese and Indo-European languages [28]. The
Systran Company, headquartered in the United States, has the most successful commercial machine translation system based upon bilingual dictionaries
on mainframe computers [10, 29]. In addition, Japan's Fujitsu uses its
mainframe machine translation system to translate manuals at three seconds
per page [28]. Fujitsu also claims quality translation can be achieved with
computer-aided translation at 20 percent human time savings. The translation system is also used for information seeking and retrieval in Japanese
language databases to identify potential articles for translation. There are
also some microcomputer-based practical machine translation systems primarily
using electronic dictionaries from Bravice International, Sharp, and other
companies in Japan.

In particular, the recent development in terminological databanks and
the introduction of electronic dictionaries on CD-ROMs have opened new
avenues of application for machine-aided human translation (MAHT) with
significant implications for human-aided machine translation (HAMT) [1,
Chaps. 2—4]. This is a very significant transition from the traditional way

of utilizing the dictionary primarily as an intermittent reference tool. The printed dictionary is not designed to facilitate in-depth references and/or research interests.

With the new electronic dictionary, in-depth reference and research interests can be accommodated with ease since information retrieval capabilities and continuous updatings are now available from the dictionary database. The conventional organization of almost all types of dictionaries by alphabetical order is still the most efficient for printed dictionaries in terms of easy access. The cost of this access efficiency, however, is the great sacrifice of close associations among semantically and syntactically related words or lexemes.

It is interesting to note that the serious drawback of alphabetical ordering of dictionary entries was discussed painstakingly three decades ago by Melton [30] in relation to the Semantic Code Dictionary project. As a counter example, Melton illustrated the nonalphabetically ordered Chinese dictionary with a much more sensible organization. Until recently, all Chinese dictionaries were indexed and arranged by radicals, which are the smallest meaning units in Chinese (see Chinese Word Knowledge Base).

The problem with alphabetical ordering that has most concerned lexicographers is the search and retrieval of multiword units or compound words. With alphabetical ordering of entries, compound words may only be found according to the first word of the compound. For example, "electronic dictionary" would be listed under "electronic" but not under "dictionary." To remedy this deficiency, massive redundant listings would be necessary. The economics of a single volume multifunction printed dictionary prohibits this expensive treatment with acceptable consistency. Users are either short-changed with a no-show or required to make repetitive trials under other entries. It would be interesting to search for "drug dealing" either under "drug" or "dealing" for the result.

MONOLINGUAL DICTIONARIES

For machine translation, the monolingual electronic dictionary might be used in the input phase to match the source language text to identify constituent words and phrases and obtain their respective linguistic information for further processing. This is true for all three generations of machine translation. However, because of operational convenience and efficiency, bilingual dictionaries were popular and the monolingual dictionaries were not known in use until the early 1980s. The European Economic Commission (the Common Market) faces the difficult task of translating all official documents into the nine languages used by its member countries [1, Chaps. 3 and 4; 8, 11]. In the planning and design stage for the joint venture Eurota machine translation project, a decision was made to deliberately separate the source language in the analysis module from the target language in the synthesis module. There were at least two good reasons for doing so: (1) This would facilitate the natural division of labor for each member country to develop an analysis and a synthesis module for her own language. (2) The concurrent development and implementation locally in each member country would result in considerable savings in time, effort, and money.

At the center of these two modules are the two monolingual dictionaries, one for input analysis and one for output generation of that particular language. These two dictionaries would have some limited redundancy regarding their keywords and linguistic information contained. Nevertheless, the functional separation into two dictionaries should allow for a more effective and efficient processing.

A more commonly acceptable usage of the monolingual dictionary for machine translation is in the editing of texts [*1*, Chap. 2; *8*, Sections 5 and 6]. The monolingual dictionary may be utilized in the pre-editing of source language text to premark rough spots for a smoother machine translation. It can also be used in the on-line editing during the translation process, most likely for the target language. For postediting, it can be used for corrections in the target language. The recent development of interactive machine translation, such as in the CULT and CMU-CMT projects, may use the dictionary for pre-editing and/or on-line editing [*31, 32*] with little or no conventional postediting.

Oxford English Dictionary

The best example of a modern electronic monolingual dictionary is probably the well-known *Oxford English Dictionary* recently available on CD-ROM [*1*, Chap. 2; *9*]. The CD-ROM contains the complete original set of the 1933 edition, twelve-volume dictionary. Funded by the British government, the Oxford University Press is in the process of revising and enhancing the original dictionary to incorporate four volumes of supplements and other new materials. The *New Oxford English Dictionary* (second edition) consisting of twenty volumes was published in the Spring of 1989. The new edition is also available on CD-ROM for machine searches.

In the machine-readable form, this *Dictionary* offers researchers as well as the general public new ways to utilize this excellent dictionary. One major contribution of the electronic version is the new capability of information retrieval through Boolean combinations of keywords or concepts. In other words, new or related concepts may be retrieved in terms of other existing or known concepts. This is possible because words or concepts hidden inside each dictionary entry may be searched electronically for comparison.

For every dictionary entry, there are several distinctive fields, including the definition and etymology fields, which are most relevant to its meaning. The definition field is common for all types of dictionaries although it varies in detail and completeness. This dictionary is unique since the etymology field contains the structure and history of words tracing their origins from other Indo-European languages including Greek and Latin. Boolean operators such as AND, OR, and NOT may be used intermixingly to formulate a logical expression of keywords to uniquely specify the intended scope of searches. Reverse dictionary searches from meaning are thus possible regressively to find an unknown word through a Boolean combination of its origins and/or related concepts. A good example illustrated by Gray [*9*] was the word nyctalopia ("nightblindness") which might be found from the Indo-European root "NEKWT (night)." The etymology of "NEKWT" will further detail the history of its Greek origin from "nuk" to "nyc" to "nyct."

Another obvious advantage with the electronic version of the dictionary is the possibility and convenience of continuous updating and revision of dictionary entries to keep up with the ever-changing world of English language usage. With the current advancement in computer technology, the automation of the dictionary updating procedure is the only sensible alternative in comparison with the traditional cut-and-paste approach. The 1933 printed first edition with its four subsequent volumes of supplements can hardly catch up with the rapid changes in the past half century. This is a particularly serious shortcoming in the fields of science and technology where constant revisions are necessary.

Although the printed dictionary is not a satisfactory reference tool as pointed out by Gray [9], its shortcomings are not due to its "strict linearity" but rather its inability to permit Boolean expression searches and quick cross referencing. However, a printed dictionary with numerous pages does not require the linear search for a given word as in the case of a magnetic tape file. Since it is arranged alphabetically, a pseudo-random probe to the approximate page of the searched word is usually performed with a few more trials necessary to narrow the scope. This is not a strict linear search but rather analogous to the binary search as in a computer file [33, 34]. Nevertheless, the electronic version is undoubtedly a versatile reference and research tool offering the unparalleled power of Boolean as well as the direct random access to headwords and other keywords. In essence, this is an innovative integration of the traditional dictionary and modern computer technology to implement a sophisticated information retrieval system augmented with database management capabilities.

Chinese Word Knowledge Base

Another monolingual electronic dictionary outside the Indo-European language system is currently under construction in Taiwan [13, 14, 35—38]. It is named the Chinese Electronic Dictionary (CED) in the Chinese Word Knowledge Base system carried out jointly by the Academia Sinica Computer Center and the Electronics Research & Service Organization of Industrial Technology Research Institute. The first objective of the system was to classify Chinese words in order to create machine-readable files. The system is divided into two subsystems: the Chinese character subsystem and the Chinese word subsystem. The latter is built upon the former due to the unique construction of Chinese words usually by combining two or more Chinese characters together [8, 30, 39—42].

In Chao's [39] authoritative book on Chinese grammar, he stated the closest linguistic unit to the Chinese "tzyh" ("tz'u/ci") is the "morpheme" which is the smallest unit of meaning in Indo-European languages. (Note: There are two types of Romanized Chinese transliteration systems, i.e., Wade-Gile/pin-yin, in use today.) Analogous to English words which are usually composed of two or more morphemes, Chinese words may frequently consist of two or more "tzyh"s. It is quite reasonable and natural for Chao to assume that "morpheme" can be treated as the translation equivalent of the Chinese "tzyh." Since this Chinese project follows Chao's book closely, the word "morpheme" is being treated as the same concept represented by "tzyh" throughout the first research report by Chang et al. [35].

However, as discussed by Melton [30], a Chinese character is an ideograph which frequently contains two or more parts called subcharacters. The subcharacters are commonly called radicals in Chinese lexicography [41]. In turn, each subcharacter or radical has its own meaning and may often be used independently as a Chinese character or even a Chinese word. In addition, almost all Chinese dictionaries are compiled and indexed according to the number of strokes in the dominant radical contained in a Chinese character. A dominant radical is usually the left or upper one within the square-shaped Chinese character. All Chinese characters with the same dominant radical are listed together in the index according to the ascending order of their number of additional strokes present in the character. In this case, would the Chinese radical be more compatible to morpheme than "tzyh"?

Furthermore, Chao extended his theory of Chinese morpheme or "tzyh" to include multiple-character terms or concepts [35, 39, Chap. 3; 43]. The strongest case and thus most interesting example is the; "p'u-t'ao/pu-tao (grape)" which is composed of two Chinese characters. Chao considered "p'u-t'ao" as a single-morpheme word because it was borrowed from the single-morpheme English word, "grape." Chao reasoned that these two characters cannot be used individually, one without another, to yield some meaning. (But the second character "t'ao" is listed separately in a popular Chinese word dictionary named "TZ'U-HAI/CI-HAI" as one kind of grass.)

A close look at these two characters reveals that each one is composed of a few radicals just as in any other Chinese character. The first character "p'u" consists of the dominant radical on top of the ideograph, the simplified character of "ts'ao/cao (grass)." Its middle part is a radical "p/b (first phonetic symbol in Chinese chu-yin/zhu-yin system." Its bottom (lower left) part is another Chinese character "fu/fu (start/begin/just)." The second character "t'ao" has the same top and middle radicals as in the first character "p'u" but has another simplified character "t'ao (ceramic container)" on the bottom left-hand corner.

Thus these two characters can be found separately under the radical "ts'ao (grass)." The second character "t'ao" is listed in the index before the first character "p'u" because its bottom part has six strokes instead of seven for the first character. The construction of these two characters may be explained as an indication to something which is a grass-based plant and shall be pronounced according to the lower-left part of the imbedded Chinese characters. Clearly these radicals and imbedded characters are smaller meaning units than each of the two characters "p'u-t'ao (grape)." Then, how can we say that "p'u-t'ao (grape)" is a single-morpheme word in the Chinese language? This same analysis can also be applied without difficulty to other two- or multicharacter morphemes in Chinese such as "mei-kui/mei-gui (rose)" and "ch'iao-k'e-li/qiao-ke-li (chocolate)."

Another question arises when a Chinese word is implanted into the English language. For example, "coolie" (hard labor) is a single-morpheme word in English. Its origins in Chinese are two characters "k'u/ku (bitter)" and "li/li (strength/labor)." The first character "k'u" has on its top the radical of simplified "ts'ao (grass)" while the rest is another character "ku/gu (ancient/old)." Through its composition, this character implies the taste of grass is bitter and it should be pronounced as the bottom character "ku." This bottom character may be further decomposed into the upper radical of "shi/shi (ten)" and the lower radical "k'ou/kou (mouth)." Should we notify all English dictionary publishers that they should indicate that "coolie" has two, three, or four morphemes? Is there a principle in lexicography that the number of morphemes of a foreign-borrowed word should follow whatever is defined in the original language?

If this is not the case, then why should we justify awkwardly that "p'u-t'ao" is a single-morpheme word which has two Chinese characters? One suggestion may be that since "p'u-t'ao" means grape and these two characters are not used separately, one without another, it should be treated as a single morpheme without any question. Further decomposition of each character into subcharacters and radicals is unwarranted because the composition of a Chinese character should not be linked with its meaning. In other words, Chao's approach to identify "tzyh" with morpheme is satisfactory and acceptable. Yeh and Hsu [44, Chap. 4] also stated that most of the time each Chinese character is the smallest language essence, but "p'u-t'ao" is a single essence word in Chinese.

With all the discussions above about "tzyh" and character and morpheme, it is suggested here that a "tzyh" should be treated and translated as a Chinese character (i.e., ideograph) and not be equated with morpheme. An English morpheme may consist of a few English characters (letters). But a Chinese character may contain several language essences or meaning units, for example, morphemes, as subcharacters and radicals. Furthermore, each square-shaped Chinese character can be arranged without spacing either in traditional form from top to bottom and then from right to left in columns, or in Western style from left to right and then from top to bottom in rows.

New Chinese words may be formed with old combinations of Chinese characters such as "yuan-tzu-tan/yuan-zi-dan (atomic bomb)" and "tian-s'uan-chi/dian-suan-ji (computer)." Occasionally, new Chinese characters may be constructed using existing subcharacters and radicals. For example, the character "lu/lu (aluminum)" is made of a left-side radical of "chin/jin (gold/metal)" and a right-side subcharacter of "Lu/Lu (legal last name)." It contains the same radical "k'ou (mouth)" on the top and in the bottom, linked by a slanted stroke in between. The composition of this character indicates this is one kind of metal and should be pronounced as right-side subcharacter "Lu."

These and other unique properties of the Chinese character should be sufficient enough to distinguish itself as a different linguistic unit. The linguistic analyses in the Chinese language does not require the substitution of Chinese characters by English morphemes. An obvious example is that the analyses of free morpheme versus bound morpheme may be carried on with free characters versus bound characters without any difficulty. It is therefore, unnecessary to identify or equate the "tzyh" (Chinese character) with the English morpheme.

MULTILINGUAL DICTIONARIES

CD-WORD

On a single CD-ROM disc, thirteen bilingual and multilingual dictionaries with five million words and five hundred million bytes (characters) of data are stored for ready reference in seconds. This modern product, CD-WORD, is the first multilingual electronic dictionary, available from Sansyusya Publishing in Japan since 1987 [45]. It includes eight languages: Chinese, Dutch, English, French, German, Italian, Japanese, and Spanish. The most amazing part is the ideograph of Japanese and Chinese characters which are nicely encoded for sharp display and printout. These nonalphabetical characters are much more complicated than Roman alphabets, and are numerous in number (i.e., about 10,000 characters). Around 2,000 of them, called Kanji in Japan, are used in the Japanese language in addition to Japan's own 50 ideographs. The Chinese and Japanese characters can be entered on the keyboard with the English alphabets as phonetic transliterations. Printouts of the Chinese and Japanese characters on paper require a NEC PC-9800 series computer system. A CD-ROM disc drive and an IBM personal computer system or its compatible will be sufficient for other languages.

Three modes of search are available: lookup dictionary, display translation, and display synonym. In the lookup dictionary mode, one may specify the desired dictionary and language to look up the full entry of a specific search term. Search terms may be entered as a single word or compound word. The search range may be selected as a headword only, subheadword with example only, headword and subheadword with example, reverse search, or search according to the last compound element. The search system will either find the location where the term should be in the alphabetical list with a blinking cursor or it will indicate that it is not found. For convenience, two or more search terms may be blocked together in the list for a single search, for example, science and scientist. The cursor may be moved to another more desirable term in the list for a full entry display. It is also possible to shift to translation mode to specify a display of translation equivalents in another language.

In the display translation mode, with additional specification of source and target languages, the search system will find and display all translations available for that term. The alphabetical list will be displayed to allow the selection of alternatives. With the same search term, one may switch dictionaries to find translations in any one of the seven desirable target languages. The display synonym mode will provide a list of synonyms in the same language for the search term.

These features offer flexibilities which are either absent or difficult to use in the printed bilingual and multilingual dictionaries. Presumably they will be incorporated into the CD-WORD-8 word processor. Its editor will allow the insertion or replacement of words in another language into a given sentence. This would facilitate the word-for-word, computer-aided-human translation using a word processor. However, this word processor with its editor is far from complete. The CD-WORD thus is currently used primarily in Japanese high schools for second language learning. It serves exactly as a multilingual electronic dictionary with no functional integration with a word processor.

Fortunately, a new version named CD-WORD 12+1 with eighteen dictionaries in twelve languages and seven million words on a single CD-ROM will be available in early 1989 [46]. The languages included are: Chinese, Danish, Dutch, English, Finnish, French, German, Italian, Japanese, Norwegian, Spanish, Swedish, and the additional American idioms in English. Correspondingly another range of search is added to allow the search of the idiom elements.

In this new version, popular word processors such as Word Perfect, Word Star, etc. may be used in conjunction with the CD-WORD search capabilities. In other words, one may compose a document using a word processor with on-line consultations to the CD-WORD for definitions, examples, synonyms, or translations. A multilingual front-end processor performs this linkage to furnish a split screen with the lower half for CD-WORD displays. Translations or synonyms may be selected for insertion or replacement in the upper screen document.

Term Banks

Term bank is the short form of technological databanks which have sprung up in most industrialized countries over the past two decades [1, Chap. 4].

The term banks are natural extensions particularly for bilingual and multi-lingual electronic dictionaries specializing in some technological domains for translation and other information needs. The existing printed version of the specialized dictionary can never keep up with the rapid changes in the terminologies used by a highly specialized domain whether in science and technology or in business. Certainly, the advancement of computer technology and the growth of user-oriented information science are also important contributing factors to the development of term banks. Users in volatile and sensitive areas such as national defense and international affairs face the requirement of up-to-date information for strategic planning and decision making.

Several user groups of term banks have been identified by Sager and McNaught [47] and Bennett et al. [1, Chap. 3]. They are: (1) professional communicators such as technical writers, abstractors, journalists, translators, and interpreters are the largest user group whose major responsibility lies in the transmission of messages to information seekers; (2) information and documentation specialists such as information counselors and brokers, librarians, and indexers who need to identify documents and to construct thesauruses accurately for the public; (3) standardization experts who establish and publish precise standards with unambiguous terminologies; (4) lexicographers and terminologists who collect, record, and disseminate existing usages of terminologies; (5) applied linguists, language planners, and educators, and machine translation researchers who require statistics on the usage of terminologies; (6) dictionary publishers who depend on the database management capabilities of the term bank for data manipulation; (7) customs officials who have to verify on the spot, the labels and documents of imported goods; (8) news reporters, legislators, and government officials who need to familiarize current usage of terminologies in their foreign visits; (9) manufacturers and marketing specialists who rely on popular and effective terminologies for foreign exports; (10) insurance agents who deal with insurance policies as well as claims in a specialized field. Other user groups may also be identified when term banks are accessible to others involved in any specialized area such as professors and students, consultants, managers, newspaper editors, television anchor persons, etc.

Equipped with database management capabilities, the term bank is a collection of database files with millions of records (i.e., entries) divided into multiple fields for data manipulation [8, 33, 34, 48]. The term bank is thus a multifunctional tool capable of various types of information retrieval and computer-aided translation. Cross reference may be achieved instantly either by terminologies (headwords or keywords) for the complete record (entry), or by attributes (fields within an entry) and values (words in the field) across all records in the file. With additional user specifications, cross reference across different files are also possible if this feature is also available in the system.

For each record of a terminology, the properties, features, translation equivalents, examples of usage, and/or synonyms may be listed as separate fields as facets, or attributes of that record [1, Chap. 3; 8, Section 7]. The number of fields of facets may vary greatly from as few as six to as many as 76 per record entry. A typical term bank may have one million records with an average of three hundred characters per record for a total of three hundred million bytes for one database file.

   Unlike the fixed number of twenty-five facets for each mathematical concept in Davis' TEIRESIAS system for mathematical discoveries [22, 49, 50], the fields in a term bank are not fixed while the individual field length may also vary. Bennett et al. [1, Chap. 3] suggested a list of twenty-four fields which would be common to a typical term bank. They are: (1) record identifier; (2) record originator; (3) date of input or update; (4) language or country code; (5) entry term; (6) source of entry term; (7) note on usage; (8) grammatical information or quality code; (9) scope note; (10) full synonyms; (11) abbreviated form; (12) synonyms; (13) conceptual links; (14) subject field; (15) definitions; (16) sources of definitions; (17) contacts; (18) sources of contacts; (19) foreign language equivalents; (20) sources of foreign language equivalents; (21) foreign language equivalent note on usage; (22) foreign language equivalent scope note; (23) foreign language equivalent context; (24) foreign language equivalent source of context. Additional fields may of course be added as the need arises, for instance, inference, class—member relationship, similar or related terms, etc. The goal of information retrieval has always been aimed at high recall and precision ratios. The recall infers the exhaustive retrieval of all relevant and pertinent data in the database file. The precision refers to the accuracy and correctness of retrieved data in relation to search request, whether it is a single keyword or a formulated Boolean expression. In addition to bibliographical and document retrieval systems, other systems such as the expert system and computer-aided instruction [1, Chaps. 4 and 5] may be considered specialized information retrieval systems augmented with other intelligent capabilities. However, as pointed out by Bennett et al. [1, Chap. 3], the success rate was averaged at 50 to 60 percent for general term bank searches. Some term banks in specialized field may reach a success rate of 75 percent to satisfy user's request. This clearly indicates that there is much room for improvements.

   As for computer-aided translation, whether it is a machine-aided human translation (MAHT) or a human-aided machine translation (HAMT), the new development and resurgence in the past decade are yet to be implemented and verified [8, 51]. The 80 percent rate of acceptable translation for the TAUM-METEO English-to-French weather reporting system of the Transfer Model rooted in syntax since 1977 is still the only exception due to a highly specialized and limited vocabulary of 1,500 phrases.

   Experimental translation systems under the new Interlingua model based on knowledge representations of concepts are at various stages of theorizing, hypothesizing, experimenting, or preliminary testing. No production system of this type is known for implementation. But interestingly enough as mentioned earlier in the introduction, the Systran systems for various language pairs under the oldest word-for-word Direct Model of machine translation continue to expand their market of productional machine translation systems [28]. Needless to say, the demand for machine translation is there and the need for more improvements is great.

DICTIONARY-BASED MACHINE TRANSLATION

Automatic Segmentation for Translation

In a broader sense, all machine translation systems were based on one or more dictionaries or lexicons. The electronic dictionary was in essence the foremost and fundamental tool for machine translation. It is much more important than the case of human translation because words in the text cannot be recognized as meaningful units and need to be segmented (fragmented) or grouped into concepts and terminologies for further processing [20, 40, 43, 52—55]. This preprocessing could be performed manually by human pre-editing as in earlier machine translation systems [8]. Pre-editing would allow manual markings of phrases so that the dictionary may be used sparingly for consultation only.

One workable automatic segmentation procedure started three decades ago for the word-for-word machine translation with the Direct Model was the use of the longest-match principle for dictionary lookups [56]. It is believed that the commercially successful Systran bilingual machine translation systems are built upon this principle. In order to have the longer text strings recognized automatically rather than the shorter string with identical characters or words, the longer string was arranged ahead of the shorter string as headwords or keywords in the alphabetical ordering of all dictionary entries.

If A, B, C, and D each represent a Chinese or Indo-European language character or word, the longer string of ABCD would be placed in front of the shorter strings in the sequence of ABC, AB, and A. A text string of CABD would be automatically segmented and looked up under three separate dictionary entries: C, AB, and D. An English word example may be: "He almost kicked the bucket twice on the highway." The phrase "kicked the bucket" would be recognized and looked up in the electronic dictionary properly instead of being treated as three separate words.

In oriental languages such as Chinese, Japanese, and Korean, the need for segmentation is much more serious since there are no spaces used in the text as word delimiters. An example in Chinese may be: "Hsiao/Xiao (small/little) lung/lung (dragon) yen/yen (eye) hen/hen (very) hao/haw (good)." These five Chinese characters are a legitimate Chinese sentence even without a verb. Depending on the arrangement of dictionary entries, that sentence could have two meanings and thus two different translations: (1) The eyes of little dragon (nickname of a boy) have very good (vision); or (2) The small dragon's eye (name of a Chinese fruit) is very good (tasty).

The first translation was the result of matching "hsiao lung" first as a popular boy's nickname. The second translation was due to the match of "lung yen" first, or the lack of the entry "hsio lung"), which indicates the name of a popular Chinese fruit. Correspondingly, the single character word "hao" may refer either to good vision for the boy or tasty for the fruit. It may be noted too that "yen" gives no indication of singularity or plurality, and no subject-verb agreement in number, gender, or tense is necessary.

Furthermore, incorrect matches from the dictionary may be corrected by adding new entries in the proper sequence, for example, "hsiao lung." However, there are cases which may still yield incorrect matches, for example, if both "hsiao lung" and "lung yen" are in the dictionary but the match of "hsiao lung" first is incorrect for the sentence "hsiao hsiao lung yen hen haw." Assuming "hsiao hsiao" is the name of a local fruit store and absent from the electronic dictionary.

One semantically interesting solution is the use of contextual information including local objectives and topics, and global goals, plans, themes, and subject matters. The translation of "The eyes of little little-dragon (boy's nickname) are very good" should be recognized as incorrect. The translation should be corrected using contextual information as "The dragon's eye (a Chinese fruit) of hsiao-hsiao (a fruit store) is very good."

Viewed from another angle, if the last character "haw (good)" in the five-character Chinese sentence is being replaced by another character, the segmentation of the first three characters "hsiao lung yen" may be determined. If "haw" is replaced by "jing (sharp)," then the first three characters should be correctly segmented as "hsiao-lung (little dragon) yen (eye)." This is because the word "sharp" can be used to describe the human vision but not a fruit. On the other hand, if the last character is replaced by "tien (sweet)," then the correct segmentation should be "hsiao (small) lung-yen (dragon's eye)." The reason is that "sweet" is often used to describe the taste of a fruit, but unlikely to describe the eyes of a human or animal.

With automatic segmentation to identify concepts in words or phrases, a minimum level of robustness in machine translation is guaranteed even without a syntactic and/or semantic grammar. For users who are experts on the subject matter but with little or no knowledge of the foreign language, ungrammatical translations with basic phrases and special terminologies would be sufficient to reveal the topical information and even the theme of the subject matter [1, Chap. 4; 8, Section 5].

This is particularly useful in information retrieval question—answering and expert systems from a foreign language database [1, Chap. 5; 57—59]. In order to provide some translations rather than no translation at all, grammars used in a machine translation system should be forbidden to stop the output due to parsing failures. Otherwise, the five-character Chinese sentence illustrated above would never be translated simply because there was no verb in existence. Similar disruptions would also occur due to missing subjects and articles, and hidden tenses, genders, numbers, and so on in Chinese as well as other oriental languages including Japanese [52a].

Lexicon-Driven Translations

Since a natural language evolves over hundreds or thousands of years, language expressions which cannot be governed by grammar are common place rather than exceptions [8, 20, 22, 49, 52a, 60]. For any machine translation system, dictionary lookup procedures were performed first at the input stage for automatic segmentation and the last stage for final output generation. During the translation processes whether in the analysis, transfer or generation module, the dictionary might often be consulted repeatedly for further clarifications.

Word-specific grammar information might be contained in the dictionary entry as facets or fields along with semantic information [30]. Other less obvious information such as word orders, contextual relations, subject matters, and speaker's attitudes should also be recorded and updated as many times as possible with the word or phrase entries in the dictionary. This would reduce the loss of information in machine translation. Knowledgable human translators always have most of this information available to perform the translation or interpretation.

Grammatical rules represented by annotated parsing trees may or may not be necessary for dictionary-based machine translations. Under the Transfer Model, translation systems such as Eurotra in Europe and MU in Japan depended heavily on tree-to-tree transfers or transformations in the translation process [52a]. As systems developed under the Direct Model, recent experimental systems under the Interlingual model were attempting to provide alternatives to reduce or eliminate complicated and not quite successful grammar-directed translations [8]. In other words, since human translators are not driven by grammar but rather by words or phrases from the source language to the target language, dictionary or lexicon-driven systems may serve information needs adequately.

The dictionary or lexicon-driven systems might appear less intelligent and thus uninteresting. This should not be of great concern. In fact, as pointed out bluntly by Nagao [52a] and others, machine translation systems in general do not require total understanding of natural languages. Interpretations of sophisticated sentences in a particular context can and should be left with the translation users. Excessive inferences made by the intelligent machine translation system could be misleading and even erroneous. Once again, human translators would not and should not use their full intelligence and world knowledge for translation tasks for the same reasons.

Furthermore, Cullingford and Onyshkevych discussed the serious problems of grammar-driven systems. One major drawback was the insensitivity or lack of robustness in translation due to the popular top-down parsing strategy. This was particularly true for irregular but common language expressions such as idioms, phrases and incomplete sentences. Another more serious problem was the de-emphasis of the importance of concept and message transfers between languages. The perfectly grammatical sentences without useful information content should not be translated in the first place.

With their experimental systems, Cullingford and Onyshkevych [20] suggested that a dictionary or lexicon-driven system would preserve the meaning in the translation. Difficult problems in the grammar-driven systems such as word sense disambiguation, anaphora resolution, and the lack of translation equivalent may be resolved. The use of the bottom-up approach for input language analyses would allow automatic fragmentation or segmentation of conceptual units in word groups or phrases. This would provide the opportunities for diagnostic evaluations and modifications to preserve the original readings of meaning.

The simplistic model of surface semantics presented by Cullingford and Onyshkevych was indeed very interesting. Without the transfer module, the analysis module for the source language and the generation module for the target language were based on word meanings alone. In place of the interlingua, an annotator bridged these two modules by annotating surface semantic forms for output. The conceptual analyzer creates a meaning structure which is a knowledge representation for each input sentence. This meaning structure is kept in the surface semantic annotator for slight modifications of concepts in order to neutralize their differences in modes of expressions among languages. The neutralized meaning structure will then be sent to the conceptual generator for the generation of target language expressions. The word sense database, namely dictionaries or lexicons, is linked to both analyzer and generator for frequent on-line consultations.

The use of surface semantics as the interlingua, furnishes a unique means to neutralize unnecessary language-specific differences. Traces from source language conceptual representations such as suffixes, cases, and functional words may be discarded since they are contained in the dictionary entry and may be looked up for target language generations. Important information such as people, time, place and things are recorded in the annotator for future references until they are replaced by the new corresponding information.

For example, the tense case information in English is not needed for the Chinese translation just as in the Ukranian-to-English translation. In

Chinese an indication of time alone, e.g., yesterday, is sufficient without further tense information to modify the verb, e.g., "-ed". The same is true for information on person, number and gender which should be stripped from the English concept words. Thus the surface semantic annotator is language independent and needs no replacement when other languages along with their conceptual analyzers and generators are included for translations. However, some additional guidelines may be added to the neutralization process when necessary. The goal is to keep the annotator small and simple by leaving all syntactic and semantic information in the concept words or phrases in the dictionary entry for output generations.

An important class of simpler inferences could be achieved with words and phrases without the use of world knowledge. These inferences include the selection of appropriate word meanings, the resolution of anaphora references, and the process of distributed target realization [20]. The distributed target realization refers to the possibility and ease of expanding single word source language concepts into multiple words and/or clauses in the target language. The same is true for the contraction from multiple word concepts to the single word concepts. This is a clear advantage of the lexically driven system over the syntactically oriented transfer system. No complicated transformation rules are required to perform the expansion or contraction. The target language expressions are realized by distributing or redistributing the concept words in the annotator through dictionary lookups in the analyzer and generator.

There are several distinctive features in the generation phase. The most unique feature in comparison with the majority of machine translation systems is the presence of a well-formed thought or message for output generation. No syntactic structure is present for the sentence. The thought or message consists of concepts organized as a meaning structure. Concepts are placed in a stack to be examined and augmented with functional words required for the target language expression.

Another important feature is the use of the top-down approach totally different from the bottom-up strategy to recognize the input concepts. This permits a total freedom to generate the output expression based on the thought or message and its concepts. Features or facets of concepts may be checked for consistency or agreement to select the most appropriate form for a given concept. In addition, this also allows for possible verifications with the theme and subject matter of the context to make sure no conflict messages are given unintentionally.

CONCLUSION

In view of the recent advancement and new developments in electronic dictionaries, a dictionary-based machine translation system presents to itself new opportunities to integrate the Direct Model with the Interlingua Model. The concept-based word and terminology databases such as the Chinese Word Knowledge Base and many terminological databanks collect and organize various aspects of word meanings for future references. The availability of monolingual and multilingual dictionaries on the high capacity CD-ROMs such as the *Oxford English Dictionary* and the CD-WORD is a blessing for further researches in machine translation on economical microcomputers.

The return to the dictionary-based system from the grammar-based system was caused by two factors. The first is due to the fact that syntactically oriented systems do not make headways in high-volume production quality machine translations. The endless linguistic irregularities and complications can never be covered substantially simply because of the evolutional nature of language development. The theoretical foundation for the Transfer Model is sound for multilingual translation systems. But its successful implementation depends heavily upon the success of the language-dependent transfer module for each one-way translation of the language pairs as specified in the gigantic Eurotra project.

Another reason was the search of knowledge representation schemes which lead to the re-examination of semantic units of concepts as in words and phrases. Properties or facets of concepts are explored and recorded. Relations between words as well as across sentences are probed for a more meaningful representation. A shift of emphasis from syntax to semantics and pragmatics in machine translation researches are underway to facilitate a more useful communication over language barriers. The use of world knowledge in human translation is analyzed and compared with the needs in machine translation.

With dictionary lookup procedures for automatic segmentations, a dictionary-driven machine translation system is possible to integrate with the Interlingua Model for new alternatives. Monolingual databases and multilingual term banks may be stored on CD-ROMs and updated periodically as new releases to the public. A multidisc CD-ROM drive system such as the InfoTrac Reference Center may be used for concurrent access to different CD-ROM dictionaries and databases for cross references during the translation process. This should provide an excellent environment for the design of an informative and message-oriented dictionary-based machine translation system.

ACKNOWLEDGMENT

I sincerely appreciate the support from Professors Allen Kent, James G. Williams, Donald L. Shirey, Roger R. Flynn, Paul W. Munro, and Charlotte Shiang-Yun Wang Yang. Many thanks are also due for the kind assistance of Ida M. Flynn, Jing-Jye Yang, Ching-Ying Pan, Ren-Jay Yin, Ting-Ting Su, Patricia E. Morgan, Donna Macortte, Shouhua Alice Kuo, Yung-Pei Philip Tsai, Fen Wang, Marty Plummer, Raymond Kin Wong, Hueiy-Fen Wang, Huey-Shing Lin, and Ya-Chen Hsieh.

REFERENCES

1. P. A. Bennett, R. L. Johnson, J. McNaught, J. M. Pugh, J. C. Sager, and H. L. Somers, *Multilingual Aspects of Information Technology*, Gower Publishing, Hamts (England), 1986.
2. A. Kent, "Machine Literature Searching and Translation: An Analytical Review," in *Advances in Documentation and Library Science: Information Retrieval and Machine Translation*, Vol. III, P. I (A. Kent, ed.), Interscience, New York, 1960, Chap. 1.
3. S. Nirenburg, "Knowledge and Choices in Machine Translation," in

Machine Translation: Theoretical and Methodological Issues (S. Nirenburg, ed.), Cambridge University Press, Cambridge, 1987, Chap. 1.

4. J. W. Perry and A. Kent, "Introduction," in *Tools for Machine Literature Searching* (J. W. Parry and A. Kent, eds.), Interscience, New York, 1958, Chap. 1.

5. J. W. Perry and A. Kent, "Logical Principles of Information Retrieval," in *Tools for Machine Literature Searching* (J. W. Perry and A. Kent, eds.), Interscience, New York, 1958, Chap. 2.

6. J. Slocum, "A Survey of Machine Translation: Its History, Current Status, and Future Prospects," *Comput. Linguis., 11*, 1 (1985).

7. A. B. Tucker and S. Nirenburg, "Machine Translation: A Contemporary View," *Ann. Rev. Inform. Sci. Technol.*, 19 (1984).

8. V. S. C. Yang, "Information Acquisition with Machine Translation," *Encyclopedia of Library and Information Science*, Vol. 45, Marcel Dekker, New York, 1989.

9. R. A. Gray, "The New Oxford English Dictionary," *Ref. Serv. Rev., 4*, 92–95 (1988).

10. F. Knowles, "Error Analysis of System Output—A Suggested Criterion for the 'Internal' Evaluation of Translation Quality and a Possible Corrective for System Design," in *Translating and the Computer* (B. N. Snell, ed.), North-Holland, New York, 1979, pp. 109–133.

11. D. Arnold and L. des Tombe, "Basic Theory and Methodology in EUROTA," in *Machine Translation* (S. Nirenburg, ed.), Oxford University Press, Cambridge, 1987, Chap. 7.

12. W. S. Bennett and J. Slocum, "The LRC Machine Translation System," *Computational Linguistics, 11*(2-3) (1985).

13. K. J. Chen, L. L. Chang, L. P. Chang, and C. C. Hsieh, "Chinese Compound Word Parsing," to be published, 1988.

14. L. L. Chang, K. J. Chen, C. R. Huang, and C. C. Hsieh, "A Classification of Chinese Verbs for Language Parsing," in *Proceedings of the 1988 International Conference on Computer Processing of Chinese and Oriental Languages*, Toronto, August 29-September 1, 1988, pp. 414–417.

15. W. L. Chiang, J. J. Chen, and I. P. Lin, "Generalized Augmented Transition Network for English-Chinese Machine Translation System," Department of Computer Science and Information Engineering, National Taiwan University, Taipei, Taiwan, 1988.

16. Sharp Corporation, Personal interview with the Machine Translation Group, Sharp Corporation, Nara, Japan, August 3, 1988.

17. Y. S. Tsai, I. P. Lin, and L. S. Lee, "Parsing Chinese Conjunctions Using SASC," presented at the 1987 International Conference on Chinese and Oriental Language Computing, 1987.

18. R. J. Brachman and H. J. Levesque (eds.), *Readings in Knowledge Representation*, M. Kaufmann, Los Altos, CA, 1985.

19. S. K. Chang, "Theory of Icons and Its Implications to Chinese Information Processing," in *Proceedings of the 1988 International Conference on Computer Processing of Chinese and Oriental Languages*, Toronto, August 29-September 1, 1988, pp. 3–8.

20. R. E. Cullingford and B. A. Onyshkevych, "An Experiment in Lexicon-Driven Machine Translation," in *Machine Translation: Theoretical and Methodological Issues* (S. Nirenburg, ed.), Oxford University Press, Cambridge, 1987, Chap. 16.

21. R. W. Langacker, "An Introduction to Cognitive Grammar," *Cog. Sci.*, *10*, 1–40 (1986).

22. J. F. Sowa, *Conceptual Structures: Information Processing in Mind and Machine*, Addison-Wesley, Reading MA, 1984.

23. J. G. Carbonell, Panel presentation, Second International Conference on Theoretical and Methodological Issues in Machine Translation of Natural Languages, Carnegie Mellon University, Pittsburgh, June 12–14, 1988.

24. A. Kurematsu, Panel presentation, Second International Conference on Theoretical and Methodological Issues in Machine Translation of Natural Languages, Carnegie Mellon University, Pittsburgh, June 12–14, 1988.

25. S. Nirenburg, R. McCardell, E. Nyberg, S. Huffman, and E. Kenschaft, "Lexical Realization in Natural Language Generation," Second International Conference on Theoretical and Methodological Issues in Machine Translation of Natural Languages, Carnegie Mellon University, Pittsburgh, June 12–14, 1988.

26. S. Nirenburg, I. Monarch, T. Kaufmann, I. Nirenburg, and J. Carbonell, "Acquisition of Very Large Knowledge Bases: Methodology, Tools and Applications," CMU-CMT-88-108, Center for Machine Translation, Carnegie Mellon University, Pittsburgh, June 11, 1988.

27. H. Nomura, "Meaning Understanding in Machine Translation," Second International Conference on Theoretical and Methodological Issues in Machine Translation of Natural Languages, Carnegie Mellon University, Pittsburgh, June 12–14, 1988.

28. J. Impoco, "Computers That to Translate Good Enough: Practical Systems are Finally Appearing," *U.S. News & World Report*, December 5, 1988, p. 72.

29. M. Masterman, "The Essential Skills to be Acquired for Machine Translation," in *Translating and the Computer*, (B. M. Snell, ed.), North-Holland, New York, 1979, pp. 159–180.

30. J. L. Melton, "The Semantic Code," in *Tools for Machine Literature Searching* (J. W. Perry and A. Kent, eds.), Interscience, New York, 1958, Chap. 9.

31. J. G. Carbonell and M. Tomita, "Knowledge-Based Machine Translations, the CMU Approach," in *Machine Translation: Theoretical and Methodological Issues* (S. Nirenburg, ed.), Cambridge University Press, Cambridge, 1987, Chap. 5.

32. S. C. Loh and L. Kong, "An Interactive On-line Machine Translation System (Chinese into English)," in *Translating and the Computer* (B. M. Snell, ed.), North-Holland, New York, 1979, pp. 135–148.

33. C. J. Date, *An Introduction to Database Systems*, Vol. I, 4th Ed., Addison-Wesley, Menlo Park, CA, 1986, Chap. 3.

34. S. C. Yang, "A Search Algorithm and Data Structure for an Efficient Information System," presented at the 1969 International Conference on Computational Linguistics, Stockholm, Sweden, September, 1969b. Also printed as pre-print No. 51, Classification: IR 1.6, Research Group for Quantitative Linguistics, Fack, Stockholm 40, Sweden, 1969b.

35. L. L. Chang, L. P. Chang, J. C. Huang, Y. H. Cheng, and W. C. Wei, *Chinese Word Analyses*, Academia Sinica Computer Center, Taipei, 1986.

36. Y. H. Cheng and C. R. Huang, "Double-Object Verb in Chinese," *Chinese World, 48*, 1988.

37. C. R. Huang, "Head-Wrapping and Possessive Objects Syntactic vs. Lexico-Semantic Treatment of Discontinuity," *Tsing Hua J. Chinese Studies, 18*(1), 161–177 (June 1988).

38. S. S. Tseng, M. Y. Chang, C. C. Hsieh, and K. J. Chen, "Approaches on an Experimental Chinese Electronic Dictionary," in *Proceedings of the 1988 International Conference on Computer Processing of Chinese and Oriental Languages,* Toronto, August 29-September 1, 1988, pp. 371–374.

39. Y. R. Chao, *A Grammar of Spoken Chinese,* University of California Press, Berkeley, 1968.

40. S. C. Yang, "Automatic Segmentation and Phrase-Structure Parsing: A Simple Chinese Parser," *Thought and Language, 6,* 324–331 (January 1969).

41. J. K. Wu and C. Wang, *Principles of Modern Chinese Vocabularies,* People's Publishing, Inner Mongolia (China), 1983.

42. S. C. Yang and C. W. Yang, "A Universal Graphic Character Writer," 1969 International Conference on Computational Linguistics, Stockholm, Sweden, September 1969. Also printed as Preprint No. 42, Classification: TG 1.2, Research Group for Quantitative Linguistics, Fack, Stockholm 40, Sweden, 1969.

43. L. L. Chang, J. C. Huang, L. P. Chang, W. C. Wei, Y. H. Cheng, K. J. Chen, S. S. Tseng, and C. C. Hsieh, "Classification and Co-occurrence Restrictions in Chinese Simple Noun Phrases," to be published, 1988.

44. F. S. Yeh and T. X. Hsu, *Outline of Linguistics,* Beijing University Press, Beijing, 1981.

45. Sansyusya Publishing, CD-WORD Operating Manual, Tokyo, Sansyusya Publishing, 1987.

46. K. Maeda and E. Clarke, Personal communications with Sansyusya Publishing in Tokyo, Japan, 1988.

47. J. C. Sager and J. McNaught, "Feasibility Study of the Establishment of a Terminological Data Bank in the UK," *British Library Research and Development Report* No. 5642, Manchester, Center for Computational Linguistics, UMIST, CCL/UMIST Report No. 81/8, 1981.

48. S. C. Yang, "A Student Record System for Primary and Secondary Schools," Area Studies, Special Issue, Vol. II, No. 2, Proceedings of the Third Tamkang American Studies Conference, Taipei, Taiwan, April, 1981, pp. 215–228.

49. R. Davis and D. B. Leanat, *Knowledge-Based Systems and Artificial Intelligence,* McGraw-Hill, New York, 1982.

50. J. L. Kolodner, *Retrieval and Organizational Strategies in Conceptual Memory: A Computer Model,* Lawrence Erlbaum, Hillsdale, NJ, 1984.

51. S. Nirenburg and V. Raskin, "The Subworld Concept Lexicon And The Lexicon Management System," 1987.

52. J. C. Dai, H. J. Lee, and T. Liang, "Deterministic Parsing of Chinese Queries Through Attribute-Dependent Grammar," in *Proceedings of the 1988 International Conference on Computer Processing of Chinese and Oriental Languages,* Toronto, August 29-September 1, 1988, pp. 363–366.

53. H. J. Lee, *Research in Chinese Intelligent Database Assistant,* Micro-electronics and Information Science and Technology Research Center, Hsing-Chu, Taiwan, 1987.

54. J. T. Tou, "CATEC—a Computer-Aided Translation of English to

Chinese System," in *Proceedings of the 1988 International Conference on Computer Processing of Chinese and Oriental Languages*, Toronto, August 29-September 1, 1988, pp. 475–479.

55. C. L. Yeh and H. J. Lee, "Rule-Based Word Identification for Mandarin Chinese Sentences," in *Proceedings of the 1988 International Conference on Computer Processing of Chinese and Oriental Languages*, Toronto, August 29-September 1, 1988, pp. 432–436.

56. T. Lee, H. T. Wang, S. C. Yang, and E. Farmer, Linguistics Studies for the Chinese-to-English Machine Translation, Rome Air Development Center, Technical Report No. RADC-TR-65-443, June 1966.

57. A. Kurematsu, Personal interview at ATR Interpreting Telephone Research Laboratories in Osaka, Japan, August 5, 1988b.

58. J. L. Melton and J. S. Melton, "A Method for Automatic Encoding for Languages Other Than English," in *Tools for Machine Literature Searching* (J. W. Perry and A. Kent, eds.), Interscience, New York, 1958, Chap. 12.

59. T. H. Rees, Jr., "Standardized Telegraphic Abstracts from Articles in New York Times," in *Tools for Machine Literature Searching* (J. W. Perry and A. Kent, eds.), Interscience, New York, 1958, Chap. 7.

ADDITIONAL READING

Lin, I. P., H. H. Chen, J. H. Liaw, C. S. Cheng, and A. K. Tang, "A Knowledge-Based Machine Translation System," 1988.

Nirenburg, S. and J. Carbonell, "Integrating Discourse Pragmatics and Propositional Knowledge for Multi-Lingual Natural Language Processing," Submitted to AAAI, 1987, Science Track.

Nirenburg, S., R. McCardell, E. Nyberg, S. Huffman and E. Kenschoft, "Lexical Realization in Natural Language Generation," Second International Conference on Theoretical and Methodological Issues in Machine Translation of Natural Languages, Carnegie Mellon University, Pittsburgh, June 12–14, 1988.

Reifler, E., "Shinese-English Machine Translation, Its Lexicographic and Linguistic Problems," in *Machine Translation* (A. D. Booth, ed.), North-Holland, New York, 1967, Chap. 10.

Rosch, E., "Human Categorization," in *Advances in Cross-Cultural Psychology*, Vol. 1 (N. Warren, ed.), Academic Press, London, 1977.

Sager, J. C., "Multilingual Communication: Chairman's Introductory Review of Translating and the Computer," in *Translating and the Computer* (B. M. Snell, ed.), North-Holland, New York, 1979, pp. 1–25.

Salton, G. and M. J. McGill, *Introduction to Modern Information Retrieval*, McGraw-Hill, New York, 1983.

Smith, E. E. and D. L. Medin, *Concepts and Categories*, Harvard University Press, Cambridge, 1981.

Su, K. Y. and J. S. Chang, "Semantic and Syntactic Aspects of Score Function," 1988.

Tomita, M., Panel presentation, Second International Conference on Theoretical and Methodological Issues in Machine Translation of Natural Languages, Carnegie Mellon University, Pittsburgh, June 12–14, 1988.

Tucker, A. B., "A Perspective on Machine Translation: Theory and Practice," *Commun. ACM*, 27, 4 (1984).

Tucker, A. B., "Current Strategies in Machine Translation Research and Development," in *Machine Translation* (S. Nirenburg, ed.), Oxford University Press, Cambridge, England, 1987, Chap. 2.

Wei, L. Y., "A Chinese Indexing System Designed for Worldwide Use," *Proceedings of the 1988 International Conference on Computer Processing of Chinese and Oriental Languages,* Toronto, August 29-September 1, 1988, pp. 316–320.

Yang, S. C., "Interactive Language Learning Through a Private Computer Tutor," 1971 International Conference on Computational Linguistics, Debrecin, Hungary. Also published in *Papers in Computational Linguistics*, Publishing House of the Hungarian Academy of Sciences, Akademial Kiado, Budapest, Hungary, 1972, pp. 565–581.

Zhang, F. J., "Library Network Development in Chinese—Should It Be Different From the United States?," presented at International Student Conference, School of Library and Information Science, University of Pittsburgh, Pittsburgh, September 23–25, 1988.

VICTOR SHOU-CHUAN YANG

ELECTRONIC MAIL

INTRODUCTION AND DEFINITIONS

In its simplest terms, electronic mail can be defined as nonsimultaneous interpersonal electronic communication. Another way to think of electronic mail is a combination of print and electronic transmission of information. Electronic mail entails three factors: origination, transmission, and reception. Any or all three of these may be performed electronically to qualify for electronic mail. In fact, only one has to be electronic to be viewed as electronic mail.

This definition covers many current and historic communication services, including telegraph, telex, fascimile, and mailgram. In fact, some experts include the telephone as a form of electronic mail. Such services have been well covered elsewhere in this publication and will only be referred to here. Rather, this article will focus on a form called computer-based messaging system (CBMS) or electronic mail and messaging system (EMS). This sort of electronic mail is electronic throughout functions of origination, transmission, and reception and will be the most likely form to develop in the future.

TECHNOLOGIES IN ELECTRONIC MAIL

Electronic mail owes its development to a multitude of technologies, many of which are still evolving. They are

Electronic technology
Origination technology
Storage technology
Communications technology
Reception technology

Electronic Technology

Great strides in digital technology have been primarily responsible for the evolution of all other technologies involving electronic mail. Large-scale integration (LSI) has permitted a cost-effective means of creating, transmitting, storing, and retrieving information in a completely electronic form. Components are now smaller in size, less expensive, more reliable, and use less power than their predecessors. The techniques of electron-beam or x-ray lithography will permit components design to continue this trend.

Origination Technology

Recently, the options for originating technology have increased significantly. In the early 1970s, dedicated dumb terminals were the only means of creating electronic information. Individuals had to type messages by relying on rudimentary text editors. Thus, the technology required access to a centralized computer, and the composition of mail became one of the computer's multitudinous functions.

More recently, communicating word processors and microcomputers have become available. They permit the creation stage to become decentralized, resulting in more sophisticated and easier to use information entry programs. Besides relieving a central computer of creation, these machines allow their users more control over information transmission. Both of these activities have helped the originator by requiring him/her to spend less time on the electronic mail system. Additionally, when one considers that they are general purpose in nature, communicating word processors and microcomputers often are more cost effective and offer more flexibility than dedicated equipment, such as fascimile machines, dumb terminals, and telex machines.

Communications Technology

Communications technology has enjoyed explosive growth in recent years. During the late 1960s and very early 1970s, dedicated lines between the user's terminal and host computer were the only means available for communication. This made for a very simple, restrictive mail system. Only those users directly connected to the computer could benefit from electronic mail. In fact, some of the earliest applications of electronic mail were system messages created by the host computer operator and distributed to all terminals.

Direct distance dialing (DDD), leased lines, packet-switched networks (also known as message switching networks) and, more recently, microwave transmission, satellite transmission, and integrated services digital networks (ISDNs) have created extremely flexible communications options. Instead of dedicated terminals, individuals can now access the mail system from anywhere, using, in many cases, standard voice grade telephone lines.

Of the various forms of transmission, communications packet-switched networks are currently the most popular for centralized CBMS. They offer quality data transmission at a low cost. Because pricing is often influenced by the unit of time chargeable, packet-switched networks often offer the smallest unit chargeable, in tenths of seconds. In comparison, the conventional phone line's smallest unit is a minute. Packet-switched networks are dedicated to data transmission exclusively.

The actual function of packet switching has many obvious benefits. Packets or, more appropriately in some cases, messages can be sent via the least traveled path regardless of distance. Each packet or transmission can take different paths. The result is a transmission that is delivered faster. In contrast, although it may take a path less traveled, a DDD cannot alter its path throughout the transmission.

Another advantage of packet-switched networks is that they often provide additional value-added services including terminal emulation and transmission padding. Terminal emulation permits a user to simulate the characteristics of other terminals even though his/her terminal may not have those characteristics. Terminal emulation is particularly beneficial with the onslaught of various originating devices; few have the same communications protocol. Padding is a means of slowing data transmission by sending null characters in place of actual content. Padding, for instance, will slow a 1200-baud transmission to, say, 1100 baud. Although such a decrease is imperceptible to the sender or receiver of the information, it is sufficient enough to permit the sending or receiving device to process the information before acting on the information following.

The speed of transmission has improved tremendously over time. At one time, 110 words (660 characters) per minute was the fastest rate; more recently, 300 to 1,200 and even 2,400 words per minute is commonplace. In fact, using a dedicated line, one can reach transmission speeds up to 9,600 words per minute. In the near future, use of fiber optics as a transmission carrier, instead of copper wires, and the digitization of all communications will permit increased transmission speeds to 10^9 characters per minute. In the near term, speeds of this nature may have little impact on the popularity of electronic mail, however, because such speeds require dedicated equipment.

Nondedicated voice grade lines require a piece of equipment to translate the information into a form that a terminal, word processor, or microcomputer can handle. Modems handle this function. In the early 1970s, communications translation was the only function a modem handled. More recently, modems have automatic dialing and automatic answering capabilities, so they are capable of connecting to an electronic mail system unattended. Modems can also detect transmission speeds and adjust to the proper speed, and they can store protocol information. These features permit automatic and unattended connection to different mail systems. Often modems may contain real time clocks to permit time-determined unattended connections. As communications lines become digitized, the need for modems will lessen.

Local area networks (LANs) are becoming a popular communications option for decentralized electronic mail. LANs now require dedicated lines and thus benefit from fast transmission speeds. However, they suffer from nonstandard technology, and LANs from different manufacturers frequently cannot be interconnected. Given that decentralized electronic mail is a popular option for intercompany communication, incompatible LAN communications protocol may not be too critical to LAN acceptance. Eventually, as all office communication, such as voice, becomes digitized, the need for a universal communications protocol will become acute and require standardization among the surviving LANs.

Storage Technology

Storage technology's developments have centered on lower costs per character stored and higher capabilities contained in the same physical space. These developments have occurred simultaneously for both internal and external storage devices. For today's microcomputers, for instance, 640,000 characters is a common limit for internal storage; some newer models are even capable of millions of characters of internal storage. This amount has increased 10-fold from a maximum of 64,000 characters only a few years ago. Similarly, external storage devices—both floppy disk drives and hard disk drives—have experienced similar increases, though not as dramatic.

This increased capacity at a lower cost has permitted originating devices to be capable of document creation, temporary storage of documents for delayed transmission, and the development of decentralized electronic mail networks. Just as important, storage technology has allowed electronic mail systems to be capable of storing messages until the recipient has had a chance to read them. This feature has permitted many centralized systems to function in a decentralized fashion because the recipient's computer contains a program that will capture all messages in an unattended mode. In this way, electronic mail becomes a tool of personal convenience. Mail can be read at one's own leisure, and, if necessary, stored in a fashion more functional than a filing cabinet.

Reception Technology

Reception technology has developed along two lines. First, a recipient can use the same devices available for originating electronic mail, that is, a terminal, a word processor, or a microcomputer. A recipient will benefit from all of the characteristics an originator experiences with these devices. Perhaps the biggest advantage for the recipient, however, is the ability to review messages at will. This option requires a reception device that can store the information until later recall. Clearly, word processors and microcomputers are ideal for this. Another benefit is the ability to modify a message and send it back to the originator. Thus, one can create a dynamic written record of communication on a particular topic.

Another option for reception technology, and a very popular one at that, is hard copy. Frequently, messages travel in one direction to a single recipient. Consequently, there is no need to keep the message in electronic form. Moreover, a message may be very long or require review by many individuals, or may require another means of portability. Like other technologies, there are many different types of hard copy devices, although they generally fall into two categories: impact devices and nonimpact devices.

Impact Devices

Impact devices are currently more popular due to cost. A drawback is the amount of noise they generate from the mechanical activity. The most popular of these devices are matrix printers. These devices are typically quite inexpensive and produce readable quality, often bordering on letter quality. Moreover, some matrix printers permit graphic reproduction, as well as text representation. Matrix printers contain a cluster of tiny pins, which are controlled by electromagnets. Matrix printers are often referred to by their print density (i.e., 7 × 9 or 9 × 9) or pin density (24 pin). Generally, the larger the number of pins there are, the greater the character or image technology. More sophisticated matrix printers can overprint a character with a slight offset and thus produce a more solid or darker looking character. Matrix printers offer the option of printing images, as well as characters. Even color printout is becoming an option with these printers.

Another popular impact device is the daisy wheel printer. These machines have a spinning device containing solid characters. The characters can be organized on a ball, on the end of spokes, or on the edges of a thimblelike device. Daisy wheel printers tend to be more expensive and slower than matrix printers. They are also unable to generate graphics. However, they always produce letter-quality print.

Nonimpact Devices

Nonimpact devices are becoming more competitive with impact devices. In general, they offer the flexibility and speed of matrix printers and the print quality of daisy wheel printers. Additionally, they are quieter than either type of impact device. This group is broken into two categories: ink jet and laser/xerographic/electrographic.

Ink jet printers actually shoot droplets of ink on a piece of paper. Therefore, low-resolution ink jet prints look very similar to that of matrix printers. Like matrix printers, ink jet printers can offset and increase density to simulate solid character generation. Also, like matrix printers, ink jet printers can produce graphics and print at fast speeds. Perhaps the biggest drawbacks to ink jets are that the paper has to be highly absorbent to minimize blotching and the ink bladders require frequent changes.

Laser/xerographic/electrographic printers actually create print through a means similar to photocopy machines. They take a "picture" of the information and either chemically or electrically affix that picture to the paper. Until recently, prices of these printers have been quite high ($20,000). Image quality is extremely high, and the printers are capable of producing high-resolution graphics—300 dots (pixels/pels) per inch. Moreover, these printers are fast. Given current prices, however, laser/xerographic/electrographic printers will not be a popular option for electronic mail.

ELECTRONIC MAIL FEATURES

Electronic mail is usually divided into two groups: centralized CBMS and decentralized CBMS. In a centralized CBMS, there is a main computer that is accessed by terminals, computers, microcomputers, and/or communicating word processors. These systems can be either direct access (i.e., dedicated) or dial-up. The electronic mail program and all electronic mail communication reside on the main computer.

In a decentralized CBMS, each machine in the system has electronic mail capability. Often, a decentralized CBMS requires direct access, although through the capabilities of microcomputers, many are now dial-up. A decentralized CBMS may be composed of stand-alone message processing workstations, intelligent peripheral devices, or software for a particular microcomputer. Messages are stored on each machine and, thus, do not require much effort to retrieve and review.

A difficulty of decentralized CBMSs is that all equipment on the system must be the same or, through software, emulate the other equipment. For instance, one cannot have a system composed of intelligent peripheral devices and stand-alone message processing workstations. As equipment becomes more standardized, this incompatibility will lessen.

Electronic mail offers many features, few of which are standard across systems. One of the reasons for the lack of standardization arises from the wide variety of products described as electronic mail. Therefore, keep in mind that some of the characteristics below may be specific to one device and one device only.

One very common characteristic is message storage and retrieval. This feature permits messages to remain in the system until they are read by the recipient. Frequently, it also means that a message remains until the recipient decides what he or she wants to do with it, and the options may be many. For instance, the recipient may decide to destroy the message or store the message under a certain category.

Another characteristic is message formatting, which is often in terms of text editing. As discussed earlier, this feature may permit sophisticated

editing/formatting capabilities similar to those found on word processors.
In fact, it is common for an electronic mail service to contain a spelling
checker with the capability of personalization.

A third common characteristic is simultaneous message preparation/
transmission. This permits an originator and a recipient to prepare messages for each other or for different individuals and send them simultaneously without any interference. In fact, many systems offer priority mailing. If one uses this feature, the recipient is notified that he/she has received a message without the destruction of work that has already been performed. At the recipient's convenience, he/she can "open his/her mailbox"
and read messages.

A characteristic working conjointly with the preceding one is that of unattended reception. An idividual does not have to be connected to have his/
her mail develivered. As described earlier, mail is stored until the individual
reads it. In most systems, an individual has an option on the amount of message he/she can read. Services often permit one to review who sent a message, when it was sent, its subject, and the length of the message. Additionally, systems offer options as to which messages a recipient can read.
A recipient can specify by position of letter (i.e., first in mailbox, etc.),
by mail status (i.e., unread), or by category (i.e., subject or originator).

Some systems offer additional communications capabilities beyond electronic mail, the most popular of which is computer conferencing. This
feature permits two or more individuals to transmit and receive information in real time. Everyone participating in the particular computer conference sees everyting else sent (although there are some systems that
permit information to be sent directly to one or a select segment of par-
ticipants). A computer conference can be thought of as a true real-time
conversation in digital form. It is replete with interruptions and side-track-
ing as well.

Finally, electronic mail systems offer various message-handling features,
including carbon copy, blind copy, delayed sending, message forwarding,
reply requested, acknowledgement requested, security mailing, and priority mailing. These features provide tremendous options for ways of handling
mail, some of which are not possible in other means of communications.
For instance, with conventional mail, it is impossible to determine whether
someone received a piece of mail from an originator without a second contact. However, electronic mail takes care of this at the originator's request.

Another feature of electronic mail is the addition of nonelectronic mail
services being offered on an electronic mail service. For example, some
electronic mail services are offering access to various types of data bases.
Others offer access to games, programming languages, and a variety of
applications programs. Frequently, these additional services integrate into
the electronic mail. It is therefore possible on some systems to retrieve
electronically full text articles on desired topics, make comments, and
"mail" them to someone else on the system.

Likewise, services not originally offering electronic mail are offering it
as an additional service. Many of the data base distributors are offering
various forms of electronic mail. Apparently, they view electronic mail as
a means to round out services already offered.

ELECTRONIC MAIL APPLICATIONS

Electronic mail is becoming an integrated part of communications systems.
In this way, like the telephone or conventional mail, electronic mail appli-

cations are endless. However, within both business and personal settings, applications can be grouped into three broad categories.

> Information dissemination
> Transactional communications
> Professional communications

These three categories are based on two features of electronic mail: the type of transmission and the size of the receiving audience.

Information Dissemination

Information dissemination takes advantage of electronic mail's ability to permit simultaneous transmission of information to a large group of users. Additionally, this group usually requires one-way transmission—to provide the recipients with information.

Electronic mail offers significant advantages over other forms of communication to disseminate information. First, it is relatively easy to create a document and distribute it simultaneously to all recipients. Moreover, the sender has options to create audit trails not only to verify that the approrieate parties were sent the information but, also, when they received the information. Finally, electronic mail permits controlled delivery of the information. Thus, the sender can control when he or she wants the recipient to receive the document.

The need to distribute information is quite popular with companies that have decentralized offices. Information, such as price changes, new product announcements, and latest changes in company policy, can be disseminated quickly and easily. A second form of information distribution is based on one of the earliest forms of electronic mail, namely notices/bulletins sent from a computer system's operator to its users. Notices/bulletins have become more sophisticated over time and still play a vital role as a means of information distribution. Finally, rudimentary forms of advertising are occurring on some electronic mail systems as a means of information dissemination.

Transactional Communications

Transactional communications are typified by the transmission of a predescribed form. Like information dissemination, this group generally takes advantage of disseminating the information to a wide audience although, in some cases, the transmission will be focused on a single recipient. However, transactional communications require response from the recipient, thus simple two-way communication.

Transactional communications take advantage of a number of electronic mail capabilities. Most commercial systems can create sophisticated forms. Additionally, a sender can control delivery and monitor for receipt of the transaction. Such a capability may be invaluable in light of customer service. Again, like information dissemination, a sender and the receiver can keep detailed audit records of the transactions. Because the transactional information is collected in computer readable form, processing the information can be immediate without keyboarding the information as would be necessary through other forms of communication.

Use of transactional communications occurs both in the business and the consumer sectors. Many companies have computerized many forms and offer the salespeople the ability to key the information in electronically and send the result electronically to a home office for approval or fulfillment. Some companies are experimenting with offering many of their customer service forms through electronic mail. Finally, some market research and other types of surveys and questionnaires have been developed on, distributed through, and responded to via electronic mail.

Professional Communications

Professional communications differ from the other two groups in two ways. First, the transmission of the communication is generally to an individual or a very limited group of individuals. Secondly, it usually requires an on-going exchange of information, not just a one-way or simple two-way exchange.

This group takes advantage of electronic mail's insensitivity to distance. Additionally, most electronic mail systems permit dynamic linking of messages, thus creating documentation and an audit trail for the duration of the particular topic. Finally, the immediacy of electronic mail permits both parties to discuss issues in a timely manner.

Scientific researchers, individuals with very specialized information, and individuals handling time-sensitive information take advantage of professional communication via electronic mail.

BENEFITS AND DRAWBACKS OF ELECTRONIC MAIL

Many experts observe that electronic mail will be a means by which office communications systems will be integrated. Electronic mail combines many of the characteristics of the telephone and conventional mail and integrates them into a single communications service. Researchers have shown that electronic mail improves productivity through its ability to capture, update, and modify information. Moreover, electronic mail tends to be handled less often. If the electronic mail service offers filing capabilities, individuals have a complete service that delivers information and permits them to digest the information at will and handle the processed information in virtually any way they wish.

Electronic mail offers faster turnaround of information. The time it takes to complete the delivery of an item is nearly instantaneous regardless of the distance. A user of electronic mail, then, needs to focus more on "when to deliver," not "how to deliver." Electronic mail has a sense of urgency that makes it an extremely effective means of communication.

It is easy to learn to use electronic mail. Many institutions have trained their clerical staffs successfully to handle electronic mail. In addition, electronic mail often provides another use for equipment that many institutions already have. The adoption of electronic mail may also offer organizations the opportunity to acquire more sophisticated equipment than they currently have.

Due to electronic mail's time and distance insensitivity, the cost of a message is constant regardless of distance. Moreover, electronic mail provides a means of an audit trail. The user generally has the option of retaining the information in electronic format or having hard copy produced.

As stated earlier, electronic mail offers the capability of sending information to one (i.e., narrowcasting) or to many (i.e., broadcasting) with relatively equal amounts of ease. Many communications require a combination of both. With the exception of graphics representation, electronic mail systems have few requirements regarding the characteristics of the information to be sent electronically. Volume is also not a consideration. Many of these characteristics provide electronic mail with an extremely good cost/performance ratio.

There are some drawbacks with the current technologies of electronic mail, however. Currently, electronic mail cannot handle graphics-oriented information. Thus, institutions generally have to rely on separate hardware, most frequently fascimile transmission, to handle graphics or combined textual and graphic information. Current trends in the terminal and communications technology indicate that it will be possible to integrate text and graphics into electronic mail in the near future.

One of the reasons that graphic and textual material cannot be combined on the same system is the lack of standards across electronic mail systems. This lack of standards plagues every aspect of electronic mail. Virtually every service has its own protocol, its own method of storing and sending messages, and its own method for identifying the destination of a message. Standardization becomes extremely difficult as more and more services are calling themselves electronic mail. Yet there are efforts toward standardization. In 1984, the CCITT started to work on the X.400 standard for CBMS. This standard covers network architecture, protocol structure, implementation structure, message transfer, and interpersonal messaging systems. Once completed, the standard will cover transmission of text, facsimile, graphics, voice, and arbitrary data structures over all electronic mail systems embracing the standard. Likewise, the United States National Bureau of Standards and ANSI are working on standards for electronic mail. How similar their standards will be to X.400 remains to be seen.

A third difficulty with electronic mail is that one must sign onto the system to determine if any mail is waiting. At present, there is no way to notify an individual that he or she has mail if the individual is not on the system. This problem, known as mailbox lag, becomes further complicated by the pricing structure of many electronic mail systems; often they charge individuals for access just to check a mailbox. Unless individuals access the mail system in a timely manner, many of the benefits of electronic mail are not realized.

Part of the difficulty of mailbox lag will be resolved when the volume of mail on the system reaches a critical mass. The current volume is often low enough that many individuals receive mail, at best, sporadically. In the meantime, systems are examining methods to encourage system access. Some are instituting additional services besides electronic mail. Others are taking advantage of auto answer modems and are attempting to contact the customers via the customer's equipment. Still others are looking at pricing structures based on the activity performed.

Electronic mail suffers from myriad policy and regulation issues. For instance, will the United States benefit from a public- or private-sector-based service? Or will electronic mail be offered by a mixture of public and private services as it currently is? Additionally, what level of privacy will users of electronic mail be benefited by? Who will be responsible for monitoring the services to ensure that no one's privacy is violated? What sort of regulations will electronic mail users be confronted with when transmitting internationally? Who will be responsible for guaranteeing equal access to electronic mail within a country? For the most part, these issues will shape the form and success of electronic mail.

The Future of Electronic Mail

Despite these current shortcomings, the future of electronic mail looks very promising. As an industry, electronic mail is expected to grow from $1 billion in the early 1980s to $150 billion by 1994. Mailboxes have grown from 5,000 in the 1970s to 200,000 in the early 1980s. By the mid-1980s there should be 3 million mailboxes. Not surprisingly, actual mail handled by electronic mail will grow as dramatically. The Office of Technology Assessment predicts that electronic mail will deliver 5 billion messages in 1985, 18 billion by 1990, and 60 billion by 2000.

Although those numbers are a fraction of the total amount of mail delivered through traditional services (approximately 2% by 1987), experts are predicting that electronic mail will have a direct impact on conventional mail by the latter part of the 1980s. From that point onward, the volume of conventional mail will decline as electronic mail becomes commonplace.

Electronic mail will have an important role as a communication's technology. Already over 18% of all U.S. businesses use some form of electronic mail, whereas another 20% are actively planning its implementation. Acceptance of electronic mail is not as impressive at the consumer level, although those who subscribe to information distributors with electronic mail features do so primarily for communication technologies such as electronic mail. Adoption of electronic mail should grow as more individuals and institutions start using electronic mail. Videotext will be a possible service to introduce electronic mail to the homes; the proliferation of microcomputers in offices will spur the acceptance of electronic mail in business. The creation and adoption of standards will speed up the acceptance of electronic mail.

Electronic mail services will begin to develop into complex communications structures. A large international electronic mail service may connect to a single node of a decentralized in-house service which, in turn, connects to a dial-up corporate centralized service. Naturally, for electronic mail to succeed, it will be necessary that communications are easy to perform throughout the whole structure. Moreover, there must be sufficient security throughout.

Advances in technology will continue to improve the capabilities of electronic mail. The integration of graphic and textual information will break down the final barrier of electronic mail as a means of communication. Also, voice- and video-activated technology will have a positive impact on the acceptance of electronic mail. Finally, the development of more sophisticated communications networks, such as LANs and ISDNs, will permit the increased flexibility of electronic mail.

BIBLIOGRAPHY

Connell, Stephen, and Ian A. Galbraith, *Electronic Mail: A Revolution in Business Communications*, Knowledge Industry Press, White Plains, New York, 1980.

Cunningham, Ian, "Electronic Mail Standards to Get Rubber-Stamped and Go Worldwide," *Data Commun.*, *13*(5) 159–168, (May 1984).

"Electronic Message Service Systems: Hearings before the Subcommittee on Postal Personnel and Modernization of the Committee on Post Office and Civil Service," *House of Representatives, Ninety-sixth Congress, Second Session*, U.S. Government Printing Office, Washington, DC, 1980.

Fersko-Weiss, Henry, "Electronic Mail: The Emerging Connection," *Personal Comput., 9*(1), 71–79 (January 1985).

Gabel, David, "Making a Habit of Electronic Mail," *Personal Comput., 8*(8), 91–97 (August 1984).

"Implications of Electronic Mail and Message Systems for the U.S. Postal Service," *Report No. OTA-CIT-183*, U.S. Government Printing Office, Washington, DC, 1982.

Nothhaft, Henry, "Making a Case for Using Electronic Mail," *Data Commun., 11*(5), 85–93 (May 1982).

Petrosky, Mary, "How to Make the Electronic Mail Connection," *Infoworld, 7*(45), 27–28 (November 11, 1985).

Potter, Robert J., "Electronic Mail," *Science,* 195(4283), 1160–1164 (March 1977).

Rafaels, Bob, "100 Links Global Business," *Portable 100/200, 2*(11), 36–42, 60–61 (June 1985).

Rivers, D. A., "Electronic Mail: Alternative for Document Distribution," *Word Process, Inf. Syst., 8*(1), 20–21, 24, 53 (January 1981).

Sachs, Jonathan, "Local Area Networks," *PC World, 2*(7), 69–75 (July 1984).

Schiappa, Barbara, "Electonic Mail Services That Really Work," *Bus. Comput. Syst., 3*(11), 45–54 (November 1984).

Trudell, Libby, *Options for Electronic Mail*, Knowledge Industry Press, White Plains, New York, 1984.

Vervest, Peter, *Electronic Mail & Message Handling*, Quorum Books, Westport, CT, 1985.

EBEN LEE KENT

ELECTRONIC MAIL MESSAGE HANDLING SYSTEMS x.400*

INTRODUCTION

Message handling systems, often known as "computer-based message systems" or simply "electronic mail," have many analogies to the regular mail system. In the regular mail system, a message is composed first, then an envelope is addressed, the message is put as a content into the envelope and both thrown into a mailbox. The mail system transports this letter from office to office and eventually deposits it in the mail box of the addressee. The addressee takes the letter out of the letter box, opens the envelope, and consumes the message.

Electronic mail will soon be an alternative to regular postal mail service. First used for simple interpersonal messages and "memo"-type communication, provisions are made such that nearly all information transmitted by traditional mail services soon will be conveyed by message handling systems.

In electronic message handling systems, the same elements can be distinguished (Fig. 1), only these are not realized with paper content, letter-box, and post office but by electronic means. The two persons involved are here called the originator and the recipient, respectively. The terms content and envelope have been carried over to the electronic message handling systems, the elements mailbox and post office, however, are designated by other terms, which we will get to know shortly.

In regular mail, a large number of content types can be communicated, for instance, letter, picture, etc. The same is true for electronic message handling systems and, although the most common application is the communication of ASCII text files, there exists the possibility to communicate teletex or telefax messages, or a mixture of both. Even complete multimedia documents can be exchanged between originator and recipient (Fig. 2).

The name "Message Handling System" is derived from the primary use of the system, namely, the exchange of interpersonal messages. Consequently, the message handling standards define fields for the recipient(s), carbon copy recipients, date and time, subject as well as references to other messages.

Message handling services have a big advantage when compared with other communication services: they offer a store and forward system (originator and recipient are not taking part in the communication simultaneously). This characteristic is especially useful when originator and recipient live in different time zones and a common usage of the system is to compose a message late in the evening, hand it over to the system, and the message is read by the recipient the following morning. Interruptions of ongoing work,

---

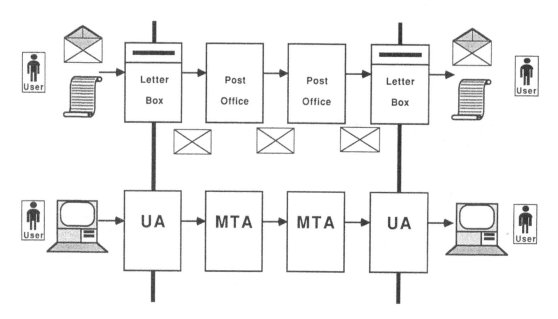

FIGURE 1 Electronic message handling systems and the regular mail. UA, user agents; MTA, message transfer agent.

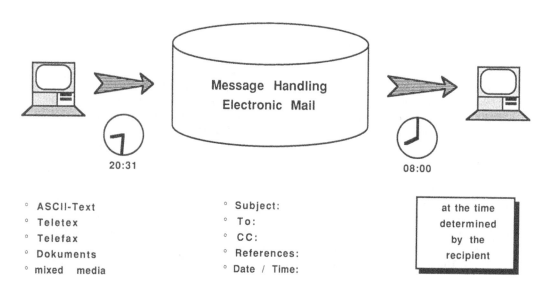

FIGURE 2 Asynchronous communication (store and forward).

as happens with ringing telephones, no longer prevails; the message is read by the recipient at his or her convenience.

In 1984, CCITT (International Telegraph and Telephone Consultative Committee) published a series of recommendations, or standards, that regulate the communication between public message handling systems as well as the communication between public and private message handling systems. These eight recommendations are issued in one volume (Fascicle is the CCITT term) of the Red Book and are commonly known under the name "X.400" (Table 1).

The 1984 standards are in some areas incomplete and have in the interim been revised by CCITT. These revisions were published in 1988 in the Blue Book and represent a major expansion of the standard. The original eight recommendations have been restructured and there are now twenty-two of them in existence. During the restructuring, some of the recommendations of the old X.400 series have received numbers in the X.200 series, that is, they now belong to the general OSI (open system interconnection) communication model. Furthermore, the recommendations describing the services have received F-series numbers. Table 1 shows the relationship between the recommendations of 1984 and the new ones.

The recommendations that are now in the X.200 series will also be published as international standards by the International Standards Organization (ISO). This indicates that the CCITT group that worked out the first recommendations between 1981 and 1984 did pioneering work for the application layer of the OSI model. On the other hand, ISO defined an interim structure for the application layer. Unfortunately, this structure is not reflected in the recommendations of 1984 and was one of the main reasons for the major restructuring of the recommendations. The new texts have a completely new appearance to the reader and also contain more precise and formal definitions of the services. Unfortunately, this formalism does not facilitate the reading and understanding of the texts.

The CCITT X.400 series recommendations of 1988 differ in appearance drastically from those of 1984. Although the model on which the definitions are based remains basically the same, subtle extensions were necessitated by the increased functionality in message handling services.

The most apparent change from 1984 to 1988 lies in the structure of the application (in the OSI sense). This modification is due to ISO's progressive work on the definition of the application layer structure, which CCITT followed in their 1988 recommendations.

A number of service elements have been added to the recommendations, many of which reflect the new functionality (e.g., postal delivery, distribution lists, secure messages, etc.). The appendix provides a complete list of all service elements as defined in X.400.

THE MODEL

Recommendation X.400 defines a model that describes the basic relations between the components of the message handling systems. This model is an onion skin model. The innermost skin, the message transfer system, relays messages from MTA (message transfer agent) to MTA. Messages enter this transfer system via a submission protocol and leave it via a delivery protocol (Fig. 3).

The middle skin, the message handling system, contains the user agents (UA). These user agents assist the user of the message handling system,

TABLE 1 The CCITT Recommendations of 1984 and 1988.

1984 →→→ 1988

1984		1988	
X.400	System Model - Service Elements	F.400	System and Service Overview
		F.401	Naming & Addressing for Public MH Services
X.401	Basic Service Elements and Optional User Facilities	X.402	Overall Architecture
		X.403	Conformance Testing
		X.407	Abstract Service Definition Conventions
X.408	Encoded Information Type Conversion Rules	X.408	Encoded Information Type Conversion Rules
X.409	Presentation Transfer Syntax and Notation	X.208	Abstract Syntax Notation One (ASN.1)
		X.209	Basic Encoding Rules for ASN.1
X.410	Remote Operation and Reliable Transfer Server	X.218	Reliable Transfer — Model and Service
		X.228	Reliable Transfer — Protocol Specification
		X.219	Remote Operations — Model, Service and Notation
		X.229	Remote Operations — Protocol Specification
X.411	Message Transfer Layer	F.410	Public Message Transfer Service
		X.411	Message Transfer System: Abstract Service Definitions and Procedures
		X.413	Message Store: Abstract Service Definition
		X.419	Protocol Specifications
		F.415	Physical Delivery Service Intercommunication
X.420	Interpersonal Messaging User Agent Layer	F.420	The Public IPM Service
		X.420	Interpersonal Messaging System
X.430	Access Protocol for Teletex Terminals	T.330	Telematic Access Protocol
		F.421	Intercommunication Telex / IPM Service
		F.422	Intercommunication Teletex / IPM Service

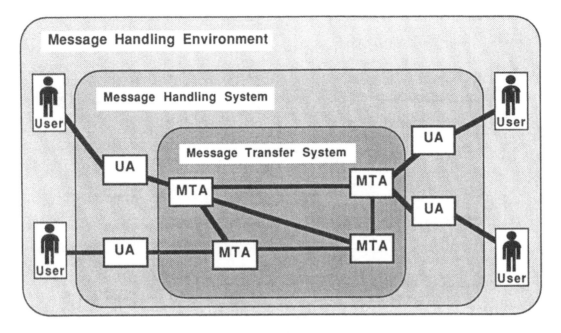

FIGURE 3   The model of the message handling system (1984).

on the one hand, and engage in submission and delivery actions with the message transfer agents.

The outermost skin, the message handling environment, is populated by the users who utilize the message handling system for the communication of messages.

In 1988 this model was enhanced and the message handling system now contains entities for message stores (MS) and access units (AU) for so-called indirect users. These indirect users normally employ other telematic services (e.g., teletex) for their daily communication. These access units have opened the message handling system to those users (Fig. 4). A special access unit (PDAU, physical delivery access unit) establishes a connection with the regular mail service.   The transition from the message handling systems to the regular mail system is defined extensively in the recommendations of 1988; these definitions provide that the special mail services (e.g., registered mail, special delivery, etc.) are employed consistently by all message handling systems.

A special feature which facilitates the integration of small computers (e.g., PCs), a new entity "message store," has been defined. Considering the limited storage capacity of a PC and the fact that a PC acting as user agent or message transfer agent has no possibility to negotiate the sequence of message transfers with an MTA results in the necessity of a system entity that can buffer messages. A definition of this entity has been repeatedly requested by users and implementors of the message handling system.

Bowing to pressure exerted by the ISO for the incorporation of such an entity, CCITT defined the message store and integrated it into the new recommendations.

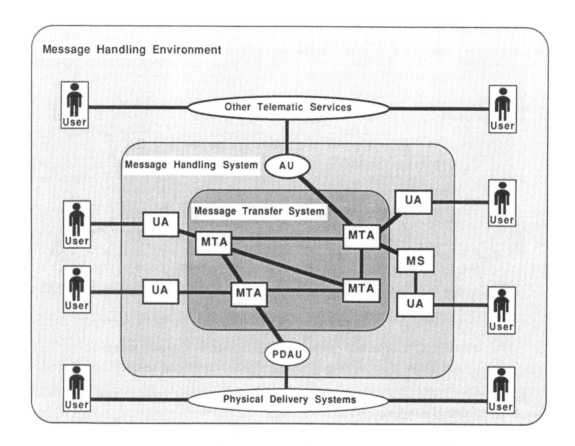

FIGURE 4   The model of the message handling system (1988).

The onion skin model makes no assumption about the physical implementations of the different entities. It is therefore possible to implement an MTA and several UAs in a single computer system via simple terminals such as VDUs of the VT100 class.

The middle of Figure 5 shows a situation where two computer systems share the functionality of a message handling system. In the system of the right-hand side again an MTA and one or several UAs are implemented that allow the utilization of the system via simple terminals. The system on the left-hand side contains an MTA and one or several MSs (message store), the UA functionality in this case is implemented in the terminal itself, which therefore, must contain some processing power (e.g., a PC).

The lower part of Figure 5 shows an implementation where in the left-hand computer system only UAs are implemented. The system on the right-hand side contains an MTA as well as one or several MSs and UAs; this provides for the possibility of accessing the system with different classes of terminals.

The three examples shown in the figure are by no means an enumeration of all possible variants of implementations of a message handling system; the intent here is to demonstrate the unlimited variety of implementation possibilities.

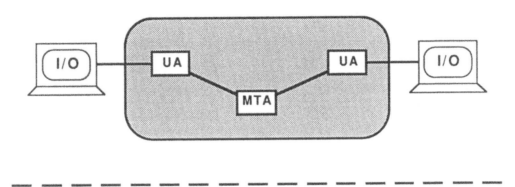

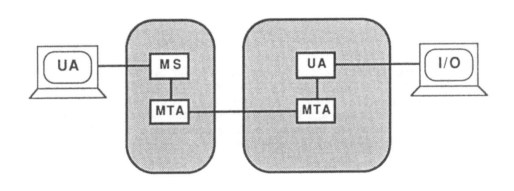

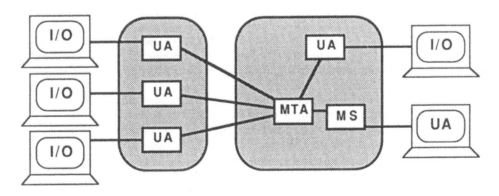

FIGURE 5 Physical realization of a message handling system.

As mentioned earlier a message is composed of an envelope and a content. The envelope part contains originator and recipient addresses as well

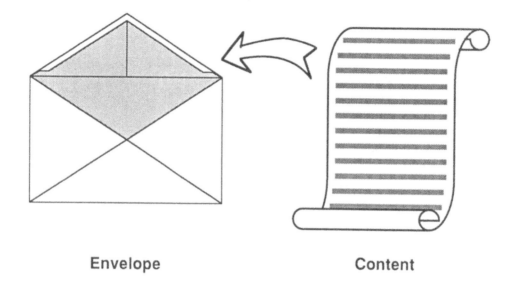

Envelope   Content

as all necessary indications to influence the transfer of the message. In particular, indications are necessary to invoke the supplementary services of the message transfer system (e.g., request for a delivery notification). The content part of a message is not touched by the message transfer system except in cases where the supplementary service of a content conversion (e.g., text to facsimile) is requested.

INTERPERSONAL MESSAGE SYSTEM

The contents of messages that are carried by the message transfer system can be coded with any chosen method. The transfer system thus can be used to establish "connectionless" store and forward communication. However, the original need was for a system that transports messages from person to person. To meet this need, the X.400 recommendations defined another skin (Fig. 6). So-called cooperating user agents, that implement this recommendation, establish for their users the interpersonal message service (IPMS).

In order to open the service for a large user community, the recommendations of 1984 already contained a specification for access protocols for the teletex and telex service. The need for this service is still present. In fact, it is envisioned that the message handling systems will become the primary interworking facilities between otherwise incompatible telematic services. It is not surprising therefore that the recommendations of 1988 have enhanced the specifications concerning this service. Together with other enhancements, an access unit for telex (TLXAU = Telex Access Unit), an access unit for telematic services (TLMA = Telematic Access Unit), and respective enhancements to the physical delivery access unit, namely, the connection with the regular mail, are defined. Also the newly introduced message store can be enhanced to an interpersonal message store (Fig. 7).

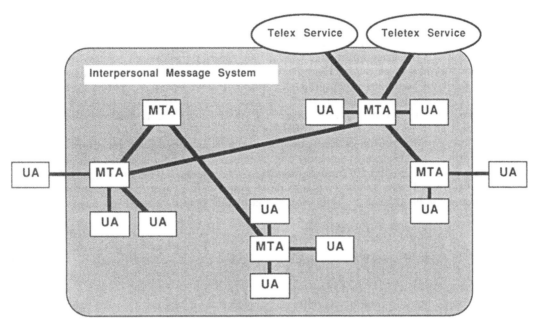

FIGURE 6 The model of the interpersonal message handling system (1984).

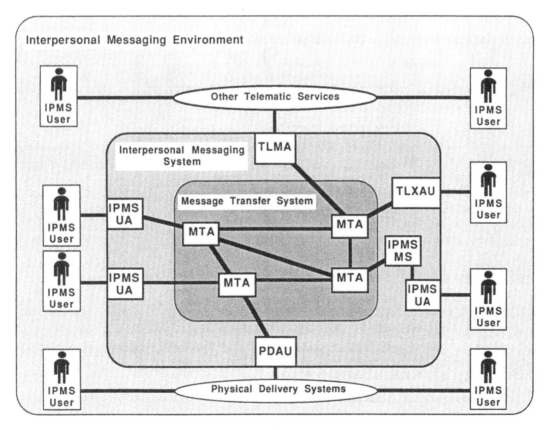

FIGURE 7 The model of the interpersonal message handling system (1988).

The message transfer system remains transparent for this application of interpersonal messages; hence MTAs can transfer messages whose content is coded according to some other (even private) definition. In Figure 6, two UAs have been drawn outside the interpersonal message system to allude to these possibilities; these UAs do not participate in the interpersonal message service, however, they make use of the message transfer system to store and forward data communication.

The content, which in the general message system model remained without further specification, received the structure for the interpersonal message system. It is divided into a heading and a body. The heading is further subdivided into fields with standard significance, e.g., "recipients," "carbon copy recipients," "subtract," "date and time," etc. (Fig. 8).

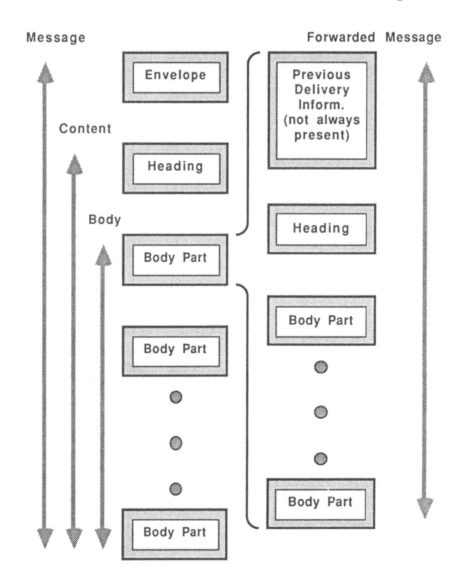

FIGURE 8   The structure of an interpersonal message.

The body itself also can be structured into one or several body parts where each part can adhere to a different coding standard. In particular, it is possible for one body part to contain a complete message consisting of envelope and content where the content again can be heading and body of an interpersonal message (Fig. 9). This message encapsulation is analogous to the situation in the regular mail where a letter that has been received is put as a whole into a new envelope, possibly an extra sheet with comments added (a further body part), and the whole sent off as a new letter.

THE STRUCTURE OF THE APPLICATION

In the recommendations of 1984 the protocol between two MTAs has been named "P1." The protocol between two cooperating user agents as "P2." A further protocol ("P3") has been defined for the communication between a remote user agent and a MTA (this protocol, however, was unsuitable for the task, has never been implemented, and hence achieved no significance).

In analogy to the layering principle of the OSI model, the message handling service has been defined in two layers: the message transfer layer and the user agent layer (Fig. 10). However, to satisfy the requirements of the layering model, an otherwise insignificant entity (SDE, Submission and Delivery Entity) for the protocol "P3" had to be introduced. Also the teletex access unit (TTXAU) as defined in 1984 presents difficulties in positioning into the layered model because this entity bears functionalities of the message transfer layer as well as of the user agent layer.

In the meantime (for 1988), ISO defined a structure for the application layer in which so-called service elements render specific services for the application. Also, the presentation layer, long a layer without portfolio, received a functionality. The layering principle of 1984 is, therefore, no

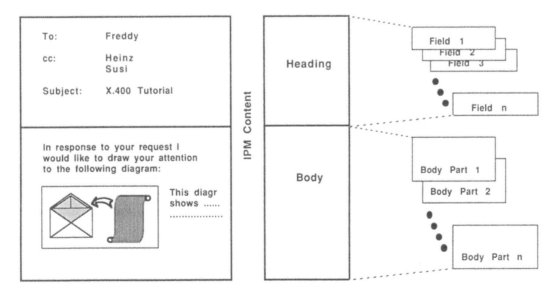

FIGURE 9 Message encapsulation.

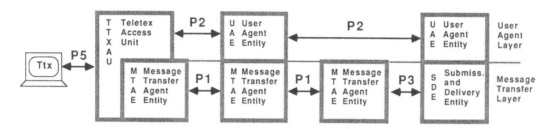

FIGURE 10   The application layer structure (1984).

longer in accordance with the general ISO structure and has been deleted
from the recommendations of 1988 and replaced with a structure containing
service elements.   Figure 11 shows the structure of two MTAs communicating
with the protocol "P1."   The message transfer service element (MTSE)
utilizes the reliable transfer service element (RTSE), which in turn makes
use of the association control service element (ACSE).   ACSE is responsible
for the establishment and release of a connection.   Both RTSE and ACSE
depend on the services of the presentation layer, i.e., layer 6 of the OSI-
model.

In the protocol between two MTAs ("P1"), in particular the protocol
of the MTSE, three service groups have been defined.   The message trans-

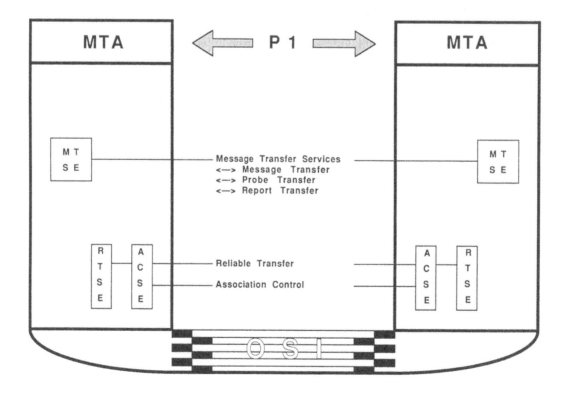

FIGURE 11   The application layer structure for the Protocol "P1" (1988).

fer group transmits complete messages (envelope plus content); the probe
transfer group enables the probe transmission, that is, transmission of an
empty envelope for checking purposes, and the report transfer group that
carries reports in the opposite direction of the probe and message transfers.
The reports indicate the outcome of a probe or message transfer, in other
words, delivery or nondelivery, the reason, and the time of the action.

The reliable transfer service element hides the particulars of the OSI
protocols. The MTSE hands over to the RTSE a complete message; this
message is then segmented by the RTSE and transmitted to the partner
MTA through the OSI layer services. The RTSE ensures that those services
are employed correctly. Even in the case of complete disruption of the connection, the message, probe, or report is neither lost nor mutilated or
doubled.

Protocols of "P3" and "P7" in addition make use of the remote operation
service element (ROSE) (Figs. 12 and 13). ROSE is a simple protocol
which permits the triggering of an action in the partner MTA. An example
of such an action is the receipt of a message. The action always responds
to the initiator with either a result or an error message. In many cases the
result contains proper message system data, for instance, if a message is
requested from the store. For these two protocols (P3 and P7) the recommendations allow the inclusion of the reliable transfer service element (RTSE),
however, this is not mandatory.

The service elements specific to protocols P3 and P7 cater to the submission of messages and probes (submission port services), the delivery of

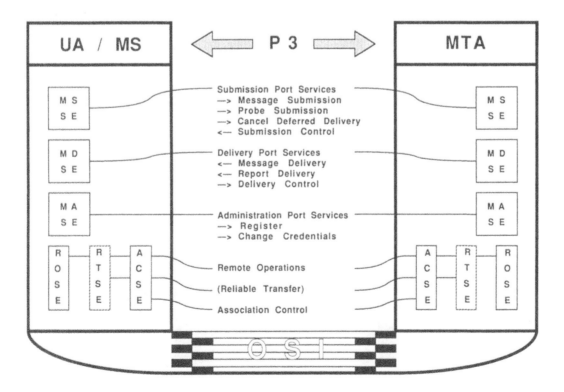

FIGURE 12   The application layer structure for the Protocol "P3" (1988).

messages or reports (delivery port services), as well as the administration
of the connection (administration port services).

Protocol P7 is nearly identical to the protocol P3 except that delivery
port services are replaced by the retrieval port services. This reflects the
fact that the message transfer system delivers a message to the message
store from where it has to be retrieved by a UA in part or as a whole.

The recommendations of 1984 knew a service element "hold for delivery."
(Note: this is a service element of the message handling service and not of
the application structure.) With this service element an MTA could be in-
structed to hold messages back that would otherwise have been delivered.
In the recommendations of 1988 this service has been refined and relegated
to the administration port services. The transmission of messages (in particular, submission, transfer, or delivery) can be restricted with respect to
their grade of service (three levels), their total length, as well as their
coding of the content (e.g., text, facsimile, etc.). This service is no
longer unidirectional but encompasses next to the known "hold for delivery"
also a "hold for submission" and "hold for transfer."

The progress of the standardization effort between 1984 and 1988 shows
clearly when the two sets of recommendations are compared with respect to
internal structure of an MTA and their respective procedural description.
In 1984 some remarks about the presence of an association manager and a
message dispatcher were sufficient (Fig. 14). In the recommendations of
1988, the enhanced functionality has been taken into account and the recom-

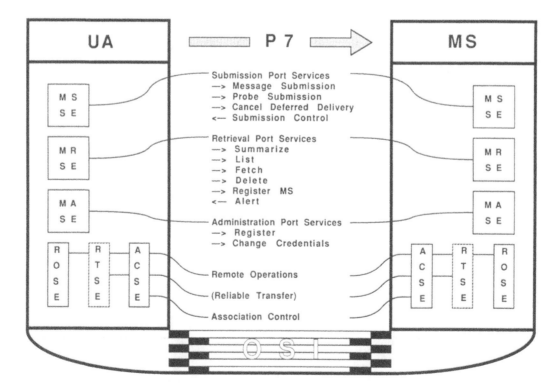

FIGURE 13   The application layer structure for the Protocol "P7" (1988).

mendations contain detailed procedural descriptions of how messages, probes, and reports are treated within an MTA (Fig. 15).

Figures 14 and 15 illustrate the big step between the two cycles of recommendations: The first figure is taken from the recommendations of 1984, the second from those of 1988. The figures serve only to illustrate the difference in the degree of details in the two sets of recommendations; an explanation of the details contained in the figures, however, is beyond the scope of this article.

MANAGEMENT DOMAINS

In the X.400 series recommendations there exists a distinction between public or administration management domains (ADMD) and private management domains (PRMD). It is foreseen that in some countries more than one administration management domain may exist.

The X.400 series recommendations cater for the standardization of the message traffic between administration management domains (within a country or across country boundaries) as well as the message traffic between public and private management domains (Fig. 16). This does not indicate that direct connections between private management domains are not possible, however, such connections are beyond the scope of the CCITT standards and, therefore, are not included in the recommendations. Omission from the standard does not prohibit such transfers.

The administrations view the message transfer system in the administration management domain (ADMD) as a central switching system. This system allows message communication between any two user agents in the world, be they connected directly to an administration domain or indirectly via

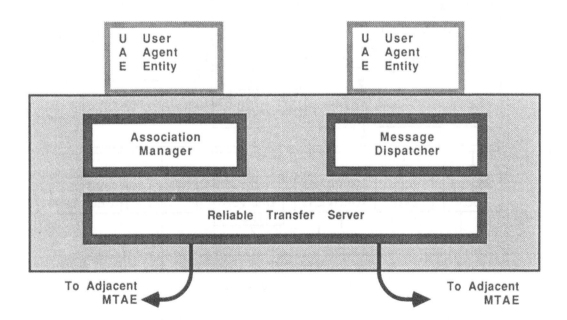

FIGURE 14 The internal structure of an MTA (1984).

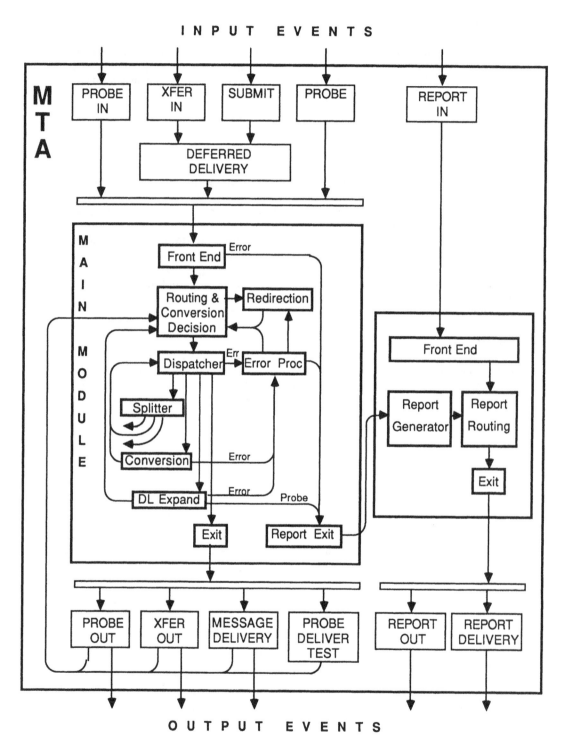

FIGURE 15   The internal structure of an MTA (1988).

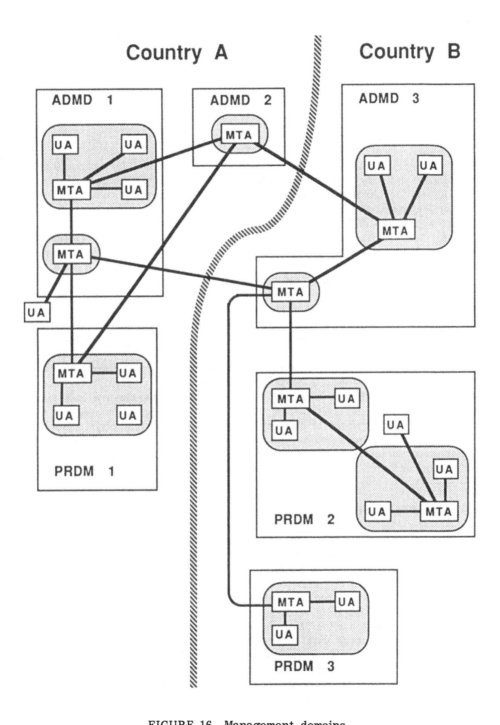

FIGURE 16 Management domains.

private management domain. However, as the addressing capabilities on the
envelope of a message allow for naming only one private management domain,
these must be connected directly to an administration management domain;
any user agent connected to a private management domain that has no direct
connection to an administration management domain is not seen by the latter,
in other words, messages destined for such a user agent cannot be transferred
through the public administation management domains, as their addresses cannot be resolved into transfer routes.

PHYSICAL DELIVERY

The value of the message handling service was increased by connecting it
to physical delivery (PD) systems such as the traditional postal service.
This allows for hardcopy delivery of messages originated within the message
handling system, and in some cases will allow for the return of notifications
from the physical delivery services to the message originator.

All users of the message handling service have the ability to generate
messages for subsequent physical delivery. This is assured by an appropriate address form, the postal O/R address, which can be used as a recipient in the envelope part of any message.

It is important to note that the physical delivery option has also been
defined for the interpersonal message service. Thus, interpersonal messages,
the (currently) most important application of the message handling service,
can form the beginning of the physical delivery possibility to be forwarded
to the physical delivery system.

A physical delivery access unit (PDAU, Fig. 3) converts an electronic
message to physical form, a process called physical rendition. An example
of this is the printing of a message and its automatic enclosure in a paper
envelope. The access unit passes the physically rendered message to a
physical delivery system for further relaying and eventual physical delivery.

A protocol between MTAs and access units has not been defined. It
is assumed that access units reside together with an MTA in the same physical system and that all interfaces are local within this system.

SUPPLEMENTARY SERVICES

The supplementary services that the transfer system can render are listed
in Table 2 (1984 set). Only a few of them will be explained here. A more
complete list is found in the Appendix (1988 set) and all the services are
described in the respective recommendations.

Compared with the regular mail service, it is a simple task for an
electronic message handling system to make multiple copies of a message.
This supplementary service "multidestination delivery," therefore, allows the
submission of a message with several addressees on the envelope; the message handling system will create enough copies of the message to deliver one
to each recipient mentioned on the envelope. For each recipient, the originator can set a flag, instructing the message system to hide all the other
recipients or if the flag is not set allow the recipient to find on the delivered
envelope the addresses of all other recipients.

The message handling system offers the supplementary service "content
conversion": It is therefore possible for a recipient having only faximile
capabilities to receive a message that originally was coded as a text message.

TABLE 2　The Supplementary Services of the Message
Transfer Service (1984)

Basic	Access Management Content Type Identification Converted Identification Delivery Time Stamp Indication Message Identification Non-Delivery Notification Original Encoded Information Types Registered Information Types Submission Time Stamp Indication
Submission and Delivery	Alternate Recipient Allowed Deferred Delivery Deferred Delivery Cancellation Delivery Notification Disclosure of other Recipients Grade of Delivery Selection Multi-Destination Delivery Prevention of Non-Delivery Notification Return of Contents
Conversion	Conversion Prohibition Explicit Conversion Implicit Conversion
Query	Probe
Status and Information	Alternate Recipient Assignment Hold for Delivery

The fact that a content conversion has been applied is reflected as an indication on the delivery envelope. Usually the conversion is implicit and determined by the respective capabilities of the originator and recipient equipment; however, the originator can also ask for an explicit conversion or he can instruct the message handling system to perform no conversion at all. Prohibiting conversions might render a message undeliverable.

A further supplementary service is the possibility of transferring a probe. A probe is basically an envelope without any content. A possible usage of the probe is in the case where a long document should be transmitted to a recipient with whom no prior communication has been taken. The delivery or nondelivery notification returned as a result of the probe transmission indicates whether the recipient address is correct (i.e., whether the transfer system can deliver the message) and it also indicates whether content conversion would be necessary when the document is transferred.

The "probe recipient" itself is oblivious to such a probe transmission. The probe travels only up to the MTA that would perform the actual delivery of a real message; there it is converted into a report that is returned to the originator.

For the recommendations published in 1988, two essential new supplementary services were defined: distribution lists and secure messages.

The address of a distribution list is no different from one of a normal recipient and an originator has no knowledge that the addresses in a message are to such a distribution list. However, when a message reaches the MTA responsible for the distribution list, the MTA expands the distribution list onto the envelope, that is, all member addresses of the distribution list are added as recipients to the envelope of the massage.

Distribution listees can themselves be members of other distribution lists. To safeguard against endless expansion loops, an appropriate system has been implemented. However, because this system works only in the MTAs adhering to the 1988 recommendations and 1984 MTAs lack this mechanism, any message arriving from (or through) a 1984 MTA is prohibited from enacting an expansion. A nondelivery notification is returned to the originator.

As soon as a message reaches the first expansion point, a delivery notification (if requested) is returned to the originator. When the replicated messages travel further through the system, they may again trigger a notification. However, these notifications are not relayed to the initial originator but are deflected to the "owner" of the distribution list (Fig. 17).

Security in the message handling system refers to the security of a message against casual or deliberate inspection by third parties. An authentication system based on the asymmetric public key crypto system, allows originator and recipient to agree on a mutual key for encyphering and decyphering of a message. The MTAs have to be included in this security concept as they need the information on the envelope to route the message and perform the requested supplementary services.

Without further explanation of the details involved, Table 3 shows which supplementary services have been defined with respect to which security aspects. The table also gives an indication as to which security aspect can be employed between which system components.

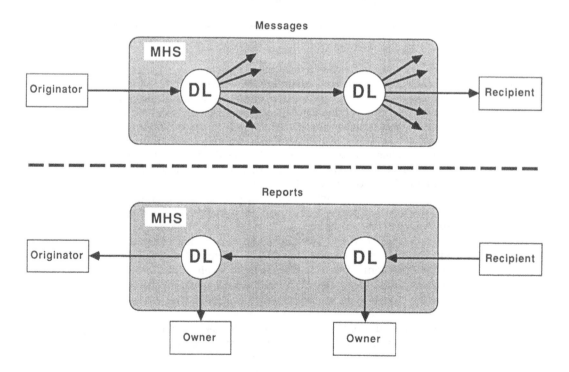

FIGURE 17   Distribution lists.

TABLE 3   The Supplementary Services of the Message Transfer Service (1984)

Elements of Service	UA to MS	MS to MTA	UA to UA	UA to MTA	MTA to MTA	MTA to UA	MS to UA
Message Origin Authentication			◊	◊			
Report Origin Authentication					◊	◊	
Probe Origin Authentication				◊			
Proof of Delivery			◊				◊
Proof of Submission						◊	
Secure Access Management	◊	◊		◊	◊	◊	◊
Content Integrity			◊				
Content Confidentiality			◊				
Message Flow Confidentiality				◊	◊		
Message Sequence Integrity			◊				
Non-Repudiation of Origin			◊	◊			
Non-Repudiation of Submission						◊	
Non-Repudiation of Delivery			◊				◊
Message Security Labelling	◊	◊	◊	◊	◊	◊	◊

HISTORY

Electronic message systems are nothing new (consider the worldwide telex service). The telex service, however, is not a store and forward service but is based on circuit switching. In addition, the functionality of telex services is way below the services of a modern message handling system. On the other hand, requests for more functinality have only been awakened by the proliferation and interconnection of data networks and the ever decreasing costs of electronic processing power and storage mediums (Table 4).

The first data network, not used entirely for a closed application and in addition with a wide geographic distribution, was the ARPA network in the United States. First the object of research itself, it soon was used for the transfer of information between researchers. This transfer was executed mainly in the form of file transfers. The researchers soon felt the need to transmit messages next to the data in the file. This need probably has arisen in large part because different researchers live in different time zones.

At first, files were exchanged with specific bilaterally agreed upon names and when such a specific name was detected in a directory, the recipient knew that it must be a message. However, this message system based on pure file transfers provided no ancillary functional services, and soon a first version of a more functional message system was developed. For the actual message transfer, this system was still based on the file transfer mechanism. Through several revisions the functionality has been enhanced and the current definition (RFC 821 and RFC 822) has probably achieved more implementations in more operating systems and on more hardware types than any other message handling system.

Following the example of ARPA, other networks, and in particular multiaccess computer systems, have implemented message handling systems;

TABLE 4 Evolution of the Message Handling Systems.

1970-1975	**Development in the ARPA-network**
1975-1980	**Introduction into main frame computers**
1978	**Establishment of IFIP WG 6.5**
1979-1980	**IFIP develops MHS-Model (UA / MTA)**
1980	**CCITT proposes the MHS topic**
	for the following study period
	(not an urgent study point)
1980-1981	**Inofficial preparatory CCITT work**
1981-1983	**CCITT develops the X.400 recommendations**
1984	**Final adoption of the X.400 recommendations**
	Splitting of the problem area into several
	study points for the new period
1985-1987	**Collaboration with ISO**
	Major restructuring of the recommendations
1988	**Adoption of the Blue Book version**
	(Compatibility of MHS'88 with MHS'84)

however, none of these systems have reached the widespread importance as has the ARPA network.

Realizing the incompatibility of systems and detecting the growing need for interconnecting the different electronic mail systems, the Technical Committee 6 (data communication) of IFIP (International Federation for Information Processing) established a working group (WG 6.5). The charter of this working group directed it to study international message handling systems. It is important to note that IFIP is not an organization that produces standards. In this case, the IFIP WG 6.5 was a forum for the open exchange of information between scientists working in the field, to develop conceptual models and architectures in anticipation of future standards work.

The North American subgroup, in which a considerable expertise was concentrated in the years 1979 and 1980, defined a model that was adopted by CCITT. This model still guides the structure of message handling systems. The transfer of knowledge from the IFIP working group to CCITT was accomplished when several members of the IFIP working group became members of the CCITT group working on the message handling recommendations.

While CCITT was completing its work on message handling systems, the IFIP Working Group 6.5 worked out a scheme for a user-friendly naming convention and researched the foundations for an international directory system. The two documents resulting from this research have both been introduced to CCITT which carried the work further. Recently, the IFIP Working Group 6.5 finished the definition of a gateway between the RFC-822 and X.400 systems. Currently, the group is studying communication, the organization of communication within groups, and has started research in multimedia multimode (real-time and non-real-time) conference systems.

CCITT works in 4-year study periods, and at the end of each period new study points for the next period are formulated in the form of questions. Thus, at the end of the period 1977 to 1980, CCITT established a question to study message handling systems. However, because the end of a period is a major interruption of the standardization process, actual work on the definition of message handling systems could not be taken up before the end of 1981. For many members of CCITT anticipating to work on the message handling system, this long delay between forming the question in the spring of 1980 and the actual start of work appeared to be too long an interval. Thus, an unofficial group was formed to start work during the "interregnum" period. This preparatory work gave the group a good headstart, and by spring of 1984 the first set of eight recommendations were completed and subsequently published in the Red Book. The last study period (1985 to 1988) is marked by the fact that the problem of message handling systems had been divided into several study points (questions) and collaboration with ISO, the International Standards Organization was achieved. The result of this collaboration was the publication in 1988 by both organizations of "aligned" texts as standards for message handling systems (they differ only in editorial conventions and some minor aspects reflecting the fact that CCITT produces "recommendations" for public service providers and ISO produces "standards" for general applications). It is worth noting that the collaboration between CCITT and ISO has not been restricted to message handling systems. It now includes open system interconnection (OSI) and the directory services as well.

APPENDIX: DEFINITIONS OF ELEMENTS OF SERVICE

Note: The abbreviations used in the definitions have the following meanings:

MT	Message Transfer
IPM	Interpersonal Messaging
PD	Physical Delivery
MS	Message Store
PR	Per Recipient (available on a per-recipient basis)

Access Management—MT. Enables a UA and MTA to establish access to one another and to manage information associated with access establishment. The element of service permits the UA and MTA to identify and validate the identity of the other. It provides a capability for the UA to specify its O/R Address and to maintain access security. When access security is achieved through passwords, these passwords can be periodically updated.
   Note: A more secure form of access management is provided by the element of service Secure Access Management.

Additional Physical Rendition—PD, PR. Allows an originating user to request the PDAU to provide the additional rendition facilities (e.g., kind of paper, colored printing, etc.). Bilateral agreement is required to use this element of service.

Alternate Recipient Allowed—MT. Enables an originating UA to specify that the message being submitted can be delivered to an alternate recipient as described below. A destination MD will interpret all of the user attributes in order to select a recipient UA. Three cases can be distinguished:

1. All the attributes match precisely those of a subscriber UA.
   Delivery is attempted to that UA.
2. Either insufficient attributes are supplied or those supplied match
   those of more than one subscriber UA. The message cannot be
   delivered.
3. At least the minimum set of attributes required by the destination
   MD is supplied. Nevertheless, taking all of the other attributes
   into account, the attributes match those of no UA.

In case 3, an MD that supports the Alternate Recipient Assignment element
of service can deliver the message to a UA that has been assigned to
recieve such messages. This UA will be notified of the O/R Address of the
intended recipient as specified by the originator. Delivery to this UA will
be reported in a delivery notification if requested by the originator.

Alternate Recipient Assignment—MT. Enables a UA to be given the capability to have certain messages delivered to it for which there is no exact
match between the recipient attributes specified and the name of the user.
Such a UA is specified in terms of one or more attributes for which an
exact match is required, and one or more attributes for which any value is
acceptable. For example, an organization can establish a UA to recieve all
messages for each country name, Administration Management Domain name,
and organization name (e.g., company name) are an exact match but the
personal name of the recipient does not correspond to an individual known
by an MHS in that organization. This permits the organization to manually
handle the messages to these individuals. In order for a message to be
reassigned to an alternate recipient, the originator must have requested the
Alternate Recipient Allowed Element of Service.

Authorizing Users Indication—IPM. Allows the originator to indicate to the
recipient the name(s) of the person(s) who authorized the sending of the
message. For example, an individual can authorize a particular action which
is subsequently communicated to those concerned by another person such as
a secretary. The former person is said to authorize its sending while the
latter person is the one who sent the message (originator). This does not
imply signature-level authorization.

Auto-Forwarded Indication—IPM. Allows a recipient to determine that a
body of an incoming IP message contains an IP message that has been auto-
forwarded. Thus the recipient can distinguish from that where an incoming
IP message contains a forwarded message in the body. As with a forwarded
IP message, an auto-forwarded IP message can be accompanied by information (e.g., time stamps, indication of conversion) associated with its original delivery.

   Note: The indication that auto-forwarding of an IP message has occurred enables a recipient IPM UA, should it so choose, to prevent further
auto-forwarding and thus the possibility of loops. In addition, a recipient
IPM UA can choose whether or not to auto-forward based on other criteria
(for example, sensitivity classification).

   When an IPM UA auto-forwards an IP message, it designates it as
auto-forwarded. If receipt/nonreceipt notification has been requested for
the IP message being auto-forwarded, the IPM UA generates a nonreceipt

notification informing the originator of the auto-forwarding of the IP message. The notification optionally includes a comment supplied by the originally intended recipient. No further notification applying to the auto-forwarded IP message is generated by any IPM UA.

Basic Physical Rendition—PD, PR. Enables the PDAU to provide the basic rendition facilities for converting the MHS message into a physical message. This is the default action to be taken by the PDAU.

Blind Copy Recipient Indication—IPM, PR. Allows the originator to provide the O/R name of one or more additional users, or DLs, who are intended recipients of the IP message being sent. These names are not disclosed to either the primary or copy recipients. Whether or not these additional recipients are disclosed to one another is a local matter.

Body Part Encryption Indication—IPM. Allows the originator to indicate to the recipient that a particular body part of the IP message being sent has been encrypted. Encryption can be used to prevent unauthorized inspection or modification of the body part. This element of service can be used by the recipient to determine that some body part(s) of the IP message must be decrypted, however, it does not itself encrypt or decrypt any body part.

Content Confidentiality—MT. Allows the originator of a message to protect the content of the message from disclosure to recipients other than the intended recipient(s). Content Confidentiality is on a per-message basis, and can use either an asymmetric or a symmetric encryption technique.

Content Integrity—MT, PR. Allows the originator of the message to provide to the recipient of the message a means by which the recipient can verify that the content of the message has not been modified. Content Integrity is on a per recipient basis, and can use either an asymmetric or a symmetric encryption technique.

Content Type Indication—MT. Enables an originating UA to indicate the content type for each submitted message. A recipient UA can have one or more content types delivered to it. An example of a content type is the contents generated by the IPM class of cooperating UAs.

Conversion Prohibition—MT. Enables an originating UA to instruct the MTS that implicit encoded information type conversion(s) should not be performed for a particular submitted message.

Conversion Prohibition in Case of Loss of Information—MT. Enables an originating UA to instruct the MTS that encoded information type conversion(s) should not be performed for a particular submitted message if such conversion(s) would result in loss of information. Loss of information is discussed in detail in X.408. Should this and the Conversion Prohibition element of service both be selected, the latter shall take precedence.

Note: This element of service will not protect against possible loss of information in certain cases where the recipient is using an I/O device whose capabilities are unknown to the MTA.

Converted Indication—MT, PR. Enables the MTS to indicate to a recipient UA that the MTS performed encoded information type conversion on a delivered message. The recipient UA is informed of the resulting types.

Counter Collection—PD, PR. Allows an originating user to instruct the PDS to keep the physical message ready for counter collection at the post office specified by the originator, or at the post office which offers counter collection service closest to the given recipient's address.

Counter Collection with Advice—PD, PR. Allows an originating user to instruct the PDS to keep the physical message ready for counter collection at the post office specified by the originator, or at the post office which offers counter collection service closest to the given recipient's address, and to inform the recipient via telephone, telex, or teletex, using the number provided by the originator.

Cross-referencing Indication—IPM. Allows the originator to associate with the IP message being sent, the globally unique identifiers of one or more other IP messages. This enables the recipient's IPM UA, for example, to retrieve from storage a copy of the referenced IP messages.

Deferred Delivery—MT. Enables an originating UA to instruct the MTS that a message being submitted shall be delivered no sooner than a specified date and time. Delivery will take place as close to the date and time specified as possible, but not before. The date and time specified for deferred delivery is subject to a limit which is defined by the originator's management domain.
    <u>Note</u>: Storage of the message shall be handled in the originating country.

Deferred Delivery Cancellation—MT. Enables an originating UA to instruct the MTS to cancel a previously successfully submitted deferred delivery message. The cancellation attempt may or may not always succeed. Possible reasons for failure are: deferred delivery time has passed, or the message has already been forwarded within the MTS.

Delivery Notification—MT, PR. Enables an originating UA to request that the originating UA be explicitly notified when a submitted message has been successfully delivered to a recipient UA or Access Unit. The notification is related to the submitted message by means of the message identifier and includes the date and time of delivery. In the case of a multidestination message, the originating UA can request this element of service on a per-recipient basis. When a message is delivered after distribution list expansion, then, depending on the policy of the distribution list, the notification can be sent to either the list owner, the message originator, or both. Delivery notification carries no implication that any UA or user action, such as examination of the message's content, has taken place.

Delivery Time Stamp Indication—MT, PR. Enables the MTS to indicate to a recipient UA the date and time at which the MTS delivered a message. In the case of physical delivery, this element of service indicates the date and time at which the PDAU has taken responsibility for printing and further delivery of the physical message.

Delivery via Bureaufax Service—PD, PR. Allows an originating user to instruct the PDAU and associated PDS to use the Bureaufax Service for transport and delivery.

Designation of Recipient by Directory Name—MT, PR. Enables an originating UA to use a Directory Name in place of an individual recipient's O/R Address.

Disclosure of Other Recipients—MT. Enables the originating UA to instruct the MTS when submitting a multirecipient message, to disclose the O/R names of all other recipients to each recipient UA, upon delivery of the message. The O/R names disclosed are as supplied by the originating UA. If distribution list expansion has been performed, then only the originator-specified DL name will be disclosed, and not the names of its members.

DL Expansion History Indication—MT. Provides to a recipient, at delivery, information about the distribution list(s) through which the message has arrived. It is a local matter as to how much of this information is presented to the recipient.

DL Expansion Prohibited—MT. Allows an originating user to specify that if any of the recipients can directly or via reassignment refer to a distribution list, then no expansion shall occur. Instead, a Nondelivery Notification will be returned to the originating UA, unless Prevention of Nondelivery has been requested.

EMS (Express Mail Service)—PD, PR. Allows an originating user to instruct the PDS to transport and deliver the physical message produced from the MHS message through accelerated letter circulation and delivery service (such as EMS or the equivalent domestic service) in the destination country.

Expiry Date Indication—IPM. Allows the originator to indicate to the recipient the date and time after which he considers the IP message to be invalid. The intent of this element of service is to state the originator's assessment of the current applicability of an IP message. The particular action on behalf of a recipient by his IPM UA, or by the recipient himself, is unspecified. Possible actions might be to file or delete the IP message after the expiry date has passed.

Explicit Conversion—MT, PR. Enables an originating UA to request the MTS to perform a specified conversion, such as required when interworking between different Telematic Services. When a message is delivered after conversion has been performed, the recipient UA is informed of the original encoded information types as well as the current encoded information types in the message.

Note 1: This element of service is intended to support interworking with Telematic terminals/Services.

Note 2: When DL Names are used in conjunction with this element of service, conversion will apply to all members of the DL.

Forwarded IP Message Indication—IPM. Allows a forwarded IP message, or a forwarded IP message plus its "delivery information" to be sent as the body (or as one of the body parts) of an IP message. An indication that the body part is forwarded is conveyed along with the body part. In a multipart body, forwarded body parts can be included along with body parts of other types. "Delivery information" is information which is conveyed from the MTS when an IP message is delivered (e.g., time stamps and indication of conversion). However, inclusion of this delivery information along with a forwarded IP message in no way guarantees that this delivery information is validated by the MTS. The Receipt Notification Request Indication and the Nonreceipt Notification Request Elements of Service are not affected by the forwarding of a IP message.

Grade of Delivery Selection—MT. Enables an originating UA to request that transfer through the MTS be urgent or nonurgent, rather than normal. The time periods defined for nonurgent and urgent transfer are longer and shorter, respectively, than that defined for normal transfer. This indication is also sent to the recipient with the message.

Hold for Delivery—MT. Enables a recipient UA to request that the MTS hold its messages and returning notifications for delivery until a later time. The UA can indicate to the MTS when it is unavailable to take delivery of messages and notifications, and also, when it is again ready to accept delivery of messages and notifications from the MTS. The MTS can indicate to the UA that messages are waiting due to the criteria the UA established for holding messages. Responsibility for the management of this element of service lies with the recipient MTA. Criteria for requesting a message to be held for delivery are: encoded information type, content type, maximum content length, and priority. The message will be held until the maximum delivery time for that message expires, unless the recipient releases the hold prior to its expiry.
Note: The Hold for Delivery Element of Service is distinct from the message store facility. The Hold for Delivery Element of Service provides temporary storage to facilitate delivery and only after a message has been transferred to the recipient's UA, is delivery notification returned. The message store facility augments the storage of a UA and can be used to store messages for an extended period of time. Unlike the Hold for Delivery Element of Service, delivery notifications are returned as soon as the message is placed in (that is, delivered to) the message store.

Implicit Conversion—MT. Enables a recipient UA to have the MTS perform for a period of time any necessary conversion on messages prior to delivery. Neither the originating nor recipient UA explicitly requests this element of service on a per-message basis. If the encoded information type capabilities of the recipient UA are such that more than one type of conversion can be performed, the most appropriate conversion is performed. When a message is delivered after conversion has been performed, the recipient UA is informed of the original encoded information types as well as the current encoded information types in the message.

Importance Indication—IPM. Allows the originator to indicate to the recipients his assessment of the importance of the IP message being sent. Three levels of importance are defined: low, normal, and high. This element of service is not related to the Grade of Delivery Selection Element of Service provided by the MTS. The particular action taken by the recipient or his IPM UA based on the importance categorization is unspecified. It is the intent to allow the recipient IPM UA, for example, to present IP messages in order of their importance or to alert the recipient of the arrival of IP messages of high importance.

Incomplete Copy Indication—IPM. Allows an originator to indicate that this IP message is an incomplete copy of an IP message with the same IP message identification in that one or more body parts, and/or heading fields of the original IP message are absent.

IP Message Identification—IPM. Enables cooperating IPM UAs to convey a globally unique identifier for each IP message sent or received. The IP message identifier is composed of an O/R name of the originator and an identifier that is unique with respect to that name. IPM UAs and users use this identifier to refer to a previously sent or received IP message (e.g, in receipt notifications).

Language Indication—IPM. Enables an originating UA to indicate the language type(s) of a submitted IP message.

Latest Delivery Designation—MT. Enables an originating UA to specify the latest time by which the message is to be delivered. If the MTS cannot deliver by the time specified, the message is not delivered and is cancelled. On multirecipient messages, the latest delivery time can expire prior to delivery to all recipients, but this will not negate any deliveries which have already occurred.

Message Flow Confidentiality—MT. Allows the originator of the message to protect information which might be derived from observation of the message flow.
    Note: Only a limited form of this is supported.

Message Identification—MT. Enables the MTS to provide a UA with a unique identifier for each message or probe submitted or delivered by the MTS. UAs and the MTS use this identifier to refer to a previously submitted message in connection with Elements of Service such as Delivery and Nondelivery Notification.

Message Origin Authentication—MT, PR. Allows the originator of a message to provide to the recipient(s) of the message, and any MTA through which the message is transferred, a means by which the origin of the message can be authenticated (i.e., a signature). Message Origin Authentication can be provided to the recipient(s) of the message, and any MTA through which the message is transferred, on a per-message basis using an asymmetric encryption technique, or can be provided only to the recipient(s) of the message, on a per-recipient basis using either an asymmetric or a symmetric encryption technique.

Message Security Labelling—MT. Allows the originator of a message (or probe) to associate with the message (and any reports on the message or probe) an indication of the sensitivity of the message (a security label). The message security label may be used by the MTS and the recipient(s) of the message to determine the handling of the message in line with the security policy in force.

Message Sequence Integrity—MT, PR. Allows the originator of the message to provide to a recipient of the message a means by which the recipient can verify that the sequence of messages from the originator to the recipient has been preserved (without message loss, reordering, or replay). Message Sequence Integrity is on a per-recipient basis, and can use either an asymmetric or a symmetric encryption technique.

Multidestination Delivery—MT, PR. Enables an originating UA to specify that a message being submitted is to be delivered to more than one recipient UA. Simultaneous delivery to all specified UAs is not implied by this element of service.

Multipart Body—IPM. Allows an originator to send to a recipient or recipients an IP message with a body that is partitioned into several parts. The nature and attributes, or type, of each body part are conveyed along with the body part.

Nondelivery Notification—MT, PR. Enables the MTS to notify an originating UA if a submitted message was not delivered to the specified recipient UA(s). The reason the message was not delivered is included as part of the notification. For example, the recipient UA can be unknown to the MTS. In the case of a multidestination message, a nondelivery notification can refer to any or all of the recipient UAs to which the message could not be delivered. When a message is not delivered after distribution list expansion, then, depending on the policy of the distribution list, the notification can be sent to either the list owner, the message originator, or both.

Nonreceipt Notification Request—IPM, PR. Allows the originator to ask that he be notified should the IP message be deemed unreceivable. In the case of a multirecipient IP message, the originator can request this element of service on a per-recipient basis. The originator's UA conveys his request to the recipient's UA. The UA automatically issues a nonreceipt notification when any of the following events occur:

1. The recipient's UA autoforwards the IP message to another user.
2. The recipient's UA discards the IP message prior to receipt.
3. The recipient's subscription is terminated before he receives the IP message.

Since receipt can occur arbitrarily long after delivery, the recipient's failure to access the IP message, even for a long period of time (e.g., while on an extended business trip) does not constitute nonreceipt and thus no notification is issued.

Note: No legal significance can be adduced from this element of service.

Nonrepudiation of Delivery—MT, PR. Allows the originator of a message to obtain from the recipient(s) of the message irrevocable proof that the message was delivered to the recipient(s). This will protect against any attempt by the recipient(s) to subsequently deny receiving the message or its content. Nonrepudiation of Delivery is provided to the originator of a message on a per-recipient basis using asymmetric encryption techniques.

Nonrepudiation of Origin—MT, PR. Allows the originator of a message to provide the recipient(s) of the message irrevocable proof of the origin of the message. This will protect against any attempt by the originator to subsequently revoke the message or its content. Nonrepudiation of Origin is provided to the recipient(s) of a message on a per-message basis using asymmetric encryption techniques.

Nonrepudiation of Submission—MT. Allows the originator of a message to obtain irrevocable proof that a message was submitted to the MTS for delivery to the originally specified recipient(s). This will protect against any attempt by the MTS to subsequently deny that the message was submitted for delivery to the originally specified recipient(s). Nonrepudiation of Submission is provided to the originator of a message on a per-message basis, and uses an asymmetric encryption technique.

Obsoleting Indication—IPM. Allows the originator to indicate to the recipient that one or more IP messages he sent previously are obsolete. The IP message that carries this indication supercedes the obsolete IP message. The action to be taken by the recipient or his IPM UA is a local matter. The intent, however, is to allow the IPM UA or the recipient to, for example, remove or file obsolete messages.

Ordinary Mail—PD, PR. Enables the PDS to transport and deliver the letter produced from the MHS message in the mode available through the ordinary letter mail service in the country of destination. This is the default action for the transport and delivery of a physical message.

Original Encoded Information Types Indication—MT. Enables an originating UA to specify to the MTS the encoded information types of a message being submitted. When the message is delivered, it also indicates to the recipient UA the encoded information types of the message specified by the originating UA.

Originator Indication—IPM. Allows the identity of the originator to be conveyed to the recipient. The intent of this IPM element of service is to identify the originator in a user-friendly way. In contrast, the MTS provides to the recipient the actual O/R Address and directory name, if present, of the originator. DL Names should not be used in Originator Indication.

Originator Requested Alternate Recipient—MT, PR. Enables an originating UA to specify, for each intended recipient, one alternate recipient to which the MTS can deliver the message, if delivery to the intended recipient is not possible. The alternate recipient can be a distribution list. For the purposes of determining success or failure (and hence delivery and non-delivery notification), delivery to the originator requested alternate recipient is equivalent to the intended recipient. If the intended recipient has requested redirection of incoming messages, and if the originating UA has requested Redirection Allowed by the Originator, the system first tries to redirect the message. If this fails, the system then attempts to deliver the message to the designated alternate recipient.

Physical Delivery Notification by MHS—PD, PR. Allows an originating user to request that an explicit notification, informing the originator of either successful or unsuccessful delivery of the physical message, be generated and returned by MHS. The notification provides information on delivery but no physical record is provided by the PDS.
    Note 1: The notification includes the date and time of delivery based on the delivery confirmation given by the delivery person, the addressee or another authorized person. This is subject to national regulations in the destination country and is also dependent on the type of delivery requested (e.g., in the case of Registered Mail to Addressee in Person, the addressee would be the confirming person).
    Note 2: This notification carries no implication that any action on the part of the recipient (such as examination of the message content) has taken place.
    Note 3: When this element of service is requested, and the physical message is undeliverable, it is either returned or destroyed depending on national regulations in the destination country, which means that the default action of the element of service B.91 is overridden.

Physical Delivery Notification by PDS—PD, PR. Allows an originating user to request that an explicit notification, informing the originator of either successful or unsuccessful delivery of the physical message, be generated and returned by the PDS. The notification serves as a record of delivery for the originating user to retain for reference.
    Note 1: The notification includes the date and time, and, in the case of successful delivery, the signature of the person confirming the delivery. The confirming person can be the delivery person, the addressee or another authorized person. This is subject to national regulations in the destination country and is also dependent on the type of delivery requested (e.g., in the case of Registered Mail to Addressee in Person, the addressee would be the confirming person).
    Note 2: This notificaton carries no implication that any action on the part of the recipient (such as examination of the message content) has taken place.
    Note 3: When this element of service is requested, and the physical message is undeliverable, it is either returned or destroyed depending on national regulations in the destination country.

Physical Forwarding Allowed—PD, PR. Enables the PDS to forward the physical message to a forwarding address if the recipient has changed his address and indicated this to the PDS. This is the default action taken by the PDS.

Physical Forwarding Prohibited—PD, PR. Allows an originating user to instruct the PDS not to forward the physical message to a forwarding address.

Prevention of Nondelivery Notification—MT, PR. Enables an originating UA to instruct the MTS not to return a nondelivery notification to the originating UA in the event that the message being submitted is judged undeliverable. In the case of a multidestination message, the originating UA can request this element of service on a per-recipient basis.

Primary and Copy Recipients Indication—IPM. Allows the originator to provide the names of zero or more users, or DLs, who are the intended primary recipients of the IP message, and the names of zero or more users, or DLs, who are the intended copy recipients of the IP message. It is intended to enable a recipient to determine the category in which each of the specified recipients (including the recipient himself) was placed. The exact distinction between these two categories of recipients is unspecified. However, the primary recipients, for example, might be expected to act upon the IP message, while the copy recipients might be sent the IP message for information only.

Note: As an example of this element of service in a typical memorandum, the primary recipients are normally designated by the directive "to:" while "cc:" identifies the copy recipients.

Probe—MT. Enables a UA to establish before submission whether a particular message could be delivered. The MTS provides the submission information and generates delivery an/or nondelivery notifications indicating whether a message with the same submission information could be delivered to the specified recipient UAs. The Probe Element of Service includes the capability of checking whether the content size, content type, and/or encoded information types would render it undeliverable. The significance of the result of a Probe depends upon the recipient UA(s) having registered with the MTS the encoded information types, content type and maximum message size that it can accept. This element of service is subject to the same delivery time targets as for the urgent class. In the case of DLs, a Probe indicates nothing about the likelihood of successful delivery to the DL members, but only whether the originator has the right to submit to the DL.

Probe Origin Authentication—MT. Allows the originator of a probe to provide to any MTA through which the probe is transferred a means to authenticate the origin of the probe (i.e., a signature). Probe Origin Authentication is on a per-probe basis, and uses an asymmetric encryption technique.

Proof of Delivery—MT, PR. Allows the originator of a message to obtain from the recipient(s) of the message the means to authenticate the identity of the recipient(s) and the delivered message and content. Message recipient authentication is provided to the originator of a message on a per-recipient basis using either symmetric or asymmetric encryption techniques.

Proof of Submission—MT. Allows the originator of a message to obtain from the MTS the means to authenticate that the message was submitted for delivery to the originally intended recipient. Message submission authentication is provided on a per-message basis, and can use symmetric or asymmetric encryption techniques.

Receipt Notification Request Indication—IPM, PR. Allows the originator to ask that he be notified when the IP message being sent is received. In the case of a multirecipient message, the originator can request this element of service on a per-recipient basis. This element of service also implicitly requests Nonreceipt Notification Request Indication. The originator's UA conveys his request to the recipient's UA. The recipient can instruct his UA to honor such requests, either automatically (e.g., when it first renders the IP message on the recipient's terminal) or upon his explicit command. The recipient can also instruct his UA, either in blanket fashion or case by case, to ignore such requests.

Redirection Allowed by Originator—MT. Enables an originating UA to instruct the MTS, if the recipient has requested the Redirection of Incoming Messages element of service, that redirection can be applied to a particular submitted message.

Redirection of Incoming Messages—MT. Enables a UA to instruct the MTS to redirect incoming messages addressed to it, to another UA or to a DL, for a specified period of time, or until revoked.
    Note 1: This is an MT element of service that does not necessitate delivery to the intended recipient before redirection can take place. It is therefore distinct from the IPM Auto-Forwarded Indication Element of Service.
    Note 2: When security provisions are in force, different incoming messages, on the basis of their security labels, may be redirected to separate alternate recipients or not redirected at all.

Registered Mail—PD, PR. Allows an originating user to instruct the PDS to handle the physical message as registered mail.

Registered Mail to Addressee in Person—PD, PR. Allows an originating user to instruct the PDS to handle the physical message as registered mail and to deliver it to the addressee only.

Reply Request Indication—IPM, PR. Allows the originator to request that a recipient send an IP message in reply to the IP message that carries the request. The originator can also specify the date by which any reply should be sent, and the one or more users and DLs to whom the originator requests (but does not demand) be among the preferred recipients of any reply. The recipient is informed of the date and names but it is up to the recipient to decide whether or not, and if so, to whom to reply.
    Note: A blind copy recipient should consider carefully to whom he sends a reply, in order that the meaning of the Blind Copy Recipient Indication Element of Service is preserved.

Replying IP Message Indication—IPM. Allows the originator of an IP message to indicate to the recipient(s) that this IP message is being sent in reply to another IP message. A reply can, depending on the wishes of the originator of the replied-to message, and the final decision of the originator of the reply, be sent to:

1. The recipients specified in the reply request indication of the replied-to message.
2. The originator of the replied-to message
3. The originator and other recipients
4. A distribution list, in which the originator of the replied-to message can be a receiving member
5. Other recipients as chosen by the originator of the reply

The recipients of the reply receive it as a regular IP message, together with an indication of which IP message it is a reply to.

Report Origin Authentication—MT. Allows the originator of a message (or probe) to authenticate the origin of a report on the delivery or non-delivery of the subject message (or probe), (a signature). Report Origin Authentication is on a per-report basis, and uses an asymmetric encryption technique.

Request for Forwarding Address—PD, PR. Allows an originating user to instruct the PDS to provide the forwarding address if the recipient has changed his address and indicated this to the PDS. This element of service can be used with either Physical Forwarding Allowed or Prohibited. The provision of the forwarding address by the PDS to an originating user is subject to national regulations in the destination country. The default action is no provision of the forwarding address.

Requested Delivery Method—MT, PR. Allows a user to request, on a per-recipient basis, the preference of method or methods of message delivery (such as through an Access Unit). Nondelivery results if preference(s) cannot be satisfied.

Restricted Delivery—MT. Enables a recipient UA to indicate to the MTS that it is not prepared to accept delivery of messages from certain originating UAs or DLs.
　　Note: This element of service can be requested in either of two ways:

1. Specification by the recipient UA of unauthorized senders, all other senders are considered as authorized.
2. Specification by the recipient UA of authorized senders, all other senders are considered to be unauthorized.

Return of Content—MT. Enables an originating UA to request that the content of a submitted message be returned with any nondelivery notification. This will not be done, however, if any encoded information type conversion has been performed on the message's content.

Secure Access Management—MT. Enables an MTS user to establish an association with the MTS, or the MTS to establish an association with an MTS user, or an MTA to establish an association with another MTA. It also establishes the strong credentials of the objects to interact, and the context and security-context of the association. Secure Access Management can use either an asymmetric or symmetric encryption technique. When access security is achieved through strong credentials, they can be periodically updated.

Sensitivity Indication—IPM. Allows the originator of an IP message to specify guidelines for the relative sensitivity of the message upon its receipt. It is the intent that the sensitivity indication should control such items as:

1. Whether the recipient should have to prove his identity to receive the IP message.
2. Whether the IP message should be allowed to be printed on a shared printer.
3. Whether an IPM UA should allow the recipient to forward the received IP message.
4. Whether the IP message should be allowed to be auto-forwarded.

The sensitivity indication can be indicated to the recipient or interpreted directly by the recipient's IPM UA. If no sensitivity level is indicated, it should be assumed that the IP message's originator has advised no restriction on the recipient's further disposition of the IP message. The recipient is free to forward, print, or otherwise do as he chooses with the IP message. Three specific levels of sensitivity above the default are defined:

Personal: The IP message is sent to the recipient as an individual, rather than to him in his role. There is no implication that the IP message is private, however.
Private: The IP message contains information that should be seen (or heard) only by the recipient, and not by anyone else. The recipient's IPM UA can provide services to enforce this intent on behalf of the IP message's originator.
Company-confidential: The IP message contains information that should be according to company-specific procedures.

Special Delivery—PD, PR. Allows an originating user to instruct the PDS to transport the letter produced from the MHS message through the ordinary letter mail circulation and to deliver it by special messenger delivery.

Stored Message Alert—MS. Allows a user of an MS to register relevant sets of criteria that can cause an alert to be generated to the user when a message arrives at the MS satisfying the selected criteria. The generation of the alert can occur as follow:

1. If the UA is connected and on-line to the MS, the alert message will be sent to the UA as soon as a message arrives at the MS that satisfies the registered criteria for generating alerts. If the UA is off line then the next time the UA connects to his MS after a message arrives at the MS satisfying the registered criteria, the user will be

informed that one or more alert cases have occurred, the details of which can be determined by performing a Stored Message Summary.

2. In addition to, or as an alternative to #1 above, the MS can use other mechanisms to inform the user.

Stored Message Auto-forward—MS. Allows a user of an MS to register requests that the MS auto-forward selected messages that are delivered to it. The user of the MS can select through registration several sets of criteria chosen from the attributes available in the MS, and messages meeting each set of criteria will be autoforwarded to one or more users or DLs. A text(s) can also be specified to be included with the auto-forwarded message(s).

Stored Message Deletion—MS. Enables a recipient UA to delete certain of its messages from the MS. Messages cannot be deleted if they have not been previously listed.

Stored Message Fetching—MS. Enables a recipient UA to fetch from the MS a message, or portions of a message. The UA can fetch a message (or message portion) based on the same search criteria that can be used for Stored Message Listing.

Stored Message Listing—MS. Provides a recipient UA with a list of information about certain of its messages stored in the MS. The information comprises selected attributes from a message's envelope and content and others added by the MS. The UA can limit the number of messages that will be listed.

Stored Message Summary—MS. Provides a recipient UA with a count of the number of its messages currently stored in the MS. The count of messages satisfying a specified criteria based on one or more attributes of the messages stored in the MS can be requested.

Subject Indication—IPM. Allows the originator to indicate to the recipient(s) the subject of an IP message being sent. The subject information is to be made available to the recipient.

Submission Time Stamp Indication—MT. Enables the MTS to indicate to the originating UA and each recipient UA the date and time at which a message was submitted to the MTS. In the case of physical delivery, this element of service also enables the PDAU to indicate the date and time of submission on the physical message.

Typed Body—IPM. Permits the nature and attributes of the body of the IP message to be conveyed along with the body. Because the body can undergo conversion, the body type can change over time.

Undeliverable Mail with Return of Physical Message—PD, PR. Enables the PDS to return the physical message without delay, with reason indicated to originator, if it cannot be delivered to the addressee. This is the default action to be taken by the PDS.

Note: In the case of "poste restante" the return of the physical message will take place after some period of time.

Use of Distribution List—MT, PR. Enables an originating UA to specify a distribution list in place of all the individual recipients (users or nested DLs) mentioned therein. The MTS will add the members of the list to the recipients of the message and send it to those members. Distribution lists can be members of distribution lists, in which case the list of recipients can be successively expanded at several places in the MTS.

User Capabilities Registration—MT. Enables a UA to indicate to its MTA, through registration, the unrestricted use of any or all of the following capabilities with respect to received messages;

1. The content type(s) of messages it is willing to have delivered to it
2. The maximum content length of a message it is willing to have delivered to it
3. The encoded information type(s) of messages it is willing to have delivered to it

The MTA will not deliver to a UA a message or probe that does not match, or exceeds, the capabilities registered.

PIETRO SCHICKER

ELECTRONIC PUBLISHING

INTRODUCTION

Electronic publishing is the electronic dissemination of information and encompasses the processes of input, storage, manipulation, composition, and display of information for presentation. The earliest forms of electronic publishing derive from office word processing and the data processing environment with the emphasis on *storage* aspects of the process. More recent efforts focus on the *manipulation, composition, and display* of electronically stored information for creation, display, and production of documents of all sizes. Electronic publishing is described below first in historical perspective focusing on the development and dissemination of electronic data base information and the evolution of office word processing. The discussion then turns to selected trends.

ELECTRONIC DATA BASES

In the early 1970s, the development of electronic publishing was spurred by the proliferation of microcomputers capable of serving as terminals connected through modems and across telephone lines to timesharing computers storing large amounts of information. This form of electronic publishing consists of computer bulletin boards, databases, and videotext or teletext information systems. The development of these systems was greatly enhanced by the development of data networks that allowed the database and bulletin board services to offer users access to systems at a homogeneous cost across broad geographic regions. Commercial services offered included news and financial information, bibliographic databases and abstracts, and marketing catalogs. Interactive services exploring the use of the system include banking and mail order catalogs.

Electronic publishing services of this type may be divided into four categories.

1. *Databases* allow many users access to an organized body of information that may be manipulated by the individual users for purposes of searching and reporting. Informational databases are the most common form of electronic publishing at this time. These systems allow a vendor to provide information updated on a daily basis to a wide variety of users. The information may be about current events or other widely dispersed activities that are not otherwise easily available. The most important feature of this form of electronic publishing is the categorization of information into a series or relatively homogeneous records with a series of fields associated with each record. At a minimum level, the user is able to select

subsets of the data for visual presentation based on matches in given fields. At the most sophisticated level, database systems offer the user the capability to search all fields in all records for given text strings including provision for matching of wild card characters and to output the selected information to screen, printer, or electronic storage medium at the local site.

2. *Bulletin boards* consist of text files stored for the purpose of sharing information among individuals with a focused common interest. The relatively focused nature of the communication generally obviates the necessity for any significant manipulation of the information that is most frequently stored as text files that may be edited or perused by all users of the system.

3. *Broadcast videotext systems* make use of special editing equipment to prepare information for storage on video disks or transmission to standard television sets equipped with processors to decode incoming signals sent via coaxial cable or the blanking interval of a broadcast television signal. The processor front end also generally includes some mechanism for frame selection from among all the frames being broadcast. These systems are most often directed at the development of electronic publishing capabilities for advertising, training, and instruction. The color and graphics capabilities of the systems allow the user to see a more varied and detailed display than is generally possible through bulletin board or database systems designed to operate effectively on the simplest terminals with a raster of 24 lines by 80 characters. A raster defines the possible locations on the output medium, in this case a cathode ray tube (CRT) screen of 24 lines, each line having 80 possible character positions. Another measure of raster is the number of points per inch at which information may be located on a given output device or media. These points are called picture elements and are referred to as PEL or pixels (see Current Trends for more information).

4. *Interactive teletext and videotext systems* are of two broad types. Teletext uses a telephone link or cable television system with upstream data transmission capability. A central computer monitors addresses on cable systems for data input from a user station. This input is used to select the appropriate subscreen of a prepared teletext display for presentation to that address on the network. This form of interactive teletext has the ultimate capability to process complex information from the remote addresses so as to process orders for materials or services.

   Interactive videotext systems make use of a microcomputer attached to a frame-addressable video playback unit to allow an individual user to proceed through an instructional sequence with the frames displayed on the screen being chosen by a program stored on a microcomputer. This technology makes use of a full spectrum of video displays from simple static text to full motion video.

A significant obstacle to the development of bulletin board and database electronic publishing has been the rates at which data may be moved across public communication facilities—generally less than 9600 bits per second (bps) and normally 300–1200 bps. (A text character is most often represented by eight bits of data, so a transmission speed of 1200 bps represents a character transmission speed of no more than 150 characters per second.) Another obstacle is the unique nature of the database structures and the differences in search and retrieval commands between the systems. Coaxial teletext systems are limited by the lack of sophisticated graphics capability in system displays, by the insufficient processing and storage capability to maintain a complex hierarchy of displays, and by the lack, in most systems, of a capability to handle upstream data from users. Video disk/microcomputer systems are currently limited by the high cost of mastering videodisks and writing control programs. In addition, the lack of an existing distribution system means that implementations of such systems must most often include the purchase of a total hardware and software system by an organizational user.

WORD PROCESSING AND OFFICE AUTOMATION

While the distribution of electronically stored information was being developed through electronic databases, parallel developments were occurring in the area of electronic preparation of information for printing. In commercial printing, computer phototypesetting and digital photoscanning and separation were developed to aid in the prepress printing processes. In the office, automated typing equipment first began to appear in the workplace during the 1960s. Taking the form of dedicated microprocessors incorporated into typewriters, they stored a limited quantity of textual information and aided in the drafting and revision process. Storage was provided by various magnetic media including magnetic cards and cassette tape. These systems evolved in the 1970s into dedicated word processors offered by a number of different manufacturers. These systems were most notable in the addition of a cathode ray display for preview and editing of the documents and the incorporation of floppy diskette storage mechanisms—generally providing greater reliability and storage capacity than the previously used magnetic media.

Most dedicated word processors offered full screen editors that also served as the first generation of What You See Is What You Get (WYSIWYG) displays, where the material entered via the editor was displayed on the screen in the final output format. Early CRT constraints mandated that this display be the standard 80 characters by 24 lines, and allowed for a WYSIWYG type display by left and right scrolling of the screen image and indications of page breaks by such conventions as dotted lines. The major limitations of these early systems was their inability to show multiple fonts—bold, italic, different point sizes, and the limitation of an 80 by 24 raster for the display of information.

Early word processing systems generally used a dedicated typewriter for printing output. Initially these devices were limited to fixed pitch elements (every character is the same width) with the later development of the capability to use proportionally spaced typing elements where each character was assigned a unique width. Initially, printers were dedicated to the system and tied closely to the development of the word processing software with unique codes being used to instruct the printer to backspace, underline, overstrike, superscript, etc. Generally, this was done via "escape sequences" (see below).

As with electronic databases, office automation was greatly spurred in the 1970s by the emergence of general-purpose microcomputers. On these systems, software and programmable function keys were used to convert microcomputers to word processors. It became easier to do a variety of work tasks on a given machine and to share the results of those tasks between programs, for example, a table produced by a spreadsheet program could be incorporated without rekeying into a word processing program for presentation as part of a report. The evolution of general-purpose microcomputers as office word processors may be traced through the development of coding techniques and screen displays, output devices, and document management. Each of these areas is described briefly below.

Coding Techniques and Screen Displays

As multipurpose machines, microcomputers had the disadvantage of having general-purpose as opposed to dedicated function keys for use by typists. Thus, most microbased editors require the typist to use either general-purpose function keys, key combinations, or multiple keystrokes to accomplish effects that are often accomplished by hitting a single labeled key on a dedicated word processor. For example, material might be bolded on a dedicated word processor by hitting a key labeled "bold." On a microcomputer, the user may use a general-purpose function key, a key combination—control key and "B," or a key sequence of keystrokes—a control key plus "F" for format followed by a "B." These codes may be displayed on the screen, or embedded in the source text with the editor displaying their effects on the screen.

There are two widely accepted character coding standards: the American Standard Code for Information Interchange (ASCII) which represents characters in a seven bit code (with an eighth bit being used for control), and the Extended Binary-Coded Decimal Interchange Code (EBCDIC) which uses eight bits for representation. With seven bits of data it is possible to represent 128 different characters; with eight, it is possible to represent 256 different characters. Figure 1 shows the general groupings of characters for the EBCDIC character set.

The first 128 characters are the same as the characters in the ASCII set. When editors display the codes as opposed to their impact, it is generally the case that the commands are special sequences of the ASCII character set. When the effects of the command are implemented on the screen, it is generally the case that the commands are stored in the source file as characters from the extended EBCDIC character set. Because characters 129—256 may be assigned special functions by word processing software, care needs to be taken when documents are exchanged to insure that the codes are understood by all the systems involved or that appropriate translation takes place.

Word processing programs may be conceived as being composed of two components—editors and formatters—editors being concerned with data input and manipulation and formatters concerned with display and output. These two components may be combined so that data is displayed during editing as it will be output or they may be maintained separately. The proliferation of word processing programs has increased the need for a document interchange format that will allow documents input by one editor to be displayed and manipulated by another editor. While some document translation programs do exist, there is no existing standard for document interchange at the current time. (The standardization of document interchange should not be confused with standards for the presentation of composed documents—page description standards—which have received much attention in recent years. Both developments are described briefly in the next section.)

Output Devices

The development of office word processing was enhanced by the development of printers that had increased capability in the form of a wider range of carriage movements. This improvement took the form of an increasingly fine vertical and horizontal raster (1/120th of an inch horizontally and 1/48th of an inch vertically). In addition, carriage movement was expanded to include reverse as well as forward movement. These two capabilities made it possible to place information at virtually any position on the printed page. These capabilities were coupled with the ability to set printing characteristics remotely from the word processing software. One widely used standard for printer control codes was established by the Diablo Corporation. By way of explanation, a few of these codes are presented in Table 1. Printers were constructed so that the reception of the escape character (the escape character, ASCII value 0011011, is written as ESC) caused the printer to "escape" from printing mode and interpret the next one or two characters as a command for movement of the carriage. (Many terminals use escape sequences in a similar way to control the characteristics of information displayed on the screen.) On a diablo-type printer, the character sequence ESC D causes the printer to reverse a half line—allowing a superscript to be typed. Following the printing of the information to be superscripted, an ESC U is sent to instruct the printer to move forward half a line. At the current time, these standards are being revised based on the development of higher resolution laser printers that introduce a new standard for rasterization. In con-

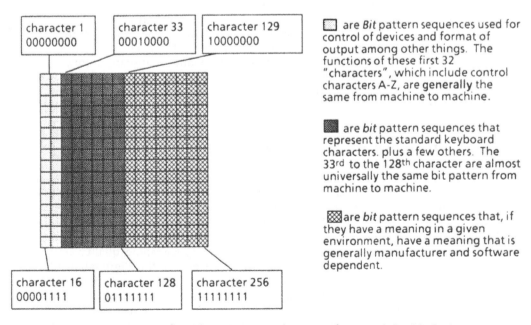

character 1
00000000

character 33
00010000

character 129
10000000

character 16
00001111

character 128
01111111

character 256
11111111

☐ are *Bit* pattern sequences used for control of devices and format of output among other things. The functions of these first 32 "characters", which include control characters A-Z, are generally the same from machine to machine.

■ are *bit* pattern sequences that represent the standard keyboard characters. plus a few others. The 33rd to the 128th character are almost universally the same bit pattern from machine to machine.

▨ are *bit* pattern sequences that, if they have a meaning in a given environment, have a meaning that is generally manufacturer and software dependent.

FIGURE 1 Schema for bit pattern assignment for an eight-bit byte.

TABLE 1 Partial List of Diablo 630 ESCape Sequences

ESC Sequence	Action
ESC 0	Set right margin at current position
ESC 9	Set left margin at current position
EWC 5	Start printing forward
ESC 6	Start printing backward
ESC LF	Perform a negative line feed
ESC FF n	Set lines per page to n
ESC HH n	Initiate horizontal tap to position n
ESC VT n	Initiate vertical tab to line n
ESC RS n	Set vertical motion indicator to (n-1)
ESC US n	Set horizontal motion indicator to (n-1)
ESC CR P	Initiate a remote reset

trast to diablo-type impact printers, which most often have a raster of 120 pel/inch horizontally and 48 pel/inch vertically, laser printers may have a resolution of 240, 300, or even 600 pel/inch vertically and horizontally.

Document Management

Current developments in the area of office automation focus heavily on document management. Standalone word processors no longer meet the needs of heavily automated offices. The proliferation of microcomputers has resulted in a growing need for electronic mail between machines and shared filing systems, communications interfaces, and printers. This need has also spurred the development of standards for document interchange between editors, formatters, and output devices (see below). Document management and interchange is one important application of local area networks described elsewhere in this volume.

CURRENT DEVELOPMENT AND FUTURE TRENDS

Database and teletext systems electronically store information for subsequent display as ephemeral data on simple CRTs. Office automation systems focused on text information output to relatively low-speed impact printers. Recent developments in electronic publishing address the storage, transmission, and display of typographic quality information integrated with images and graphic information. Specifically, it includes scanning of typographic quality text in complex formats, interactive composition of graphics, the digitization of analog images, composition of integrated text and graphic information, screen display of formatted multiple font and graphic output, and printing of multiple font output including graphics to all points-addressable devices. Because extensive amounts of information are involved, electronic publishing in this form is generally limited to the transmission of information across relatively small distances (circa 2 km) using local area networks. Figure 2 depicts the domain of disseminated information and provides a rough picture of which forms of electronic publishing may be used to disseminate the information. As shown in Figure 1, electronic database dissemination of information is restricted to low-quality and relatively low-volume output. Traditional office word processing accommodates small volumes and low-quality output. New developments in electronic publishing that allow the incorporation of graphics, use of multiple font sizes and styles, and high-speed output opens up a significant area of the publishing domain. Those applications requiring extremely high-quality, e.g., color and/or very high volumes, remain outside the domain of electronic publishing.

A modern electronic publishing system may include a number of subprocesses such as those shown in Figure 3. Text information is input along with coding information to determine presentation characteristics. Vector-defined graphics and analog images are input to the system and converted to a digital representation. Some systems allow for composition of graphics with the resulting composition being stored either as vector or digital information. Generally text is stored in a normal file format and graphic and image information is stored in separate nonstandard files that are merged with the text at the time of output. Font information is also stored separately with information about its characteristics available during composition and information about construction of characters available at the time of printing. Generally, the composition process translates user-provided copymarks into an intermediate code which is subsequently interpreted by one of a family of subprocesses that prepares specific instructions for a given device. Electronic publishing in this form is currently still in the process of being standardized and there are several areas in which vendor definitions are competing to become the standard. The following issues characterize the ongoing development.

Text Coding

The coding of information for electronic publication may be handled in any number of ways. A general trend in the field is toward coding schemes that are independent of the ultimate output device. Coding schemes may be characterized by how they are implemented, the type of demarcation, and the degree of intentionality.

1. *Implementation* of coding is most often by explicit coding of source text on a standard display with implementation of those commands waiting until the text is processed. More recent developments allow implementation of codes from menus on a bit-mapped display screen that shows either the precise form of the output or some approximation of it. User-typed commands are normally associated with large-scale text processing systems that require the user to employ a standard editor to prepare the text which is then composed into a print image by a separate text processing program. Integrated text editor/processors are normally associated with dedicated work stations employing bit-mapped screens.
2. *Demarcation* may be by toggle switching, delimitation, or explicit commands. Toggling implies that the first instance of a command turns a feature on and second instance turns it off. With delimita-

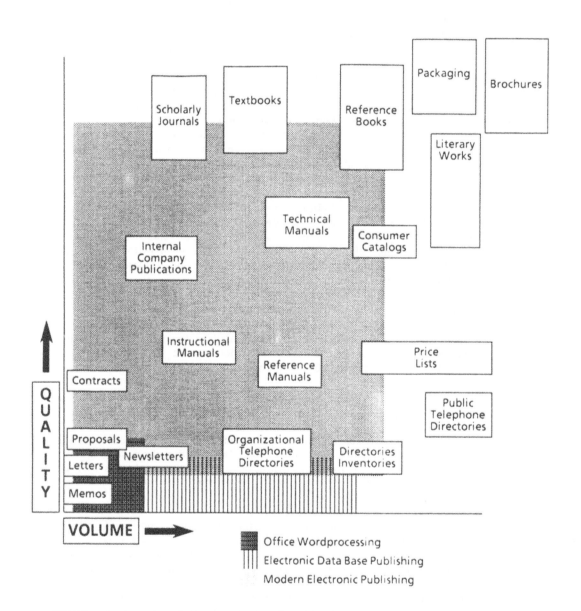

FIGURE 2 Domain of disseminated information showing selected applications of electronic publishing.

tion, the command is associated with delimiters which specify the extent of the command's effect. With explicit commands, a given command is in effect until a counter command is given.

3. *Intentionality* refers to the nature of the command specified by the user. At one end of the continuum, the user functionally specifies information as detailed as the machine font to be employed by the output device; more *intentionally*, the user specifies that the text is to be bold, leaving the choice of the specific font or technique for bolding to the composition program; and finally, a fully intentional command would specify that given text is to be emphasized or that it is a heading, leaving it to the composition system to decide what array of output characteristics on a specific device will best display the intent of the user.

Handling of text coding is complicated by three factors: the growing diversity of input devices, the growing diversity of users, and the growing diversity of output devices. For example, input from a user on a simple microcomputer who is unaware of typographic fonts, which are proportionally spaced and some in multiple sizes, may be output to a typographic engine that can do both. In the absence of specific coding from the user, it must be decided whether, and if so, how, the composition program should make best guess decisions about the user's intent.

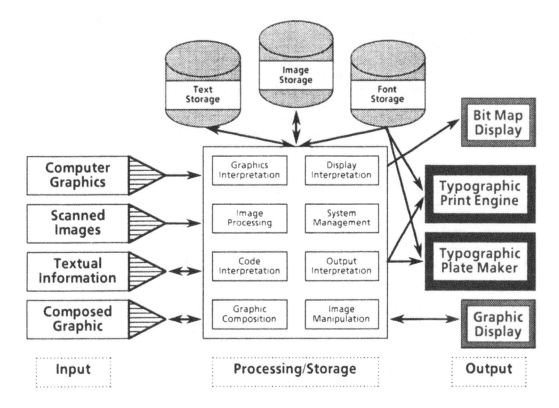

FIGURE 3 Processes in electronic publishing.

Nontext Information

As the universe of documents considered appropriate for electronic publication expands, the need to include nontext information in output is also increasing. Nontext information falls into two categories: that which may be described economically by vectors and that which may be described only through pixel by pixel description. There is a growing tendency to label those entities stored as vectors *graphics* and those stored as digital information *images*. Historically, vector-described graphics were the first to be stored electronically. They had the advantage of being economical to store and transmit across limited capacity communications facilities. Instructions stored as vectors were translated at point of display into the appropriate set of commands or the appropriate bit map. With the advent of higher speed communications facilities (coaxial and optical fiber cable) it is possible to consider the transmission of compressed or raw bit-mapped images from site to site. The scanning, processing, and display of bit map or rasterized images involves several distinct decisions which are at this point far from standard across the industry. However, they have the following characteristics in common. The image is scanned at a given level of resolution which involves two decisions: the number of samples per inch, and the gray scale employed to describe each sample. Each sample is referred to as a picture element (a pel or pixel). Table 2 shows the number of bits of information required to depict a series of 8.5 × 11 inch images at varying levels of physical resolution (pel/inch), varying levels of contrast resolution (gray tones per pel), and in compressed and uncompressed form. (Because most images do not require a pel by pel description, techniques have been developed to compress bit map images.) Compression formulas are most useful for line art which is more amenable to statistical description and prediction. When applied to continuous tone images, certain effects may be generated, particularly when there is a discrepancy between the scanning resolution and the output resolution. For this reason, much energy is currently being devoted to the development of algorithms for image enhancement to eliminate display effects such as staircasing and worming. Graphics handling is tending toward the digital storage of images of all kinds. As yet there

TABLE 2 Comparison of Image Storage Requirements

Size (Y" × X")	PEL/inch (YPEL/in × XPEL/ln)	Gray Tones (in 2^n Jumps)	Bits/image	Bits/image (8:1 Compression)
8.5 × 11	300 × 300	2	8,415,000	1,051,875
8.5 × 11	300 × 300	16	33,660,000	4,207,500
8.5 × 11	300 × 300	64	50,490,000	6,311,250
8.5 × 11	300 × 300	256	67,320,000	8,415,000
8.5 × 11	240 × 480	2	10,771,200	1,346,400
8.5 × 11	240 × 480	16	43,084,800	5,385,600
8.5 × 11	240 × 480	64	64,627,200	8,078,400
8.5 × 11	240 × 480	256	86,169,600	10,771,200

is no set standard for the resolution of the mechanisms employed to scan or reproduce images. At the current time, most scanning, storage and transmission schemes are vendor dependent. Xerox has proposed a subset of the *Interpress* page descriptor language (see below) called the *Raster Encoding Standard (RES)* for the interchange of raster images in a device independent form.

Storage and Transmission of Information

Given text, graphic, and image information, electronic publishing systems must be able to store, manipulate, and transmit the information between the various devices that comprise the system. To accommodate the growing number of editors that embed coding in the text section specific to the editors, some effort has been made to define a standard format for source code that allows different editors to effectively work with the same source text with interpreters maximizing the quality of the display generated from the source code. *Interscript* from Xerox is one example of such a standard for document interchange. A significant subproblem is the need for foreign characters and special symbols in higher quality documents. If these additional characters are included, neither the ASCII character set (128 characters) nor the ISO 646 character set (256 characters) are sufficient. The Xerox Character Code, a 16-bit code, and the Xerox *Interscript* standard describing the logical structure, layout structure, and content of a document, represent an effort to develop a standard in this area.

In contrast to a standard for the exchange of source documents between editors, some progress has been made in the development of standards for composed pages so as to minimize the need for device interpreters that can translate the metacode of the composing system to any of a number of output devices. The two leading candidates at the current time are *Postscript* and *Interpress*. These systems assume all point-addressable output devices and consist of a number of primitives which describe the placement and characteristics of information to be used to compose any given page. In both cases, it is the responsibility of the software doing the composing to develop output in the page format standard and the responsibility of the software driving the print engine or plate maker to translate that code into output. As indicated previously, standards have also been proposed for the interchange of raster images and for the interchange of source documents. In all these cases, device-independent coding is simply a mechanism that reduces the need for interfacing software packages with a large number of devices. More basic transmission software is concerned with the encapsulation of all these forms of data with the appropriate protocols to allow it to be transmitted meaningfully across some intermediate media. At the current time, most systems are limited to transmission to an output channel of the CPU, requiring no protocol encapsulation or to vendor-specific networks requiring encapsulation only with protocols known to all the vendor's network devices.

Display Mechanisms

While current electronic publishing systems allow the generation of hard copy output within minutes or hours of composition, there is ongoing demand for screen display systems that allow the user to see the document in final form on a screen—to allow for *soft-proofing*. This speeds the design and composition process and reduces the problem of collating errors in the output with the source of those errors in the input text stream. Several systems offer facilities for this kind of composition. In the typographic/multiple font arena the Xerox Star and Apple Macintosh provide examples of an editor integrated with the composition program so that *What You See* (on the screen) *Is What You Get* from the printer. This kind of display system is often referred to as a WYSIWYG display. Mainframe text processing systems such as the Document Composition Facility from IBM or the Xerox Integrated Composition System (XICS) offer this option through an interpreter capable of preparing output to a bit-mapped screen. Much energy is currently being devoted to the development of screen displays that show the output interactively and that allow modification of the input stream simultaneously. This may be done either by a split screen display that coordinates input and output streams or by an interactive output display that translates the user's manipulation of the output display into the appropriate changes in the underlying source code.

Output Devices

As indicated above, output devices for electronic publishing have included a standard TTY for electronic data bases, a standard CRT for microcomputer-based word processing systems, and letter quality printers with a 48- by 120-pel/inch raster. As electronic publishing has developed, a variety of different output devices have been used for the final composition of materials. In addition to those mentioned above, these include optical phototypesetters, machines which photographically transfer a character image on a negative to some medium such as photographic paper; digital phototypesetters, like phototypesetters but replacing the photographic negative with a digital bit map representation of each character; and laser printers that function like digital phototypesetters but use a dry chemical process that is generally of lower resolution but higher transfer speed. The most basic characteristic of these last three output devices is *all-points addressability*. This means each device is capable of placing information at any point on the medium on which printing is being done. In reality this refers to a high level of rasterization such that the impression is one of being able to address any given point. For optical and digital phototypesetters this raster is most often at the level of 600, 1200, or 1800 pel/inch. For laser printing, the broadest industry standard at this point in time is set by Xerox, which uses a raster of 300 points per inch, both horizontally and vertically for laser printing. IBM has introduced a device with 240 and 600 pel/inch rasters vertically and horizontally. The speeds of most laser printers are acceptable for making masters and compare favorably, excepting the lower level of resolution, with other mechanisms for producing masters. In terms of production, laser printers are relatively slow compared with traditional printing presses, with laser printers being 10- to several 100-fold slower than the fastest web offset presses. They are, however, fast enough to produce low volumes of production work (4,000 to 12,000 pages per minute). Several efforts are currently underway to define a standard intermediate coding agreed to by all text processing systems as well as all printers. Such an intermediate code eliminates the combinatorial explosion of unique code translations. As indicated above, two such output page definition standards offer promise: *Interpress* by Xerox and *Postscript* by Adobe Systems Inc. These standards work by proposing a language that may be used to describe an output page. Such a language describes page locations, character and graphic information, font information, etc. in a way that it is device independent.

User Interfaces

Significant difficulties in electronic publishing currently exist in the area of the user interface. Early electronic publishing systems such as bulletin boards required little user sophistication. The seven bits of information provided by a user striking a key on the keyboard were sufficient. With the possibility that a letter be any point size from 4 to 36 points (32 possibilities); four type faces (roman, bold, italic, or bold italic); 100's of different type families; and non-European character sets, the user or the software needs to define which of 1,000s of characters might be intended by a given keystroke.

In addition, systems may establish preset standards which allow even the casual user to get some results, but which then frustrate the knowledgeable user. On the other hand, the lack of such a system makes the system too complicated for all but highly trained users. These kinds of concerns create difficulties for the designers of electronic publishing systems in that they must decide on the appropriate level of user decision-making requirements which will correlate with the amount of learning required for a user to manage the system. The more learning required of the user, the less widespread the use of the system is likely to be. The more automated a system the less likely it is to be accepted by sophisticated publishing users.

System Management

Additional concerns at a more macroscopic level are introduced by the management of the entire process of electronic publishing. Systems must have facilities to insure appropriate document security as well as for monitoring progress on all the various component parts of the process. Users must have some simple mechanisms for controlling the editorial process to know what changes have been entered by who, when they were done, and how to handle conflicting systems. More recent systems from the major corporations have added additional levels of software that aid in the management of document production and creation.

The future of electronic publishing will be tied closely to the development of standards for document interchange, the refinement of image manipulation software, and increases in the speed and resolution of output devices. It is possible that such systems will eventually be integrated with video disk technology to allow the option not only for graphics but for motion. The ultimate development of the technology into the home will be closely linked to the development of high-speed data transmission systems. It is possible that such electronic publishing systems, given the availability of appropriate output devices affordable for personal use could include electronically delivered mail and newspapers, as well as digitized voice information. Finally, the addition of program code with the information to microprocessors at the end point will allow the sender to include additional information about organization and presentation of the information at the point of display that would be interactive for a given user. At the current time, these directions are being driven primarily by business needs to rapidly create documents that have to be modified frequently and produced on demand. It is unlikely that the high costs of such systems and the need for special processing equipment at the user endpoint will allow such applications to have much impact on the educational or the entertainment/home market in the foreseeable future.

SELECTED BIBLIOGRAPHY

"Aesthetics vs. Technology: Typography for Electronic Printers and Video Displays," *Seybold Report, 11*(11) (February 8, 1982); *11*(12) (February 22, 1981).

Character Code Standard, XSIS 058404, Xerox Corporation, April 1984.

Gencode and the Standard Generalized Markup Language (SGML), GCA Standard 101-1983, Graphic Communication Association, Arlington, VA.

Interpress Electronic Printing Standard, Version 2.1, XSIS 048404, Xerox Corporation, April 1984.

ISO Open Systems Interconnection—Basic Reference Model, International Organization for Standardization, ISO/TC97/SC 16 N 719, August 1981.

Nothmann, G. A., "Is There an Electronic Press in Your Future," presentation to the Graphic Arts Technical Foundation International Congress on Lithography, April 9, 1984, Pittsburgh, PA.

Proposed American National Standard for Videotext/Teletext Presentation Level Protocol Syntax, American National Standards Institute, ANSI X3-110-1983.

Raster Encoding Standard, XSIS 178412, Xerox Corporation, December 1984.

Roberts, T. L. and T. P. Moran, "Evaluation of Text Editors," *Proceedings of the Conference on Human Factors in Computer Systems*, March 1982 15-17, Gaithersburg, MD, pp. 136—141.

MICHAEL BLAISE SPRING

ELECTRONIC SPREADSHEETS—See Decision Trees on Electronic Spreadsheets

THE ELECTRONIC TIMESHEET

The Electronic Timesheet (ET), a VAX-based office automation package from fbn Management Science Corporation of Toronto, Ontario, offers a computerized solution to time accountung, project costing and client billing. *ET's* target market is professional services organizations, such as consulting firms and project-oriented environments.

    ET permits data entry on employee time, employee expenses, external expenses and interdepartmental transfer charges. Both time and expense data can be entered by individual employees from workstations or centrally by a data entry operator. Error reduction is achieved through a variety of logical checks. Also, the program catches and rejects unauthorized charges before they are posted against a project. After the charge ceiling has been reached for a particular project, the project manager may decide whether additional charges should be rejected. In addition, the project manager may disable charging to any project at any time.

    Because *ET* permits direct and immediate data entry by employees, a completely up-to-date database is possible. Thus, *ET* can produce up-to-date reports on demand that center on:

1. The Employee
   a. Detailed Labor Report—This report format lists all time entries in sorted order by employee name and then by project.
   b. Daily Hours Charged Report—This type of report lists all time entries in chronological order for a particular employee.
   c. Summary Labor Report—With this report format, it's possible to list hours charged by a particular employee for a specific reporting period.
   d. Detailed Expense Report—An itemized listing of expenses incurred by a particular employee during a specific reporting period is given by this report format.
2. The Project
   a. Detailed Project Cost Report—This report lists daily time and expense charges for activities in a project.
   b. Summary Project Cost Report—This report summarizes time and expense charges for a particular project durng a specific reporting period.
3. The Client
   a. Detailed Client Charges Report—This report itemizes daily time and expense charges to a particular client.
   b. Client Billing Report—This format yields a summary of all labor and expense charges for all projects belonging to a particular client. Thus, this report can be used for billing purposes.

---

*Reprinted by permission of Professional Press, 921 Bethlehem Pike, Spring House, PA 19477.

ET is basically a menu-driven package with plenty of easily understood online help available. The menus and help enable persons with minimal computer sophistication to use the system effectively in a short period of time. The available online help is structured so that it reduces the potential for the uninitiated user to get caught in a maze of menus.

Training is provided via two online tutorials, the User Tutorial and the System Manager Tutorial. The User Tutorial teaches data editing, how to post entries against projects, conducting online enquiries and how to generate individual time and expense reports. The System Manager Tutorial tells the system manager how to set up the system and track the definition of employee, clients, projects, activities (project subdivisions), project teams, suppliers and expenses. In addition, the system manager assigns system users and their privileges.

FEATURES

ET offers plenty of features, among them:

1. Time Charging

The following sequence ilustrates how you would charge time to a project. First, you log on and select "ENTER time" from the Functions Menu (see Figure 1). Next, enter time-charge data (see Figure 2).

During data entry, *ET* performs a series of logical checks, and echoes a project description along with the number of hours already charged by the employer on that date (see Figure 3). Last, you approve the transaction, assuming the logical checks are completed successfully.

2. Online Enquiries

If you're entering data on the screen and forget a needed datum that's in the system, you can use the Online Enquiries feature. Online enquiry per-

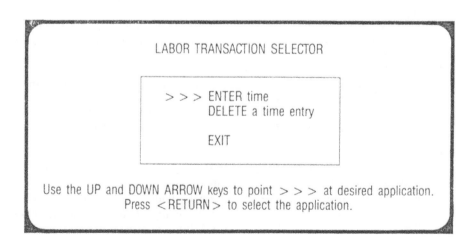

FIGURE 1   Select time-entry function.

```
┌─────────────────────────────────────────────────────────┐
│                      ENTER TIME                          │
│                                                          │
│   Employee number: 1      MIKE GONZALES                  │
│                                                          │
│   Project number: 22335   COMPUTING RESOURCES — MEMO ACCOUNT │
│                                                          │
│   Activity number: 07     TUNING & OPTIMIZATION — COMPUTER RESOU │
│                                                          │
│   Date: 7-FEB-86          Prior charges (today) 7.00 hrs.│
│                                                          │
│   Time code: 1                                           │
│                                                          │
│   # hours worked: .50                                    │
│                                                          │
│        Memo:              ADJUST RESHASHTABLE            │
└─────────────────────────────────────────────────────────┘
```

FIGURE 2   Input of time-charge information.

```
┌─────────────────────────────────────────────────────────┐
│                      ENTER TIME                          │
│                                                          │
│   Employee number: 1      MIKE GONZALES                  │
│                                                          │
│   Project number: 22335   COMPUTING RESOURCES — MEMO ACCOUNT │
│                                                          │
│   Activity number: 07     TUNING & OPTIMIZATION — COMPUTER RESOU │
│                                                          │
│   Date: 7-FEB-86          Prior charges (today) 7.00 hrs.│
│                                                          │
│   Time code: 1                                           │
│                                                          │
│   # hours worked: .50                                    │
│                                                          │
│        Memo:              ADJUST RESHASHTABLE            │
└─────────────────────────────────────────────────────────┘
```

FIGURE 3   *The Electronic Timesheet* performs checks, echoes information.

mits you to suspend data entry, obtain the needed information from the system and then return to data entry.

For example, Figure 4 shows a data entry screen for initiating projects. To proceed you must enter a client number, but if you don't know what the number is, you can press a key and obtain a list of clients and their numbers on the screen (see Figure 5). After finding the appropriate client number, you press <CR> and you're shown Figure 4 screen again. You then resume data entry where you left off.

3. Logical Checks

ET performs a number of logical checks during data entry. Take a time-entry transaction, for example. *ET* checks that the employee, project and activity exist. Also, it checks to see if employees must be assigned specifically to the project team to charge time or expenses to the project. If assignment is required, *ET* checks that the employee in question has been assigned. In addition, checks are performed to verify that the project isn't charge-disabled, and whether processing the transaction will cause a charge overrun.

Finally, a check is done to alert the user that the current entry is a duplicate. This is a useful check. (Did I already return this call? Did I already send out that memo?) *ET*'s final check eliminates uncertainties by flagging duplicate entries.

4. Password Security

Data integrity is maintained through password security implemented with several privilege classes.

5. Flexibility

ET is flexible in that it easily accommodates special cases. For example, if the charge ceiling has been reached for a particular project, but it's decided

```
                              ADD PROJECT

     Project number:                  Client number:

     Profit center:                   Billable (Y/N): Y

     Description:

     Manager's employee number:       Charge-enable (Y/N): Y

     Enforce ceiling (Y/N): Y         Require assignment (Y/N): Y

     Labor ceiling: 9999999.00        Expense ceiling: 9999999.00
```

FIGURE 4   Project initiation.

that charges might be posted beyond the ceiling, the system manager readily can implement this new decision. *ET* informs you that the ceiling has been exceeded but will still accept the posting of the charge.

LOGICAL DESIGN OF ET

The *ET* logical entities are:

1. System Users—Included here are both regular users and privileged users.
2. Clients.
3. Projects—These are client-specific contracts. A client may have many projects; however, a project is associated with only one client.
4. Activities—These are further subdivisions of a project.
5. Employees.
6. Suppliers.
7. Project Teams.
8. Expense Categories—Included are such expenses as travel, meals, etc.

CLIENT LISTING ENQUIRY

number	name
59774	M. C. S. S. ONTARIO:PENS
54307	MACK CANADA — COMMUNICATI
54305	MACK CANADA INC -PENSION
54306	MACK CANADA-GRP
54687	MANCHESTER LINERS
54765	MANITOBA POOL ELEVATOR
55118	MARKEL FINANCIAL -GEN INS
55220	MARR ELECTRIC : PENSION
55349	MARSHALL DRUMMOND MCC PEN
55348	MARSHALL DRUMMOND MCC:GRP
55356	MARSHALL STEEL -
55386	MARUBENNI
48094	MARVA JEMMATT
55619	MASSEY COMBINES — GROUP
55618	MASSEY COMBINES — PENSION

FIGURE 5   Client listing enquiry.

USER CLASSES

ET ensures data integrity and confidentiality of client-related data via the use of user classes. These classes are:

1. User—This class allows an individual to input his own charges and expenses, conduct enquiries and generate reports relating to himself only.
2. Privilege Classes—All privilege classes include the User privilege.
   a. Project Manager—Within this class, the user can produce labor reports for employees in his resource center, produce project cost reports, initiate projects and assign employees to projects.
   b. Data Entry Operator—An individual with this class may enter charges on behalf of himself as well as others.
   c. Operator—The operator class allows you to maintain control files. These files contain data on system users, clients, projects, activities, employees, project teams and expense categories.
   d. System Manager—This class can perform all functions available under *The Electronic Timesheet*. Thus, the system manager can enter transactions, product reports and listings and maintain data files.

DOCUMENTATION AND TUTORIALS

ET comes with a well-written, easy-to-understand users manual, containing seven chapters. Chapter 1 is an overview and summary of *ET*. Chapter 2 details *ET* features. The third chapter describes *ET* from the standpoint of logical design. Chapter 4 is titled "Installation and Initiation of the Electronic Timesheet." The issues involved in setting up a functioning system are treated in Chapter 5. Chapters 6 and 7 document the User Tutorial and System Manager Tutorial, respectively.

To use either Tutorial, you need the appropriate chapter from the users manual. Both tutorials are segmented into separate lessons, concentrating on some specific function of *ET*.

ET is a neat office automation package. Some formalities require concentration, such as the requirement that the TAB key, not RETURN, be pressed after filling certain fields. These were minor inconveniences, however.

In its promotional material, fbn Management Science Corporation claims that *ET* offers several advantages over a manual system. These advantages include:

1. Productivity gains through reduction of unnecessary paper work by facilitating automatic and systematic collection of data.
2. Reduction of errors.
3. Project cost control.
4. Improvement in cash flow by providing up-to-date client billing and project costing report on demand.

As you become familiar with *ET*, you'll realize that *ET* does fulfill each of these advantages.

This package is pleasant and fun to use and I recommended it enthusiastically.

MICHAEL G. GONZALES

ENERGY MANAGEMENT

INTRODUCTION

Energy management is a very complex concept which subordinates distinct but multiple aspects with the aim of achieving efficiency and readiness to assist consumers in fulfilling a business's production goals under a constant set of production constraints (e.g., economical, technical, environmental, risk and uncertainty, time, etc.).

This article considers the dimensions of energy management, from planning procedure to education policy.

The main topics covered are:

Penetration/substitution mechanism for energy systems (a paradigm of energy management); mathematical description and examples at different strata of energy systems

Planning for energy systems (linear programming and other complex models)

Systems analysis for energy management; objectives, modeling techniques, actors involved in a systems analysis task force, pitfalls in energy systems analysis

Indicators for energy management (e.g., quantitative, qualitative, semiotics, synergy, the inherent multidimensionality of energy indicators, limits and frontiers of indicators, etc.)

Socioeconomic risk in energy development programming and management

Risk-safety dichotomy for energy systems design and management

Optimal siting for obnoxious technologies (nuclear power stations)

Waste management, part of an energy management program for complex energy technologies

Energy storage, part of a sustainable energy management program

Energy conservation and economics of introducing new energy technologies

Centralized vs. decentralized systems to achieve reliability and safety in energy systems

End use energy management

Dispatcher concept for energy management at the territorial, regional, or enterprise level

Energy management information systems (online and offline energy management and the impact of microprocessors)

Energy costs for pricing (e.g., electricity, heat, cogeneration systems, etc.), and tarriffs (finance and equity)

Price of decommissioning for nuclear power stations; a basis for a better pricing of energy

Information and microelectronics in energy management

Hardware/software/orgware/brainware—the evolution of applying computers to the field of energy management

Office automation and energy end use management (technologies for
office automation, how to optimize the use of energy at a factory
level)

Net energy content and WELMM (water, energy, land, materials, manpower); complex indicators to assess different energy strategies

Rate of return on projects and associated engineering-economic models

Energy management vs. legislation and environmental impact

Effect of TIME in energy management (e.g., macrotime and microtime
dimensions)

Artificial intelligence for power production management; KIPS; expert
systems, and decision support systems

Educational systems and programs for energy management

ENERGY SYSTEM MANAGEMENT

This term is used mainly to define efficient use of energy (or of the finite
energy resources) at macroeconomic as well as microeconomic levels by
adequate actions such as energy savings, rational use of energy, substitution of one form of energy by other (e.g., fossil fuels by solar, wind, geothermal, photovoltaic) energy. The means used may be regulating, incentives, political, economic, or innovative.

There are several diversifications of this concept, and it is difficult to
adopt a single point of view in defining energy management. Some people
draw a neat distinction between governing and managing energy problems.
Within the decision-making process, one faces negative and positive feedback as well as a strong interwave connection between these two concepts
and types of actions.

Within the "complex" arena of energy system management and government policies one must consider the relationship between a decision maker
(e.g., manager, executive, planner, politician, public) and an energy
systems analyst. A systems analyst should be able to propose alternatives
and produce rules to establish an adequate hierarchy among these alternatives.

Figure 1 presents the framework for energy systems management procedures by special means: introducing goals and constraints, as well as
new tools for decision making (e.g., information sciences, learning procedures, risk-safety attitude formation, cultural and moral). Energy management implies basic and specific features such as forecasting and planning,
organization, motivation, coordination, and control. An adequate meaning
of information sciences and computers is widely accepted today in the field
of energy and power engineering.

As an alternative term, energy saving represents adequate measures,
passive or active, on the effect of such measures taken by suppliers and
users of energy (e.g., insulation, utilization of waste heat or gas that
would otherwise be flared) to limit wastage of energy; organizational measures are also possible (e.g., changes in transportation mode or information
data handling).

Rational use of energy is a management concept with associated organizational tools which enable the utilization of energy by consumers in a manner
best suited to the realization of economic/energetic objectives, taking into
account short-/medium/long-term social, political, financial, environmental,
etc. constraints at the enterprise, branch, or national level.

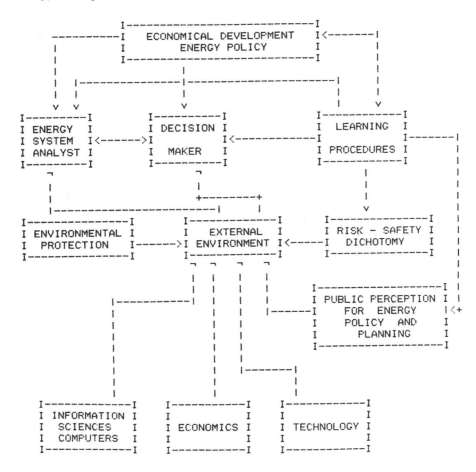

FIGURE 1 Framework for energy systems management.

Over the last 10 to 15 years, the concept of energy content (net energy analysis) has been introduced within the energy management framework and is defined as the quantity of energy (direct and/or indirect) that has been consumed in the manufacture of a product measured at the production point or in the provision of a service measured at the point at which the service is provided. Additional aspects should be stated regarding each of the following parameters: the energy content of machines, materials etc. (indirect energy), the energy used to produce or deliver products or services etc.

GOALS IN ENERGY MODELS AND POLICIES

New terms such as flexibility, resiliency, freedom of action, and robustness are appearing more and more in sectorial or national energy policy analysis as a prerequisite to modeling and systems analysis. Linkage between energy models and policies to facilitate the use of robustness analysis is recommended (e.g., linear programming models are possible analytical means to deal with robustness). One can consider robustness as a measure of the benefits and costs of an energy project (policy) and the opportunity costs of adjustments to future demand conditions. It can also be considered as the maintenance of flexibility or a type of adaptivity that relates to the number of decision options remaining after an initial decision for energy policy and management.

Robustness, as a measure of economic performance, requires that a probability distribution over forecasted parameters (e.g., demand or price) be estimated. When such probabilities are known, a suitable measure of robustness is of the following form:

$$R_p = \text{Prob}[C(d/P) < (1 + p)L(d)]$$

where $C(d/P)$ is the cost of satisfying a given demand condition d with the specific energy policy P, p a certain fraction over the original minimum cost $L(d)$.

While energy planning is viewed as sequential, robustness analysis identifies initial decisions that preserve as many future decision alternatives as possible. The robustness of a decision is defined as:

$$R_i = \frac{n(S_i)}{n(S)}$$

where $n(S_i)$ is the number of alternatives remaining after an initial decision di and $n(S)$ represents the total number of alternatives initially considered. Opportunity cost with robust decisions is given by

$$QCR = C(d/PR) - \min C(d/P)$$

where PR is the sequence of planning decisions based on robustness that meet the demand d. Some authors define robustness as a certain type of adaptivity that considers available alternatives subsequent to an initial decision without considering associated probabilities.

MACRODYNAMICS OF ENERGY PENETRATION AND SUBSTITUTION

It has been proved that energy technologies obey a substitution process which is remarkably regular on the world level as well as on the national level whether or not the market is centrally planned. Time plays a substantial role in the energy substitution process.

A given energy technology undergoes three distinct phases: growth, saturation, and senescence. Marchetti [1] and Peterka [see Ref. 2] developed the phenomenological model by devising the logistic equation among competing technologies (e.g., wood, coal, oil, natural gas, nuclear, solar). For a group of n energy technologies, the logistic equation is:

$$\frac{f_i(t)}{1 - f_i(t)} = \exp(\alpha_i t + \beta_i) \qquad (i = 1, 2, , , ,, n)$$

where α_i and β_i are the estimated coefficients from historical data and $f_i(t)$ is the market share of the i-th energy technology at time $t (\sum_{i=1}^{n} f_i(t) = 1)$.

If $y_j(t) = \log [f_j(t)/(1 - f_j(t))]$, then the energy technology j completes the saturation phase when $y'_j(t) < 0$ and $y''_j(t)/y_j(t) \longrightarrow$ min.

The diffusion of a specific technology i is determined by the available investment b_i, the costs c_i, and the growth rate, such that:

$$f_i(t) = f_i(t_o) \exp [\psi_o(t) - \delta_i(t)] a_i \; ; \; i = 1, 2, \ldots, n$$

where $a_i = \alpha/b_i$, $\delta_i = (c_i + b_i\rho)(t - t_0)/\alpha$, and $\alpha = (\sum_i 1/b_i)/(\sum_i 1/b_i^2)$;

$\psi_0(t)$ is the root of $\xi(\psi) = \sum_i f_i(t_0) \exp(\psi - \delta_i)*a_i - 1 = 0$, which can be computed by the Newton-Raphson method.

According to Marchetti [3], "it is to be observed that the main characteristic of the primary energy substitution of the world is the extreme regularity and slowness of each substitution. It takes about 100 years to go from 1% to 50% of the market. We call this length of time the time constant of the system. . . The regularity refers not only to the fact that the rate of penetration (. . .) remains constant over such very long periods when so many perturbing processes seem to take place, but also to the fact that all perturbations are reabsorbed elastically without influencing the trend. It is as though the system has a schedule, a will, and a clock." This is emphasized with respect to the energy technologies dynamics at the international level (Fig. 2), market economies such as the United States (Fig. 3), planned economics such as the Soviet Union (Fig. 4), or even medium-sized countries such as Romania (Fig. 5) [3].

FEATURES OF ENERGY MANAGEMENT

Energy planning is a complex and difficult task, a formalized and direct outcome of policy analysis. It is effective only as an integral part of development planning (e.g., energy use and energy supply are not ends in them-

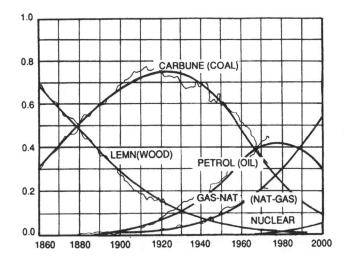

FIGURE 2 World primary energy substitution.

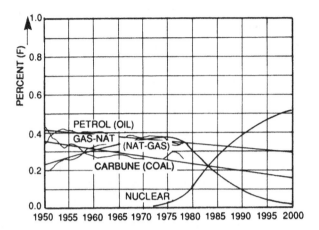

FIGURE 3   U.S. primary energy substitution.

selves). The objectives of energy policy must be subordinated to wider
goals and strategies; links between energy plans and overall development
strategy are to be emphasized and included in the subsequent analysis.

Analysis/planning activities can be divided into two parts: descriptive
and decision oriented, either at the national, regional, sectorial, or enterprise levels. A coordinated process is shared across the board. Figure 6
shows a possible scheme for analysis in the energy planning process [4].

As summarized, "energy planning, broadly interpreted, denotes a
series of steps or procedures by which the myriad of interactions involved
in the production and use of all forms of energy may be studied and understood within an explicit analytical framework. Planning techniques range
from simple manual methods to sophisticated computer modeling. The complexity of energy problems and the enhanced capability of low cost micro-
components has led to increasing on the latter approach" [4].

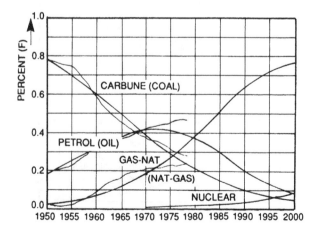

FIGURE 4   USSR primary energy substitution.

The energy planning and decision process has some intrinsic characteristics [5, 6].

Complexity

An energy system could never be brand new. One has to build on the previous energy technologies new infrastructures to meet the growing needs of the consumers. Old technologies (e.g., coal, oil, hydro, etc.) and new ones (e.g., nuclear, solar) do coexist for a period of time while the system looks coherent enough under given technical and economical constraints. The energy system has an internal clock and technologies do experience a complex substitution process over a span of time. The complexity index for the energy system involves certain reliability, availability, and safety figures which have to be met in order for the system to maintain operation and be viable at the interface with the consumer.

Dynamics

It is evident that the time dimension of an energy system development or involution is a primary characteristic. It has a very relevant weight in the overall judgement of strategies, policies, and success.

Inertial Behavior of Consumers

It seems strange to a "rational" decision maker when an energy consumer does not totally react as it was agreed, planned, or asked that he do. Sometimes, the consumers do not sustain enough of a conservation policy effort to decrease, for instance, oil consumption as requested by social planners. They manage to bypass the regulations, to afford paying for a higher price structure for the energy consumed, and in the beginning, are less motivated to modernize and seek robust engineering solutions to decrease national energy consumption. Consumers always find ways to fulfill their energy need in accordance with their preconceived image of that need.

The Planning Appeal

Today the energy problem is closely related to the concepts of national security and independence. Government's in their peculiar way, pay a great deal of attention to planning the future energy scenario for their country. They sometimes find it necessary to update their forecast to keep in stride with new technological achievements, the balance of foreign debt of the country, sudden increases of fuel and material prices, or to redefine the political and social goals of their country. Within the implementation process of an energy program the decision maker is faced with fuzzying constraints.

High Capital Costs

Even if energy resources were very abundant, the investment of capital cost requires a careful analysis for each possible energy scenario. At the time a decision is taken to develop a certain technology, the capital cost estimation looks different from the time of the actual implementation; this is true regardless of the value of the project (e.g., discounted costs for energy projects).

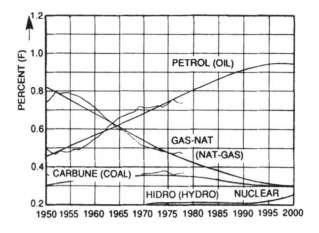

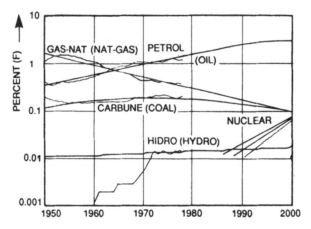

FIGURE 5   Romania primary energy substitution.

Societal Impact

The consumer is directly dependent upon the energy supply system with a
special emphasis on electrical power. Socioeconomic development relations
and risk perception problems are potential "noise" in the relationship between consumption and supply.

Environmental Impact

A strategic energy planning model is unable at the decision point to reflect
all consequences either economic or environmental. Environmental effects
could have a lag time before becoming manifest, and eventually will irre-
versibly deteriorate the surroundings (e.g., acid rain).

All the above characteristics underline the fuzzy character of the goals
and purposes which a social planner has to deal with in connection with the
normative approach of the energy system structure and its future evolution.

Sectorial analyses are used to plan for basic energy requirements
(e.g., quantity and type) and assess the impact of pricing policies, conservation investments, regulations, as well as the possibility of energy

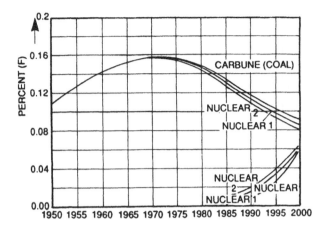

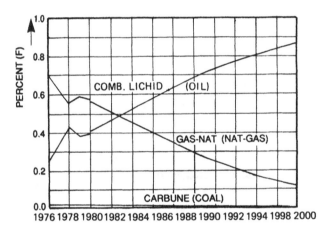

FIGURE 5 (Continued).

substitution. National policy analysis and planning must include fuel pricing, taxes, investment policies, land and water use planning, materials and manpower. A multicriteria model used in such instances is WELMM (Water, Energy, Land, Materials, Manpower) [2].

The main objective of energy supply planning is to meet demand requirements for various energy types in a cost-effective, environmentally acceptable manner. Consistent energy policy and planning require the integration of the previous stages (e.g., establishing the conditions for a balance of energy demand—supply and evaluating the manifold impacts of each alternative), leading to determination of the size and mix of the energy system. Such balances provide the basis for establishing the attributes or impacts of the energy plan (e.g., costs, human resources, financing, material, etc.). At this stage, microcomputers offer special assistance to the energy systems analyst/planner team concerning data processing and energy scenario development. The energy planning process is iterative and must be direct and transparent for adequate success of practical implementation.

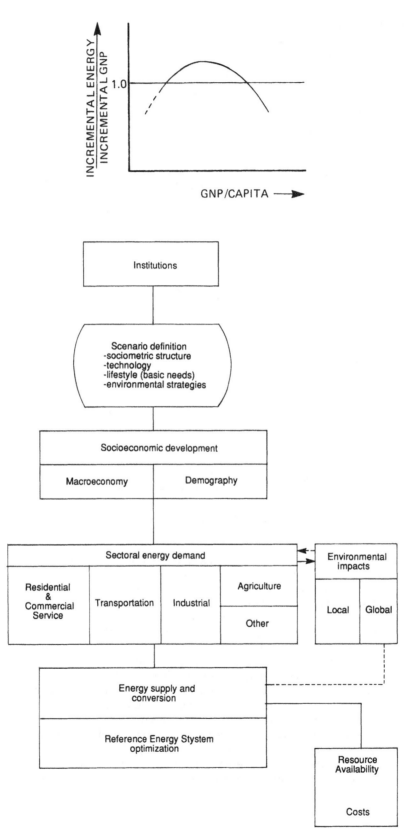

FIGURE 6   Analysis and planning activities in the framework of energy management.

As stated in the literature concerning energy planning, priority must be given to flexible and adaptive policies and that "in any planning program it is always necessary to expect the unexpected" [4].

Operations Research Models

Two analytical tools widely used in the field of energy planning and optimization are operations research (OR) models and linear programming (LP). For a power system planning problem LP is characterized by the following patterns:

> The objective function introduces the discounted present values of the investment and operations costs
>
> The load-flow could be expressed in the form of power balance constraints
>
> The system operation can be given by means of dynamic peak demand energy and capacity constraints, taken also into consideration the reverse margin

A typical LP energy model is of the following general form:

Objective function (minimize the discounted costs of investment)

$$\sum_{v=1}^{T} \sum_{j=1}^{J} c_{jv} x_{jv} + \sum_{t=1}^{T} \sum_{v=0}^{t} \sum_{j=1}^{J} \sum_{p=1}^{P} f_{jvtp} u_{jvtp} Qp$$

Constraints:

(a) peak demand constraints:

$$\sum_{v=0}^{t} \sum_{j=1}^{J} a_{jv} x_{jv} >= d_t (1 + m); \qquad t = 1, \ldots, T$$

(b) energy constraints:

$$\sum_{v=0}^{t} \sum_{j=1}^{J} u_{jvtp} >= g_{tp}; \qquad t = 1, \ldots, T; \qquad p = 1, \ldots, P$$

(c) capacity constraints:

$$u_{jvtp} <= a_{jv} x_{jv} \qquad j = 1, \ldots, J$$

$$u_{jvtp} >= 0 \qquad v = 0, \ldots, t$$

$$0 <= x_{jv} <= n_{jv} \qquad t = 1, \ldots, T$$

$$x_{jv} - \text{integer} \qquad p = 1, \ldots, P$$

where

T	=	number of internals in period of study
J	=	number of different types of plant
P	=	number of subperiods in each interval
v	=	date of installation of a plant (v = 0 identifies existing plants)
x_{jv}	=	number of plants of type j installed in interval v
c_{jv}	=	discounted capital and fixed charges for one plant of type j installed in interval v
u_{jvtp}	=	level of production in subperiod p of interval t of plant type j installed in interval v
f_{jvtp}	=	discounted cost of production of one unit of energy for u_{jvtp}
Q_p	=	duration of subperiod p
a_{jv}	=	available capacity of plant type j installed in interval v
d_t	=	peak demand in interval t
m	=	reserve margin as a percentage of dt
g_{tp}	=	average demand in subperiod p of interval t obtained from the load-duration curve of interval t
n_{jv}	=	maximum number of plants of type j that can be installed in interval v

A large variety of models integrated into a system analysis framework have been used for energy planning purposes. It must be mentioned the work done at IIASA-Laxenburg, in the United States with particular note to the model work at the National Center for Energy Systems Analysis at the Brookhaven National Laboratory, the GULF-SRI model, and the work of the members of the Energy Modeling Forum. A great deal of work has been performed as well in other government departments in France, the United Kingdom, Denmark, as well as in Eastern European economies (e.g, Romania) and the Soviet Union. Among the well known models for energy policy and planning are MEDEE, IMPACT, and MESSAGE.

Decisions to run national economies are assisted these days to a large degree by computer models. One can assess them as being hard computer models embedding hard programs (i.e., many variables, advanced econometrics, large amount of input or output data, etc.).

By extension, one can identify the difficulties in devising, implementing, and operating such models, particularly by the decision maker (DM) who generally has little input as far as the engineering of such sophisticated devices.

It becomes more and more difficult to extract a simple and good decision from an array of output data. OR by itself offers limited advantages when one wishes to assist the DM with dynamic modeling and control. If a hard model is designed by a team of systems analysts with only weak interaction with the DM, the result is a decision which is not entirely trusted even by the DM (the decision maker is not assisted by the model, rather the model forces decisions upon him or her). By extension, the DM draws upon his feelings and experience more than is necessary—management as an art—losing the synergy of input and output data.

Progress in computer technology, and particularly in personal/professional computers (PC), urges the DM closer to the concept of soft programming.

Soft programming for computing implies the use of rather simple models (i.e., less input and output data, fewer variables, less structured coherency, etc.), but in turn allows the DM to toy with the models, offering forecasting results in the same range of precision as the dedicated models.

In this way to DM can be effectively assisted by such computer programs. The user does not need large data files and can even bring his or her experience, wishes, and perception online. A fuzzy approach fulfills such requirements.

The fuzzy approach is used to quantify the preferences and/or the given information states which are neither deterministic nor certain, and so they must be dynamically approached.

This approach is used to compute and evaluate end use energy demand on a time scale as well as appropriate investment efforts (Fig. 7).

The management-oriented results illuminate further dimensions of the complex problem of energy use management by means of models and the interaction with the social planner, its way of thinking and preferences.

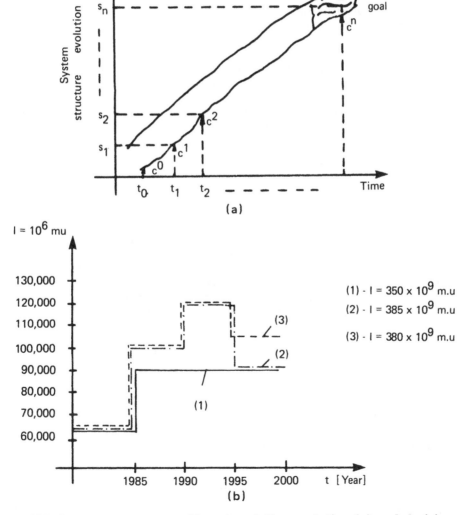

FIGURE 7 System structure (fuzzy) and time evolution (a) and decision alternatives features over a definite horizon (b).

SOCIAL EFFORT EVALUATION FOR AN ENERGY STRATEGY:
A COMPLEMENTARY FUZZY REPLICA TO EXPLORATORY
FORECASTING

As already accepted in the theory of large-scale systems, the goal of a
future development for a given energy system is described as "fuzzy".
The forecasting process always embeds fuzziness and uncertainty.

One may consider a fuzzy goal G defined as:

"Continuous improvement" of the energy system structure, which means
that the social planner would like to get as close as possible to the "self-
reliance" state:

$$G = 0.2/s1 + 0.4/s2 + 0.8/s3 + 0.9/s4 + 1/s5$$

The state of the system is given by a vector, which includes the primary energy resources. The states represent the structure of the system
as it is to be achieved by the corresponding year. In order to achieve a
given state at a specified future date, appropriate efforts are required. A
good measure for quantifying this is in monetary terms. It is evident that
at discrete points in time the decsion maker has to implement the effort by
means of capital. We shall define these controllers (c_i, i = $\sqcup$ 1,...,I).

A transition matrix is defined by the way the system behaves under
several controllers. Despite the classical approach, the fuzzy constraints
are introduced to show that in the real managerial process one does not
know with certainty, for each decision moment, that he will be able to allocate the exact amount of capital as given by c_i, i $\in$ I. The following fuzzy
constraints are therefore considered:

$$C^o = 0.5/c_1 + 0.5/c_2 + 1/c_3$$

$$C^1 = 0.6/c_1 + 0.9/c_2 + 0.8/c_3$$

$$C^3 = 0.8/c_1 + 0.7/c_2 + 1/c_3$$

In using a fuzzy model one defines X as the set of the system states
($x_t \epsilon X = \{s_k\}$, $k \epsilon K$; t >= 0); U as the set of the controllers ($u_t \epsilon u = \{c_p\}$,
$p \epsilon P$; t >= 0); $C^t <= U$ is a fuzzy set of U and represents the fuzzy con-
straint at time t and $G^{t_k} <= X$ is a fuzzy set of X which represents the
fuzzy goal at the final moment t_k which is non-fuzzy defined.

A fuzzy decision D, D <= X, is characterized by the membership
function:

$$\mu_D(x_o, u_1, u_2, \cdots, u_{t(k)-1}) = \min[\mu_c o(u_o), \mu_c 1(u_1), \cdots,$$
$$\mu_c t_k - 1(u_{t(k)-1}), \mu_G t_k(x_{t(k)})] \qquad (6.1)$$

where x_o represents the final state of the system, and

$$x_{t(k)} = f(x_o, u_1, u_2, \cdots, u_{t(k)-1}) \qquad (6.2)$$

is the final state of the system.

The state transition function is of the form:

$$x_{t+1} = f(x_t, u_t) \qquad (6.3)$$

Let T = 0, 1, 2, ..., t_k the set of the final moments; $T \varepsilon T$ is the fuzzy final time characterized by $\mu_T(t)$.

The computational algorithm solves the problem by finding the maximum decision as a sequence $u_0, u_1, ..., u_{t(k)-1}$, which maximizes μ_D from (6.1).

Considering (6.1) and (6.3), we obtain a system of recurrent equations

$$\mu_G t_k - i(x_{t(k)} - i) = \max \{\min[\mu_C t_k - i(u_{t(k)} - 1), \mu_G t_k - i + 1(x_{t(k)} - i + 1)\}$$

$$x_{t(k)-i+1} = f(x_{t(k)-i}, u_{t(k)-i}) \quad ; \quad i = 1, 2, ..., t_k \qquad (6.4)$$

The solution of system (6.4) offers a maximum decision for a fixed t_k. It is convenient to express the solution as a policy function $u_t = P_t(x_t)$, t = 0, 1, ..., t_{k-1}.

To solve the dynamic fuzzy estimation of optimal effort distribution to meet the self-reliance goal for the energy needs, a computer program named FUZZY has been implemented on a PC system.

To achieve energy self-reliance status requires significant financial expenditures. Using the above model one is able to find the optimal allocation of investments in time and to assist the management planning process in the power engineering sector.

System states are represented by the electrical production structure; the controlled states are represented by the corresponding allocated investments to meet the given structure (10^6 m.u./5-year period) the time moments for the fuzzy constraints are chosen as 1980, 1985, 1990, 1995, and 2000.

Table 1 gives the states for the analyzed system.

The controlled states are represented by the investment levels in the energy field. They were computed as a function of specific investments in different kinds of power stations (e.g., nuclear, hydro, thermo, solar). It was assumed that no extra investments are made in thermal power stations

TABLE 1

	Hydro	Thermo coal	Thermo gas + oil	Nuclear solar	Total %	Total MW
s1	13	31	54	2	100	11,600
s2	17	40	40	3	100	16,000
s3	20	55	20	5	100	20,100
s4	22	56	18	4	100	20,100
s5	24	44	5	27	100	24,200
s6	23	46	15	16	100	24,200
s7	25	40	3	32	100	28,500
s8	25	41	5	29	100	28,500
s9	26	35	3	36	100	32,500
s10	26	38	3	33	100	32,500

which run on hydrocarbons, since that share is gradually being assumed by coal energy units per five-year period and they were computed as:

$$c_1 = 50{,}000; \quad c_2 = 65{,}000; \quad c_3 = 85{,}000; \quad c_4 = 95{,}000;$$
$$c_5 = 100{,}000; \quad c_6 = 120{,}000; \quad c_7 = 130{,}000$$

The fuzzy constraints are chosen as a function of the adopted investment policy and they are given by the following relations:

Time 0

$$C_0 = 0.4/c_1 + 0.8/c_2 + 0.4/c_3 + 0.2/c_4 + 0.15/c_5 + 0.1/c_6$$
$$+ 0.0/c_7$$

Time 1

$$C_1 = 0.1/c_1 + 0.3/c_2 + 0.8/c_3 + 0.5/c_4 + 0.4/c_5 + 0.7/c_6$$
$$+ 0.3/c_7$$

Time 2

$$C_2 = 0.3/c_1 + 0.5/c_2 + 0.85/c_3 + 0.7/c_4 + 0.3/c_5 + 0.2/c_6$$
$$+ 0.1/c_7$$

The fuzzy goal is defined as achieving energy self-reliance. This is quite similar to being in either state s7, s8, s9, s10, by 2000. The membership function of the fuzzy goal was chosen as:

$$G_4 = 0.0/s1 + 0.1/s2 + 0.2/s3 + 0.25/s4 + 0.4/s5 + 0.45/s6 + 0.6/s7$$
$$+ 0.65/s8 + 0.9/s9 + 0.95/s10$$

The transition matrix for the system is given by:

$$u_t = \begin{array}{c} \\ c1 \\ c2 \\ \cdot \\ \cdot \\ \cdot \\ c7 \end{array} \left| \begin{array}{cccccc} s1 & s2 & .\ .\ . & s9 & s10 \\ s2 & s3 & .\ .\ . & s9 & s10 \\ s2 & s3 & .\ .\ . & s9 & s10 \\ \cdot & \cdot & \cdot\ \cdot\ \cdot & \cdot & \cdot \\ \cdot & \cdot & \cdot\ \cdot\ \cdot & \cdot & \cdot \\ \cdot & \cdot & \cdot\ \cdot\ \cdot & \cdot & \cdot \\ s3 & s4 & .\ .\ . & s10 & s10 \end{array} \right|$$

Using the FUZZY computer program to solve the above problem, the maximum decisions were found to be:

Initial state	Maximum decisions
$x_0 = s1$	$D = c_2c_3c_2c_1$ or $c_2c_4c_3c_2$
$x_0 = s2$	$D = c_2c_4c_4c_4$ or $c_2c_5c_6c_5$ or $c_2c_5c_6c_4$
$x_0 = s3$	$D = c_2c_4c_6c_1$ or $c_2c_5c_6c_2$
$x_0 = s4$	$D = c_2c_4c_6c_2$ or $c_2c_5c_5c_3$

The state s is of interest for the present study and corresponds to the year 1985.

The chosen maximum decisions are:

(1) $D = c_2 c_4 c_6 c_1$ (final state x = s8)
(2) $D = c_2 c_5 c_6 c_2$ (final state x = s10)

A graphic representation for the corresponding investment effort over time could be drawn accordingly (see Fig. 7,b).

FUZZY MODELS AIDED

Energy Demand Management

Estimation of the energy demand at the national or the regional level presents a strong challenge to the energy planner. The dedicated models (e.g., OR, econometrics) and others require a large set of complex data, careful handling of information, large memory, and computer facilities. They are quantitatively oriented studies, requiring specialized staff and processed information at quite large-scale costs during the compilation stage.

We should note however that the decision maker may sometimes be unable to control the development of the model and its outputs at any stage. Instead, he has to trust the systems analyst's judgement in the correctness, the articulation of all assumptions, and programming tricks during the modeling and running steps. Additionally, several difficulties arise in getting input data; some of these are obtained through careful, cumbersome computation from routine environmental data. The output information is cardinally oriented, while the decision maker is concerned with trends, and so is interested in ordinal information.

Large-scale energy models do not include the options and "attitudes" of a decision maker. Likewise, they do not reflect to a sufficient degree of flexibility the appropriate technological changes over a forecasting horizon, nor the "possibilities" of the sociotechnological environment. Next, a fuzzy linguistic model for demand evaluation is described.

Total fuel needs are predicted by industrial branches and are expressed by the so-called "pattern structure." The contribution of each industrial branch toward the overall output is expressed in linguistic terms. The most probable pattern structures will be given by fuzzy methods. A brief account of the methodology employed is given here.

Given a set $A = \{a1, a2, . . ., an\}$ of symbols (e.g., industries) and an orderly set $G = \{g0, gi, . . ., g(m - 1)\}$ (e.g., the values of gi ϵ [0,1]) one may generate a pattern structure: $B = \{a1, \mu_B(ai)/i = 1, 2, . . ., n; \mu_B(ai) = G\}$, where $\mu_B(ai)$ represents the membership function of the appropriate element in set A.

With the designed pattern construals, one may further select those which imply the most probable desirable state. This allows the decision maker to attach linguistis terms to the components of the total fuel industrial needs.

Thus, in the steel industry, for instance, one may envisage the need for coal as very large, while in the chemical industry it is lower. It is a natural method of forecasting evaluation; since intuitive expert feelings are usually adequate, such linguistic estimations can be converted into exact figures. One has to define basic linguistic terms such as low, medium, large; the derived terms are computed under appropriate rules.

The steps involved in the forecasting:

1. Linguistic estimation of required amount of coal by each individual industry
2. Building up of the transition mapping from linguistic to membership values
3. Quantitative computation for the required amount of coal by industries (in T. E. C.)

The energy demand forecasts at the national level may raise our concern for the case of coal. The horizon chosen covers the span to the year 2000 in five-year steps. Nine industries were identified for analysis [food (1), paper (2), chemical (3), petrochemical (4), building materials (5), steel (6), nonferrous metallurgy (7), machine building (8), others (9)].
The G-set is expressed by:

$$G = \{0, 0.045, 0.090, 0.135, 0.225, 0.270, 0.315, 0.360, 0.405 \}$$

and a V set was chosen so as to divide the [0, 1] into equal shares with a 0.05 step:

$$V = \{0, 0.05, 0.10, \ldots, 0.95, 1.00\}$$

Thus, the basic linguistic terms are defined as shown below:

low = 1/0.0 + 0.85/0.05 + 0.80/0.10 + 0.70/0.15 + 0.60/0.20 +
       0.40/0.25 + 0.0/0.30 + 0.20/0.35 + 0.10/0.40 + 0.05/0.45 +
       0.0/0.50 + 0.0/0.55 + . . . + 0.0/1.0
medium = 0.0/0.0 + 0.0/0.05 + 0.0/0.10 + 0.2/0.2 + 0.3/0.25 +
       0.4/0.3 + 0.45/0.35 + . . . + 0.5/0.8 + 0.3/0.85 + 0.20/0.9 +
       0.10/0.95 + 0.0/1.0
large = 0.0/0.0 + . . . + 0.05/0.45 + 0.10/0.50 + . . . + 0.70/0.85 +
       0.80/0.90 + 0.85/0.95 + 1.0/1.0

If large, medium, and low represent three basic linguistic terms, then the derived terms can be obtained by using specific fuzzy rules such as: very large = $(large)^2$; very very large = $(large^2)^2$; large and low = min large,low); not large = 1 − large, etc.
The elements of G are obtained by virtue of the above rule such that:

Linguistic term	Number
very very low	0.00
very low	0.045
.	.
.	.

Based on the linguistic description, we can compute the following results for the case of coal (see Table 2).

TABLE 2

Industry year	1	2	3	4	5	6	7	8	9
1975	very low 144	very low 144	low 288	very low 0	very low 144	low 288	very very low 0	very low 144	very very low 0
1980	very low 144	low 288	low and medium 432	low 288	low 288	low and medium 432	very very low 0	very low 144	very very low 0
1985	194 very low 144							197 low 288	114 very low 114
1990	233 low 288							230 low 288	165 very low 144
1995	255 low 288							255 low 288	294 very low 144
2000	270 low 288							275 low 288	206 low 288

TABLE 3

Industry year	1	2	-----	8	9
1980	very low 144	low 288	-----	very low 144	very very low 0
.	.	.		.	.
.	.	.	-----	.	.
.	.	.		.	.
2000	low 288	very low and not medium 576	-----	low 288	low 288

This approach reveals the following observations:

Difference between econometric and fuzzy forecasting are less than 10%
These differences are getting smaller, as the forecasting horizon gets larger
The fuzzy expert resoluton is of paramount importance

Linguistic Sensitivity

Linguistic sensitivity allows the decision maker to quantify the changes in his or her value options.

As an example, one can idealize the above problem, assuming that the following changes are likely to occur: (1) the paper industry is requested to decrease coal consumption against the use of secondary resources, (2) the petrochemical industry increases coal use and this induces a decrease in oil consumption, (3) in the nonferrous metallurgical industry, coal consumption increases with lower use of electricity.

Because the above assumptions are extremely time consuming to satisfy, linguistic sensitivity will furnish distinct future estimation for the corresponding linguistic terms (see Table 2, which changes accordingly in Table 3).

TABLE 4

Year	Total demand	
	Previous	Changed
1975	1152	1152
1980	1728	2016
1985	2880	2880
1990	4032	4032
1995	4464	4464
2000	5184	5320

Advances in modeling and simulations of complex engineering economic systems brought into use the fuzzy models with their advantages and limitations. The energy systems were among the first to be investigated by means of such flexible and handy analytical tools.

Comparing such models to classical energy OR/econometric models shows that the difference in output estimation is shrinking as the forecasting horizon and investment policy expand.

The total coal consumption at different time periods and in alternatives (a) and (b) is given in Table 4.

SOCIOECONOMIC RISK IN ENERGY DEVELOPMENT PROGRAM AND MANAGEMENT

A great deal of attention over the last twenty years has been given to elaborating scenarios enabling energy systems to take the "right" path in meeting the future energy requirements of society. A pervasive lack of consensus on the meaning of the energy crisis has reduced the assertion of planners into postulates emerging mostly from group or individual convictions, motivations, and attitudes. It is generally agreed that energy conservation management is a long-term challenge resulting from a given order based primarily on such factors as: (a) the energy-intensive nature of modern society, either production, or service oriented; (b) oil monoculture; (c) misuse and mismanagement of energy resources.

Concerning the general attitude toward energy, it is agreed that today (i) the traditional energy status quo of the 1960s is untenable, particularly in the long run, and (ii) energy systems must be made technically, economically, and socially more adequate through changes in their nature, structure, and management.

There is a conspicuous perception of risk entailed by changes shared in various degrees by those advocating changes and those opposing them. It goes with the classic dilemma of to do or not to do what, how, where, and when, in what depth, with what results—be these direct, indirect, foreseen, and also unforeseen. It is probably this perception that makes energy assessment and planning a favorite topic in pertinent decision media, and risk analysis and management an indispensible built-in component of today's process of decision making and energy conservation policy.

Energy management considers the fact that energy, technology, the economy, and society are closely intertwined and there is a need to look more analytically at the intricacies of this relationship. "Hard," econometric, operating research, and "soft" rather qualitative, approaches merge in this respect.

Oversimplified models described as soft models (e.g., catastrophy theory) were able to explain some facets of the behavior of energy systems, as well as to define attitudes toward structural changes of these systems that entail risks not only by virtue potential results, but also be the very way in which these changes are (or are not) performed, including the timing factor. The model recognizes stochastic and cooperative features in the collective behavior of the decision media, and claims that these features are of consequence as far as the outcome of the decision makers (e.g., how much money should be allocated to any given option in energy technology and policy).

Disruptive, discontinuous evolutions within the hierarchy of energy systems management are perceived as risky by society; visualizing such risks

can naturally be connected with the resilience of the system (a concept
used to describe the capability of a system to absorb perturbations without
changing its very integrity and nature). By going beyond this concept one
may eventually arrive at policy judgements that would be inspired by mathematical forms, rather than be sheer numbers.

Such models represent a "topological" assessment of strategies (energy
policies). It is plausible to assume that the exchange interaction of deciding
bodies may be indirectly measured by the indicator—energy demand per
capita of a given society. The more intense the interaction of labor and
capita and production entitles (public and/or private), the greater the exchange of information and communication between social groups and individuals. Looking at trends now looming in real life, it may well be that the
future will bring about the indicator information demand per capita (or even
information processing capacity per capita) as a relevant substitute for
energy per capita in describing intersocietal interaction.

Topological models show that the less one knows about the connections
between the energy economy and energy technology and about the technological impact of the overall energy policy, the greater the chance of an
"unpredictable" (in effect not duly predicted) structural change in the
energy system management.

Through a variety of paths the energy economies will probably strive
toward a status of maximum energy security, or even "oversecurity" (net
importers turned into net exporters on the account of coal, nuclear, fuel,
electricity etc.) taking advantage of their increased margins of resilience as
their energy intensity increases. From the point of view of energy management it is said that all paths would in principle require timely adjustments
in the technological infrastructure of the energy economy. Some paths,
when followed persistently and blindly, can drive the energy system and
economy into critical states of disruption. It is clear that a prompt and
correct perception of the need and size of structural adjustments in the
energy system is a prerequisite of a sound and smooth energy management
policy.

The fact that while there is a cost and risk to any change, there is
also a cost and a risk to ignoring the need for changes seems inescapable.
Such an attitude that treats alternatives not as subversive to the existing
establishment, but as safeguards of its stability and also formative germs of
future, ever more appropriate, patterns, is of great importance for both
the planner's and the public's peace of mind.

Deriving policy arguments from mathematical models may bring wry
smiles in some segments of the decision media. One solid objection is that
models are always poor—mathematical modeling might indeed, never have
straight access to applications in effectively building up operational energy
management strategies. In the long run, it can certainly induce new motivations and attitudes in the planner's mind, increasing his reverence as to
decisional risk problem.

STRUCTURAL CHANGE IN THE ENERGY ORDER: A TOPOLOGICAL APPROACH

It is important to understand the discontinuities in an overall energy development program, due to appropriate human decisions. The major impetus for
developing energy policies originates from the interdependence of the exhaustion of energy resources and the desired rate of economical and social

development measured by aggregated indicators (e.g., energy use per capita). Energy systems will never be "brand new"; technologies of different eras will coexist.

To ask for change is untypical conduct for a planner. Social planners would ask questions like "What if we don't accept a change?" or "Can a structural change be forced upon us?" before taking any firm steps to restructure the energy infrastructures.

Answering such questions is extremely important. This helps the planner and the consumer to understand the need for changes in the energy systems.

Models of catastrophe theory can prove that, in principle, a structural change in the energy system can be forced upon us and that macrotime plays an important role in efficiently managing such transitions.

Let us postulate that the structure of the energy system for a given economy can be appropriately described as a collection of weighted technologies. In terms relevant to decision making the weight of a given technology or group of technologies can be qualified by the amount of money put at each moment into research, development, demonstration, and deployment of a particular technology, relative to the total amount of money available for the development of the system.

We assume that the total amount M of money allocated to the energy sector is practically constant. We suppose that all energy technologies can be split into two groups; (1) actually used, as against (2) potentially useful ($M1 + M2 = M$ = constant, where Mi, $i = 1$, 2 are the funds allocated to the two types of technologies).

Making a decision that leads to a potential structural change in the energy system is equivalent to redistributing the fixed amount M between technological group 1 and group 2. Every allocation of the type $(M1, M2) \longrightarrow (M1 - 1, M2 + 1)$ is a transition which enhances group 2 and an allocation $(M1, M2) \longrightarrow (M1 + 1, M2 - 1)$ enhances group 1.

The decision process is stochastic and cooperative, since a given decision is the result of a complex interaction of opinion between individuals or groups, sensitive to the momentary power of influence and to external circumstances (market, policy, etc.).

A complex model is given by Gheorghe and Purica where a distribution of function f at time t for deciding upon an allocation (M1, M2) is of the form [7]:

$$f(\xi) = k[(1/m)w21(\xi) + w12(\xi))]^{-1} * \exp[2m \int_{-1/2}^{\xi} (w21(x) - w12(x))$$

$$/(w21(x) + w12(x))dx] \qquad (9.1)$$

where

$$w12(\xi) = (1.2 + \xi) \exp((-1/\theta)(I\xi + B)) \qquad (9.2)$$

$$w21(\xi) = (1.2 - \xi) \exp((1/\theta)(I\xi + B)) \qquad (9.3)$$

$$\xi = (M1 - M2)/2M \qquad (9.4)$$

and k is a constant. Here I is a measure of the intensity of the energy system, B is a "preference parameter" accounting for the external influences on the decision process, and θ stands for a "decision climate" parameter: the higher θ the higher the "temperature" of the debates, owing to a higher perception of the crisis. For large M the continuous variable ξ is an "order parameter," featuring the structure of the decision.

A numerical analysis of f for B = 0 and various values of 1 and θ shows some interesting features (Fig. 8): (a) beginning with a certain value of I/θ the function f displays pronounced groups of opinions; (b) for θ small, the sharp, single peaks show that one-sided decisions should be expected when the intensity of the debates is low.

When u = I/θ and v = B/θ, one obtains f(ξ, u, v), so that bifurcation in the plane (u, v) (Fig. 9) suggests that f can be approximated by a jet bundle of corank one and the topological manifold is corresponding to the cusp-type catastrophe. By choosing appropriately u and v from the possible economic indicators related to the energy systems, the decision maker may predetermine in principle the structure toward which the system is attracted in the case of sudden (catastrophic) changes.

The natural evolution of the energy system in the (u, v, ξ) space is represented by the surface F in Figure 10. This surface displays borders (Fig. 10a,b) which can be naturally interpreted as being the resilience limits (separatrices) of the different phases of the system.

It means that a system with a dominant "group I" technological structure accepts continuous reallocations of money from the group 1 technologies to the group 2 without essentially changing its 1-kind profile until the resilience border is crossed due, for example, to a continuous disturbance of its traditional energy trade balance (imports–exports). Then the system structure undergoes a sudden transition to a dominant group 2 profile, thus facing the undesirable consequences of sudden changes. It is clear that the same applies for an evolution from 2 to 1 in connection to the other resilience border.

The "topological behaviorism" suggested here is a way to keep the planner thinking and to help communication of ideas. In fact it is a paradigm. It shows that the less we know about the connections between the energy economy and energy technologies, and about the technological impact of the overall energy policy, the greater the chance of a catastrophic structural change in the energy systems.

As we have seen, moves in the space of the energy intensity of an economy (E/C) and its energy trade balance ((I −E)/C), even with no apparent connection to technology create stresses in the technological infrastructure of the energy policy. The energy system may collapse either if

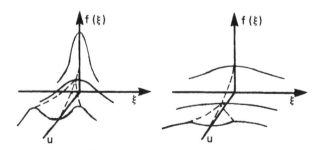

FIGURE 8 Distribution function of the probability of decision.

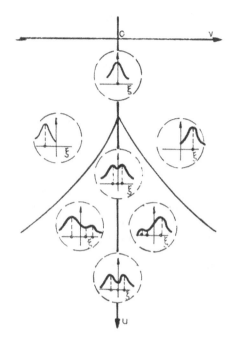

FIGURE 9 Topology of the most probable decisions.

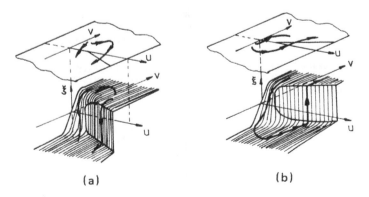

FIGURE 10 Smooth (a) vs. disruptive (b) possible paths.

traditional paths are indefinitely pursued, or if excessive changes are made in the energy policy.

Referring to the intuitive model discussed, one can see that the plan of action (E/C, (I — E)/C) of the energy policy falls naturally into four different categories (Fig. 11). In principle one can make a distinction between high-energy-intensive, import-dominated, low-energy-intensive, export-dominated, low-energy-intensive, import-dominated and high-energy-intensive export-dominated economies. Such a classification had to do with the choice of definition for the otherwise abstract parameters u and v of the model.

The energy constraints induce the economies move in this space, according to specific, understandable driving forces, as presented in Figure 11.

Thus, the actual path of a low-energy-intensive export-dominated economy could be chosen anywhere between still increasing exports (driving forceprofit), diminishing energy exports (driving force-caution about premature resource exhaustion) and increasing the domestic energy affluence, roughly related to welfare. Similarly, a high-energy-intensive import-dominated economy may wish to follow a path somewhere between still increasing imports for security storage, still increasing energy affluence, and discouraging imports by caution about sustainability of supply. Low-energy-intensive import-dominated economies will, most probably choose a path

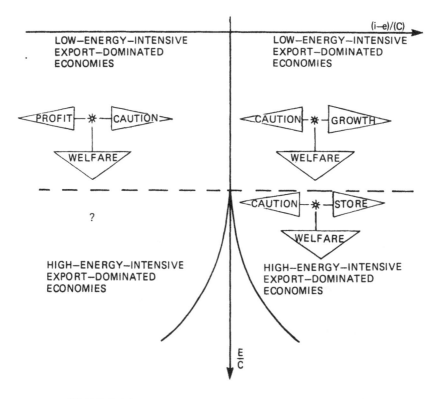

FIGURE 11   Patterns in the space of energy policy.

ensuring an increase of energy affluence, doubled by efforts to diminish the dependence of the foreign supply. It is unlikely that an economy will really choose to reduce drastically its per capita energy consumption in absolute terms which roughly translates in slowing down the development and degrading the standard of living.

Since indefinite increase of energy exports or imports is not sustainable, it is to be expected that the paths in the energy policy of many economies will resemble the trial paths hinted of in Figure 12. It should be mentioned that these paths do have strategic targets or attractors.

The line of convergence $(I - E)/C = 0$, which implies no energy trade at all is one possible attractor; it is called the line of "energy security." It goes through the origin of the separatrices which shows that once this Y status is approached the distribution $f(\xi)$ has a maximum plateau. A whole mix of technological decisions is compatible with the energy status of the economy and financial resources and it can be interpreted as freedom of choice. One may call this singular status "energy independence."

An extended remark of this paradigm is that while the target of energy security is more achievable and sustainable by appropriate policies of economic and technological adjustments, energy independence is rather difficult to achieve and probably even more difficult to sustain: a wrong move in the economy space can easily drive one way down on the verge of the separatrix, where even small fluctuations can drop the energy system beyond its resilience limits.

CENTRALIZED VERSUS DECENTRALIZED DECISIONMAKING

Within the energy management (conservation) process it requires joint ventures of government and individual consumers, the willingness of both parties

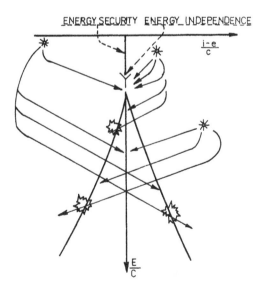

FIGURE 12 Making decisions in the energy policy.

to act coincident with their interests. There are different definitions of the term energy conservation. While engineers view energy conservation as efficient use of energy, within the bounds of physical laws and processes, economists consider energy conservation as the efficient use of energy in a given process of activity in terms of cost-benefit analysis, both for economy and society. Two types of energy conservation are generally considered: behavioral (e.g., changing in the behavior of the final consumer) and technological (e.g., reducing the level of final energy—a choice of energy mix and utilizing devices).

From the perspective of individual consumers (decentralized decisions) energy conservation means minimizing costs, while government (centralized decision making) seeks to optimize the overall energy system (multicriteria decision process); their overall perspectives are not necessarily identical. A diagrammatic representation for the consumers versus government perspectives is given in Figure 13. The horizontal axis represents the ranking of n energy carriers (e.g., coal, oil, solar), ready to provide energy service (according to the cost for the individual consumer from the least expensive to the most expansive one) and the vertical axis represents the share (in cumulative percentage points), of the same energy carriers in an optimal mix with the same final energy services. In an overall energy system analysis one must take into consideration the economic aspects of a particular energy service given a fuel mix as well as various constraints of the energy system (e.g., interdependence of its subsystems, reliability, environment, etc.) and the goal of the centralized decision body (e.g., government) responsible for a robust, flexible, and resilient overall energy policy.

Curve A in Figure 13 indicates that carrier (the least expensive one, for an individual consumer in cost-benefit terms) provides after an energy system optimization, 40% of the given energy service under consideration.

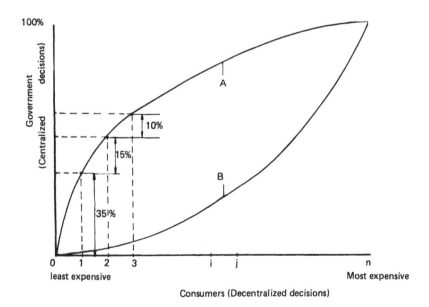

FIGURE 13 Centralized vs. decentralized decision making.

The second least expensive energy carriers provide 20%, the third 10%, and so on. It can be argued that "the more expensive an energy carrier is, the lower its share in providing the particular energy service (....). In this specific case one can see that the economic behavior of an individual energy consumer is in agreement with the overall goal of the energy system (the centralized system/government). Curve B indicates a situation of conflict between the individual consumer (a cost minim actor) and the general goal of the centralized energy system. One can easily argue that the latest cannot rely the economic behavior/judgement of the final energy consumers (e.g., the fuel which optimizes the global energy system objective is expensive to the consumers; they will be reluctant and nonparticipative in using it). It is argued and has been demonstrated that the energy system (i.e., conservation) cannot be based solely on one set of decisions taken by one set of decisionmakers, but must be an interplay of factors, prices, incentives, regulations, private initiatives, public awareness, and new attitudes and points of view" [7].

RISK ANALYSIS AND THE COMPLEXITY INDEX FOR ENERGY TECHNOLOGIES

It is already recognized that risk analysis of energy production and management plays an important role in energy technology design. Safety measures are imposed to assure the public or to circumvent any possible damage to the environment or to surrounding assets. The risk-safety dichotomy is present in the energy policy evaluation for technical, social, and political reasons. This directly affects the design effort and time associated for developing flexible and robust energy technologies. Concerning energy production risk, within the framework of energy management, it is recognized that "analyses of energy production risks play a role in the formation of national energy policy as well as in specific decisions about plant selection and siting. The context in which (. . .) risks are considered apparently changes more rapidly than do the technological characteristics given rise to the risk" [8]. It is considered that a difficult task is conceived with the numerical evaluation of the risk, "rather than with the issue of how to weigh catastrophic risks relative to routine risks." Risk is an inherent characteristic of energy technologies and systems (Table 5).

TABLE 5

Fuel	Equivalent no. 1000 MW(e)	Estimated deaths	Estimated disabilities
Coal	128	1,900–15,000	25,000–39,000
Oil	44	88–4,400	4,000–7,900
Gas	45	6	600
Nuclear	26	18–42	130–470
Totals	243	2,000–19,000	29,000–48,000

Source: Ref. *10a*

Risks are also associated with the reduction of emissions such as SOx, NOx, and CO_2 (the greenhouse effect). Novel horizontally integrated energy systems (NHIES) have been emphasized in recent literature [9], which interact with methanol to meet the needs of the heating market and CO for electricity generation. By implementing this new concept it is envisaged that the risk from emission could be diminished. Relative emissions as a function of time in different scenario development for NHIES are presented in Figure 14 [9].

In a continuous effort to improve the efficiency of industrial infrastructures, information theory plays an important role in estimating the informational content of machines, plants, equipments, technologies, and processes. Using low-level information (negentropy) and computers along the whole chain of the energy systems and technological infrastructures, large quantities of high potential energy could be saved. The information content (info-cap) of some or all parts of equipment is determined by multiplying each specification (e.g., length, materials, angles, etc.) by the logarithm of the appropriate information content (i.e., reciprocal relative tolerance) [10]. Innovation and human creativeness in an adequate energy management program and the use of CAD/CAM/CAP/CIM/CAE/CAQ/JIT/OA techniques are conceived as information flow. One can go the limit with empirical energy management/development programs according to some Pareto optimal rule; after that the information content of labor (infolab) has to increase quantitatively. Infocap in systems engineering management required for a given project can describe the possible substitution of infolab [10].

Complexity of energy systems influences their operational performances (e.g., reliability, safety, and availability). Complexity is inevitable, is very sensitive of system size, and it can be considered already as an attribute of the energy chain.

EFFECT OF TIME IN ENERGY MANAGEMENT

This can be considered in two ways: macrotime and microtime. The first case was previously investigated, primarily within the context of penetration/substitution mechanism for systems management. This has not been exten-

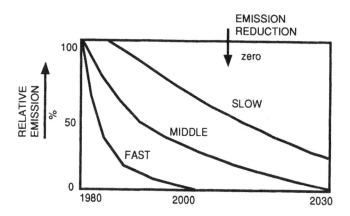

FIGURE 14 Possible emissions in a NHIES under different environmental policies.

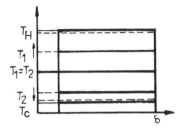

FIGURE 15   A classical energy conversion cycle.

sively analyzed yet, but future engineering design of power equipments would incorporate this aspect.

The conversion of primary energy into final energy forms (e.g., electricity) can be achieved in a variety of ways and by using different engine types. Comparison of conversion engines is usually done by means of an ideal machine characterized by maximum efficiency (i.e., engine operating on Carnot cycle). The cycle presented in Figure 15 operates between two temperatures T1 and T2 which are infinitely close to TH and TC, the hot source and the cold source temperature, respectively. Practical achievement of such an engine is impossible, and even if it were possible, there is no interest in using it. It is well known that the maximum conversion of a finite quantity of energy (one may imagine a very small quantity) into useful work requires an infinite time interval.

It is clear that useful energy should be obtained in the shortest possible time interval; time has a relevant significance for energy conversion. When the task is performed in a finite time interval, an irreversibility develops which increases in some unspecified way the faster the task is performed. A rapidly performed task (less efficient thermodynamically), overall may be more useful than would be the more slowly performed task. Purica introduced the Minimum Noncompensated Action Principle (MNAP) to specify the irreversibility production; it can be used to determine the maximum power cycle.

The cycle with non-negligible temperature difference TH − T1 and T2 − TC having a finite time interval is presented in Figure 16.

When the time interval of the expansion and compression is negligible to that of isothermal heat transfer (assuming the global heat transfer coeffi-

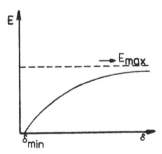

FIGURE 16   A conversion cycle with nonnegligible temperature difference.

cient K constant) then for cycles with the same heat input Q1 the conditions corresponding to the maximum power can be derived.

The cycle time interval and the available power per cycle are given by the relations:

$$\zeta = \frac{Q1}{K}\left[\frac{1}{TH - T1} + \frac{T2}{T1} \cdot \frac{1}{T2 - TC}\right]$$

$$P = K\frac{(T1 - T2)(TH - T1)(T2 - TC)}{T2\ TH - T1\ TC}$$

If $\delta P/\delta T1 = 0$ and $\delta P/\delta T2 = 0$ one obtains the maximum power:

$$P_{max} = \frac{K}{4}\left(1 - \sqrt{\frac{TC}{TH}}\right)(TH - TH\ TC)$$

for an optimal duration given by:

$$\zeta^* = \frac{Q1}{K}\frac{4}{TH - \sqrt{TH\ TC}}$$

and the associated efficiency figure:

$$\eta^* = 1 - \frac{TC}{TH} < \eta Carnot = 1 - \frac{TC}{TH}$$

Computing the entropy variations

$$\delta S_{ir} = Q1\left[\frac{1}{T1} - \frac{1}{TH} + \frac{T2}{T1}\left(\frac{1}{TC} - \frac{1}{T2}\right)\right]$$

and using $Q2/Q1 = \sqrt{TH/TC}$ one obtains:

$$\delta S_1^{ir}\ T_1^*\ \zeta_1^* = \delta S_2^{ir}\ T_2^*\ \zeta_2^*$$

If $\delta E^{ir} = \delta S^{ir}T^*$, then one may define the product $\delta E^{ir}\zeta^*$ as the noncompensated action. The MNAP is defined as:

> Within a finite time interval cycle the variation of the non-compensated action is null if the conversion system operates at maximum power.

The reciprocal statement is not true since the principle gives only a single relation between temperatures $T1/T2 = \sqrt{TH/TC}$. The second relation needed for the maximum power cycle evaluation is given by an original appliance to the Prigogine—De Groot theorem for closed systems.

The graphical representation of the energy versus cycle time interval is given in Figure 17.

The power dependence on time is plotted for T1 rising from (TH + TC)/2 to TH and simultaneously T2 decreasing from (TH + TC)/2 to TC.

For T1 = T2 = (TH + TC)/2, one has $E = E_{min}$ and the energy conversion cycle degenerates into two superpositioned isothermal processes and no power is available. For T1 = TH and T2 = TC, we get $E \longrightarrow \infty$. This corresponds to a Carnot cycle which has maximum efficiency and, therefore, maximum useful energy but the available power is null. It is to be empha-

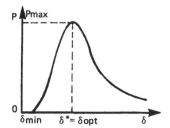

FIGURE 17   The energy vs. cycle time interval relationship.

sized that the power function has a single maximum for C = Copt (Fig. 16). Energy is a monotonous function of time and gets its value maximum for C = ∞ (the Carnot cycle).

The energy cycle conversion process may be analyzed from two points of view, depending on the way in which useful energy is to be obtained:

1. Conversion with maximum available power per cycle
2. Conversion with maximum efficiency (maximum available energy per cycle)

Each viewpoint implies a criterion for cycle comparison.   Neither the power maximization nor the efficiency maximization can be set as the single criterion governing cycle processes.

Each criterion has its own limits.   According to Stoica [*11*]:   "The first involves operation with low efficiency and therefore wastes the available finite resources; the second implies an infinite cycle time interval".

It is clear from the above conclusions that it would be desirable to imagine and design an engine working with high efficiency and at the same time getting maximum work in a finite time.   This implies a bicriterial approach.   The "best cycle" should be found among "good cycles."

In Figure 18, one may observe two particular points; the maximum power and the maximum energy cycle, which give the criteria of judgement. The good cycles are characterized by values for the available power per cycle and the useful energy both less then P_{max} and E_{max}.   From Figure 19 one can see that the best cycle is to be found closer to P_{max} than to E_{max}.   The choice of the good cycles and then among them of the best

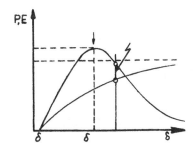

FIGURE 18   How to choose among the best energy cycles.

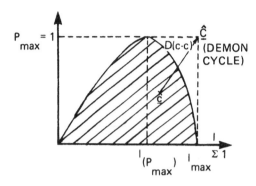

FIGURE 19   The Demon cycle.

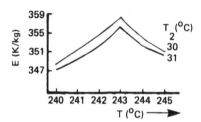

FIGURE 20   Computational results for the CANDU nuclear power station.

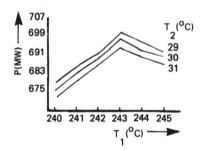

FIGURE 21   Computational results for the CANDU nuclear power station.

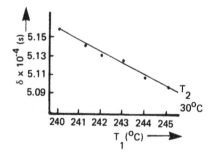

FIGURE 22   Computational results for the CANDU nuclear power station.

cycle frames into so-called vector maximization problem (VMP) whose mathematical model is of the form:

max f(x)

g(x) <= 0, x ∈ Rn

The methodology to solve this problem is based on the Holder norm for the evaluation of the distances in Rn, the space of criteria. The procedure consists of setting up an ideal point within the criteria space. The ideal point represents a "Demon" cycle working at the same time with Carnot efficiency and maximum power. This ideal cycle is a reference point and real cycles which are closer to it are "better." A hierarchy of cycles using the hot and cold sources is achieved.

Resolution of the optimization problem requires power and energy normalization. This can be achieved in different ways, all involving a diffeomorphism: I ⟶ [0, 1], where I is the domain of interest (the power and energy values domain).

Practical examples were developed for the case of a CANDU nuclear power station. Some results plotted in Figures 20−22 show the influence of the hot source level on the microtime needed for the heat exchange.

INDICATORS FOR ENERGY DEVELOPMENT AND MANAGEMENT STRATEGIES, POSSIBILITIES, AND LIMITATIONS

General Outlook

Dealing with energy planning and management is a long-term challange. It is a very costly one too. Efficient decisions require stringent energy indicators, either technical or/and economical.

Today, we use very simple indicators to understand the complex issue of energy development and society as a whole. Indicators such as installed MW, energy production (TWh), and investment capital (10^9) are sometimes too limited in value to produce a profound understanding of modern day energy problems.

It is agreed that simple historical energy figures cannot explain current phenomenological aspects of energy system dynamics; what happened to the system to produce a crisis state. Is this a structural crisis or a "statistical" crisis? Indicators needed to explain the complex problem of energy development should go well beyond the simple, statistical, nonmotivated set being proposed.

A simple reading of an annual yearbook on energy will give you official figures, rough dynamics on the economical system in which the energy infrastructures operate, but will give no hint on the way in which structural energy patterns operate and interact in order to profoundly improve them.

The present work deals with the problem of identifying the indicators (statistical, structural, etc.) which will give a better understanding of the development proces with regard to energy. It also emphasizes the danger inherent from misuse of simple statistical indicators in planning complex energy networks, which involve electricity as well as oil, coal, natural gas, or renewable resources. The relevance of indicators to different strata of energy decision makers and users is also discussed.

The commonly used present indicators are limited in effecting an understanding of the interplay between society, economy, and energy. The argument for more elaborate categories of indicators is put forth.

Examples that emphasize the limits of simple statistical indicators in the process of energy systems development are presented.

Before proceeding with our analysis we shall emphasize the main aspects concerning the present report:

a. There is an obvious need for a system of indicators when dealing with complex systems (e.g., energy systems)

b. Energy system indicators are complex and usually interact at the macrolevel of the economy with other integrated indicators (e.g., watt/$ GNP, etc.)

c. Detailed analysis of energy system dynamics cannot be gained through existing indicators from an annual yearbook

d. In many situations, statistical indicators can mislead the decision maker; complex indicators could have an appropriate managerial impact

e. The addressability of indicators should be considered; some indicators are relevant only to energy experts or decision makers, while indicators for general population use should be compact, comprehensive, and should impact positively on energy conservation attitude formation

f. The semiotics of indicators should be fully considered for a very viable and persuasive energy program and its appropriate implementation procedure

g. Excess use of indicators could be detrimental to an energy program; one should not play with figures to justify spot decisions which, in turn, could harm a medium or long-term energy program

h. Of great importance is the accessibility of indicators to the public and the use of indicators for establishing a relevant local, national, or regional policy

i. It is desirable to design a set of actions for the convergence of indicators for a resilient medium and long-term energy policy

j. One should appropriately consider the relevance of indicators for different strata of energy decision makers and users (e.g., supply, demand, conservation, quality, etc.)

The main interest in the present study was to point up the importance and the need for a system of indicators for energy strategies. Clearly, there are inherent limits to the manouverability of indicators, which emphasizes the importance of a systems analyst to assist the decision maker.

Our primary interest is to emphasize the dimensionality and special features which a set of indicators should possess. We deal with new indicators such as risk, complexity, and phase-portrait. Future studies should analyze in-depth the influence of nonstandard indicators (e.g., risk-safety of energy technologies) on medium and long-term energy policy and strategies. Such "soft indicators" could have a very significant impact on planning indicators and management actions.

It is our intention to make clear that the present work simply structures the multidimensionality and variety of elements in an indicators system. More work has to be devoted to understanding the mechanism through which one can urge management and planning to consider appropriate indicators for energy equity.

Statistical Indicators: A One Hundred-Year
Experience

There is no doubt that statistical indicators make a very direct impression
on people's perception concerning the dynamics and the economy of scale of
large systems such as energy systems.   Statistical indicators are old enough
to be embedded in our way of thinking, in the decision-making process, etc.
    The structure of installed powerline systems in Romania is given in
Table 6.   Table 7 shows statistics for overhead lines.   These indicators are
reported with some regularity for the sake of compiling statistics as well as
for making managerial decisions.   It is a simple way of expressing results
and then processing them in a more elaborate way.   Similiar ways of expressing figures could come from presenting data sets on primary energy
consumption.
    Another way of presenting indicators is to use a diagrammatic repre-
sentation.   To be more explicit, one can image an energy system through
the "Reference Energy System" (RES) diagram.
    A RES is a network representation of all the technical activities required
to supply various forms of energy to end-use activities.   Technologies are
defined for all operations involving each specific fuel including its extraction,
refinement conversion, transport, distribution, and utilization.   Each of
these activities is represented by a connection in the network for which
efficiency, environmental impact, and cost coefficients may be specified.
    A RES could be formulated for any given year for which one can take
into consideration the introduction of new technologies which are based on
forecasts that are available from various sectors of the energy department.
These energy indicators are used primarily in the decision-making process;
to determine how energy can be most efficiently used within society.

TABLE 6

	1938	1950	1965	1975	1980	1985
(a) Installed power in power stations in the Romanian energy system						
Total 10^3 kW out of which:	501	740	3,258	11,578	16,109	19,576
Thermal	453	680	2,797	8,945	12,654	15,154
Hydro	48	60	461	2,632	3,455	4,421
Per capita /W/	32	45	171	545	726	861
(b) Electricity production						
Total 10^6 kWh out of which:	1,130	2,113	17,215	53,721	67,486	71,819
Thermal	982	1,944	16,210	45,009	54,849	59,922
Hydro	148	169	1,005	8,711	12,673	11,896
Per capita /kWh/	72	130	905	2,529	3,040	3,160
(c) Electricity industrial consumption (kWh)						
Per capita	—	1,846	7,061	13,237	14,916	15,597
Per worker	—	2,345	8,210	14,509	16,387	17,624

TABLE 7 Overhead Lines

Voltage	Length (km)
400 keV—total	3,377
Double circuit	226
Operation at 220 keV	1,174
220 keV—total	3,550
Double circuit	1,493
110 keV—total	15,697
Double circuit	6,684
30—60 keV—total	1,954
Double circuit	111
15—25 keV—total	72,165
Double circuit	612
Low voltage—total	103,834
Multicircuit	1,821
Total	203,051
Multicircuit	10,991

Simple indicators, even in their dynamics are sometimes misleading. They do not emphasize the internal structure of the system or possible changes within it. The complexity of energy systems must be described using structural models. Their outputs can be treated as structural indicators and should be processed accordingly within the decision-making process.

Dynamic Indicators for Energy Resources Substitution and Penetration

As considered above, primary energy resources and their associated technological infrastructures tend to follow a compound logistic curve with repect to their existence, penetration, diffusion, and decline. As a main parameter and indicator in analyzing the dynamic substitution process of different energy technologies, the fractional market share of a new competitor, f, can be used. It is interesting that introduction of such an indicator can produce a significant learning experience regarding energy systems; "the fractions of market share exhibit a much higher regularity that the absolute values of particular production."

New competitors could be introduced in a given energy scenario, and it is possible to determine under which conditions an energy technology (e.g., geothermal, solar, etc.) may enter the market and what role it will play within the energy scenario.

The final judge in the struggle for existence of a technology is defined not only by a simple penetration and diffusion process. The analysis has to be articulated with the development goals of a given economy (e.g., energy self-reliance) as well as the behavior of the international primary resources market. It seems that the penetration and substitution process in the energy field takes place regardless the size of the system.

Structural Technological Changes in Electricity
Transportation Networks

The rapid development of all branches of a national economy is leading to a spectacular rise of energy consumption, in particular, of electricity. Vast changes must take place in every aspect of the power system. The continuous growth of bulk power and the difficulty of producing it nearer to the consumption centers implies a rapid development of the transmission network. Table 8 defines the history and the dynamics within the structural changes of the electricity transportation network with regard to the Romanian power grid [12].

Looking at the historical evolution of the analyzed network several relevant changes can be noted which are not easy to identify using simple statistical figures.

New technologies broke through (number of circuits and voltage level) and old ones have been replaced. Parallel with the penetration process one may also envisage a substitution process.

A common indicator used to compare at a given moment different competitors, is the length of the transmission line multiplied by its transport capacity (km × GW).

By inspecting the results of such investigations, special conclusions could be drawn concerning the technological dynamics and the interplay among different competitors.

Such structural indicators enhance simple statistical indicators, which are not relevant enough on their own. In this respect, indicators can extract specific information because a cross correlation between particular technologies can be taken into account.

Discontinuities in an Energy Development Program: Indicator for Structural Change

Recent acceptance that "one may be able to arrive at policy judgement that would be based on mathematical models and not numbers," encourages that such models be envisaged as "topological comparisons of strategies" (energy policies).

Using results from catastrophy theory one can investigate in a formal model the fast behavior of the internal variables (indicators) of a given qualitative process by means of the slow behavior of the quantitative exter-

TABLE 8

Electrical line type	Vintage year	Length of the first line (km)	Share of the line type (year) 1981 %
110 keV (sc + dc)	1930	127	68.49
220 keV sc	1961	191	9.08
400 keV sc	1963	206	6.45
220 keV dc	1965	51	15.26
400 keV dc	1977	4	0.71

Abbreviations: sc = single circuit; dc = double circuit.

nal variables or indicators (e.g., energy per capita, export/import ratio, etc.). In this way one can find a way to understand the discontinuities in the behavior of an overall energy development program due to appropriate human decisions. The topological comparison of energy policies lies in the interdependence between the exhaustion of energy resources.

Indicators and models show how the energy crisis will make economies move in a complex decision-behavior space. Existing trajectories should be explored by manipulating indicators as well as appropriate energy infrastructures. Such an approach reveals the value of indicators within the content of models of discontinuity. The result has to be treated as a special global indicator for energy system dynamics within the space of constrained parameters (see Fig. 12).

Energy-Population Indicators for a Taxonomy of National Economies

Indicators from distinct fields do interact in a dynamic way. There is a special relationship between the population of a given country and the energy consumption for that country.

The dynamic relation between such parameters has been included in a mathematical model of a general form: for the assumption that the energy consumption, q, is in linear dependence of the population:

$$\frac{dq}{dt} = u_1 \, q(t) + u_2 \, q(t) \, P(t)$$

where P(t) is the population at time t; for the assumption that the population ratio is linearly dependent on the energy consumption:

$$\frac{dP}{dt} = v_1 \, P(t) + v_2 \, q(t) \, P(t)$$

The above equations represent an acceptable concept of the reality, therefore, v1, v2, u1, u2 are complex functions of a set of very independent and distinct parameters such as morbidity ratio, birth ratio, quality of life, type of economy (planned of market economy), etc.

Applying the model population-energy and using data for different economies gives an appropriate classification (see Table 9). Generally the hyperbola type of trajectory indicates a stable energy system (e.g., status quo in production, consumption structure at the national level).

The use of the energy phase-portrait (the diagrammatic representation for the solution of differential equations for the energy population model), facilitates identification of the trajectories and future tendencies concerning the energy systems. The phase-portrait is understood in the context of the present paper as a global structural indicator for the overall energy system dynamics. It gives hints regarding the way in which different energy infrastructures will interact with the population level to assist in establishing an appropriate energy comfort level (see Figs. 23–29).

Complexity: A New Indicator for Energy Technologies

Energy technologies induce complexity at different levels within the energy system (e.g., engineering level, environmental relationship, interaction with the economy). Recently, scientists have argued for a view of "system complexity as a property arising from the interactions of the system with its

TABLE 9

Description of a given economy	Country	Type of the trajectory
Developed countries with abundent energy resources	Canada	Hyperbola
	United States	Ellipse
	Soviet Union	Hyperbola
	United Kingdom	Hyperbola
Medium developed countries with abundant energy resources	Poland	Ellipse
Developed countries with limited energy resources	Czechoslovakia	Hyperbola
	Sweden	Hyperbola
	German Democratic Republic	Hyperbola
	France	Hyperbola
	Japan	Hyperbola
Moderately developed countries with limited energy resources	Hungary	Ellipse
	Bulgaria	Hyperbola
Developing countries with limited resources	Romania	Hyperbola
	India	Ellipse
	Nigeria	Hyperbola
	Cuba	Ellipse
	Mongolia	Ellipse
	Vietnam	Hyperbola

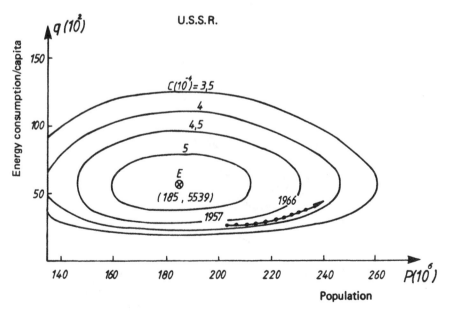

FIGURE 23 Phase-portrait for U.S.S.R.

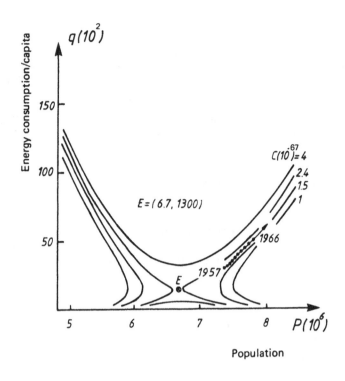

FIGURE 24   Phase-portrait for Sweden.

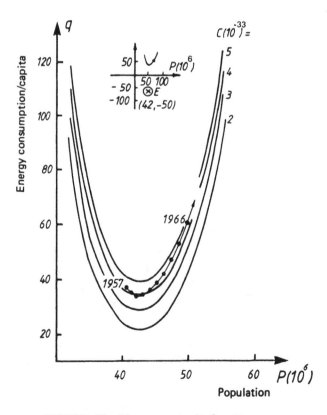

FIGURE 25   Phase-portrait for France.

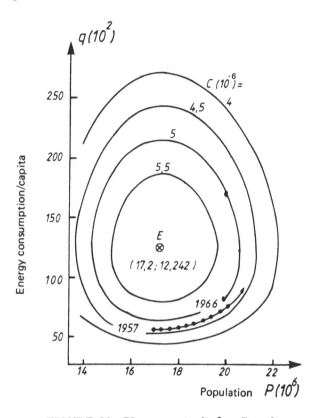

FIGURE 26   Phase-portrait for Canada.

observer/regulator rather than as an intrinsic property of the system itself."
Indeed, one can agree that "complexity, like beauty, is as much a property
of the beholder as of the object being observed."

The main problem is computing complexity for an energy technology to
make it possible to express it in indicator form. In this effort to characterize the complexity of an energy system (technology), S, one must (1)
reflect in a mathematical representation—a mathematical model M—the features
of S that are of interest, (2) associate the complexity of S with appropriate
mathematical properties of M.

Next, we identify the design complexity denoted by Co(S) and the
control complexity of S denoted by Cs(O), where (O) stands for the obser-
ver (Fig. 30). According to Casti "it is the relationship between the
qualities Co(S) and Cs(O) that provides the basis for a theory of complexity
management."

The model used to quantify the complexity of an energy technology is
adapted from Ferdinand and is fully implemented so to be able to be treated
as an indicator in an energy development program. In the present work,
we completely agree with the balance between the design complexity Co(S)
and the complexity Cs(O)."

Determination of the complexity index for an energy technology is
based on the use of the maximum entropy concept so that one can write:

$$H(\sigma,m) = \ln Z(\sigma,m) - E(\sigma,m) \ln \sigma$$

where

      σ = coefficient of complexity
      m = maximum number of faults
      H = informational entropy
      Z = expected entropy
      E = mean number of expected faults

    A complete mathematical model can be found in Gheorghe et al. (1986); an appropriate computer program has been written to compute the indicator σ for a variety of energy technologies. The complexity index for a system is correlated with the number of measuring points within an energy production system. Table 10 gives appropriate examples.

    To compute the complexity index, for a practical application of the complexity indicators, two types of nuclear power stations were chosen, namely PHWR (Candu) and GCR (EdF3), both of comparable output. Results extended to other engineering and economic aspects of complexity are summarized in Table 11.

    One can realize that it is possible to obtain an energy saving by using systems with a higher technical level (systems with a bigger coefficient of complexity, σ).

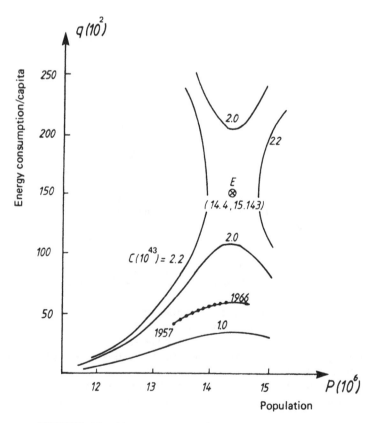

FIGURE 27   Phase-portrait for Czechoslovakia.

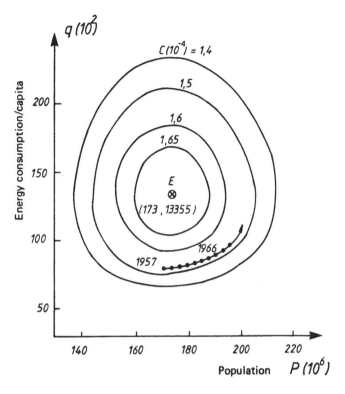

FIGURE 28 Phase-portrait for the United States.

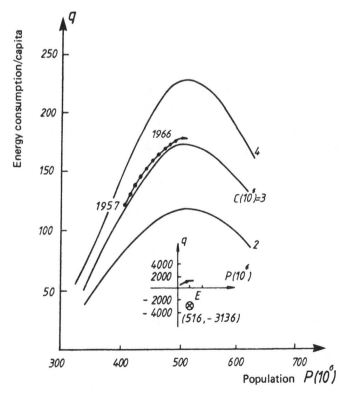

FIGURE 29 Phase-portrait for India.

FIGURE 30 Risk-cost evaluation.

TABLE 10

Type of power station	Hydro	Diesel	Gas turbine	Thermal[a]	Thermal[b]	PWR	GCR	PHWR	LHWR
Number of measuring points	20—30	15—40	40—100	70—120	200—800	2000	3000	5000	10,000

TABLE 11

Type of nuclear power station	PHWR (Candu) 634 MWe	GCR (EdF3) 780 MWe
Number of measurement points, m	5000	3000
Degree of burning B (MW day/t)	9750	3100
Specific power p (MWt/t)	16.68	3.28
Weight of one (t)	41.6	475.6
Campaign T (days)	585	945
Combustion over a 25-year period (t)	649.24	4594.95
Energy consumption in 25 years (TJ)	546,919.78	1,230,711.4
Complexity coefficient, σ	2.9094	2.9229
H (σ, 200)	0.9804	0.9765

The energy saving due to complexity increase which, in turn, is due to informational entropy is expressed by

$$\frac{\Delta E\ 25}{\Delta H} = 9.927 \times 10^6 \ [\text{TJ/IEU}]$$

where (IEU) stands for informational entropy units.

Complexity induces risk, and this is not to be neglected as an intrinsic indicator when designing a resilient long-term energy strategy.

Risk Analysis for Energy Technologies

It is recognized that risk analysis of energy production plays an important role in the design of energy technologies. Risk is now an outstanding indicator in the evaluation of energy systems or technologies. Safety measures are imposed to ensure public safety or to minimize possible damage to the environment or to surrounding assets. The risk-safety dichotomy is included in energy policy evaluation for technical, social, and political reasons. This has a direct effect on design efforts of flexible and robust energy technologies.

Risk is an inherent characteristic of energy technologies and systems. Today a clear perception and a positive attitude toward reducing nuclear risk must be enforced. Concerning energy production risks, Whipple [8] points out that "analysis of energy production risks play a role in the formation of national energy policy as well as in specific decisions about plant selection and sitting. The context in which (. . .) risks are considered, apparently changes more rapidly than do the technological characteristics given rise to the risk."

Risk assessment represents a difficult task for a designer or a decision maker, more so than the issue of how to weigh catastrophic risks relative to routine risks (see Fig. 31).

A Synergetic Approach to Safety Indicators of Energy Technologies

Few, but dramatic abnormal concurrences have haunted the nuclear debate on the issue of safety. While Quality Assurance/Quantity Control mainly

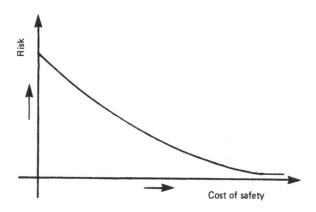

FIGURE 31 Risk-cost evaluation.

provide for failure-proof components and subassemblies, it is the manmade
and operated nuclear power plant (NPP) which makes foolproof achievement
elusive. Sound ways and means of monitoring and reacting properly to the
behavior of the highly complex, nonlinear system of an NPP seems to be
one key to more rigid nuclear safety, thus to more confidence in the viability
of nuclear power and less resistance to its expansion.

Beyond the ability to read gauges is the integrative perceptiveness of
an operator, of the "state" of the system, of the reactor eventually approaching its safety boundaries, critical regimes, etc. The "hard" approach consisting of relying on the plant automation is irreplaceable, but there is
increasing evidence that complementary procedures, meant to observe the
necessarily holistic nature of the man—machine relationship are required.

A second critical factor is the time of response. It is well known that
system operators react adequately to a huge, but finite set of abnormal
situations. A nuclear reactor is characterized by nonlinear behavior. This,
in turn, could lead to the possibility that small but aggregated variations
in some of its many parameters may entail a chain of sudden dramatic
developments.

According to practical experience, a finite set of events are most relevant to safety. Assessing during design stage and/or during the licensing
procedures the range of situations which may occur in the operation of a
NPP, can be helpful in raising the degree of confidence on the decisions
taken while shortening lead times.

A mathematical model of structural and dynamic stability is used to
visualize the resilience of a nuclear reactor, allowing in principle the continuous monitoring of its state within the resilience boundaries, delivered
as critical curves of discontinuity in a space of adequately chosen parameters [13].

The reactor system may be described in a first approximation by a
system of three equations corresponding to the well-known reactor model
with two temperature zones and ignoring the delayed neutrons effect.

The main assumptions made to simplify analytic treatment while not
sacrificing the essential nonlinearity of the system are (1) the power density, q, in the reactor is a fast variable: in contrast, the temperatures in
both zones 1 (fuel and clad) and 2 (coolant) follow the power density fluctuations with enough of a delay to make possible an adiabatic approximation,
and (2) the total reactivity, including feedback from fuel and coolant, is
linear in zone temperatures with linear coefficients in temperatures as well.

On these assumptions, the following equation describes in an integrative manner the evolution of the reactor systems:

$$lq = q^3 + uq + v$$

This equation involves the fast variable q (the reactor power density)
and two control parameters, u and v; l is a constant proportional with
lifetime of the prompt thermal neutrons, of the order of 10^{-4} s.

The control parameters aggregate in a some intricate way: operational
monitorable parameters such as the coolant flow and control rods reactivity,
as well as other design parameters such as fuel volume, specific heats, and
heat transfer characteristics.

The representation in the space (q, u, v) of the equation

$$q^3 + uq + v = 0$$

is a folded surface made up of all possible states of the reactor system.
The actual state of the reactor is a point anywhere within this surface,
except the inner zone of the S-shaped fold. This is to say that continuous,
thus easily monitorable, predictable, and controllable evolutions of the reactor state stay with only those variations in the primary variables aggregating the control parameters u and v, which amount to trajectories not
crossing the cusplike boundaries in the (u, v) projection plan of the surface. On the contrary, even small variations of the primary variables,
when aggregating in such a way that, through u and v, the trajectory of
the system's state cross the said boundaries, force the whole system into a
disruptive evolution—a hazardous jump from the upper to the lower sheet
associated with a chain—jump in many interrelated, even distantly essential
parameters pertaining to the effective control of the system. One may call
such an undesirable occurrence a shock.

A graphic display of a minicomputer properly fed with simulated or
real input data on a reactor operation will dramatically expose both the
imminence of such an occurence and the event itself. It will also monitor
continuously the point state of the system, localizing with respect to dangerous critical borders, which makes the solution predictive, thus increasing
the operator's ability to cope with the event, in turn, increasing the plant
safety.

The degree of confidence of this solution depends obviously on the
quality of the model. There must be an optimum of its refinement and
gradual sophistication, reflective of a trade-off between accuracy and mastering capacity. The assumptions of the present model were purposely the
simplest: again, this only hints at a possible complementary approach.

A preliminary test of the model contrived a series of case histories and
transcribed them in the model's logics. The sample cases here describe
possible behaviors of a BWR.

Small power variations may occur from long-term reactivity change,
during steady-state full-power operation, caused by fuel burn up. The
variation is compensated by the reactor power control system via the coolant
flow. Intermittently, the control rod settings are adjusted to reset the
pump speed and this the core coolant flow to recommended values.

Reactor isolation, following an accidental pipe break inside the reactor
containment or in the steam lines, resulting in a complete interruption of
the steam flow is automatically executed by closing the mainstream line
isolation valves.

The same signals which initiate the steam line isolation actuate also the
reactor scram and a fast reduction (in about 4–5 seconds) of the recirculation and the feedwater flow. The relief valves are opened to blow off the
steam to the condensation pool. As a consequence of the scram and the
reduction of the recirculation flow the neutron flux is rapidly reduced.
The thermal power decreases more slowly because of the fission product,
decay heat and the ceramic fuel's ability to store heat. This is a typical
example of a system evolution trajectory crossing the critical borders.

Turbine trip may be initiated under certain abnormal conditions such
as turbine overspeed, high-condenser pressure, generator faults, etc.
Tripping causes all turbine control and stop valves to close. The reactor
power is rapidly decreased by reducing the recirculation pump speed to a
minimum within 5 seconds. Pumping of reactor steam to the condensor is
initiated by opening the dump control valves which control the reactor

pressure (it is assumed that the condenser has a bypass capacity to recieve the steam produced at 60% of reactor power or more).

The fission power is rapidly reduced, apart from a small pressure-induced increase during the first second. The feedwater flow is reduced by the feed water controller and steam production decreases. The reactor power temporarily stabilizes on an approximate level of 50%. However, the turbine trip reduces feedwater temperature from 180°C down to about 30°C in a few minutes after feedwater reheating ceases. The acompanying increase of core inlet subcooling causes the reactor power to rise slowly. If the power reaches a specified value (60%) while the feedwater temperature is still below 100°C, a "partial scram" is actuated (only one scram group is inserted). This partial scram protects the fuel from any cladding failure that may result if the global power is allowed to increase on top of the spatial power redistribution that the cold feedwater gives rise to.

Power oscillations can also be accommodated in the model. Crossing the critical boundaries, in the above and other possible examples is for the reactor to undergo shocks.

Shocks erode the reactor's resilience. How many shocks can a system afford before reaching the limit of its ever-diminishing resilience?

Beside providing for shock avoidance, the implementation of models of the nature described also offer a normative answer to the question. Indeed, the number and amplitude of shocks can be quantified. And on this basis one may assess to what extent the generation of power has influenced, in time, the system's ability to further work safety. This can help to redefine the in-service inspection plans for an NPP.

There are basically two ways to pursue the line of thinking introduced in this article. One is to elaborate further the mathematical model, on more refined assumptions and to jump at incorporating the resulting soft in some hardware able to screen before the eyes of an operator a red spot (reactor state) drifting in the straits of some cusplike resilience separatrices. The alternative and the author's preference, is to give more thought to the variety of ways and means to decouple the many techniques of controlling the nuclear power generation, performance, and safety, from their traditional reputation of inaccessibility, to design new approaches to make this unforgiving technology more tolerable, from a human point of view. This is not only a question of engineering, ergonomy, and economy, but also, as our feeling goes, a question of the future of nuclear power.

The total reactivity ρ is composed of the reactivity of the 30 control rods, which includes the effect of the fuel burn up, (ρ_0) and two feedback terms:

$$\rho = \rho_o + \alpha_f t_f + \alpha_c t_c$$

Data in the literature show that the coefficients of reactivity in the first approximation vary linearly with the temperatures:

$$\alpha_c = a + bt_c$$

$$\alpha_f = c + dt_f$$

By adequate analytical manipulations, one has:

$$l\dot{q}_1 = \rho_o\, q_1 + (Ac + Ba)\, q_1^2 + (A_2 d + B_2 b)\, q_1^3$$

$$l\dot{q}_1 = cq_1 + bq_1^2 + aq_1^3$$

With a change of variable

$$q = q_1 + \varepsilon$$

the condition that the coefficient of q^2 is zero gives the equation

$$l\dot{q} = q^3 + uq + v$$

where

$$\varepsilon = -b/(3a)$$

$$u = c/a - b^2/(3a^2)$$

$$v = 2(b/3a)^3 - bc/(3a^2)$$

The system of equations describing a reactor with two temperature zones and neglected neutrons reads:

$$\dot{q}_1 = (\rho/l^x)\, q_1$$

$$(\gamma_d V c_p)_f \dot{t}_f = V_f q_f - k_s S(t_f - t_c)$$

$$(\gamma_d V c_p)_c \dot{t}_c = k_s S(t_f - t_c) - G c_p \phi t_c$$

where

q_1	=	power density (kW/m3)
t_f	=	temperature in zone 1 (fuel + clad) (°C)
t_c	=	temperature in zone 2 (coolant) (°C)
V_f	=	fuel volume (m^3)
V_c	=	coolant volume (m^3)
$c_{pf,\ c}$	=	specific heats (kJ/kg/°C)
k_s	=	global coefficient of heat transfer (W/m²/°C)
S	=	surface of heat transfer (m^2)
G	=	coolant flow (kg/s)
ρ	=	total reactivity
l^x	=	10^{-4} s (for thermal neutrons)
ϕ	=	a constant of proportionality
$\gamma_{df,\ c}$	=	densities

The adiabatic approximation reads:

$$\dot{t}_f = 0; \qquad \dot{t}_c = 0$$

One obtains the system of equations:

$$V_f\, q_1 - k_s S(t_f - t_c) = 0$$

$$k_s S(t_f - t_c) - G c_p\, \phi t_c = 0$$

Solving this system one has:

$$t_f = V_f(1/k_s S + 1/W)\, q_1 = A q_1; \qquad t_c = V_f)1/W)\, q_1 = B q_1$$

where $W = G c_p \phi$.

The Semiotics of Energy Indicators

Nadin's very interesting study on the sign and value of energy emphasized that [14]:

> The energy crisis is part of a general crisis of man's values. It has no local character or political color, although the signs of this crisis vary enormously from one country to another, from one system to another and have led to different ideologies.
>   Semiotics, as a logic of the vague, can approach the problem of the analytical means at its disposal permit operations using fuzzy concepts—and crisis is such a concept—not to say that semiotics actually attracts our attention to the fact that in reality what we call "clear-cut" is the exception the vague dominating our whole perception and explanation of the world.

Within this context, energy indicators are influenced by their semiotic value. The informational message of an indicator, a flow diagram, or a figure could play an important role in an energy conservation program or the participation of people in implementing new energy sources and technologies. The message, the informational content of a variety of energy indicators should be analyzed through their semiotic value, the way in which, in an efficient mode, they can alter the system to meet their goal.

Limits and Frontiers of Unicriterial Indicators

Indicators are needed to describe any system. The more complex the system, the more indicators become accessible at "simple" integrative levels. A special attempt should be made to indicate a set of indicators which will better characterize an energy system for a given complexity index.
    Indicators for an energy system vary from technical form (kWh, Gcal, btu, Quads, etc.), to economical and of a system engineering type (e.g., reliability, availability, safety, risk, etc.).
    Indicators should be integrated to produce new kinds of measures for system performance (e.g., the technical level of equipment is determined by its technical parameters, reliability, efficiency, etc.). Such indicators would be used to choose from among alternatives decisions.

There are limits to the variety of indicators that can be produced for a system or a collection of equipments. For a variety of reasons, they cannot be easily processed at the same time. Therefore, structural indicators should play an important role.

Indicators are coming in for a larger role in a variety of situations where one has to find new approaches to the system, to bypass its discontinuous behavior to effect resilient and flexible survival.

The concept of identifying indicators for energy systems should be augmented by incorporation of signs and values with a powerful semiotic content. Managing energy systems via controlling indicators minimizes their entropy. That is reason enough to explore the limits and the frontiers of indicators.

Bicriterial Indicators for Decision-Making-Aided Energy Cycle Conversion Systems Design

Thermal energy cycle conversion engines are designed today as to respond to one major thermodynamic criterion: to be highly efficient; that is, to operate as close as possible to the Carnot cycle. This means that all real conversion systems are compared against an ideal engine in which all transformation is reversible.

Practical achievement of such an engine is impossible, and even if it were, there is no interest in using it. Indeed, the conversion of a finite quantity of energy (heat), even a very small one, implies an infinite time interval of usefulness. It follows that TIME has an important significance for energy conversion. This has been noted in several reports.

Purica [15] has established a new criterion for energy conversion which deals with the time problem; it is the Minimum Noncompensated Action Principle which determines the maximum power available per cycle. He says that each real conversion system should be compared not with an engine working on a Carnot cycle, but with one working at maximum power available per cycle. The present work shows that both criteria of comparison have some disadvantages, so they have to be considered simultaneously.

As previously suggested, an energy cycle conversion process may be analyzed from two viewpoints, depending on the way useful energy is to be obtained, namely (a) conversion with maximum available power per cycle and (b) conversion with maximum efficiency (maximum available energy per cycle). Each viewpoint implies a criterion for cycle comparison and thereby a comparison between different energy resources (for the same engine).

Neither the power maximization (giving the maximum power cycle) nor the efficiency maximization (giving the Carnot cycle) can be used as the single criterion governing processes. Each has its shortcomings. The first involves operation with low efficiency and therefore wastes the available finite resources; the second implies an infinite cycle time interval (i.e., no useful work can be done is a finite time).

It would be highly desirable, therefore, to design an engine working with high efficiency and concomitently getting maximum work in a finite time, in other words, an engine using a conversion cycle which is the best energy (efficiency) power (productivity) compromise.

The answer to such a problem involves a bicriteria approach, and therefore some multicriteria decision-making concepts are to be used.

The "best cycle" is to be found among "good cycles" which are elements of the set of nondominated solutions of the problem. In Figure 18, one may

observe the two particular points: the maximum power and the maximum
energy (Carnot) cycles, which give the criteria of judgement. All cycles
between these two points constitute the set of nondominated solutions and
are therefore "good cycles." The good cycles are characterized by values
for the available power per cycle and the useful energy, less than both
P_{max} and E_{max}. Intuition indicates the best cycle is to be found closer to
P_{max} than to E_{max}. The selection of the good cycles and the choice among
them of the best cycle forms the so-called vector maximization problem (VMP).

A methodology was set up to solve such a problem [11]. The solution
procedure consists of setting up an ideal point within the criteria space.
The ideal point represents a "Demon cycle" working at the same time with
Carnot efficiency and maximum power (see Fig. 19). Nevertheless, this
ideal cycle constitutes an excellent reference point and real cycles which
are closer to it are "better" than the distant ones. In this way, a hierarchy
of cycles using the same hot and cold sources is achieved. The methodology
may help the design of cycle conversion systems by determining the optimal
values for the different parameters such as: upper and lower temperatures
for the working fluid of the cycle, the mass of fluid within the system,
characteristics of the condenser and the hot source system (e.g., nuclear
reactor, boiler etc.). The methodology takes into account the importance
assigned by the decision maker to each criterion (productivity or efficiency)
by means of the coefficients of importance of each criterion.

For example, if one is interested in obtaining large quantities of energy
in a finite time (for industrial development in a period of some years), then
the coefficient of importance associated with the productivity criterion must
be high.

One may envisage even a design of a condenser with the capability to
vary the lower temperature of the working fluid. Raising it may obtain a
higher productivity (which must be paid for unfortunately by a decrease
in efficiency, therefore a waste of resources). Decreasing the lower working fluid temperature produces higher efficiency, but lower productivity
(power per cycle).

From the point of view of indicators, under the specific analysis from
this paragraph one can conclude that productivity and efficiency do not
mean the same thing to the cycle conversion processes (as in other industrial branches); further, design optimization for cycle conversion processes
means finding the best power-energy (productivity-efficiency).

The Inherent Multidimensionality of Indicators
for Energy Management

We start by considering two different points of view, both of which will
lead eventually to the same conclusion, namely energy indicators should be
multidimensional; when we want to "describe" an energy system we have to
use systems of indicators.

A Former Approach to Inherent Multidimensionality

The former point of view is theoretical; the so-called "impossibility theorem
of indicators aggregation" in Paun [16]. The framework is the following:
consider more initial socioeconomic indicators conceived as functions:

$$f_i : S \longrightarrow R. \ 1 \leq i \leq n$$

associating real numbers to "subjects" in a given "population" S, and consider the aggregation problem for these indicators. We look for a mapping $f : R_n \longrightarrow R$, which will again associate a real number to each element in S, through the scheme

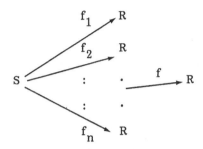

The mapping f has to intuitively "synthesize" the primary indicators $f_1, f_2, \ldots, f_n$ (think of some global indicator of the quality of life, which would start from a set of indicators of the type "hospital beds per capita," "TV sets per capita," "refrigerators per capita," food indicators, and so on).

From a formal point of view, such an aggregation mapping f (hence an aggregated indicator) has to observe at least the following general conditions (stated otherwise, in numerous practical circumstances, such conditions are naturally to be imposed, an indicator would be considered "good" if it will fulfill them):

Sensitivity: The aggregated indicator to record the large variations of the input indicators (to increase when the value of the positive initial indicators will increase, to decrease when the value of the negative initial indicators will increase and conversely)

Anticatastrophism: The aggregated indicator must be stable, in the sense that it has to remain unchanged when small modifications of the initial indicators are produced

Noncompensation: The initial indicators do not compensate each other to any great degree (the aggregated indicators do not equalize two very different situations)

The quoted theorem says that there is no aggregated indicator which simultaneously observes all three conditions. Stated otherwise, every sensitive, anticatastrophic aggregated indicator is (excessively) compensatory.

Most (probably all) the usual socioeconomic indicators are sensitive and anticatastrophic (they are sums, products, ratios, averages of initial indicators), therefore they are compensatory. (In some sense, this makes it "impossible" to build—by aggregation—a set of good indicators for describing global concepts of the type "quality of life", "the level of development," etc., because all such indicators will excessively compensate essential facets of this concept, thus considering equivalent, for instance, the development level of two countries with visible nonequivalent socioeconomic situations).

In conclusion, if the violation of one of the three conditions in the theorem is a disturbing fact, then we cannot aggregate. A prime argument for using packages of indicators. Consider now the concrete frame of energy systems. In most cases, such systems can illustrate perfectly the principle: "the strength of a chain is equal with the strength of the weakest

chain loop." Indeed, in energy systems all subsystems are important.
(For instance, at a nuclear power station, what part is more important, the
nuclear reactor, the water circulation system, the control devices, or the
radioactive waste elimination subsystem?) Implicitly, a set of indicators can
be considered which neither can be hierarchized, nor substituted for others,
thus compensated. (The pressure, temperature, and many other parameters
in a control system of a nuclear station are equally important, we cannot
aggregate them, working, for instance, with the average temperature or
with similar indicators. . . .)

The use of multidimensional indicators packages is a must for many
(perhaps all) energy systems. A conclusion which also follows from the
"impossibility theorem of aggregation," taking into account that for energy
systems, all three conditions in the theorem are desirable.

Here, a problem arises: the packages of indicators cannot be used for
comparing two (energy) systems or two different stages in the evolution of
the same system. The only relevant order relation for such a multidimensional case is that of Pareto (the componentwise comparison): if $A = (a1,
a2, . . ., an)$ and $B = (b1, b2, . . ., bn)$, $n \geq 1$, ai, bi real numbers,
we write $A \leq B$ if and only if $ai \leq bi$ for all i, and $A < B$ if and only if
$ai \leq bi$ for all i and there is no such indicator as $a_{io} < b_{io}$.

Unfortunately, these relations are not total [$A = (1, 2)$ is incomparable
to $B = (2, 1)$]. In other words, from the negation of $B \leq A$ (or $B < A$,
respectively) we cannot infer that $A < B$ (or $A \leq B$). From a practical
point of view, Pareto ordering does not allow the comparison of two given
energy systems (of two countries, for example).

When considering the evolution of a given system and the need of comparing two stages of it, we can adopt the following negation of the above
relation $\geq$: Let us remenber that we deal with energy systems and with
sets of independent and equally important indicators (which do not compensate each other). Let us suppose that at some given time, the system is
described by a vector $A = (a1, a2, . . ., an)$ (the values of n indicators
at that time), whereas the next time, the system is identified by the vector
$B = (b1, b2, . . ., bn)$, where $bi \geq ai$ for $2 \leq i \leq n$, but $b1 < a1$.

What can we say about system states at these two moments? At least
on one account, the situation described by B is worse and according to the
principle "the strength of a chain . . .," we can conclude that the global
situation described by B is worse (it is not important that energy production
has increased, consumption has decreased and so on if the workers' exposure
to radiation in a nuclear station has increased).

Thus, we can define the following relation, negation of Pareto ordering:
for $A = (a1, a2, . . ., an)$, $B = b1, b2, . . ., bn)$ we write $A < B$ if and
only if there is i_0, $1 \leq i_0 \leq n$, such that $a_{io} < t_{io}$ (the other components
are ignored).

Clearly, for each couple of vectors A, B, $A \neq B$, we have either $A < B$,
or $B < A$, or both of these relations. The relation $Z < Z$ does not have
significant mathematical properties; it is not reflexive (we never have $A < A$),
it is not symmetrical ($A < B$ does not imply $B < A$), it is not antisymmetrical
(we can have $A < B$ and $B < A$ without having $A = B$: take $A = (1, 2)$,
$B = (2, 1)$, and, finally, it is not transitive (from $A < B$, $B < C$ it does
not follow $A < C$: take $A = (2, 3)$, $B = (3, 1)$, $C = (1, 2)$).

Two conclusions must be emphasized:

1. The energy systems must be approached by using multidimensional
    packages of indicators

2. This makes difficult the comparison of energy systems, whereas the systems evolution involves the use of the relation A < B (in spite of its "severity" and mathematical nonelegance)

Limits in Using the Multidimensional Indicators:
A Case Study from Energy Area

As we have already noted, the indicators are mainly used for comparing various systems and the various stages of a given system, in order to characterize the system evolution. Such comparisons are also involved in the decision-making process, when we have to choose "the best" alternative from a set of given action alternatives.

However, we have seen that the energy systems request the use of indicators packages, which, in turn, makes comparison difficult. Unfortunately, the multicriterial decision (the building of a synthese hierarchy of decision alternatives, starting from a set of initial hierarchies—possibly contradictory) is faced with many inherent difficulties. Remember the Condorcet paradox, the Arrow theorem, or the similar theorems proved in Paun [17]. It is known that these "impossibility" result in low frequencies [18].

However, and this is quite interesting, such an example from the energy area was found, namely the results of a public investigation entered upon in Austria some years ago, concerning five sources of energy: nuclear (N), solar (S), hydro (H), coal (C), and oil (O). Five main categories of criteria have been considered in evaluating the five energy strategies [19]:

1. Indirect risk
2. Economic benefit
3. Environmental risk
4. Psychological and physical risk
5. Technology development

Clearly, criteria 2 and 5 are positive types (greater values correspond to better situations), and the others are negative.

The authors of the quoted investigation do not intend to aggregate the obtained results, they do not aim at producing a unique hierarchy of the five energy strategies, but they discuss the hierarchies given by each criterion separately. These hierarchies are the following ones (we denote by > the strict preference and by ~ the indiscernability):

Indirect risk: H > (S ~ C) > O > N
Economic benefit: O > H > N > S > C
Environmental risk: S > H > N > C > O
Psychological and physical risk: S > (H ~ C) > O > N
Technology development: N > S > H > O > C

Let us try here to obtain a synthese hierarchy. (Which is the global hierarchy of the five energy strategies in the opinion of the interviewed persons?) We may suppose that such an objective is considered implicit by the authors of the investigation, and it is certain that if one energy strategy proves better than the others from all points of view, then this finding would be stressed and commented upon.)

There are many methods for aggregating hierarchies [20]. We shall use two of the most frequent ones, namely the simple majority rule and the Borda method [17] for discussions about the "rationality" of these methods.

The first method consists of comparing each alternative against the others and of composing the obtained relations with the aim of obtaining a total ordering over the alternatives set. In our case we obtain

        S > H with score 3-2
        S > N with score 3-2
        S > O with score 4-1
        S > C with score 4-0
        H > N with score 4-1
        H > O with score 4-1
        H > C with score 4-0
        C > O with score 3-2
        O > N with score 3-2

The last three relations lead by transitivity to

        N > C > O > N

which is exactly the Condorcet paradox. Using this method we can infer that S is the best alternative, H is next, but we cannot go farther; we cannot distinguish N, O, and C by the simple majority rule.

Using the Borda method: reward by 5, 4, 3, 2, and 1 points ranks 1, 2, 4, and 5, respectively, in the starting hierarchies, sum these points for each alternative, and order the alternatives according to these totals. (In our case, hierarchies 1 and 4 are assigned 3.5 points to S and C, respectively, H and C, considering these alternatives as occupying together ranks 3 and 4.) We obtain

        S: 3.5 + 2 + 5 + 5 + 4 = 19.5 points
        H: 5 + 4 + 4 + 3.5 + 3 = 19.5 points
        N: 1 + 3 + 3 + 1 + 5 = 13 points
        O: 2 + 5 + 1 + 2 + 2 = 12 points
        C: 3.5 + 1 + 2 + 3.5 + 1 = 11 points

The obtained hierarchy is

        (S ~ H) > N > O > C

Let us note the equivalence of S and H, contrasting the result given by the simple majority rule.

The Borda method does not lead to cycles (Condorect paradoxes) as the majority rule does, but violates the independence condition in Arrow theorem. In short, this condition requests that the order of two alternatives not depend on the presence/absence of a third alternative.

Let us check this condition for the above example (if the independence would be violated, then confidence in the hierarchy given by Borda method will be diminished). As we shall see, the independence is strongly violated, which is both surprising and unpleasant.

  a. Remove S. The initial hierarchies become

        H > C > O > N
        O > H > N > C

```
        H > N > C > O
        (H ~ C) > O > N
        N > H > O > C
```

Therefore,

```
        H:  4 + 3 + 4 + 3.5 + 3 = 17.5 points
        N:  1 + 2 + 3 + 1 + 4 = 11 points
        O:  2 + 4 + 1 + 2 + 2 = 11 points
        C:  3 + 1 + 2 + 3.5 + 1 = 10.5 points
```

The synthese hierarchy is

```
        H > (N ~ O) > C
```

and we have already obtained an independence violation case: N > O in the presence of S and N ~ O in the absence of S!

b. Remove H. We obtain

```
        (S ~ C) > O > N
        O > N > S > C
        S > N > C > O
        S > C > O > N
        N > S > O > C
```

Therefore,

```
        S:  3.5 + 2 + 4 + 4 + 3 = 16.5 points
        N:  1 + 3 + 3 + 1 + 4 = 12 points
        O:  2 + 4 + 1 + 2 + 2 = 11 points
        C:  3.5 + 1 + 2 + 3 + 1 = 10.5 points
```

which implies

```
        S > N > O > C
```

and the independence is satisfied.

c. Remove N:

```
        H > (S ~ C) > O
        O > H > S > C
        S > H > C > O
        S > (H ~ C) > O
        S > H > O > C
```

Therefore,

```
        O:  1 + 4 + 1 + 1 + 3 = 9 points
        C:  2.5 + 1 + 2 + 2.5 + 1 = 9 points
```

which implies

S > H > (O ~ C)

Again an independence violation is obtained; in the presence of N we have S ~ H and O > C and in the absence of N, O becomes equivalent with C and S becomes better than H!

d. Remove O:

H > (S ~ C) > N
H > N > S > C
S > H > N > C
S > (H ~ C) > N
N > S > H > C

Therefore

S: 2.5 + 2 + 4 + 4 + 3 = 15.5 points
H: 4 + 4 + 3 + 2.5 + 2 = 15.5 points
N: 1 + 3 + 2 + 1 + 4 = 11 points
C: 2.5 + 1 + 1 + 2.5 + 1 = 8 points

that is

(S ~ H) > N > C

and the independence is observed.

e. Remove C:

H > S > O > N
O > H > N > S
S > H > N > O
S > H > O > N
N > S > H > O

Therefore

S: 3 + 1 + 4 + 4 + 3 = 15 points
H: 4 + 3 + 3 + 3 + 2 = 15 points
N: 1 + 2 + 2 + 1 + 4 = 10 points
O: 2 + 4 + 1 + 2 + 1 = 10 points

that is

(S ~ H) > (N ~ O)

and for the third time the independence is violated: in the presence of C we have N > O and in the absence of C we obtain N ~ O!

Three of five cases lead to nonindependence (and when N is eliminated two relations are modified). A significant result!

Of course, we considered here only the relations between energy strategies, and not numerical values representing the concrete results of the quoted investigation. This loses some information, because we retain only the preferences not the strength of these preferences. As the report of Thomas et al. [19] does not contain such figures, we cannot avoid this loss of information here. Nevertheless, we have to emphasize that all Borda-type methods still remain under the influence of Arrow theorem, and similar paradoxical results could be obtained (perhaps not for the practical problem considered here).

MICROPROCESSORS AND PARALLEL PROCESSING IN POWER SYSTEMS MANAGEMENT

Microprocessors have been extensively used by electric power utilities since the early 1970's.

Applications are being considered to offline analysis of large systems based on new techniques (e.g., parallel processing and hierarchical computation) which use dedicated microprocessors.

In the field of online control applications include power system protection (high reliability, excellent accuracy, and high speed).

Among the advantages of microcomputers suitable for large-scale energy management one can consider: small size, large number of computing functions, high reliability, low cost, and hardware standardization. The trend in the performance to cost ratio of microcomputers is given in Figure 32, and the performances are expected to improve due to advances in VLSI technology.

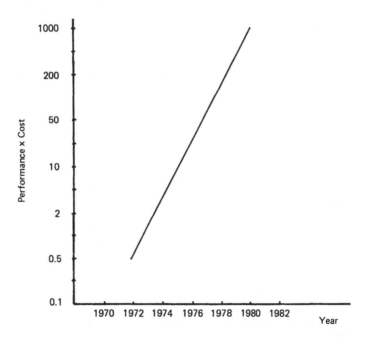

FIGURE 32 Trends for performance and cost of microprocessors.

TABLE 12

Hardware block	Type of diagnosis	Execution timing
Analogue input	Zero-sequence detection	Every sample
Microcomputer	Diagnosis program	Every N sample
Memory	ROM/RAM check	One word every sample
Man-machine interface	Memory comparison and rationality	Every sample or at setting change
Total system	Automatic inspection	Once every day

Typical applications in electric power systems are presented in Table 12, and in the near future they will assume more direct online control of power stations and systems (e.g., boilers, nuclear reactors, ten lines, generators). The response time needed for control action is in the range of seconds to minutes, and one must maintain a high degree of reliability to prevent large-scale discontinuities within the system.

Concerning digital protection relays, they can be characterized by: miniaturization, ease of maintenance, unproved performance, flexibility and expandability, increased reliability, leading finally to resource savings.

Electric power systems applications of microprocessors started in mid-1970s as prototype or laboratory-scale equipment (e.g., Westinghouse Electric Corporation and University of New South Wales, Australia). In Japan, the Tokyo Electric Power Company (1971) tested protection systems using microcomputers and Kansai Electric Power Company developed tests for the 154 keV transmission line protection by means of digital protection and microprocessors. The development of form-bit and bipolar microprocessors in 1971 and 1974, brought them to the fore as main components of digital-relay hardware. It should be mentioned that such applications require dedicated, high-speed microcomputers.

Operating algorithms need special requirements such as: high-speed fault detection, short operating times, filtering functions, as well as immunity to data error.

Microprocessors enable self-diagnosis and automatic inspection functions, which increases the reliability of the system under operation. Examples of self-diagnosis functions are given in Table 12.

Main areas for the use of microprocessors include digital protection supervisory control, data acquisition systems, as well as alarm logger using fiber optics.

Problems which must be solved in the future concerning the application of microprocessors in energy management are:

New theories and protective relaying schemes for the use of digital technology which should finally satisfy the requirements of the electric power system

Miniaturization of the hardware (e.g., peripheral equipment), new transducers, and a systematic effort to improve software reliability

Greater integration, higher function (32-bit machines, floating-point operation, high-speed execution), lower power dissipation

Decentralized processing, multiprocessing, and network technology

The concept of parallel processing (supercomputers, array processors, and multiprocessors networks) influences computer architectures and may have an important influence on power-system computing and management. To take advantage of the new supercomputer technology, one must adjust the investigation methodology (e.g., power-flow and stability simulations) to the machine architecture which uses data in vector form. Few tests have been developed before now; and these emphasize that a large amount of specialized programming may be needed to take full advantage of the new equipment.

Array processors (specialized machines for performing high-speed arithmetic operations) have been used to solve power system problems. Survey studies indicated that improvements in array-processor hardware as well in the software (e.g., an efficient FORTRAN compiler) would profoundly affect its cost effectiveness.

Multiprocessor networks are usually analyzed in the framework of the micro, mini, and midsize computer networks for power system computation and hierarchical management in interconnected systems. The concept of "joint computing" is used to emphasize the contribution of each computer to the total computing function. In 1973 the diakoptics (power flow—stability) algorithm was introduced to deal with the computer hierarchy, or a cluster of minicomputers, in power systems management.

Computational techniques used in von Neumann architecture (sequential) machines are not adequate for use in parallel processing hardware. Energy systems analysts will have to produce an optimal methodology for the new generation of the computers (hardware costs decrease while programming costs increase dramatically); also hardware must be dedicated to particular energy management applications (e.g., power-flow-stability, optimal power flow, etc.).

Software Developments in Energy Management Systems (EMS)

A common description for an EMS considers that the data concerning the operational state of the power system are transmitted and displayed in an alphanumerical or graphical way to the operator in the control center. Adequate calculations are performed to estimate the steady-state condition of the power system, to calculate unmeasured parameters, to detect bad data, and to reconsider the online measurements.

Future developments in the field of EMS will have to find positive answers to the following aspects:

EMSs must develop data exchange between control centers
They must be database and more user-friendly oriented

EMSs must answer properly and interfae accordingly with the user in emergency (critical) situations (e.g., a blackout in a large power system). Because the operator can process only a limited amount of information at any given moment, the specifications from the EMS are useful in identifying the state of the system and not handling emergency situations.

System control management in large power systems is becoming more difficult "since the consequences of interventions (e.g., switching) are difficult to assess. . . Independent of the complexity of the power system, power system control should translate power system behavior in all operating conditions with respect to data and time in a way that allows the operator to fulfill his duties efficiently and easily."

An operator's tasks are in accordance with the power systems' state mainly: (a) normal and secure, (b) vulnerable, (c) emergency, (d) restorative.

Normal operating state is characterized by lack of contingency and the operating constraints are not violated, so that the system is in a reliable state (e.g., adequate quality (f, U), high reliability, minimal operational costs).

When there is at least one contingency which could lead the system into an unsafe (emergency) state, then the operational limits are violated and the power system is in a vulnerable operating state. The system operator must "pull-back" the system into a normal state of operation or at least to try to minimize the potential damage (e.g., reduce the final effect of critical contingencies, operate emergency strategies in the case of a critical contingency, prepare postemergency corrections).

A power system is in an emergency state when the operational constraints are violated (e.g., mismatch between production and load, transmission capabilities are not enough). Protective relays must operate in order to avoid the damage to the power system as well as to the end users.

In the restoration state, the operator must remove loading constraints and bring the power system back into reliable cost-effective operation (minimizing the amount of untimely delivered energy for a disconnected consumer or power station).

There are definite ways in which the control system can assist the operator:

a. In the normal state, the automatic generation control is provided (e.g., power system topology, state estimation network equivalent, etc.). Local or global security (dynamic stability, security voltage stability, security) show the difference between the present state of operation and the security boundaries of operation. Management objective functions under this state of operation might be minimal production costs, minimal transmission losses, minimal environmental contamination, etc.

b. Preventive measures to avoid the system from entering a vulnerable state are connective rescheduling of generation, postcontingency corrections, and emergency strategies. Postcontingency corrections could involve network islanding, load shedding, etc.

c. Emergency state is defined by the degree of violating operating constraints, therefore "as soon as there is an equilibrium between generation and consumption for active and reactive power within the constraints of energy transmission the emergency is removed. The power system has reached a stable working point."

d. For the risky and complicated task of restoring the power system the operator must be informed about the elements which are energized, islands, and the black start areas.

Research directions given in the literature for developments of the so called "user-oriented software" are data flow according to system state, man—machine communications, application functions (e.g., improvements of the existing algorithms and the development of new algorithms).

ENERGY MANAGEMENT INFORMATION SYSTEMS

Information technology defined as the encompassing electronic technologies associated with data collection, storage, processing, and communications has been widely used in the field of energy management by electric and gas utilities since the mid-1960s. Today the oil industry is considered as the heaviest civilian user of information technology expressed in terms of installed computing power per employee. Information technology will raise the energy efficiency of systems and production processes independently of the energy price. It is considered that "information technology may have an effect on the energy efficiency of advanced economics similar to that of the electric motor and the internal combustion engine in the first half of the century." This advanced technology has direct and indirect effects on energy consumption and will continue to be directly applied in different practical applications for reducing energy costs in a variety of sectors of the economy.

A transition is taking place today from local process control to integrated systems control greatly assisted by microcomputers (Figs. 33 and 34).

The concept of process control is as old as Watt's governor from the 1790s; in the late 1960s, controls to multiple energy systems of some complexity had been applied. Integrated systems control allowed coordination within and between systems under a given strategic management. This led also to the possibility of integrating and controlling subsystems previously considered to be independent units. Therefore, today, the whole power conversion chain is not considered simply a mechanical and electromechanical linkage. CAD/CAM/CIM concepts allow engineers and managers to design so-called built-in energy management systems (see also Office Automation).

If the energy system is viewed as a set of independent subsystems of oil/gas, coal, nuclear, hydro, electricity, information technology then has many applications (Table 13).

The introduction of (micro)computers as well as software associated with it in the field of energy management opens manifold aspects: data processing, word processing, voice processing, image processing, human engineering,

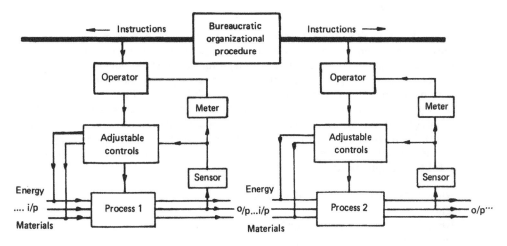

FIGURE 33 Local process control systems.

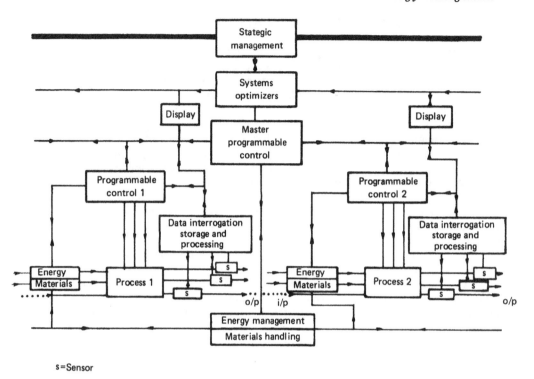

s=Sensor

FIGURE 34   Integrated control systems.

telecommunications, robots, office automation, KIPS, all associated with a dynamic evolution in time.

ARTIFICIAL INTELLIGENCE FOR POWER PRODUCTION MANAGEMENT: DECISION SUPPORT SYSTEMS AND EXPERT SYSTEMS

The EMIS (Energy Management Information System) in a power system organization represents a collection of all application subsystems (e.g., forecast, planning contingency evaluation, engineering-economics). It is, in fact, an integrative procedure of all the existing systems which make information available to decision makers in useful form. EIMS must be assisted by an adequate and versatile database management system (DBMS) and language capability to retrieve energy management data. An adequate EIMS must be developed at different hierarchical levels on the energy chain (e.g., production stage, end users) and it should be able to respond to the following questions:

What information is needed and when?
Who needs it?
Where and why is it needed?
How much does it cost?
How much is the overall reliability of the system improved?

TABLE 13

	Oil/Gas	Coal	Nuclear	Electricity
Sensor and instrumentation offshore monitoring	Geophones and hydrophones in seismic surveys	Geophones in seismic surveys; coal quality control	Plant performance radiation detection waste monitoring and safeguards	Monitoring system/plant conditions
Data storage	Geological/ Geophysical/ Design Databases	Coal records Plant maintenance records	Safety performance; fuel accounting	Plant design and maintenance records
Data processing	Seismic processing and interpretation	Mine simulation models	Reactor safety simulation models	Coal management
Data communication	Remote operation; network integration	Remote monitoring	Power plant operation; system integration	Coal dispatch
Control systems	Platform operation	Automation of coal preparation	General operation of nuclear systems	Operation of electricity system
CAD/CAE	General design, maintenance of capital goods	General design of production equipments	Plant licensing	Design, manufacture, maintenance
Robotica	Undersea installation and maintenance		Plant monitoring maintenance decommissioning	

Decision support systems (DSS) have become subsystems of EMIS. The main characteristics are:

It assists (energy) managers at the upper levels
It is flexible and can assist managers with specific questions
It displays the interactiveness of the decision-making process by providing "what if" management scenarios
It could be designed to take into consideration the personal decision-making styles of management

A DSS could interface in different ways with the EMIS:

a. By providing routine detail summary and exception reports
b. When coupled with DBMS, it provides nonroutine information using ad hoc query facilities

    c. With the help of more complicated modeling techniques, it provides feedback capabilities to management

Within the framework of this article, "machine intelligence is understood . . . to mean the capability of recognizing external environment, solving problems to realize some goal, and acquiring new knowledge from past experience." Expert system for EIMS are designed to perform a variety of processes such as interpretation, prediction, diagnosis, design, planning, and control, all related to the cognitive (decision-making) process.

There is some agreement in the literature that EIMS represents a computerized control for a power system and it is designed "to meet requirements at the normal/alert states" as well as "to include emergency/restorative state operation." Expert systems are considered to adequately represent practice in an explicit form, to improve it with regard to power systems, and to enhance the operator's cognitive capability.

A good survey on prospects of expert systems in power system operation and management is due to Sakaguchi et al. [21].

It is recognized that the number of faults which operators experience within a power system (e.g., national grid) is diminishing, while the number of operators with little experience is increasing. Due to recent large-scale accidents in energy systems, one must consider the need "for friendly assistance when the operator has to understand the situation and to make a correct decision in time during an unforeseen event."

Future EIMS must include some methodological innovation derived mainly from large computer programs (e.g., with more than 106 steps for recent EIMS) as well highly advanced microcomputers.

Expert systems could deal with knowledge in computer software in two major ways, namely via logic- and heuristic-based systems.

The logic-based methodology uses first-order predicate logic or the deontic logic. Problem solving using predicate logic is accomplished by using automatic theorem proving. For example, in the field of power system, one can apply first-order predicate logic to generate a switching sequence for substation equipment. Such applications are easily represented in the conditional part of a logic formula, but it is necessary to ensure global correctness. For dynamical systems, one can use temporal logic, designed to describe a property over a time sequence $(t0, t1, . . ., tn, ...)$. Deontic logic can handle several duties such as: no power interruption, no overload, and safety operation.

A system control can also be described from a semantic point of view.

Logic-oriented expert systems have advantages (e.g., precise, flexible, modular, facilities; incremental growth of a knowledge base, it naturally represents declarative knowledge) and disadvantages (e.g., writing procedural knowledge is a complicated task, inefficient development; and it is time consuming).

Heuristic-based methodology uses the rule-based system (knowledge is represented in a form called the production rule, which has a premise part and an action part; IF—THEN), frame-based system (which allows an expert system to facilitate data management at run time and maintenance), as well as an object-based system (when all data are distributed within each object).

An important aspect of expert is the representation and processing of uncertain knowledge. There are means of solving these aspects by using a certain factor or fuzzy logic (when exact modeling is impossible or ineffective). A software hierarchy for expert systems with great potential in the field of

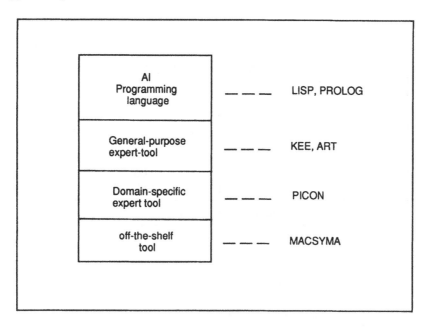

FIGURE 35 Software hierarchy for expert systems.

energy management is given in Figure 35. Expert systems developed for
use in energy management are summarized in Table 14.

Of special interest is the human interface which must be designed for
an expert system. It must enhance human cognitive capability so that the
AI software will become the most important tool to achieve the goal of user-
friendly expert system.

Next, a few pointers should be given concerning evaluation and future
potential of expert systems:

> The present generation expert system is not sufficiently sophisticated
> to define a problem (e.g., in the case of system diagnosis, a
> problem is well defined if one assumes single fault and single
> failure in relays and breakers, but not double failure).

> Expert systems are to be used for problems where (a) no analytical
> method is know, (b) the analytical method is partially know, (c)
> the analytical method is known but operations is very inefficient.
> Different kinds of applications are appropriate for the spectrum
> of the expert systems.

> Some implementation issues must also be considered. A scheme to
> integrate an expert system in the EIMS environment is given in
> Figure 36.

The attitude toward expert systems could be described in the following
way [21]:

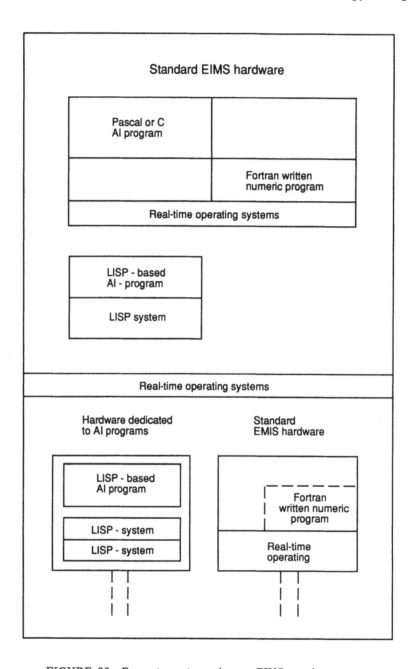

FIGURE 36 Expert systems in an EIMS environment.

TABLE 14

Application field	Phase		
	Research	Development	Demonstration for practical use
Planning and scheduling	Network maintenance scheduling	Short-term load forecast	Load flow planning
System control	Reactive power control	Unit commitment; Network restoration	Contingency selection
Diagnosis	Network fault diagnosis	Alarm processing	Network fault diagnosis

one extreme . . . is that power system operators will be at risk if they fail to consult them. The other extreme is that, . . ., people are in danger of losing their jobs with expert systems. In between lies a moderate view that the new system will be accepted once it has proved to be useful for the job. . . Expert systems become an intellectual tool for human operators.

Future trends indicate that expert systems will be designed, developed, implemented, and evolved by users (e.g., managers, engineers, operators).
Real-time expert systems will probably be developed as C-based systems.
The general attitude toward expert systems and DSS in the field of energy management is positive. An expert system will be used as a decision-making aid by the power system operator or the energy system manager.

ENERGY MANAGEMENT FOR TECHNICAL (COOLING) SYSTEMS

Weather conditions in many countries make air conditioning (AC) an absolute necessity.
For the sake of energy management measures, the economics of such AC systems could be expressed in terms of present value of life-cycle cost per ton-hour of refrigeration output.
By discounting the equivalent present value of the life-cycle cost of the i-th cooling system one has the following relation:

$$PV_i = (I_i - S_n^i a^n) + \sum_{t=1}^{n} [M_{it} + R_{it}]a^t + (P_1 \cdot E_{it})b^t + (P_2 \cdot W_{it})g^t]$$

where:

I_i = the initial cost of the i-th cooling system
S_n = the salvage value at the final year n
M_{it} = maintenance cost in year t
R_{it} = repair cost in year t
P_1 = initial price of electricity

P_2 = initial price per gallon of water
E_{it} = electricity consumption by the i-th system in year t
W_{it} = water consumption in year t
a,b,g = present values of cost parameters

Considering 15 years to be the system life, the life-time present value of cost per (t-h) of refrigeration output of the i-th system is:

$$PVT_i = PV_i/15Q$$

where Q represents the annual refrigeration output ($Q = \alpha K$ T1T2) where K is the design refrigeration capacity of the cooling system, T1 is the daily duration, T2 is the number of days of cooling demand in a year, and α is a design parameter.

Initial cost for a cooling system could be calculated using the following relation:

$$IC = C_1 K$$

system (b), so one can have the following relations:

$$E_a = 1.3Q; \qquad E_b = 1.75Q$$

Water consumption for the (a) system could be calculated by the relation $W_a = 2.5Q$. Maintenance costs for the system must also be considered.

One can finally evaluate the extra initial cost (ΔIC) for the cooling system (it is assumed that the cost of maintenance and water consumption in the (a) system remains constant during the period that conservation measures are in effect).

A CURRICULUM FOR AN INTEGRATED UNIVERSITY EDUCATION PROGRAM ON ENERGY MANAGEMENT

The problem is one of managing transitional processes in higher education in such a way as to match the rate of change in science and technology and to create anticipatory structures for successfully dealing with the anticipated changes the future will inevitably bring.

A university curriculum for higher education in power engineering is given:

Heat and Mass Transfer
Nonelectric Measurements
Energy conversion and General Principles of Energetics
Energy Production in Power Plants
Power Systems Reliability
Fuels and Primary Energy Resources
Thermal and Hydropneumatic Networks
Cogeneration Systems
Thermal Equipment for Thermal Power Plants
Thermal Power Stations
Electrical Networks
Thermal Equipment for Industrial Use

Heat Use and Secondary Energy Recovery
Electrical Power Use in Industrial Applications
Optimization and Energy Audits in Power Systems
Nuclear Reactor Physics
Nuclear Reactor Safety and Control
Nuclear Reactor Operation
Energy Production from Renewable Energy Systems
Direct Energy Conversion Technologies
New Energy Sources used in Industry, Agriculture, and Households
Water Processing Systems
New Technologies for Energy Conservation
Automation in Hydroenergetics
Numerical Methods in Power Engineering
Systems Engineering and Decision Analysis
High Voltage Techniques
Electrical Equipment
Electrical Energy Use and Automation
Optimization and Computers in Power Engineeering
Electrical Power Transmission and Distribution
Electrical Systems
Power Networks and Systems
Electronics of Power in Energy Systems
New Technologies in Energy Transmission Systems
Electrical Networks and Energy Use
Electrotechnical Materials
Organization and Production Management
Management Information Systems

APPENDIX: THE MATHEMATICAL FORMULATION OF THE IMPOSSIBILITY THEOREM FOR INDICATORS AGGREGATION

Let R+ be the set of positive real numbers.

Definition A1. A fuzzy set χ: R+ $\longrightarrow$ [0, 1] is said to be increasing (decreasing) if the mapping χ is increasing (decreasing, respectively) in the usual sense. Let us consider four fuzzy sets, $\chi1$, $\chi2$, $\chi3$, $\chi4$, with the following properties:

(a) $\chi1$ is decreasing and $\chi2$, $\chi3$, $\chi4$ are increasing
(b) $\chi1 \subseteq C\chi2$ ($C\chi$ is the complement of the fuzzy set χ, $C\chi(x) = 1 - \chi(x)$)
(c) $\chi4 \subseteq \chi3 \subseteq \chi2$

Consider also a significance threshold $\lambda \varepsilon$ [0.5, 1]. A number x = R+ is said to be small if $\chi^1(x) \geq \lambda$, x is said to be significant if $\chi^2(x) \geq \lambda$, large if $\chi^3(x) \geq \lambda$, and it is said to be very large if $\chi^4(x) \geq \lambda$.

The sets $\chi1$, $\chi2$, $\chi3$, $\chi4$ give the meaning of the terms small, significant, large, very large, and they will be implicitly used in the next definitions.

Definition A2. A set $A \subseteq$ R+ is said to be consistent if:

P1. The set A is χ^1—dense, that is, for any xεA for which there is yεA, y $<$ x(y $>$ x, respectively), there exists zεA, z $<$ x(z $>$ x, respectively) such that the number $|x - z|$ is small;

P2. The set A is $\chi 4$—consistent in the sense that there exist x, y εA such that $|x - y|$ is a very large number.

Definition A3. Let us consider a mapping:

$$g: \quad A1 \times A2 \longrightarrow R, \quad A1, A2 \subseteq R+$$

C1. The mapping g is called sensitive if it is monotonous in each argument.

C2. The mapping g is called anticatastrophic if for all x, yεA1 (x, yεA2, respectively) for which $y - x$ is small, the number $|g(y,z) - g(x,z)|$ (respectively, $|g(z,y) - g(z,x)|$) is also small for any zεA2 (zεA1, respectively).

C3. The mapping g is called noncompensatory if for all x, y εA1 (x, y εA2, respectively) with the difference $y - x$ very large we have $|g(y,z) - g(x,w)|$ (respectively, $|g(z,y) - g(w,x)|$) is a significant number for any z, wεA2 (respectively, z, wεA1).

THEOREM: Let A1, A2 $\subseteq$ R+ be two consistent sets. There is no mapping $g: A1 \times A2 \longrightarrow R$ which is simultaneously sensitive, anticatastrophic, and noncompensatory in the sense of Definition A3.

REFERENCES

1. C. Marchetti et al., "The Dynamics of Energy Systems and the Logistic Substitution Model," IIASA, Laxenburg (1978) AR-78-1A.
2. W. Hafele, *Energy in a Finite World*, vols. I and II, Ballinger, Cambridge, MA, 1981.
3. A. V. Gheorghe, *Paradigms in Energy/Time Relationship* (W. van Gool and J. J. C. Bruggink, Eds.), North-Holland, Amsterdam, 1985, pp. 81–103.
4. M. Munasinghe, *Energy J.*, 9, 1-17 (1988).
5. A. V. Gheorghe and M. A. Stoica, *Found. Contr. Eng.*, 12, 153–165 (1987).
6. A. V. Gheorghe, *Modelling, Simulation & Control*, 1, 1–54 (1984).
7. I. Ursu, D. Vamanu, A. Gheorghe, and I. Purica, *Risk Analysis*, 5, 315–327 (1985).
8. C. Whipple, *Risk Analysis*, 1, 29–37 (1981).
9. W. Hafele et al., *The Concept of Novel Horizontally Integrated Energy Systems, The Case of Zero Emission*, Kernforschungsanlage Julich, West Germany, 1984.
10. A. Thoma, "Energy, Entropy and Information," IIASA, Laxenburg (1977), RM-77-32.
10a. L. D. Hamilton and A. S. Manne, "Health and Economic Costs of Alternative Energy Sources," in Proceedings of the International Conference on Nuclear Power and Its Fuel Cycle, IAEA-CN-36/448, IAEA, Vienna, 1977.
11. M. V. Stoica, *Energetica*, 31, 27–35 (1983) (in romanian).
12. A. V. Gheorghe, C. Zeilicovici, M. Stoica, P. Postolache, and M. Eremia, *Energy*, 9, 341–349 (1984).
13. I. Ursu et al., "Towards More Safety; A Synergetic Approach," *IAEA*, Vienna (1982).
14. M. Nadin, *Kodikas (Code)*, 3(3) (1981).
15. I. I. Purica, Un nou principiu in conversia ciclica a energiei termice, A IX-a Conferinta a termoenergeticienilor din Romania (1982).

16. Gh. Paun, *Fuzzy Sets Sys.*, *9*, 205—210 (1983).

17. Gh. Paun, "Participation, Social Chance Aggregation of Preferences (Hierarchies): Inherent Limits," The UNU Project Economic Aspects of Human Economics, Tokyo, Japan, Working Paper (1968).

18. H. F. Weisberg, *Behav. Sci.*, *13*, 317—323 (1986).

19. K. Thomas, D. Maurer, M. Poshbein, H. J. Otway, R. Hinkle, and D. Simpson, "A Comparative Study of Public Behavior About Five Energy Systems," IIASA, Laxenburg (1980), RR-80-15.

20. C. L. Hxang and L. Yaxn, *Multiple Attribute Decision Making. A State of the Art Survey*, Springer Verlag, New York, 1981.

21. T. Sakaguchi et al., *Elec. Power Energy Sys.*, *10*, 71—82 (1988).

ADRIAN V. GHEORGHE

ENGINEERING APPLICATIONS — See also Industrial
Engineering Microcomputer Application

INTRODUCTION

The engineering profession would be expected to make more use of micros than any other; the very symbol of engineering, formerly the slide rule, and now the calculator, indicates its deep involvement in mathematical calculations and scientific techniques. When the handheld calculator first arrived on the scene, in the late 1960s, engineers were so quick to adopt them that the slide rule became obsolete in only a few years.

Paradoxically, though, no such revolution accompanied the next major advance—the development of the microcomputer. In fact, engineers make less use of microcomputers than many less technical professions, and any discussion of the use of micros in engineering must start by considering the reasons for this anomaly.

DIVERSITY OF ENGINEERING

The first obstacle to the use of micros for engineering is the very diversity of the profession. Engineering comprehends many different disciplines, from the four mainstreams: civil, mechanical, electrical, and chemical, to their many more specialized subdivisions, as exemplified by structural, aeronautical, electronics, and biochemical engineering. This diversity means that there are very few common problems, and that programs and methods worked out on the micro by one engineer are likely to be of interest to relatively few others. While engineers use micros for word processing and database management, their use of such programs is, in general, not a specifically engineering application. However, there are few applications in engineering that have the universality that word processors, spreadsheets, databases, or financial accounting have in the general business world.

THE HERITAGE OF THE MAINFRAME

Another hindrance to greater use of micros in engineering is that the mainframes got there first. In the early days of computing, when these machines were merely giant calculators, engineering applications were among the few that could make use of their capabilities with some financial return. Thus, engineering was one of the first disciplines to use computers; and the use of computers in engineering was largely shaped by the requirements of the mainframe. Some results of this are:

A predilection to the use of FORTRAN for programming

A tendency to consider computers for only large or complex problems,
    where the potential economic benefits are large—this is necessary
    on the mainframe to justify the high cost of computing
A trend in research toward development of complex mathematical pro-
    cedures and correlations, and in teaching toward much more
    mathematically rigorous design methods

The failure in many companies, especially larger ones, to appreciate
that micros are not just mainframes of limited speed or capacity, and that
the general guidelines and procedures developed for use on mainframes are
irrelevent when using micros, has retarded the use of micros both in their
own work, and, as a result of their large influence, in the industry generally.

CURRENT STATUS

As a result of the circumstances already described, microcomputers are not
universally used in the engineering profession. The widest use is by individual engineers, and in smaller corporations, where there is no corporate
mainframe, and where the modest cost and flexibility of the micro make it
an asset, not only for engineering, but also for word processing and accounting. Larger corporations have not, in general, realized that there are many
engineering problems that can be handled economically by a microcomputer,
without tying up the mainframe.
    The leadership position of smaller companies has made cost a major
factor in the development of engineering applications. While micros are
relatively cheap, and are getting cheaper (and more powerful) every year,
software has not followed suit. As a result, purchased engineering software is not, in general, very cost-effective. The large variety of problems
faced by any particular engineer means that many programs are needed,
each of which may only be used a few times a year. To be of value, the
programs have to be ready to use, and thus must be purchased ahead of
time, in case they are needed. With a current program cost minimum of
about $50, it is quite conceivable for an engineer to need several thousand
dollars of program inventory, just to cover most of the normal program requirements. Such an investment is out of the range of individuals and
smaller companies.

OBSTACLES TO WIDER USE

Apart from the difficulties that have already been discussed, there are a
number of other problem areas. Some are inherent in engineering applications—many more are the result of deficiencies in current software.
    While most engineers have a good understanding of how computers work,
and of basic programming principles, they are not by nature hackers, or
even enthusiastic programmers. Engineers will use the micro as another
tool in their profession, but the current state of development of software
for micros makes the micro an awkward and inconvenient tool in too many
cases. Some of the problems are:

Poor operating systems. MS-DOS, and, indeed, all of the other oper-
    ating systems for micros, contain too many arcane and cryptic

commands, provide poor error recovery, and require the operator to do many things that the computer ought to do for itself. When using a variety of applications programs, not specifically designed to be used together as a single package, it is impossible to avoid interaction with the DOS, if only for making backups and file copies.

Typing skills. At present, communication with micros is primarily by keyboard, and some familiarity with a typewriter keyboard is essential. Many engineers do not have this skill, and are not prepared to learn it.

Programming is tedious. Owing to the large variety of problems in engineering, many computer applications are specific to an individual. However, to write, debug, test, and verify such a program is a chore that many engineers are not prepared to attempt, given the current state of computer languages.

Lack of standards. Microcomputers lack standards for programming language, data interchange, commands, and operating systems. The only near-universal standard is the 5¼" floppy, and, even for that, formats vary widely. Engineering is a profession that depends heavily on interchange of data and ideas, and this lack of standards militates greatly against the use of micros. The few standards that do exist, for example, language standards, are so simplified and generalized as to be unusable, so that they act merely as cores on which variants are built.

Lack of software. There are thousands of engineering problems that could profitably be solved on a micro, but very few available programs. Many of the programs that are available are simply programmed calculations, with primitive input and output procedures, no error-trapping, and little flexibility; such programs would be completely unacceptable in the business world, yet are offered to engineers, because their needs are perceived to lie in the calculations themselves, rather than in convenience of use, and usefulness as a working tool. So far, the concepts of public domain software, shareware and special interest group BBS do not seem to have made any inroads into engineering.

Yet, in spite of all these difficulties which have retarded engineering applications of microcomputers, there are some interesting ones to discuss. Some of these follow.

STANDARD BUSINESS APPLICATIONS

The availability of many fine standard business programs for word processing, database management, and spreadsheets has encouraged engineers to make use of them. In some cases, the programs have been successfully adapted to engineering uses, or suitable modifications have been made; in others, the need to make the application fit the program, instead of having a program to fit the application, has limited the potential because engineers are unwilling to accept the inconveniences involved.

Word Processing

The flexibility of good word processing software has been a real benefit to engineers, in allowing the preparation of highly technical reports, with many tables and figures, in attractive, and accurate form. The ease with which technical material can be corrected and reprinted, has resulted in substantial reduction in the number of typos, and handwritten corrections, which were so necessary in the days of manual typing.

In addition to this, the advent of high-quality dot-matrix and ink-jet printers has encouraged the development of software to allow use of their graphics capabilities in generating technical fonts (Greek and Hebrew symbols) and mathematical fonts which allow proper presentation of equations intermixed with regular type; previously, such facilities were limited to typeset manuscripts. Typical of such programs are PCTex [1] and MicroTex [2], both of which are based on the Tex type formatting system [3].

Some programs attempt to use dot-matrix capabilities to incorporate graphics within the text; at present, the quality of such graphics is marginal for technical reports, especially in comparison with pen-plotter graphics (see CAD, below).

Database Management

There are numerous opportunities for using database programs in preparation and organization of the many schedules on which engineering relies so heavily, such as equipment lists, parts lists, bills of material, piping schedules, and door and window schedules. Unfortunately, most databases seem to be designed by programmers whose imagination stops at mailing lists. As a result, many commercial database programs have defects which prevent effective use in technical applications. Some of the problems are:

Inability to use common engineering symbols, like '#,' '%,' and nonkeyboard symbols in field names.

Inability to sort in proper numerical order; the standard ASCII sort puts 11 after 1, and 2 after 19. This is fatal in sorting the number-based lists so common in engineering.

User-unfriendly operation, with complex command structures, that make the programs difficult for the occasional user.

There is, at present, no really acceptable technical database management program suitable for engineering use; the profession could certainly use one.

Spreadsheets

There are many engineering applications that can use spreadsheet programs, either because the same procedure has to be repeated many times, or because of the need to do 'what-if?' calculations. A big advantage of the latest and most comprehensive spreadsheets, like Lotus 1-2-3 [4], is the ability to graph data taken from the sheet, thereby saving additional time in presentation of results. A number of specific spreadsheet applications have been described, including economic evaluations [5], solving differential equations [6], and controlling refinery operations [7]. See also Bibliography for other spreadsheet references.

Disadvantages of spreadsheets in engineering include the inability to perform iterative calculations, which are so common in engineering, and, as with databases, the complex and difficult-to-recall command structure, which makes use of spreadsheets inconvenient on an occasional basis. Only those engineers who regularly do calculations on a spreadsheet become familiar enough with the commands for the programs to be of real benefit. For the majority, who may need such programs once a month, the benefits are far outweighed by the time spent searching through the manual for the necessary commands.

Spreadsheets are of limited application in engineering, but are useful for some repetitive calculations.

MATHEMATICS AND DATA ANALYSIS

Engineering is very math oriented, and numerous occasions arise where there is a need for correlation or analysis of data. This is an area in which micros excel, with their ability to handle and manipulate large amounts of data. As a result of the overlap with mathematics, statistics, and the other physical sciences, a number of good quality programs are available in these areas.

Curve Fitting

A frequent requirement in engineering is the determination of an explicit equation relating two or more variables from a set of data points. In the past, much engineering design has been based on tables of data in various handbooks and standards, but for use in computer programs, such data tabulations require a lot of memory, and require look-up routines and inter-polation procedures. There is thus considerable interest in correlating such data in the form of one or more equations. In general, such programs use the standard least-squares techniques to fit various equations, such as linear, exponential, power or polynomial to the data.

In addition, research data and plant data often need correlating for evaluation, and frequently need statistical analysis, especially if several variables are involved. While these applications are not unique to engineering, they are applications of value to engineers.

Available software of this type includes Allcorr [8], Flurp [9], and X-Stat [10]. In addition, many public domain programs and techniques have been presented, especially in Access [11] to allow individual engineers to prepare their own routines.

Matrices

Many engineering problems involve the solution of a number of simultaneous equations; if there are more than three of these, solution by matrix inversion is usually the most convenient. However, this technique is rather tedious if done by hand, whereas it is an ideal application for a microcomputer. One problem, in older microcomputers using 8-bit chips has been loss of accuracy when using single-precision real numbers, since matrix inversion often involves the quite small differences in very large numbers. As a result, 8-bit matrix routines usually operate in double-precision mode, which tends to slow them down. This is being offset in the latest machines by 16- and 32-bit chips, higher speeds, and use of math coprocessors.

Most of the programs for matrix manipulation have appeared in the public domain, as these routines are usually incorporated as a subroutine in other applications programs. One standalone program for matrix manipulations has been published [12].

Algebra

A number of programs have been developed to solve algebraic problems, in particular differential equations, using computer techniques, and these are of value to engineers. Of more use are programs to allow solution of equations, even when the unknown variable is not explicit. This has great potential in engineering, as many of the iterative procedures used by engineers are required because of inability to obtain the desired variable in explicit form.

Programs of this type include Calfex [13] and Eureka [14], which facilitate the evaluation of mathematical expressions. Expressions are entered once, and can then be evaluated for dependent or independent variables, or a range of variables.

DESIGN (MATHEMATICAL MODELLING)

Design calculations occupy a major part of an engineer's technical working time, and anything that can improve either the speed or accuracy of performance of such calculations is necessarily of interest. Engineers have long used mathematical design procedures, formulae, and equations to, typically: determine the size of foundations and structures; calculate the stresses in vessels or airframes; analyze power distribution networks; or find the size of a distillation column. With the advent of computers, such design techniques have become more mathematically rigorous, and the procedures used are now frequently referred to as mathematical models. This upgrade in name, has, regrettably, not always been accompanied by any improvement in accuracy, as the design methods are still based on the same type of physical data and measurements used in the days of hand calculation. One of the major problems encountered in the use of engineering software is the generation of results that are specified to many more significant figures than is justified by the original data.

The application of microcomputers to design work is so natural, that design programs have been developed and offered for sale from the earliest days of micros. Many of the earlier attempts were little more than programmed calculation procedures that took no advantage of the inherent ability of the micro to display messages, handle text, or produce formatted output. Recently, authors have begun to produce properly designed, interactive software that is of real utility; the ensuing discussion illustrates the importance of such changes.

Structure of Engineering Programs

In order for a program to be of use to an engineer, it must:

   Be easy to use without reference to a manual
   Require a minimum of data preparation and input
   Facilitate repetitive calculations using similar data
   Be accurate, and founded on sound, easily verified, theory

A program rarely represents the whole design function; it is only one step in the usual design sequence, which is:

Analyze the problem
Decide how to solve it
Collect data
Design calculations
Analyze the results, technically and economically
Repeat the last two steps until a satisfactory design is achieved

Thus, a designer's interest in the middle of the design process is in completion of design as quickly and as accurately as possible. For a program to be of value, it must be constructed so that it can be loaded and used immediately, without training or reference to manuals. Desirable features of engineering programs are:

Instructions. The program should contain brief instructions about its purpose, input data needed, and design procedure used.

Input. Input should be in standard units, or in one of a user-selectable set of units (e.g., imperial or metric); the units should be specified in the input prompts. Full-screen input, with unlimited editing is ideal, but, in any case, the program should allow correction of input errors without having to reinput all data. Input data should be recallable and editable after each program run, and should preferably be saveable to a user file, to minimize future data entry time.

Output. Output should be available in hard copy, at the users' option. All hard copy should be identified by title and date, and should include relevant input data.

Interaction. The program should make repetitive calculation easy by allowing fast return to data entry after each run, and simple editing of input data for different run conditions.

A significant problem in engineering design programs is the need for verification. Most standard business software is easily verified by simply running a test case to which the answer is known. Unfortunately, engineering design methods are not sufficiently standardized to allow this method of testing, except to indicate that the procedure is approximately right for one specific case. Verification of a program thus depends on the individual engineer's review of the theory on which the program is based; this normally requires the author to produce a fairly comprehensive technical manual outlining the basis of the calculation method used. For a detailed review of what is involved in software verification see Ref. *15*.

There have been a number of references recently to design errors having arisen consequent to use of inappropriate or erroneous computer programs, although the exact problems encountered have not been documented. The professional responsibility of the individual engineer is to ensure that the design techniques used are appropriate to the problem and this makes it difficult to rely on software written by others. At present the engineer must either write the software (a tedious and time-consuming business), or spend time reviewing the program theory, and testing its accuracy in order to be satisfied that it is a proper and accurate tool. This, of course, largely negates the benefit of using the computer, especially when the program may only be used at long intervals, which is commonly the case.

This problem of software verification, especially in relation to professional responsibility, is now being addressed by the professional engineering societies. Until some consensus is reached, the problem of verification may well prove to be a major obstacle to the wider use of micros in the design process.

Specific Applications

As indicated in the introduction, there is an almost unlimited variety of engineering problems, so it is difficult to generalize. There are few tasks in engineering that have the almost universal applicability of word-processing, database management, or accounting in the business world. Instead, each engineer has a specific set of problems and procedures for solving them—these applications are only of use to a limited number of other engineers, so that to attempt a comprehensive survey of engineering applications would involve reference to an enormous number of examples, with no discernable pattern. As an alternative, some classification will be attempted, and some examples of specific applications presented as an illustration of areas in which micros have actually been used in engineering design.

Codes and Standards

Many engineering designs are done in accordance with industry codes, or with ANSI, CSA, or other national standards. In many cases, these codes specify the exact method of calculation to be used, and computer programs can easily be written to incorporate the code structure.

A secondary advantage is that, by incorporating a logical structure, and specific menus, the many conditions and alternatives that occur in codes can be evaluated, and the appropriate calculation method determined. This minimizes the possibility of overlooking some little-used code requirement, or using the wrong method of design.

While the national standards organizations do not yet seem to have taken any active part in preparing such computerized codes, industry bodies are now beginning to produce programmed versions of part or all of their standards. A related area is the programming of government regulations in technical areas. An example of this is the air pollution law for the Province of Ontario, Canada [16]. This act sets out quite specific formulae for the calculation of ground-level concentrations of pollutants from the stack emission rates. Since the formulae are quite complex, and the calculation has to be done many times for various wind speeds and distances from the source, a computer is a great time-saver. Some other jurisdictions (e.g., Alberta and Québec in Canada) have similar requirements for air pollution calculations, and at least one commercial program is available for this purpose [17].

Networks

This refers to flow or force networks, rather than computers! Almost all branches of engineering are faced with systems in which force, material, or power is transmitted through a group of interconnected paths, so that there are a large number of possible routes. Typical of this situation are: electric circuits; structural trusses; piping systems; and air ducting, as in heating or industrial ventilation.

Most of these problems are solved by making an initial assumption of the flux, checking the resulting effect from each branch at each joint, and then adjusting the fluxes until the effects balance. In the case of electric circuits, the flux is current and the effect voltage; for pipe or duct systems, the flux is flow, and the effect pressure; and for trusses the flux is load, and the effect deflection.

The calculations required in such networks are usually simple, but extensive. Use of a computer allows rigorous solution for a number of different fluxes, and makes rapid evaluation of the effect of changes in the network, or variations in the system, much faster and more accurately than is possible by hand calculations.

Equipment Design and Selection

There are an almost unlimited number of pieces of equipment, designed by engineers, that employ fairly standard methods of calculation. Such calculations occupy a major part of an engineer's technical working time, and anything that can improve either the speed or accuracy of performance is of great potential value. The large variety of requirements is a major problem due to the very limited range of software available. In general, however, engineers tend to encounter the same or similar design problems at regular intervals, as a result of the natural tendency to specialize within specific industries.

In some cases the work is, in itself, specialized. Special purpose programs are in common use by equipment vendors for such purposes as: heat exchanger rating; building heat-load calculation (for sizing boilers, heating, and air-conditioning systems); and fan selection and design. In such cases, the engineer's job is to define the problem and collect the necessary data, while the computer prepares the design according to established parameters, or selects from a standard line.

For an individual engineer, design applications may vary from a quick piece of code, written to solve an iterative or repeated calculation, with only crude input and output, to a full-fledged program, complete with full-screen input, printed output, error-checking, and documentation. The structure of such programs has been discussed above; many programs of this type are available, although there is a regrettable tendency to market several different programs aimed at solving the same design problem, and none for many other problems, rather than a wide spectrum of programs.

In general, however, for all but the broadest based design programs, the engineer will have to use self-written or public domain programs. Although the professional societies have shown no interest in encouraging the exchange of software, there are a number of journals that do publish scientific and engineering programs on a variety of subjects [11,18]. In addition, some books of programs have been published [19—21]. Generally, computers are used in one or both of two ways in design. First, for interactive design, corresponding to the 'what-if?' approach used in business. A design is prepared, and the output analyzed in relation to external constraints, such as space availability, cost, operational flexibility, or safety. After evaluating these factors, a revised design is prepared and analyzed, and the process is repeated until an optimum result is achieved. In the past, the intermediate designs would tend to be approximations, made to minimize the manual computing time required; with a computer, each design is quickly and rigorously completed, so that the results are completely accurate and reliable (assuming, of course, that the correct calculation procedure is used).

Second, the computer is an aid in trial-and-error, or iterative calculations. Many engineering design calculations do not have explicit solutions, and must be solved by assuming the answer, and then seeing if all conditions are satisfied by it and if they are not, the solution is modified accordingly, and the calculations repeated, until the solution converges.

A special case of trial and error, which is also related to networks, discussed above, is relaxation. This is a technique used to solve problems which would normally involve the solution of a set of very complex differential equations. Instead, an arbitrary grid is imposed on the system, and the problem solved by evaluating the effect of changes at one intersection on the surrounding intersections, while observing known boundary conditions and the basic system mathematics. Typical of such problems are determining the time variation in temperature in a solid body heated or cooled externally, and determining stresses in a complex shape under various load conditions.

Process Simulation

An area in which there is intense interest at present is process simulation, where a group of interrelated operations are combined into a process, in which material, force, or energy flows between individual operations. In many cases, there are recycle streams that can only be determined by trial and error.

A simple version of this is electric circuit design, where currents and voltages have to be calculated in many branches, between components of the circuit [22]. Fortunately, most electric circuits are mathematically well-behaved, and this is not a complex job, although it is well-worth using a computer to reduce drudgery and save time.

At the other end of the scale lies the simulation of chemical processes. Here, each stage alone represents a major, complex, mathematical model, which could tax the powers of a microcomputer. Until recently, process simulation programs of this type were restricted to mainframe and minicomputers, because of the very large physical property databases, and extensive calculation required. Recently, however, vendors of this software have announced microcomputer versions [23, 24], made possible by the faster hardware, extended memory, and cheap hard-disk drives now available for micros. There is, in addition, at least one public domain process simulation program project underway [25].

Design Examples

As indicated above, there are an almost unlimited number of design examples from all fields of engineering. To illustrate some of the points discussed, here are three specific applications, from three different fields of engineering, all from published sources, and therefore in the public domain.

Pin-Jointed Truss Analysis [26]: This is a program of the network type described above, used to determine the stresses in the members of plane structures. It is a full-feature program, with proper, full-screen, input editing, including a graphic display showing the structure and the assigned element data. The program not only generates a table of stresses for the given load conditions, but also a graphic display of the loaded structure, with the deflections exaggerated, and with overloaded members identified.

Voltage Regulator Input Filter Design [27]: This is a simple program designed to solve one specific design problem; the design of filters to smooth the voltage output from a rectifier before it enters the voltage regulator in a power supply. The design of such filters is an iterative procedure, which may need to be repeated several times, if the voltage ripple is not within allowable limits. Input is made in answer to a number of prompts, and the program then computes the design, and lists the resistor and capacitor sizes, the transformer specifications, and the rectifier diode data; output is on the screen.

Distillation Tray Efficiency [*28*]: This is a full-featured program to allow calculation of binary system efficiency of sieve trays or bubble-cap trays in distillation or absorption. Input of tray and system data is by full-screen editing, and may be in imperial or metric units. The program includes a routine for estimating diffusivity of the components from other physical properties, which is required for the calculation, but frequently is not available. Output is initially to the screen, but may also be in hard-copy, and the data are saved for additional calculations. The value of the program lies in the extreme complexity of the calculation, which involves the evaluation of 23 expressions for each efficiency estimate.

For further references to design applications, see the Bibliography, with special reference to the review articles.

ELECTRICAL APPLICATIONS

In addition to the typical engineering uses for microcomputers already described, electrical engineers have adopted some other applications for these small machines. The following three broad classes summarize these activities:

Signal analysis and processing
Circuit analysis, simulation, and design
Embedded processor system development and emulation

None of these applications are new. Originally they were implemented on the larger mainframe systems popular throughout the 1960s and early 1970s. However, each application has found a niche in the current micro-computer environment.

Signal Analysis and Processing

Signal analysis has long been a popular field of electrical engineering. Before the era of microcomputers, signal analysis/processing was primarily a development tool. Specialized measurement instruments (usually analog) were used to study and manipulate waveforms in a laboratory environment in an effort to design waveform processing circuitry for a particular appli-cation. Now this type of work can be done on microcomputers and the portability of micros has made signal analysis in the field possible. This gives engineers the capability to debug analog signal irregularities at the site of the problem.

Signal analysis involves determining the characteristics of a given waveform. For simple periodic signals, an analog oscilloscope will suffice as an analysis tool. However, for more complex waveforms it is often more cost effective to digitize the analog waveform and work with the resulting data. Microcomputers provide a very good environment for this type of work. The addition of a data acquisition board to the microcomputer's bus is usually all the hardware modification that is necessary to perform practical analysis/processing of typical signals. Such a board acts as an interface between the microcomputer and the analog signals to be studied, sampling the signal and storing the resulting data. The microcomputer takes the role of the user interface, allowing various standard functions to be selected via menus and displaying resulting data, usually in the form of graphs. It often handles any incidental calculations as well. Serious calculating is usually done in parallel on another processor.

There are a number of data acquisition boards available for the common microcomputers. These are general-purpose boards in that they are not specifically setup for particular applications such as process control, audio signals, etc. It is often necessary to add custom interface circuitry to ensure nonobtrusive measurements for each individual application. A review of some of the data acquisition boards available for the IBM-PC family can be found in Ref. *29.*

Many of these boards not only do the analog-to-digital conversion required for analysis, but also perform the digital-to-analog conversion needed for signal processing. This allows numerical simulation and testing of a processing function that, when verified, will be implemented in hardware, again, often using a microcomputer (as outlined in the next section). The manufacturers of the data acquisition boards usually supply software that gives access to all the functions of their particular piece of hardware. Typically the common processing functions such as FFTs, Bessel functions, and various filters are provided; however, there is signal analysis/processing software available that is sufficiently configurable to execute most of the functions of any of the common boards. ASYST and ASYSTANT from Macmillan Software are good examples of such packages. The latter is reviewed in Ref. *30.*

Circuit Analysis, Simulation, and Design

The ability to analyze and/or simulate an electrical analog circuit has been available for many years on large mainframe computers. ECAP (Electrical Circuit Analysis Program) and its more popular variant PCAP (Princeton Circuit Analysis Program) were used extensively on IBM 33xx's during the early 1970s. Normally this type of program is used to design a circuit to achieve a specified output for a given input. This often involves just a little trial and error. The batch environment of mainframes made simulating a circuit a painfully slow process. When microcomputers with enough speed and memory to handle a practical circuit became available, their interactive nature made them very attractive for circuit analysis software; an engineer can work on an independent computer to make as many adjustments as necessary, as quickly as desired, to refine the circuit.

Often the circuit analysis packages include the ability to simulate the circuit's operation by displaying graphs in either the time or frequency domain. The simulation allows a design engineer to check that the circuit design functions properly in concept. Under no circumstances does it exactly simulate how the real circuit will work after it is built. No two components have exactly the same characteristics, and certainly no component available has the ideal characteristics that the simulator uses to derive its output. Some of these simulating packages have the ability to implement noise functions. This helps to simulate a more realistic environment. A designer can test the robustness of the circuit in this manner, which is important because it is difficult to predict the tolerances of components that will be used when the circuit goes into production.

More recent circuit analysis packages have allowed for the integration of yet one other function, hardware layout. Since analysis and simulation requires that each component and its operating characteristics be known to the computer, it entails only a little extra work to type in a physical description of each component. This adds enough information to generate layout of the components for a wire wrap or printed circuit board. A parts list is also created from the database of information.

A number of software packages are available to design both analog and digital circuits and then their corresponding printed circuit boards. Two separate packages, Micro-CAP [31] and Micro-Logic [32], are used to design analog and digital circuits, respectively. smARTWORK [33] has proved to be a popular printed board designer for small to medium applications, and PCB-3 [34] is a comprehensive schematic editor and printed circuit board designer that integrates smoothly into an industrial-grade computer-assisted design (CAD) environment.

Embedded Processor System Development and Emulation

This application is moving more and more into the realm of computer science even though it traditionally has been the work of electrical engineers. Many products today have microprocessors or microcontrollers embedded somewhere in their design. As improvements are made to the product or as faster/more powerful processors/controllers (the term processor will be used to represent both microprocessor and microcontroller) become available, the current processor is replaced with another, more suitable one. This usually involves some amount of software revision or maybe a total redevelopment. It is apparent that software development must take place in an environment that is tolerant to such changes. In the past, when processors had a lifetime longer than a couple of years, system development was done either on a native system or on a large development system equipped with the necessary development tools for the processor of interest. These tools include cross compilers, linkers, locators, downloaders, and librarians. In addition to these tools, the large development system had to interface with a target system or an in-circuit-emulator (ICE) unit. Each time a new processor is selected, a complete set or subset of new tools and target system/ICE unit must be purchased. It takes longer to write these tools for large computers (IBM, DEC, etc.) because their operating environment is more complex. The same argument applies to interfacing hardware with these larger systems. Because the move to new processors occurs more frequently now than in the past, many companies are moving their software development to microprocessor-based systems. It is much easier to write development tools for these small systems because their operating environment is typically a trivial, single-user operating system. Unfortunately, the gain in mobility means a loss in cost effectiveness. Networking many small systems costs more than purchasing a single larger multiuser system, but the cost of *not* moving to a more advanced processor each time one becomes available is greater than the one-time savings of a larger development system.

This trend toward development on microcomputer systems is substantiated by many vendors of the development tools. Intel, one of the major producers of microprocessors and microcontrollers and their associated software tools, implements their products on all common computer systems, large and small. Invariably the products are released for use with microcomputers first.

In general, the manufacturers of microprocessors tend to market and support their own development systems. Only recently have they begun to target their products for use on common general-purpose microcomputers. However, many of the standard tools for software development have been ported over to microcomputers by independent companies who have worked out a resale agreement with the manufacturer. For example, RTCS Corporation has implemented Intel's popular iRMX operating system and its associated utilities on the IBM-PC family of microcomputers [35].

The transition of software development tools to the microcomputer environment is progressing smoothly, although rough territory has been encountered in the area of adequate source code control and maintenance utilities. As might be expected, it is much easier to maintain a system's software in a centralized (mainframe) environment than in a distributed (network of micros) environment. Eventually more appropriate maintenance tools should be developed to make the life of a software department's librarian a little less hectic.

COMPUTER-AIDED DRAFTING

Drafting is the activity that unifies all branches of engineering. The final product of engineering is the production of things: buildings, power, chemicals, and consumer goods, and the lifeblood of this production activity is design drawings. The drawing is the means whereby the engineer's design is conveyed to the tradesmen who will actually construct it. Although an increasing number of manufactured goods are now built by programmed machines, rather than tradesmen, it is unlikely, in the foreseeable future, that the engineering drawing will become obsolete.

For the machines, drawings are unnecessary, in fact, useless. The machine requires electronically coded instructions. For human owners, builders, and designers, drawings are more necessary than ever to allow visualization and optimization of the ever more complex constructions that are needed.

Engineers realized, from the early days of computers, that the computer had tremendous potential as a drafting tool. However, until very recently, this tool was financially out of reach to all but the largest companies, and could, even for them, only be justified by departments that had very large drafting loads. Drafting required, at the very minimum: a minicomputer with a large hard-disk drive; a very expensive and space-consuming plotter; and a lot of air-conditioned space. The availability of the IBM-XT and -AT type computers, and cheap, reliable hard-disk drives has provided enough power to support professional CAD systems in microcomputers, and has resulted in an explosive proliferation in the number of CAD systems in use. This, in turn, has prompted the development of more reliable, smaller, and less expensive plotters, which are needed to turn the computer output into drawings.

The widespread use of computer-aided drafting is so recent that even the nomenclature has not yet been standardized. Abbreviations like CAD (computer-aided drafting or design), CADD (computer-aided drafting and design), CAM (computer-aided manufacturing), and CAE (computer-aided engineering) are used in various branches of engineering, in some cases interchangeably. In this discussion, the term CAD will be used, and will refer strictly to the generation of drawings using microcomputers.

The basic operation of CAD is the generation of drawings in computer memory and on a cathode ray tube (CRT), instead of on paper. The same techniques needed for manual drafting are used, but with a cursor in place of the pencil, and the CRT instead of paper. The computer has a lot of advantages over manual drafting, such as:

Errors and changes can be erased very simply, and without leaving any trace on the drawing; manual erasures are often time-consuming, and leave marks on the paper.

Items that appear many times on the drawing (e.g., electronic components) need only be drawn once, and can then be rapidly copied as many times as required; manual drawing requires each item to be drawn individually.

The various views on the drawing can be easily moved, so that the drawing is more neatly or logically arranged; on manual drawings, this would involve tracing a new drawing.

Related items on the drawing can be grouped on layers (see below), which can be activated or deactivated at will for plotting or display. One drawing will thus serve several purposes, whereas putting all the material on one manual drawing would result in a very complex, and probably unreadable, document.

Drawing views can be easily enlarged, reduced, or rotated; in manual drafting they would have to be redrawn at the new scale or orientation.

Drawings can be drawn to exact scale, limited only by the accuracy of the computer's internal numbers; manual drafting is limited to the accuracy of the drafter's ruler.

Printing is always tidy, uniform, and legible; in manual drafting printing is of very variable and uncertain quality.

Small details can be enlarged to the limit of the computer's accuracy, and can thus be comfortably worked on; in manual drafting, a separate, enlarged, view has to be drawn.

These points are technical comparisons. Taking a wider view, the advantages of CAD are:

Accuracy
Productivity
Standardization
Ease of modification
Drawing quality

Accuracy

As indicated above, drawings produced on the CAD have the lines drawn to the accuracy with which the computer stores its numbers, usually 14 to 16 decimal places. This means that the drawing can be scaled, and dimensions taken off with a confidence impossible on a manual drawing. Hand drawings are not only inaccurate due to the limitations of the tools used, but the time and effort involved in making changes is so great that parts of the drawing are often drawn 'not to scale' when dimensions are changed, but the picture is not. Such short-cuts are unnecessary in CAD, because changes are so easy.

Productivity

CAD is inherently faster than manual drafting, although the factor of improvement varies from about 1.3 for mechanical drafting to as much as 14 for standardized electrical schematics. The differences between disciplines depend on two factors: the degree of repetition and the degree of design.

Electrical schematics (and similar drawings, like process flowsheets and printed circuit boards) are faster because they contain many repetitions of identical or similar objects, frequently in a geometric pattern. Manually, each item has to be drawn; on the computer, it can be copied quickly and accurately.

Mechanical drawings, in contrast, have a minimum of repetitive items and require a lot of design work, involving thought, and possibly calculations, on the part of the draftsman or designer, and possibly trial layouts and scrap views. These items are not speeded up by the use of a CAD system, so the corresponding gains in productivity are not so dramatic.

Another gain in productivity derives from the accuracy, which results in not having to do such rigorous checking, especially of trigonometrical dimensions; these things are done by the computer quickly and accurately, and can be checked in the computer just as quickly. In addition, the use of automatic dimensioning relieves the checker of the need to add up internal dimensions, and the use of standard, predrawn and prechecked parts (blocks) means that these need no checking at all.

Standardization

Manual drafting is still very much an individual skill as far as such matters as lettering, layout, and detail are concerned, and it is very difficult for engineering firms using contract drafters to impose appropriate standards. Such standards are necessary both internally, to ensure that standard design features are used exactly as designed, and externally, to meet customer requirements for lettering size and style, or part-numbering systems. CAD systems can have these standards built into standard template drawings, and, even if the standards are not followed, corrections that would take many hours by hand can be accomplished in minutes.

Ease of Modification

Drawings frequently require modification during the design process, and it is usually the most complex ones that require the most changes. Changes in manual drafting are time consuming, and often lead to errors due to shortcuts and not-to-scale items; in addition, the drawing vellum tends to deteriorate after several changes, making for poor copies, and leading to the possibility of mistakes in manufacturing. On the CAD, changes are made quickly; shortcuts need never be taken, as it is simple to change the drawing properly to scale; and, after each change, a new, clean and easy to copy plot can be produced.

Drawing Quality

Since all changes are made in the computer, all drawings can be done in ink, which gives sharper and better-looking prints. Line weights are always even; dashed lines are uniform; hatching, however complex, is correct in every detail; lettering is perfect, of uniform size, and legible. These factors mean a superior product which is not only visually attractive, but which is less likely to be misunderstood or misread.

Lest it be felt that all is perfection in the CAD world, some problems do remain to be solved. One is that the 14" CRT monitors that are presently dominant on microbased systems can only show a small part of the drawing in detail; if the whole drawing is shown, the detail is lost. This means frequent zooming, panning, and view changing, which makes it difficult to keep track of the drawing, or to get a coherent feel for the layout. Larger CRTs are available, but they are expensive, and are still not big enough to allow detailed work while viewing the whole drawing.

Another problem is obtaining quick hardcopy, especially for check plots. Dot-matrix printers are quite fast, but with the exception of one recently developed [36], and currently rather expensive, printer, the product quality and small size make such plots of little value. Pen plotters, in contrast, produce excellent product, but it is not unusual for a single plot to take up to an hour to complete, tying up the drafting computer for a good portion of this time. This plotting problem also makes users reluctant to make minor changes to drawings; frequently, the change is made in the computer, but the drawing alteration is done by hand, to avoid replotting.

A significant problem in plotting is the choice of plotting medium and pen. There seems to be no industry agreement on the best combination, and, as a result, each new user seems to go through the same trial-and-error development process. This is largely because there are no independent vendors of these supplies; each vendor thus tends to recommend his own product, rather than the most suitable one. Most engineers use liquid ink pens, which give a good quality drawing, and are available in a variety of pen widths. Unfortunately, these pens are messy, but the recent development of disposable, sealed cartridge points has overcome this to some extent. It is still not uncommon, however, for even these pens to run dry in the middle of a plot, requiring either a replot, or a certain amount of ingenuity in repairing the defective one. Selection of a plotting medium is another area requiring experimentation, although the plotter manufacturers are often quite helpful and knowledgeable.

Hardware

The basic hardware requirements for a professionally used microbased CAD system are:

    A computer of at least IBM-AT level
    A high-resolution monitor
    Some kind of device for moving the cursor about the screen
    A device for producing hard-copy of the finished drawing

These requirements have been intentionally listed in fairly general terms, as the exact specifications depend on the work to be done by the system.

Although computers—even slow ones—do things much faster than people, even short delays in program operation are irritating, and interrupt work flow. Thus, for a system that is to be used every day in production drawing work, the fastest possible machine is required. CAD systems will work—slowly—on XT-type machines with no 8087 chip, but they work a lot more satisfactorily on an AT-type computer with a coprocessor. This is because the computer stores the drawing entirely as coordinate geometry, and *calculates* the whole drawing every time it is regenerated. For a large drawing, this takes a lot of computing, especially for text, hatching, or dashed lines as each individual line has to be computed. At the time of this writing, the 80386 machines are just coming on to the market, and there is already intense interest in taking advantage of the potential increase in speed using this CPU. At present, there are no widely used CAD programs for use on 68000-based machines.

To run full-featured drafting software effectively requires as much random access memory (RAM) as the machine can have (currently 640K). Even this is barely enough for maximum speed, and there is interest in expanded memory systems, although opinion is divided at present as to whether current systems actually give any advantage. There is no doubt, however, that a hard disk is almost essential. CAD systems can be run from floppys, but only with serious limitations on drawing size, and with frequent disk access. When one relatively simple drawing can have a file size of over 200K, even a 1.2 Mb floppy can only store a few drawings, with backups and support files.

A high-resolution monitor is essential for graphics work, and, although CAD systems work in monochrome, the use of a color monitor opens up possibilities of color-coding layers, as well as making it easier for the drafter to differentiate between overlapping items. At present, most micro-based CAD systems use 14" monitors, owing to the substantial jump in cost involved in going to a 19" monitor. Some systems have two monitors: a high-resolution color unit for graphics, and a regular, low-resolution mono-chrome for text, instructions, or menus.

In CAD work, the drawing is usually done by moving a cross-hair or target on the screen. While this can be accomplished with the arrow keys on a keyboard, this is awkward, and it is much more convenient to use some kind of pointing device. Devices that are used for this include: the mouse, light pen, and digitizer pad. At present, the digitizer pad is most commonly used, because it not only allows movement of the cursor, but also supports the use of tablet menus, which have many advantages over on-screen menus. The pad can also be used to input graphics (e.g., existing drawings) to the CAD.

Output from a CAD system may be to a dot-matrix printer, or to a pen plotter. Dot-matrix printer output is fast, but of poor quality [but see Ref. *36*], and small, showing little detail. Pen plotters produce a good quality product, up to E-size, depending on the model, but take longer for the computer to process the file, and even longer to plot. At present, most of the larger size plotters used in microbased CAD are drum-type; smaller, fixed-bed plotters are available, at low cost, up to B-size. The choice of plotter depends on the demands of the industry as regards plotting medium, quality, and drawing size. As discussed above, the plotting media and pens are still a point of weakness.

Software

There is no doubt that the leading microbased CAD software at present is
AutoCAD [*37*], which has reportedly sold up to 50,000 copies, and is the
standard of the industry. However, the market is growing rapidly, there
are new entries in the CAD market every month (see Bibliography). Some,
like AutoCAD, are general-purpose drafting packages, not tied to any
particular technical branch; several are designed simply to produce sketches,
diagrams or charts; others are special-purpose drafting packages, aimed at
one particular field, for example, smARTWORK [*33*] for printed-circuit
board drafting.

How CAD Systems Work

Entities and Their Manipulation

Whatever the software, all drafting programs work in more or less the same
way. Drawings are made up of individual lines, arcs, or circles, called
entities, just as in manual drafting, except that these entities can be easily
copied, rotated, moved, or erased.

In order to allow the operator to draw, the CAD software has a large
number of commands (AutoCAD has about 130). Typically, these commands
are themselves quite complex, and usually require the operator to enter
various data items in response to prompts. For example, if a line is to be
drawn, the command 'line' is given; the program asks for 'Start point,'
which is normally selected by pointing with cross-hairs on the screen, but
may also be given as absolute coordinates relative to the drawing origin, or
as relative coordinates from a previous point. Then the program wants to
know the 'end point,' which again has to be picked. Of course, this procedure is the same as the procedure for drawing a line manually, except
that the progression is much more formal, and the operator is much more
aware of the individual steps than when drawing manually.

With so many commands, the CAD would be very confusing without
organization in an easily accessible or selectable way. This is usually done
through some sort of menu, in which the commands are in groups of similar
functions: one group contains the drawing functions, like 'line,' 'arc,'
'circle'; another contains editing functions like 'erase,' 'move,' 'copy,'
'extend'; other groups will relate to text, dimensioning, and general utilities.
The menus may be on the screen, and selected by pointing to command words,
in which case the menu is usually built of small segments, only one of which
is displayed at any time; this minimizes encroachment on the drawing space.
Menus may also be displayed on a separate, low-resolution screen, but the
most common professional arrangement is the tablet menu, an overlay of
squares representing different commands mounted on the digitizer pad, from
which the commands can be selected by picking the appropriate square. A
tablet menu is faster to use than an on-screen menu, and does not take up
any drawing space on the screen; it can have as many as 300–400 commands,
without crowding, thus providing for not only the basic command structure,
but also for frequently used sequences, and custom-designed sequences and
routines.

A CAD drawing is constructed using the same principles as a manual
drawing, by building up images from basic entities. These entities may be
manipulated by moving, copying, rotating, trimming, scaling, or erasing.
The ability to erase simply and completely is a valuable feature of the CAD,

as objects can be inserted to see how they look, and then erased, if the result is not acceptable. All manipulations can operate on single entities, or on selected groups of entities, so that whole sections or views can be worked on.

In a drawing, after the first line is placed, almost all other objects on that view are located relative to some existing point (an end point, an intersection, or a midpoint). In manual drafting, these points are selected by eye, but the extreme accuracy of the CAD, combined with the small screen, makes such a process unacceptable in CAD work. The software therefore has a snap facility that allows the user to pick the endpoint, intersection, midpoint (or some other property) that is nearest to the cross-hairs; usually, when this option is chosen, a box appears at the crosshairs indicating the area of the drawing that will be searched for the desired point. As long as the user gets the desired point in the box, the CAD will find it, and use the exact location as the selected point. In addition, the CAD has a snap grid that can be turned on or off at will; when on, only points on the grid can be selected, so that lines and points are spaced in even multiples of the basic snap unit.

Layers

A valuable feature of CAD systems is the ability to use layers; these are like transparent overlays, which are perfectly aligned with each other. Each layer has its own color and linetype, and the layers can be turned on and off at will. A common use of layers is to allow all aspects of a plant or building layout to be put on one drawing. One layer has the basic building plan; another has the equipment; another the electrical; another the plumbing; and so on. By turning off appropriate layers, the electrical system alone can be displayed, modified, or plotted; or the different layers can be plotted in different colors or pen thicknesses.

Standard Symbols

CAD systems increase productivity by speeding up repetitive drawing, and by allowing the user to have libraries of symbols or blocks. These are pieces of a drawing that may be used many times, such as a standard W beam cross-section in structural, a resistor in electronics, or a door in a building layout. If the symbol is of use only in the current drawing, it may be saved inside the drawing; if it is of general use, it is saved as a separate symbol, so that it can be inserted into other drawings. Individual users can build up libraries of symbols that are commonly used in their designs, and so speed up future drawings.

Symbols not only save drawing time, but they help to standardize designs and reduce errors. In addition, use of a standard symbol in a drawing means that, if that particular detail changes, only the one symbol needs to be altered, all references within the drawing to that symbol are automatically updated.

Customization

Most professional systems offer the ability to customize the system to suit the requirements of individual users. This includes a choice of menu systems (on-screen, split-screen, or tablet), a means of calling frequently repeated sequences of commands, some kind of programming procedure to allow new commands to be designed and used, and the ability to define new shapes or symbols. Typical uses of these features include: design of different text styles, additional text characters, or special symbols; parametric drawing, in which a drawing of an object with a specific shape, but variable dimensions, a pipe flange, or a W beam section, for example, is generated by entering the dimensions, and letting the program do the drawing; and automatic scaling and insertion of borders and title blocks.

Extracting Data from CAD Drawings

As has been pointed out recently [38], a CAD file is not only a graphical representation, but also a potential database: as such, CAD drawings lend themselves readily to automatic generation of reports, lists and schedules. The drawing file is actually an organized list of drawing elements, so, in theory, it should be possible to extract any information about the drawing by searching the file. In practice, the engineer is mostly interested in specific objects, which are usually inserted as symbols, or blocks. To make the ability to extract lists of symbols more valuable, CAD systems allow the assigning of 'attributes' to a specific symbol. For example, a valve symbol on a flow diagram can have a size, material, type, manufacturer, model number, and cost associated with it. The attributes will not normally be displayed or plotted on the drawing, but they exist in the drawing file in association with the symbol, so that it is a simple matter to search the file, and extract a list of valves, along with the associated information, to prepare a bill of material or cost estimate. Professional CAD systems (like AutoCAD) have extraction commands that will sort out the attributes as a database file that can be used by a standard database program to prepare suitable reports.

At present, attribute extraction is the responsibility of the individual user, and there is no general-purpose software to allow complete flexibility in report format. Specific software exists in the building field to allow automatic generation of door and window schedules, or lists of furniture. A number of programs exist for inserting text from ASCII files into drawings, so it should not be long before the user can create a bill of material from the drawing, and then insert it into the drawing, without any manual effort, other than transferring a few files. This offers not only productivity increases, but also greatly improved accuracy, especially after a drawing is revised—always a fruitful source of error, and extremely time-consuming for the checker.

Potential fields where this capability can be used are: piping and valves; structural steel details; electrical conduit; HVAC; and electrical controls and panels. All of these involve numerous individual items, which must be listed and specified on the drawing both for construction and costing purposes.

Standards and Drawing Interchange

As with so many other types of software, CAD program designers have developed various file structures for drawing files. Fortunately, with all CAD programs working in basically the same way, a common interchange standard has been agreed: the Initial Graphics Exchange Standard (IGES). This is a standard file format designed to allow drawings to be exchanged between systems. Thus, system A user would write an IGES file using a

command in the A software, and system B user would read this file from
IGES and convert it to B format using a command in the B software.

Differences between software do not allow perfect interchange of drawings. Clearly, if system A has features that do not exist in system B, such
data are meaningless to B; however, the basic geometry can be transferred.

In addition to the IGES route, there is a large amount of software aimed
at converting one specific software file to another. This is particularly the
case at present as new entries challenge AutoCAD; almost all vendors offer
utilities to directly convert their files to and from AutoCAD format. There
are also programs to convert microbased CAD drawings to mini- and mainframe-
based software, but these have tended to be expensive, and only worthwhile
if there are a large number of drawings to copy over.

CAD as an Adjunct to CAM

The advent of programmable or computer-controlled machines and production
facilities inevitably raises the possibility of sending the designer's output on
the CAD directly to the manufacturing machine, without any intervening hard
copy. At present, this is only feasible for numerically controlled (NC)
machines, and software already exists to take a part drawing and automatically
generate the NC program without any manual participation.

Other, slightly less complete CAD/CAM interfaces which reduce the
manual work between design drawing and manufacture include automatic
generation of masks for printed circuit boards, and (a direct development
of the discussion on attribute extraction, above) generation of cutting
instructions for automatic machines preparing timbers for prefabricated
wooden houses [39].

This is an area of intense interest and active development in CAD, in
which rapid advancement can be expected.

3D Modelling

An area that offers great potential in the CAD field is the ability to move
away from working in a single plane. In manual drawing the information
is limited to a single plane. Isometric or perspective views may be added,
but they represent only one possible three-dimensional appearance. The
CAD drawing, being a mathematical, as opposed to a physical, model, can
have three-dimensional properties in its database, and offers the potential
of providing rapid access to views of solid objects from any direction.

Such three-dimensional systems are already available on mini- and
mainframe systems, but three-dimensional systems implemented on micros are,
at present, very limited and slow. The reason for this is that three-
dimensional representations involve tremendous amounts of calculation,
especially if hidden line removal is required. At present, the extreme slowness, and the complex input required to create views makes use of three
dimensions unsatisfactory on microbased systems. However, the arrival of
faster machines with more memory and faster access times will eventually
make this feature attractive to micro users.

Three-dimensional capability is useful in designs where appearance is
a factor, as it gives a much better idea of the product than an orthographic
drawing. It also helps check for interferences, for example, in piping layouts and plant arrangements. However, it is more help in the planning and
drawing stages than in the manufacturing process, where true views and

true dimensions are needed. Since most engineers and drafters are familiar with two-dimensional representations, and have little difficulty in visualizing the object from such views, there is no great demand at present for three-dimensional systems (which are more expensive, and slower). However, three dimensions is the next major area for improvement in microbased CAD, and, once familiar, should prove a great asset for all users.

ENGINEERING MANAGEMENT

The information-organizing abilities of micros have been harnessed to aid in the management of engineering projects, plant engineering, plant record-keeping, and utilities control. Almost any task that was once done with manual filing or card systems can be done more efficiently by computer, and, while many of the larger plants have these systems tied into company mainframes, the accessibility and convenience of standalone micros is leading to greater use of these in the management function. For a detailed description of the use of micros in project management in a larger organization see Ref. 40.

Project Organization

CPM and PERT

The large amount of calculation needed to generate schedules for optimum use of time and resources, using such techniques as critical path method (CPM) or Program Evaluation and Review Technique (PERT), makes them a natural computer application. There are many commercial and public-domain programs available that will generate CPM charts, bar charts, and project activity reports from the input data.

Material Lists

Engineering project management is largely organization, and involves numerous tables and lists. Standard microbased database management systems (DBMS) have been adapted to preparation of various schedules, such as bills of material, pipe and valve schedules, conduit and cable schedules, and equipment lists.

The inherent organizing ability of the DBMS allows one central list to be maintained, and then sorted or subdivided for project use; a valve schedule, for example can be split into: valve types and sizes for purposes of procurement; working conditions, for purposes of insulation or gasket selection; or process location, for operational purposes—all using the same basic list.

In addition, backward integration into CAD systems can allow the database file to be extracted directly from the drawing, while forward integration into a spreadsheet program allows direct preparation of material and/or labor cost estimates.

Cost Control

Project cost control requirements are very similar to those for material lists, and are handled in much the same way, using a combination of database, to sort individual costs to cost centers, and spreadsheet to compute totals, percentage completions and deviations from budget. There are not a large number of commercial programs specifically for engineering cost control, as this is largely an individual preference, and is, to some extent, out of the hands of the engineers, especially in larger companies. In smaller operations, the user mainly adapts standard programs to suit project needs.

Plant Engineering

Maintenance Management

Microcomputers are widely used in maintenance management. A recent survey of available programs [41] listed 60 maintenance management programs.

Most of these are combination database/scheduling/inventory programs, although some are aimed at specific individual tasks. However, most users prefer an integrated system that will handle all maintenance functions. Typically, the database maintains details of the plant equipment, specifications, model numbers, manufacturers, and the equipment history. The scheduling section allocates the tasks to optimize the available labor, availability of parts, plant priorities, and the needs for both breakdown and scheduled maintenance; this generates the work-orders for the next work period. The inventory program keeps track of parts usage and demand, and automatically generates purchase orders or requisitions when stock falls below minimum. It also keeps track of special parts orders, and may produce reminders for follow up if these are delayed. In addition to these functions, the program will generate historical and, sometimes, predictive cost data for the maintenance program.

Of all engineering tasks, plant maintenance is the area that has adapted quickest to computers, because of the large amount of record-keeping and organization involved. Many companies use mainframe computers for this task, but smaller departments have found micros well-suited to the task, adaptable, and cost-effective.

PLC Documentation and Programming

Many plants and machines are now controlled by programmable logic controllers (PLC), rather than by mechanical relays. The PLC can perform all the normal tasks handled by instantaneous, latching, or time-delay relays, as well as providing built-in timer and counter circuits, and math capability. PLC makers have facilitated the changeover from relays by using familiar ladder diagrams for programming PLCs, but the capabilities of PLCs are such that programming them can be quite a complex task. Even more important, since there are no wires to trace, and since programs can be erased by power failure or electrical damage, proper documentation of the control circuit is crucial for maintenance and trouble-shooting.

Most PLCs have only fairly primitive programming and documentation features built-in, but micros have proved ideal for this purpose. Documenting programs with a micro can be done without any special software [42], but there are now several commercial packages available that combine programming and documentation of various manufacturers' PLCs, using microcomputers [43].

Electrical Load Shaving

Most plant electrical billings include a demand charge based on the maximum load drawn during the billing period. In plants that have heavy electrical demands, like large compressors, electric furnaces, or induction heaters, electrical costs can be reduced by scheduling large power users to minimize this peak. It is necessary, however, to keep constant watch on the plant load, so as to ensure that large loads are not inadvertently turned on at the wrong time; the effort involved in scheduling and monitoring power demand is rapidly repaid in power cost savings.

It is not difficult to interface a microcomputer to the plant meter, and allow this to supervise the demand. Depending on the organization of the plant, and the type of equipment, the micro may be limited to giving a warning of plant overload, or it may actually turn off nonessential equipment to keep the total demand to a minimum. Commercial software is available to allow a micro to be used for demand monitoring. Direct control of equipment requires a suitable interface to accept the micro output and implement actual load switching.

COST ESTIMATING

Cost estimating appears to be a natural computer application, involving a lot of simple math, and frequent reference to standard cost data and tables. Many of the simpler cost-estimating procedures can most easily be handled using standard spreadsheet programs, and little has been published about such applications. Such applications would be of use in small manufacturing concerns where a limited number of specialized parts are made, or where there are a small number of machines of known productivity.

Three factors have slowed the more general application of micros to cost-estimating:

1. The very large database of material and labor costs necessary for even a simple estimating program. For example, even a crude piping estimating procedure involves keeping labor and material data on 40 to 50 fittings and valves in 15 or more sizes, and per-haps 6 materials of construction—4500 sets of records. This amount of information involves either a lot of memory, or a lot of rather slow disk access.

2. The effort of keeping the database current, as costs and technology change. In particular, it is time consuming to document the source and date of all cost data, in order to validate the database.

3. The lack of flexibility in a program designed to breakdown estimates in a particular way. Most estimators use a combination of unit costs, factors, vendors' quotes, past estimates and detailed labor/material breakdowns in building up an overall estimate, to which are added other factors to take account of the risk, the site conditions, and the current shop load. It is very difficult to build this kind of flexibility into a general cost-estimating program.

One recent entry into the estimating market [44] attempts to address these problems in a plant engineering environment by providing a user-definable project definition, and regular cost database updates.

Computers have found widest application in two specific areas: building construction and standard production items. Most building construction contracts are firmly based on unit costs and detailed material take-offs, using fairly well-established cost data. Some companies [45] specialize in regularly updating unit costs, and are now making their databases available on disk for use in estimating programs.

Micros also provide a fast, and more accurate, way for sales engineers to quote packages made up of standard production items, like fans. A purchaser will typically purchase a fan, with various optional items like cleanouts, casing drains, shaft seals, motor, and V-belt drive. Most fan manufacturers have a range of standard fans, so it is a simple matter for a program to take as input the fan specification, and produce the optimum fan selection, a cost estimate, and, sometimes, a performance curve for the selected model. In fact, the computer can even estimate several different fan options with minimal effort; something a human may be reluctant to do. Similar estimating possibilities exist for any manufacturer of standard production-line equipment, like pumps, heat exchangers, HVAC systems, transformers, or switchgear.

TECHNICAL DATABASES

The development of inexpensive, good quality, modems has encouraged many owners of microcomputers to use them as smart terminals for electronic communications. Few of these applications relate directly to engineering; there have been a few attempts to set up Bulletin Board Systems (BBS) specifically for technical groups, but these are not in widespread use. The main engineering use of computer communication has been to access technical databases.

The solution of many engineering problems begins with a search for data; specifically, what has been done previously in the field, and the basic properties of the materials, or equipment involved. This information is widely dispersed in the numerous technical journals and magazines that are published. In the past, it was necessary to locate a good technical library, often a university library, some distance away, and then spend several hours searching the relevant indices and journals.

In the past few years, the major indices and abstracts have been placed in publicly accessible databases. Many of these are available through Dialog [46] in California. Once an account is opened, databases can be accessed remotely and at any hour of the day or night, using cheap rate long-distance services such as Tymnet or Dialnet. The engineer can call up selected databases, search for information based on key words, have an immediate printout of selected abstracts, or, alternatively (and more cheaply), have them printed out off-line, and mailed.

Although this is a very valuable, and time-saving, capability, there are still a number of shortcomings. One is cost; with communications, print-out and on-line charges, costs can amount to $100 to $200 per hour for the more common databases, and even more for specialized ones. Normally, a specific subject can be searched in 15 to 20 minutes, but a widespread search can take a long time, and be quite costly.

Another deficiency is that, at present, the searchable databases do not go back much before the late 1960s, and they only cover abstracts. This means that it is still necessary to obtain the text of the original article, in order to obtain the details, and the illustrations. Some databases, physical properties of compounds, for example, now provide the actual data, or the actual text. At present, however, there is no system that will transmit the illustrations, and graphs which are frequently the most important part.

The major stumbling block to complete accessibility of the literature via electronic communications is the huge backlog of past literature, and the continuing deluge of new technical publications, most of them in hard-copy form. Whether this material can ever be made available for direct access— if only because of the enormous labor involved in transferring it to a data-base—is questionable. At present, remote access to technical databases provides a good starting point and summary of the recent literature. By obtaining the abstracts, and then the original articles, past references can be located with much less time and effort than a complete manual search.

CONTROL OF PROCESSES

Microcomputers have seen quite extensive use in both the design, and the actual control of processes.

In design applications, they have proved very useful in alleviating the extensive (but standard) calculations involved in sizing orifice plates for flow-metering—there are numerous public-domain and commercial programs available for this—and also in sizing control valves. Again, the procedure is fairly well-established but the calculations are time-consuming, especially if compressible or flashing flow is involved. At least one commercial program [47] is available that combines both these functions.

Another design application is in the stability analysis of control loops, which again involves extensive math. Use of a micro allows the effect of disturbances on the operation of the controls to be studied in advance of plant construction, and thus indicates areas where control changes are needed for safe or reliable operations; it also speeds plant startup, by reducing the time needed for setting up the loops.

Micros have been applied in actual plant control conditions, too. They are robust, reliable, and relatively inexpensive, especially in comparison to most other electronic instrumentation. One of their main benefits in plant control has been the ability to do fast calculations, and to display results on the CRT.

One major use has been as an adjunct to PLCs which are excellent sequential controllers, but are very poor at both data handling and math, and have essentially no output capabilities. By tying a micro into a PLC system, the micro can handle any math, the storage of data, and the communications between operators and plant, while the PLC does what suits it best—logical control.

Micros are also used for data logging in plant applications, as they are an inexpensive means of storing large amounts of data, and can be easily programmed to deliver reports, statistical summaries, or quality control reports. An extension of this, requiring a fairly fast machine that can operate in real time, is the use of a micro to analyze plant data, and optimize operations in accordance with pre-established criteria by adjusting plant controls. At present, optimization is limited to dedicated control computers, but the latest micros are becoming powerful enough to handle this kind of application.

FUTURE DEVELOPMENTS

Engineering use of micros is in a very active stage of development, after quite a long incubation period. The hardware is reliable and powerful; software is generally sparse, and often inadequate. Future developments must, therefore, be in the software area if major advances are to be made.

By far the most enticing prospect is the integration of design and manufacturing. This is already a reality in some limited applications, but the extension of this idea to all areas will take a long time, and will be hindered by the absence of automatic machines in the custom-build sector. At present, emphasis is on the integration of design and drafting, both of which are under the control of the engineering function. Complete integration of these operations with manufacturing offers the opportunity of faster completion, less errors (due to less human involvement), and a better, more uniform, product quality.

The design function, that is, the definition of the problem, and a conceptual solution, will still remain a human task, but the micro can aid in this, too. Development of three-dimensional CAD systems for micros will expand the availability of this technique, and allow faster, and better, visualization of designs. Artificial intelligence and expert systems, which have made almost no impact on engineering so far, should be useful tools in the design stage, in startup/troubleshooting and in hazard/operability studies, which are becoming increasingly important in the face of growing public concerns about the safety and health aspects of industrial operations.

For the individual engineer, two major software improvements will greatly expand the use of micros. At present, there is a significant shortage of software, and, as discussed previously, little incentive for commercial developers to produce it, due to the limited market. Thus, some means of simplifying the programming of micros is essential, to allow engineers to use them quickly and easily. One feature that will help is voice-communication; this will avoid the need to type, and speed-up input. The other is the development of either program generators, or a language, that can accept a description of the problem, and turn it directly into a program, without all the struggle with syntax, logic, and debugging that normal programming requires.

In the field of third-party software, the handbooks, design manuals, and codes, on which all engineers rely, will inevitably be issued with computer programs for all calculations, and probably in electronic, rather than hard-copy, form. This is technically feasible now, but the sheer amount of work required will delay implementation for some time. Owing to the large technical effort involved, it is probable that such a development will be contingent upon agreement on standards for hardware, operating system, and language. This may well prove to be the major factor in determining the speed with which engineering will fully accept and use the microcomputer. It all comes down to humans, in the end.

ACKNOWLEDGMENT

Thanks are due to Steve Fox P. Eng for the section on electrical engineering applications.

REFERENCES

1. PCTex, Personal Tex Inc., Mill Valley, CA.
2. MicroTex, Addison-Wesley Publishing Co., Reading, MA.
3. H. Varian, "Review of PCTex and MicroTex," *Byte*, *11*(4), 267 (April 1986).

4. Lotus 1-2-3, Lotus Development Corp.

5. J. F. Ferrall et al., "Process Analysis on a Spreadsheet," *Chem. Eng.*, *93*(5), 101 (March 3, 1986).

6. S. M. Goldfarb, "Spreadsheets for Chemical Engineers—Solving Differential Equations by the Relaxation Method," *Chem. Eng.*, *93*(8), 93 (April 15, 1986).

7. J. R. White, "Use Spreadsheets for Better Refinery Operations," *Hydrocarb. Proc.*, *65*(10), 49 (October 1986).

8. *Allcorr*, LEDS Software, Research Triangle Park, NC.

9. *Flurp—Regression Analysis*, LEDS Software, Research Triangle Park, NC.

10. *X-Stat—Statistical Experiment Design*, Wiley, New York.

11. *ACCESS, The Journal of Microcomputer Applications*, Research Triangle Park, NC.

12. B. Flynn, "Mat-man matrix manipulator," *ACCESS*, *4*(1), 26 (1985).

13. *Calfex*, Interlaken Technology Corp, Minneapolis, MN.

14. *Eureka: The Solver*, Borland International, Scotts Valley, CA.

15. W. K. Oliver, "Evaluating CAE Software," *Hydrocarb. Proc.*, *64*(2), 51 (1985).

16. Environmental Protection Act, RSO 1980, Chapter 141 & Regulation 308.

17. *Alberta/Ontario Dispersion Models*, Cerca Conversions, St. Catherines, Ontario.

18. *Microsoftware for Engineers*, Computational Mechanics Publications, Southampton, UK.

19. *Microcomputer Programs for Chemical Engineers*, Vols 1 and 2, McGraw-Hill, New York, 1984, 1986.

20. P. D. Smith, *BASIC Hydraulics*, Butterworths, London, 1982.

21. J. Heilbron (ed.), *Science and Engineering Programs*, Osborne-McGraw-Hill, New York, 1981.

22. W. Blume, "Computer Circuit Simulation," *Byte*, *11*(7), 165 (1986).

23. *Hysim*, Hyprotech Ltd., Calgary, Alberta, Canada.

24. *Process*, SimSci International, Stockport, UK.

25. *PaChESi*, Co-ordinator D. E. Voit, 4447 St. Ives Ct, Santa Maria, CA 93455.

26. C. Pedicini, "Engineering on a Micro—a Bridge-Truss Analysis Program in BASIC," *Byte*, *11*(7), 145 (1986).

27. S. Fox, "Voltage Regulator Input Filter Design," *ACCESS*, *4*(5), 41 (1985).

28. J. N. Stone, "Tray Efficiency Calculation," *ACCESS*, *5*(3), 5 (1986).

29. E. M. Miller, "Digitizing Analog Data," *PC Tech. J.*, *4*(5), 52 (May 1986).

30. V. E. Wright, "Desktop Data Acquisition," *PC Tech. J.*, *5*(2), 106 (February 1986).

31. W. H. Murray, "Review," *PC Tech. J.*, *2*(3) (March 1984).

32. W. H. Murray, "Digital Designs," *PC Tech. J.*, *3*(3), 112 (March 1985).

33. W. H. Murray, "Drawing Circuits," *PC Tech. J.*, *3*(5), 113 (May 1985).

34. R. Angell, "End-to-End Design," *PC Tech. J.*, *4*(11), 97 (November 1986); "End-to-End Design, part 2," *PC Tech. J.*, *4*(12), 155 (December 1986).

35. R. M. Foard, "PC Versions of iRMX," *PC Tech. J.*, *4*(6), 127 (June 1986).

36. *JDL-850 EWS*, JDL Inc., Westlake Village, CA.

37. *AutoCAD*, Autodesk Inc., Sausalito, CA.

38. V. M. Steiner, "Selecting and Managing CAD Systems," *Plant Eng.*, *40*(21), 52 (1986).
39. B. Hechter, "Solid Wood Computing—CAD/CAM for Log Homes," *CADalyst*, *3*(3), 50 (July 1986).
40. P. A. Teas, "Improving Engineering Productivity with Personal Computers," *Hydrocarb. Proc.*, *64*(2), 57 (1985).
41. J. Katzel, "Microcomputer Applications Software," *Plant Eng.*, *39*(12), 48 (1985).
42. J. N. Stone, "Documenting Programmable Controller Programs," *Plant Eng.*, *39*(8), 66 (1985).
43. J. Katzel, "Microcomputer Applications Software (Survey)," *Plant Eng.*, *39*(12), 48 (June 27, 1985).
44. *Quest*, Icarus Corp., Rockville, MD.
45. R. S. Means Co. Inc., Kingston, MA.
46. *Dialog Information Services Inc.*, Palo Alto, CA.
47. Kenonics Controls, Calgary, Alberta, Canada.

BIBLIOGRAPHY

The intense interest in engineering applications has resulted in publication of many papers, books, and articles, with more appearing daily. Most of this material is in the technical journals, because information becomes outdated very quickly as new hardware and software appears. The following list gives references to many of the topics mentioned in the text, which will serve to augment the specific references cited.

This is by no means intended to be an exhaustive list, but will act as a starting point for anyone interested in researching a particular topic.

Surveys, Reviews, Books

A. I. Ch. E. Applications Software Survey for Personal Computers, A. I. Ch. E., New York, 1986.

Balfour, J. A. D., *Computer Analysis of Structural Frameworks*, Wiley, New York.

Charlwood, R., "1986 CADD Systems Survey," *Can. Cons. Eng.*, Nov./Dec. 1986, 25.

Chemical Engineering Software Guide 1987, CAE Consultants, New York.

Cheremisinoff, N. P., "1987 Environmental Software Review," *Pollution Eng.*, *19*(1), 30 (January 1987).

Computational Methods for the Solution of Engineering Problems, Halstead Press, New York.

Holland, R. C., *Microcomputers for Process Control*, Pergamon Press, New York, 1983.

Lipowicz, M. A., "Fluid Flow and Flow Network Software," *Chem. Eng.*, *92*(24), 59 (November 25, 1985).

Mechanical Engineering Software Guide 1987, CAE Consultants Inc., New York.

Milner, D. A., *Computer-Aided Engineering for Manufacture*, McGraw-Hill, New York, 1987.

Newsletter of Engineering Analysis Software, Frank Maga Assoc., Sepulveda, CA.

Journals

Computers and Industrial Engineering, A. Wheaton & Co., Exeter, UK.
Computers and Electrical Engineering, A. Wheaton & Co., Exeter, UK.
Computers and Chemical Engineering, A. Wheaton & Co., Exeter, UK.
Computers in Mechanical Engineering, AIME, New York.
International Journal of Mini- and Microcomputers, ACTA, Anaheim, CA.
International Journal of Modelling and Simulation, ACTA Press, Anaheim, CA.
International Journal for Numerical Methods in Engineering, Wiley, New York.
Software Engineering Journal, IEE.

Word Processing

'Exact,' Technical Support Software Inc., Brookline, MA.
'forMath,' Shantha Software Inc., New York.
MacKay, P. A., "Typesetting Problem Scripts," *Byte, 11*(2), 201 (February 1986).
'T^3,' TCI Software Research Inc., Las Cruces, CA.

Spreadsheet Applications

Goldfarb, S. M., "Spreadsheets for Chemical Engineers—Design Calculations," *Chem. Eng., 92*(8), 91 (April 15, 1985).
Johnson, T. S., "How Spreadsheets Aid Process and Control Engineering," *Hydrocarb. Proc., 64*(2), 61 (February 1985).
Sawyer, P., "Integrated Software for Process Engineering Calculations," *Chem. Eng.,* 32 (November 1986).
Schmidt, W. P. and R. S. Upadhye, "Material Balances on a Spreadsheet," *Chem. Eng., 91*(25), 67 (December 24, 1984).
Selk, S., "Spreadsheet Software Solves Engineering Problems," *Chem. Eng., 90*(13), 51 (June 27, 1983).
Sowa, C. J., "Engineering Calculations on a Spreadsheet," *Chem. Eng., 94*(3), 61 (March 2, 1987).

Math and Statistics

Hsiao, F. S. T., "Gauss Quadrature Numerical Integration—a Comparison of the Programming Method and the Spreadsheet Method," *ACCESS, 5*(5), 38 (1986).
Krant, J., "Program ODE—a Generic Ordinary Differential Equation Solver," *ACCESS, 5*(5), 43 (1986).
Nixon, L. R., "Gauss-Seidel Iterative Method for Large Matrix Systems," *ACCESS, 3*(2), 48 (March/April 1984).
Wright, V. E., "Equation Solving by Formula/One," *PC Tech. J., 4*(6), 110 (June 1986).

Engineering Design

Chemical

"Computer-Aided Design Zeros in on ChE Needs," *Chem. Eng., 93*(17), 15 (September 1, 1986).
Kimmel, S., "Vapor-Liquid Equilibrium Program," *ACCESS, 2*(3), 44 (May/June 1983).

Kirkpatrick, H. L., "Program Designs and Prices Vessels," *Hydrocarb. Proc.*, *66*(3), 41 (March 1987).

Lipowicz, M., "Selecting Personal Computer Software," *Chem. Eng.*, *93*(11), 75 (June 9, 1986).

Lipowicz, M., "Heat Exchanger Software," *Chem. Eng.*, *93*(15), 101 (August 4, 1986).

Shammas, N. C., "New Root-Seeking Scheme to Solve Flash Calculations," *ACCESS*, *4*(4), 10 (July/August 1985).

Shammas, N. C. "Basic Program for Shortcut Multicomponent Distillation," *ACCESS*, *4*(6), 16 (November/December 1985).

Sparks, L. E., "Particle Collection Using a Venturi Scrubber," *ACCESS*, *1*(5), 24 (September/October 1982).

Sparks, L. E., Program for Isothermal Compressible Flow," *ACCESS*, *4*(1), 38 (January/February 1985).

Stone, J. N., "Cyclone Efficiency Determination," *ACCESS*, *2*(3), 35 (May/June 1983).

Stone, J. N., "Sieve Tray Design," *ACCESS*, *3*(6), 10 (November/December 1984).

Stone, J. N., "Small Scale Engineering Applications," *Byte*, *11*(7), 253 (July 1986).

Tsai, T. C., "Flare System Design by Microcomputer," *Chem. Eng.*, *92*(17), 55 (August 19, 1985).

Watson, A., "Flowchek/bas—a Program for Quick Orifice Calculations," *ACCESS*, *5*(5), 18 (September/October 1986).

Civil

Alim, S. and J. Munro, "PROLOG-Based Expert Systems in Civil Engineering," *Proc. Inst. Civ. Eng.*, *83*, 1 (March 1987).

Elton, D., "Microcomputer Solution to Calculation of Settlement of Building Foundations," *ACCESS*, *5*(1), 20 (January/February 1986).

Horvath, J. A., "Finite Element Analysis Using a Microcomputer," *ACCESS*, *5*(6), 36 (November/December 1986).

Johnson, R. W. and F. G. Loygowi, "Structural Analysis," *Byte*, *11*(7), 199 (July 1986).

Petersen, D. L. and S. L. Crouch, "Stress Analysis," *Byte*, *11*(7), 219 (July 1986).

Stevens, G. J. et al., "A Computer Aided Discharge Determination Technique," *Microsoftware Eng.*, *1*(2), 127 (October 1985).

Electrical

Blume, W., "Computer Circuit Simulation," *Byte*, *11*(7), 165 (July 1986).

McNeill, D., "Analog Circuit Analysis," *Byte*, *11*(7), 170 (July 1986).

Trammell, L., "A Simple Radial Power Flow Program," *ACCESS*, *4*(5), 26 (September/October 1985).

Mechanical

Fields, C., "Diameter of a Series Pipe System," *ACCESS*, *4*(5), 10 (September/October 1985).

Frey, D. J. and M. J. Holz, "Use of Microcomputers for Performance Evaluation of (Solar) Residential Buildings," *ACCESS*, *5*(2), 19 (March/April 1986).

Kao, T., "Solving Hydraulic Transient Problems on a Microcomputer," *ACCESS*, 4(2), 28 (March/April 1985).

Li, K. W. and W. K. Lee, "Computer Programs for Condenser Thermal Analysis," *Microsoftware Eng.*, 1(2), 97 (October 1985).

McMillan, H. K. and J. Kim, "A Computer Program to Determine the Thermodynamic Properties of Moist Air," *ACCESS*, 5(1), 36 (January/February 1986).

Rose, G. K., "Computer Programs for Heat Exchanger Design," *C. E. P.*, 82(9), 53 (1986).

Sawyer, T. and M. Pecht, "A Material Selection Program," *Byte*, 11(7), 235 (July 1986).

Process Simulation

Chemcad, Coade Engineering Software, Houston, TX.

Glaser, D. C., "The PC Simulator," *C. E. P.*, 82(9), 45 (1986).

Parton, L. R., "Software for Improving Productivity," *C. E. P.*, 82(9), 49 (1986).

Seader, J. D., "Computer Modelling of Chemical Processes," AIChE, 1985.

Waye, D., "Dynamic Simulation for Modelling and Control of Industrial Processes," Process Ind. Canada, 7 (November 1986).

Computer-Aided Drafting

CADkey, Micro Control Systems, Vernon, CT.

Hollifield, W. R., "Applying Microcomputer-Based CAD Systems to Plant Engineering," *Plant Eng.*, 62 (December 24, 1986).

Personal Designer, Computervision Corp., Bedford, MA.

Sawyer, P., "Getting to Grips with the Nature of CAD," *The Chemical Eng.*, 22 (October 1986).

VersaCAD, T & W Systems, Huntington Beach, CA.

Wright, V. E., "Microcomputer CAD Systems," *Chem. Eng.*, 92(14), 99 (July 8, 1985).

Plant Engineering

Billis, P. et al., "Open Learning on the Factory Floor," *The Chemical Eng.*, 24 (July 1986).

Jenkins, J. H. and G. W. Luce, "Improve Plant Operations with Personal Computers," *Hydrocarb. Proc.*, 65(9), 149 (September 1986).

Nolden, C., "Maintenance and the Computer," *Plant Eng.*, 39(17), 34 (August 22, 1985).

Waterman, A. P. and A. P. Sperry, "Desktop Computer Based Energy Management," *Plant Eng.*, 39(20), 64 (October 24, 1985).

Engineering Management

O'Neill, M. V., "Implementing a Chemical Process Plant Expert System," *ISA Trans.*, 26(1), 19 (1987).

"Putting Personal Computers to Work at Allegheny-Ludlum," *Plant Eng.*, 41(3), 44 (February 12, 1987).

Cost Estimating

"CAD/Cost—Computer Assisted Building Design and Costing," R. S. Means
    Co. Inc., Kingston, MA.

J. NEIL STONE

ENGINEERING ECONOMY SOFTWARE

The literature of Engineering Economy and Managerial Economy abounds with proposed methodologies for selecting among proposed capital investments. However, in a paper which Horowitz [1] was invited to write for *AIIE Transactions*, he asserted, "Engineering economists have a perennial obsession with devising new ways to approach the problem, and new arithmetic procedures for practical implementation old ways. This, despite the fact that the *economic* criterion for choosing among mutually exclusive investments, in the absence of risk, is straight-forward and indisputable; namely, select that alternative having the highest net present value. . .(at) the maximum rate at which present and future revenues could be invested.. . ." With certain qualifications, Bernhard [2] had come to the same conclusion.

Most available software recognizes the net present value (or, as it is often called, the net present worth) method as valid, but many offer the rate of return method, either as *the* method, or as an alternative approach. As Horowitz [1] put it, ". . .there is considerable intuitive appeal and comfort attached to the philosophy that choosing alternatives that yield the highest rate of return (1) cannot be all that bad, and, moreover (2) should maximize the overall return on an investors capital. Indeed, managers that have not enjoyed the advantage of being educated otherwise. . .are easily seduced by this attractive, if erroneous, rate of return argument."

Since it is a trivial task to write a program to calculate the net present value of a series of cash flows (this is the sum of their discounted values), programs which do offer this have proliferated, often appearing as one of a series of utilities.

Unfortunately, in one sense, it is only a little more difficult to solve for that rate of return which reduces the net present value to zero. This rate is defined as the rate of return by some; as the internal rate of return by others. Programs making rate of return calculations have also proliferated. They generally employ a systematic trial and error method, though the method of successive approximations could also be employed.

Finding "the" rate of return requires a solution of a polynomial of the n-th degree, where n is the number of cash flows in the series. Therefore, one should anticipate n rather than one solution: hence using the term "the rate of return" could be misleading. All rate of return programs known to the author deal with the problem of multiple rates of return in one of the following ways:

1. By ignoring the problem and offering the first solution found as "the" rate of return.
2. In recognition of the fact that Descartes' rule of signs promises that there will not be more real roots than there are changes of sign in the series of cash flows, print out some sort of message warning that any root found is meaningless if more than one change of sign exists. It should be noted that proponents of the rate of

return method either ignore or differ on the answer to the question of whether or not this is appropriate if multiple changes of sign lead to only one real root or on whether or not multiple roots have any meaning.

3. No rate of return program known to the author seeks out and reports all real solutions when more than one exists.

The Capital Expenditure Analyst,[*] is a unique program which offers graphs showing net present values (or their surrogates, net future values, or uniform annual equivalents) as a function of the interest rates at which these values are calculated. (The graphs are in color, but print acceptably on black and white.) This software, which permits very rapid revision of the range of interest rates presented, offers the following advantages:

1. In general, much uncertainty exists over the interest rate at which a net present value should be determined. This program has a built-in sensitivity study over a range of interest rates. (As Swalm and Lopez [3] show, this interest rate must be the opportunity rate for an organization if its objective is to maximize its wealth.)
2. It encourages the user to examine more than one alternative.
3. The graphs offered permit complete and unambiguous analyses of mutually exclusive investment opportunities. An example to illustrate this is offered in Figure 1, which shows the plot of net present values for two mutually exclusive projects over an appropriate range of opportunity rates. (This plot was produced by an early version of this software: the final version will substitute NET PRESENT VALUE for NET PRESENT WORTH and will permit the user to select his own term for the abscissa.)

The first of these projects, which we have termed INCREASING, costs $30,000. It is projected to produce net cash flows starting at $2,000 at the end of the first year and increasing by 100% in each of the next four years. The second, termed DECREASING, costs $24,000, and is projected to pro-

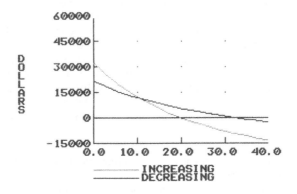

FIGURE 1 Net present worth.

---

[*]Soon to be offered by B.E.S.T., 11525 S.W. Durham Road, Tigard, OR 97223 (800) 368-BEST.

duce net cash flows starting at $13,000 at the end of the first year and decreasing by $2,000 per year for each of the next four years. The graph shows clearly that INCREASING is the better choice for any opportunity rate upgrowth of about 10%, that DECREASING represents a better choice for any opportunity rate expected to fall between about 10% and 31%, and that neither project should be undertaken if one's opportunity rate exceeds 31%. For those addicted to rate of return calculations, the graph shows the rate of return on "decreasing" to be about 31% (remember, the rate of return is that rate for which the net present value is zero). It also shows the rate of return on INCREASING to be about 20%, and the rate of return at which both are equally attractive to be about 10%. (In addition, it clearly demonstrates why the rate of return on INCREASING is irrelevant to the choice between the two alternatives.)

Values of interest can be read more accurately by using the upward and downward pointing arrows on the keyboard to zoom in and out and the left and right pointing arrows to select the desired range of interest rates. Using this feature, results such as those shown in Figure 2 can be obtained. This figure shows why anyone who feels that their after-tax opportunity rate falls between, say, 5 and 9% would probably feel comfortable in selecting the INCREASING option, whereas DECREASING would probably be chosen by those projecting a growth rate between 12 and 16%. But what if the growth rate were projected to fall between 8 and 12%? Zooming in a bit further yields Figure 3, which would probably lead to a decision to choose DECREASING (unless one felt that the distribution of growth rates was badly skewed).

Now suppose it was felt that the opportunity rate fell in the 12% range, and that INCREASING had the intangible value of having greater flexibility. By zooming in still further, and placing a 12% growth rate at the vertical axis, it can be seen that the difference in net present value in favor of DECREASING at this opportunity rate is projected as about $1,200. One might then be able to decide whether the additional flexibility offered by INCREASING were worth $1,200. (This approach recognizes the fact that it is easier to make comparisons than it is to judge absolute magnitudes.)

For simplicity, the example discussed above was evaluated on a before-tax basis, although the program permits ready evaluation on an after-tax basis. (When selecting this option, an after-tax opportunity rate must be

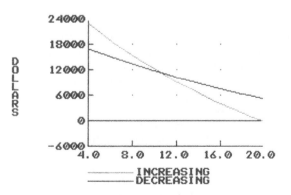

FIGURE 2 Net present worth.

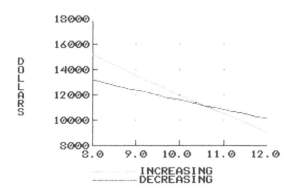

FIGURE 3 Net present worth.

considered when making decisions, of course). It also permits sensitivity (or "what if") studies to be made on all parameters. Additional features included are options to use continuous compounding, the inclusion of inflation considerations, and it is even possible for the user wishing to base decisions on the cost of capital or the minimum attractive rate of return, etc. to label the abscissa appropriately. In addition to a very complete manual, a fairly extensive tutorial on the basics of capital expenditure analysis is provided. This latter offers many examples of the use of this program.

For those who wish to go beyond sensitivity studies and to include the explicit consideration of probabilities in their analyses, two techniques present themselves. The first, risk analysis (as defined by Hertz), requires the assessment of probability distributions on all parameters. Based on these distributions, a Monte Carlo simulation is used to generate a probability distribution on the rate of return (technically incorrect, as noted above) or on the net present value.

Since it is difficult to write a program covering all situations and even more difficult to obtain meaningful distributions on a host of input parameters, it is not surprising that this technique has not, to the author's knowledge, been implemented on any general-purpose, publicly available software.

Decision analysis, on the other hand, has, despite its complexity, been offered by at least three developers. These offer interesting contrasts. First, Decision 1-2-Tree, version 2.0, published by Fast Decisions Inc.,[*] costs less than $200. The Arborist, published by Texas Instruments,[†] costs about three times as much, and Supertree, published by Strategic Decisions Systems,[‡] costs several times more again. There were wide differences between the power and features offered in the first versions of these three programs, but these, except for the costs, have been markedly reduced in the current versions. Each offers advantages not found in some of the others, and each has disadvantages. Decision 1-2-Tree has a very obvious cost advantage, but lacks the probability wheel (used in assessing

---

[*]P.O. Box 264, Cambridge, MA 02238, (617) 314-4901.
[†]P.O. Box 2909, M/S 2151, Austin, TX 78769 (800) 847-2787.
[‡]100 Sand Hill Road, Menlo Park, CA 94025-7127, (415) 854-9000.

subjective probabilities) that the other two offer. The Arborist has unusually fine color graphics, but lacks the ability to "flip the tree" found in the other two. (This ability is useful in calculating the value of perfect information and in making the Baysean analyses so often needed to evaluate the value of imperfect information.) Supertree is the most powerful of the three, but offers only "typewriter plots," an anachronism in today's computer programming. Also, its greater power is paid for by rather long delays while the computer grinds away. All three offer Lotus 1-2-3 compatibility, and all offer site-licensing agreements and special student editions at attractive rates.

Supertree comes with an exceptionally fine tutorial on decision analysis, and the Strategic Decisions Group offer a magnificent two-volume, boxed paperback set entitled "Readings in Decision Analysis." A number of these readings are by Ron Howard, the founder of what has become known as the Stanford school of decision analysis; others are by leading practitioner proponents of this school. No one with more than a passing interest in decision analysis should be without these readings and one of the three fine decision analysis programs now available.

REFERENCES

1. I. Horowitz, "Engineering Economy: An Economist's Perspective," *AIIE Transactions, 8*(4) (1976).
2. R. H. Bernhard, "A Comprehensive Comparison and Critique of Discounting Indices Proposed for Capital Investment Evaluation," *Eng. Economist, 16*(3) (1971).
3. R. O. Swalm and J. L. Lopez, *Engineering Economic Analysis: A Future Wealth Approach*, John Wiley & Sons, New York, 1984.

RALPH SWALM

THE ENGINEERING WORKSTATION AND
THE ENGINEERING SUPPORT SYSTEM

INTRODUCTION

In the early 1950s, the engineering and scientific community was the primary source of innovation in the computer industry. However, in the latter years of that decade, business data processing emerged as a major influence on computer system design. With banking applications at the forefront, the early 1960s became an era of rapid development of computer systems primarily designed for accountants. Real-time transaction processing systems with on-line databases provided businesses with exactly what was needed for improved management control in the face of explosive growth. Some large users actually required their engineers to confine their computing time to third shift so that the engineering work would not cause poor response time for order entry clerks during the first and second shifts. Hence, many engineers and scientists believed that computer manufacturers and computer center managers were ignoring their problems and needs.

However, in the mid-1960s some visionary faculty members and talented students at Dartmouth College developed computer timesharing. Engineers and scientists quickly recognized timesharing as an answer to many of their frustrations. Timesharing provided them with a way to perform their computing work without the aggravation of having to interact with a large computer operation. Timesharing fulfilled their desire to be "computer-do-it-yourselfers." In the past twenty years, the timesharing market has grown to a multibillion-dollar annual level. Yet the past two decades have seen very few innovations made specifically to benefit engineers and scientists. Several leaders in the computer industry have publicly expressed their wish that engineers and scientists be more effective in influencing new product developments. Recently, however, the computer industry has been displaying a much greater interest in engineering workstations and engineering and scientific support systems.

Most agree that the need for increased productivity of engineers has never been greater. Most also recognize that one key to successfully meeting this need is the efficient use of computing resources, resources which are rapidly becoming more powerful and less expensive. At Arizona State University, an Engineering Joint Study was sponsored by IBM to investigate the requirements for a computerized workstation that would allow engineers to fulfill their tasks more quickly and effectively. The study also considered the development of highly specialized powerful, sole-source CAD/CAM workstations. Although giant strides have been made in developing engineering workstations for geometric design work and engineering

This article is based on several white papers from two Arizona State University Workshops on Engineering Workstations held on April 26–27, 1984 and February 7–8, 1985.

drawing production, much less progress had been made for other important application areas such as design computation, data acquisition and analysis, documentation, communication, and engineering management. The concept of the engineering workstation evolved into an even more improtant concept—that of the engineering support system (ESS) in which several engineering workstations are interconnected through a central computing facility to form a fully integrated system. Workstations are being integrated with office automation tools to form comprehensive engineering support systems.

The purpose of constructing the computer-based workstations contained in an ESS is to provide tools to increase productivity. Current limitations on productivity result from repetition and inefficient transfer of information. Information takes many forms, including letters and memos, reports, charts and graphs, and engineering drawings, as well as experimental and analyzed data. The speed with which a manager or professional can produce a technical paper or document is restricted by manual paper handling, repetitive editing of and corrections to drafts prepared by secretaries, and the final manual distribution of the finished material. In manufacturing plants and industries these restrictions can also apply to the preparation of engineering drawings. Original sketches and specifications are reproduced by draftsmen, copied, and manually distributed to contractors of fabrication facilities.

The inefficiency of this process lies not only in preparation and distribution but also in the method of feedback of discrepancies and modifications to the designer. When discrepancies or modifications reach the designer, the entire process must be repeated. And if this feedback does not occur, then the original mistakes tend to propagate into other projects and designs, and stored records can misrepresent the finished product. It is in this way, then, that productive engineering design and construction becomes limited in both the long and short term. Other phases of engineering, such as the collection and analysis of experimental data, also require productive transfer of information. Data must be able to be easily stored, retrieved, and transferred between field and laboratory personnel, and between engineers and managers.

An effective engineering support system can greatly increase productivity by providing an integrated system of electronic information transfer capabilities. In addition, the productivity of the individuals at each workstation can be enhanced by on-line data analysis, documentation, and graphics capabilities. Although centralized computer systems have improved the transfer of information, these systems frequently become overloaded by multiple simultaneous users, causing unacceptable delays in the flow of constructive activity. In these systems the occurrence of a hardware or software failure can take everyone off-line, halting production altogether. A properly designed and implemented ESS, on the other hand, can reliably and efficiently transfer data and can distribute the information processing capabilities of the workstations.

In the succeeding sections we first state the objective of an ESS and then define an ESS, its users, and their requirements. We then discuss obstacles to meeting ESS user needs and the results of not meeting them, and make some concluding observations.

OBJECTIVES OF AN ENGINEERING SUPPORT SYSTEM

The purpose of an ESS is to enable the engineer to make more productive use of time. Essentially, the ESS enables engineers and other ESS users to supplement their human thinking capabilities with complementary computer capabilities. This is sometimes referred to as synergism of the user and the support systems [1]. The objectives of an ESS are to provide users these additional capabilities in the most effective way, i.e., to take a minimum of additional user time, and to provide a maximum amount of assistance in performing tasks.

Minimum Additional User Time

The amount of time spent by the user learning to operate an ESS and to incorporate new enhancements or software releases needs to be minimized. This may require standardization of most ESS components, in particular software, hardware, user interfaces, operating system functions, program-to-program and program-to-storage formats, and databases. Standardizing these functions will form a common ESS kernel, i.e., a least-common denominator on which divergent applications can be run.

Other methods of minimizing user time and effort include providing extensive on-line assistance, which can be configured to the user's level of ability. Constructive feedback, good documentation, and high system reliability will also provide a friendly environment for the ESS user.

Maximum Assistance in Performing Tasks

Assistance in performing tasks is provided by an ESS that can run a variety of application software, provide text processing, transfer mail, documents, and figures or programs electronically, and provide computational power. Graphic drawing aids, including ones that enable graphic input and output of data, are also essential. A database common to managers, engineers, office and production personnel, and other ESS users should be concurrently usable and updateable.

A common database can be used to store partial results for reports, proposals, papers, and other documents. Thus, several people can work together (e.g., engineer and secretary, professor and graduate student) in the iterative generation of a document. High-quality output for documents (multiple fonts, attractive formatting, and correctly spelled words) is also desirable. To accomplish these goals, the ESS must provide sufficient storage capacity for such items as picture and test files, databases, and computational algorithms.

The ability to share resources such as letter-quality printers, high-resolution interactive graphic display stations, analog I/O stations, and databases also maximizes the ESS's ability to provide assistance in problem solving.

A final objective of ESS is to improve the quality as well as the speed of work, by means of tools that promote accuracy, readability, legibility, organization, and attractive visual format.

DEFINITION OF AN ENGINEERING SUPPORT SYSTEM

An engineering support system is any one of several levels of computer-based workstations that provides support for engineers and the people they work with, including secretaries, managers, designers, and marketing personnel. Basically, an ESS is a complete computer system configured to fit into the workplace of each of these persons, one that has the computational power, communications and peripheral support, and software needed to assist in most, if not all, of their work. A similar definition applicable to workstations in a local area network (LAN) environment is given by Yalamanchili et al. [2]. Engineering support systems consist of engineering workstations as well as the less powerful workstations at the desks of secretaries, managers, and others with whom engineers work. Essentially, an ESS is a concept better described by example of itself and its user [3].

The components of an ESS resemble the components of a personal computer, and the ESS and personal computer have many of the same hardware and software components in common. As we will define it here, an ESS will include not only these minimum components, but also all the elements that must be available to an ESS user should he or she require them. The section below on ESS user requirements provides a shopping list or menu of available services, displays, printers, communication methods, etc. The difference between this menu and what one sees on the shelves of a computer store is that the items on the menu absolutely must be able to work together in a completely integrated system, if needed.

A basis or minimal requirement of an ESS is that it allow the exchange of data from any one workstation to any other workstation within the system. Various forms of hardware support for interchange of data may be offered. These can range from transfer via diskettes or RS-232 or IEEE 488 ports, to transfer via a local area network.

In general, an ESS consists of various layers. There is an inner layer of distributed computing hardware—CPUs, memory, disks, and so on. This is surrounded by operating systems and language support software. The latter is, in turn, surrounded by network graphics, and database manager software. At the outermost level are application software packages such as those for engineering design and word processing. Dhar [4] discusses this model.

USERS OF AN ESS

The potential users of an engineering support system include a wide range of personnel. The proposed ESS must serve as a universal tool for increasing the productivity of a diverse group of interacting users (e.g., managers, professionals, secretaries, draftsmen, designers, operators, and laboratory technicians) collectively engaged in a variety of information processing tasks. These tasks include

> The creation, modification, printing, archiving, and distribution of engineering designs and related documents and drawings [5]
> The collection, analysis, utilization, archiving, and distribution of experimental data from laboratories, test stations, pilot plants, and production plants
> The training of new personnel

Typically, an ESS is in an engineering or technically oriented environment, whether the organization or institution is doing basic research, accomplishing design, training technicians, educating engineers, or manufacturing a product. Users range from the technically sophisticated engineer or research scientist to the person performing clerical duties. Personnel with requirements for information processing will range from those in the highest levels of management, including the board chairperson, to those at the lowest levels of the company hierarchy. Requirements for accuracy, timeliness, detail, and volume of information will also vary within this wide range of users.

The configuration of each workstation comprising the ESS will vary, depending on the needs of the user. A design engineer, for example, may need a complete set of drawings, but a clerk may require only a letter or memo. Hence, a computer-aided design capability will be a must for the engineer, though not for the clerk.

The software needs of users depend on their responsibilities and level within the organization. One basic requirement exists: information for all users should come from a common database that can be concurrently accessed and updated by all.

By recognizing and understanding the wide range of ESS users, the varying levels of system performance they require, and the basis need of all of them to be able to process and receive information from a common database, ESS developers can establish parameters and criteria for an ESS. To accomplish this, they must listen to users. If user needs seem to be totally different from one another, then perhaps the common points of those needs have not been clearly defined or understood [6].

One thing is clear, no matter what his or her level, the user will not be working in an isolated environment. Gomes's quote [1] is relevant here:

> Synergy is an increasingly important concept for persons working with computer systems. A score of unattached workstations scattered about a research center will, no doubt, go a long way towards increasing the productivity of their individual users. But link them together and suddenly a new creature emerges. What was once a single group of individuals toiling away in isolation can become a single, robust unit, sharing the same information and proceeding in parallel towards the same goals. One of the guidelines we use is that by 1990 or so virtually everyone that is employed will have some access to a computer.

Our view is that these statements about the user are probably true and that we must plan, design, and produce hardware, peripherals, networks, interfaces, and software that will be able to support wide ranges of users.

There is another reason for providing a wide range of services. If we look just at the engineering workstation component of the ESS and examine the work that an engineer performs at that workstation, we find that design and analysis—though the traditional tasks for which engineers are educated—account for only 15 to 25% of the engineer's workday [6]. Studies conducted at Hewlett-Packard's Colorado facilities [3] showed that as much as 80% of an engineer's time was spent doing nonengineering work, with often as little as 20% actually spent in engineering. A typical breakdown of an engineer's workload was

Design: 10%
Test and evaluation: 10%
Planning: 15%
Documentation: 25%

Although percentages varied somewhat from department to department,
clearly most of the engineers spent the largest amount of their time doing
engineering support work. Hence, an engineering workstation should have
software and hardware features to support all the tasks an engineer does.
At the same display at which an engineer draws a schematic and analyzes
circuits, he should be able to generate documents, prepare reports, send
mail, interact with databases, and easily develop special-purpose software.

REQUIREMENTS OF AN ESS USER

The general nature of the needs of an ESS user is well known. Pyke [7]
identifies eight factors associated with "user service quality": functional
fidelity, level of performance, ease of use, reliability, availability, upgrade-
ability, maintainability, and data confidentiality. Hardware and software
designers express the need in terms of ESS hardware and software that
provides them with a development environment that enables them "to design
more easily than ever before" [8]. Meeting user needs requires a combination of hardware, software, database management, standardization, and extensibility. We will discuss each of these in turn below.

Hardware

There is considerable agreement on the major features that should be required in ESS hardware. Dhar [4] refers to these features as "computational performance, network communications, and graphics." We restate
these more specifically as a need for a mainframe architecture, an integrated
local area network capability, and a high-resolution, bit-mapped interactive
graphics capability.

Hardware for an ESS must serve as a universal tool for increasing
the productivity of a diverse group of interacting users engaged in a variety of tasks. The hardware, along with its associated software, encodes,
processes, stores, and decodes information coming from a variety of sources
and going to a variety of destinations. Information as diverse as dimensional views, speech, procedures, and mechanical motions must be handled
by workstations comprising an ESS. Doing so requires a menu of standard,
preintegrated I/O devices, each with preintegrated device drivers and
diagnostic software, from which a user can select as his needs dictate.
Standard hardware interfaces and software communication protocols between
an ESS workstation and its associated I/O devices, or between the workstation and another ESS workstation, must be transparent to the user and
permit rapid installation, testing, and use.

The hardware for model ESS workstation can be divided into several
categories:

The central processing unit and associated high-speed memory
Low-speed memory
Input devices

Output devices
Communication devices

The central processing unit should be a microprocessor from a 16- or 32-bit
microprocessor family that provides a stable architecture and a substantial
third-party software base. Important characteristics of a candidate microprocessor include

A large, directly addressable memory range
Virtual memory capability in at least one microprocessor in the family
Existence of a family of coprocessor and peripheral chips that offload
    CPU functions and permit parallel processing [9] as well as net-
    working
Adequate exception handling capabilities
Existence of standard firmware kernels for operating system modules,
    graphics, and communications
Existence of multiple sources

High-speed memory consists of semiconductor read/write memory and
read-only memory. The ESS workstation should have at least one megabyte
of high-speed memory and should be designed so that expansion to at least
16 megabytes of high-speed memory is possible.
Low-speed memory will be primarily magnetic. Current technology
favors the high-capacity hard disk for file storage, the floppy disk as the
transfer medium, and various media as the backup store. The integration
into the workstation of a variety of powerful software packages and the implementation of an "engineering database" will place enormous demands on
low-speed memory capacity. Capacity in the 100-to-1000-megabyte range
is not an unreasonable extrapolation for today's technology. Several options
may be considered for the backup store: communication to a central computer for archival storage, high-capacity soft disks or removal hard disks,
streaming tape, one-megabyte semiconductor memory cartridges with built-in
microprocessor, or write-only digital video media. At this time it is difficult
to predict which option is most appropriate.
Input devices can be viewed as encoding devices that convert nonbinary information into binary code. Such devices can be divided into several categories:

Those that a user can manipulate
Those than can encode the voice
Those that can encode images
Those that can encode analog data

Devices in the first category include the keyboard, soft function keys,
the light pen, the mouse, the touch screen, the trackball, the joystick, the
Koala Pad, and the bar code reader. It should be understood that there
will be a variety of users of the workstation and that different input devices will be appropriate for different individuals and different applications.
An engineer may prefer a keyboard, a manager a mouse or touch screen,
and an operator a keyboard and trackball.
Devices in the second category include inexpensive speech encoders
able to accept speech input from any individual. The speech encoder
promises to be a critical workstation component for users who want to enter

text into the ESS but who do not know how to type and do not wish to learn. Voice encoding can replace dictation and eliminate the tedious task of transcribing text from a dictating machine or from stenographic notes.

Image encoding can be performed by a variety of devices. Image-encoding device technologies are advancing rapidly, and image-encoder costs are declining. Included in the image-encoder category are video cameras, optical character readers, CCD arrays, and laser scanners. Video images have the advantage that they can be stored in analog form on magnetic media and then converted to binary and entered into the ESS.

Analog data encoders function as on-line data acquisition devices in laboratory, pilot plant, and factory systems. Included in this category are analog-to-digital converters, voltage-to-frequency converters, timer/counters, and digital multimeters. A real-time clock falls into this category as well, but has general utility even in the absence of a plant or laboratory.

Output devices can be viewed as decoders that convert binary information into nonbinary form. Output devices can be divided into the following categories:

> Text displays
> Graphics displays (both black-and-white and color)
> Voice and sound generators
> Printers and plotters
> Digital-to-analog converters
> Interfaces to electrostatic and magnetostatic copiers

Text displays should have the capability to display uppercase and lowercase letters, boldface letters, italic letters, underlined letters, superscripts, half-superscripts, subscripts, and half-subscripts. They should be able to display Greek symbols, diacritical marks, and other special characters through software or firmware. These abilities allow engineers to manipulate both soft- and hard-copy representations of technical data with minimal effort.

The value of graphics cannot be overstated. The speed, accuracy, and information content of user communications can be tremendously increased through the use of graphics. Graphics is "the communciation medium" [6]. There is general agreement that the minimum acceptable resolution should be about 512 × 512 for raster color displays. In addition, 60 frame/sec noninterlaced scanning and a bit-mapped graphics memory with several planes are needed to supply suitable response time, color, and avoidance of flicker. Monochrome displays are acceptable for many purposes and are standard on many current workstations.

Printers should be able to reproduce the characters and symbols that appear in the text display. The ability to print high-quality characters and symbols, and the ability to reproduce bit-mapped graphic images, should be combined in a single printer, if possible. The ability to handle both tractor-fed paper and single 8.5 × 11-inch sheets is also important.

Plotters should provide resolution of at least 0.01 inch, and be able to handle paper of up to at least D size (and perhaps larger sheets in some applications). Built-in software that allows image manipulation such as expansion, reduction, rotation, and translation is desirable.

Communication devices, which are classified in the general category of I/O devices, deserve special mention. Communications will become an indispensable characteristic of the ESS, since ESS workstations will be networked throughout organizations. Standard communications hardware such as RS-232C, RS-449, and IEEE 488 multibaud-rate modems, and hardware that supports a standard local area network, should be employed.

Software

"User service quality" is provided by ESS software that incorporates certain key features and meets certain key user requirements.

User Interface Features. The software used to provide the interface between the man and the machine is the single most improtant aspect of a productive engineering support system. The software must be capable of supplying applications and data to the entire spectrum of engineering and support personnel. The ease of use of the tools available must not depend heavily on the frequency of their use or on the level of expertise of the user. The format and sequence of commands should be natural, easy to learn, and easy to remember. The number of commands or interactions needed to perform a high-level function should be as few as possible [7].

The following features are required for the system software:

Easy execution: The software should provide menus for activity selection. The menus should be designed to flow logically and branch to other menus as required. Each screen should indicate how one should proceed forward, return to the previous menu, obtain on-line assistance, or exit to the main menu. The information presented on the screen should eliminate the need for the user to remember a "glossary" of available commands and the proper format for each.

User-defined interface: The user should have the ability to adjust both the level of prompts and the defaults provided in the menus. The user should also be able to directly enter commands and bypass the menus. These features are needed to increase the productivity of the more experienced user.

Use of macros: The software should make extensive use of macros. A macro reduces a series of commands to one command or to a single keystroke.

Training Requirements. At least the following training aids are required:

On-line assistance: The available software should be autoinstructional. The user should not need a manual or a formal training course to effectively use the software package. The software should provide on-line assistance for each panel. An integral on-line tutorial should be included to aid the new or infrequent user.

Documentation: Documentation should be provided to assist support personnel, who will use it for system troubleshooting, installation, and modification.

Software Interchange Capability. When new software is developed to provide desired features, the new software released must be capable of interfacing with existing software and files.

Required Applications Software. The applications software required in an ESS can be broken down into four categories: [11]

System software
Administrative software
Engineering analysis software
Engineering design software

The following application software is typical of that required for specific tasks on some or all of the workstations in an engineering organization:

Word processing programs (with the ability to handle equations and
     sub- and superscripts)
Report writing programs (with the ability to insert artwork in text)
Electronic mail and communications packages
Real-time data acquisition programs
Graphics development packages
Program development packages (including compilers, assemblers, linkers,
     librarians, etc.)
Operating system utilities (copy, sort, file management, directory display
     utilities, etc.)
Terminal emulation programs
Spreadsheet programs
Accounting packages
Drafting packages
Electronic, mechanical, and chemical
Process control and simulation programs
Scheduling programs
Project management programs
Discrete and continuous modeling programs
3D viewing and visualization programs (with the ability to perform
     rotation)
Educational programs

No single workstation will have all these applications. A real-time data acquisition station, for example, may not require extensive word processing software. Additional packages may be required and can be provided by the hardware supplier or by third-party software suppliers.

The operating system, or at least the lowest level of software that is common to all workstations, should support tools for the workstation environment [3]. The tools to be supported suggest that the operating system should provide low-level mechanisms for concurrent processes, virtual memory, and file or record locking, as a start. It should also directly support tools for electronic mail, text editing, file management, and graphics. In addition, the operating system should provide tools to simplify system management and transportation and software. And finally, the operating system ought to be one that is implemented on many systems. There is general agreement today that UNIX and its lookalikes and workalikes are becoming (or already have become) the de facto standard operating system for small computers [12]. With an installed base of over 200,000 systems [13], UNIX is currently the dominant system in all sections of the market except the single-user and large mainframe system sections [14].

Database Management

An ESS deals with large masses of data containing many records. The virtue of a "database manager" is that it allows a record to be randomly and automatically entered. The data can then be selected according to one or more criteria, formatted, and sent on to the next operation. The database manager is considered by many to be the "hub" of an ESS.

Types of data include ASCII correspondence files, numerical data indexed to other sources, and graphic data. The data can be made more useful if it is stored as a shared resource on a large high-speed storage device. (Graphic data, in particular, use many bytes and require a large store.) The database should be relational and it should also efficiently handle the problem of contention (for updating) created by multiple users. Last, a database management package should interface well with other software and operating systems.

Some packages already provide limited integration of database-like functions with other capabilities, at least on small systems.

Command files, DO files, and friendly error trapping, correction, and reporting features tend to enhance the ease of database use in a large, compelx multiuser and multitasking environment. Most database management systems are used to do inventorying, accounting, job costing, timekeeping, and many of the other applications anticipated in an ESS. Database management systems are available in many versions, some with graphics and menu enhancements that simplify their use.

The price, speed, and performance of database managers have become most attractive. The large storage requirements are cheaply and reliably satisfied by floppy disks, Winchester disks, and videodiscs. If additional speed is needed for multilevel sorts on megabyte files, a local, dedicated CPU is a cost-effective addition. Many existing local area networks provide dedicated "file server" CPUs for reasons such as this. File servers also make it economical to provide "diskless workstations" in high-data-rate local area networks [15].

Standards

Incorporating standards into workstation architectures frequently simplifies the task of supplying the latest technology to ESS users [4], although the opposite argument is often heard. Standardized buses, communication protocols, operating systems, and languages provide a base for hundreds of products, whereas proprietary architectures lock users into a given system's technology. Standards make application software more transportable by providing a common base for applications. One reason for the enormous increase in UNIX-based systems is that there have been no major changes at the system-interface level since 1979 [16]. Therefore, workstation designers should provide an architecture that incorporates the standards on which ESS applications have already been built, and that provides a structure for absorbing the latest technology [4].

The use of nonstandard microprocessors, and of operating systems other than that selected as a standard, will aggravate the already serious fragmentation problem. We should select one hardware system, one operating system, one database kernel, and one set of hardware interfaces. Once this has been done, software vendors will begin to develop application programs for the ESS, assured of its stable architecture and of a large and expanding marketplace. The technical societies should form committees to evaluate and report on the performance of these programs. Experts in the application areas should review them for content, and other reviewers should provide information on their ease of use, degree of integration, and so on. It is possible that the application area will engender its own journal, newsletter, or special interest group.

Once standards have been agreed on, it will be possible to allow them to evolve as new hardware emerges. Standards are not intended to stultify the development of the ESS, but only to halt the widespread fragmentation of effort caused by differences in media, microprocessors, bus structures, communication protocols, data formats, and operating systems. The development of standards will protect the interests of users. Users need better direction and counsel than can be obtained from vendors' sales personnel or literature. Standards development may be a proper role of professional societies, special interest groups, and national electronic mail.

The ESS that results from this process may not reflect the state of the art in every hardware element. However, this shortcoming is more than compensated for by the benefits obtained from well-debugged, integrated, easy-to-use software.

Few of the required standards should be particularly difficult to develop. Standards committees should set specifications for

Microprocessors, ROMs, RAMs, and soft and hard disks
Operating systems
Hardware systems
Database kernel designs
I/O interfaces
Graphics interfaces
Buses and backplanes
Local area network interfaces
Printer and plotter interfaces

Once such efforts gain momentum through pressure, the various hardware and software vendors will support them because of the obvious rewards, such as a ready marketplace and constancy of environment.

Extensibility

A system is extensible if it can be incrementally upgraded with hardware or software components to provide greater performance. Such an upgrade must be able to be accomplished in a way that does not require the replacement of other major elements or render obsolete a significant number of the applications that run on the system. Thus, if ESS users find it necessary to add hardware or software, they should be able to do so without having to perform major system modifications.

Programs added to the system should use familiar interactive tools (e.g., tablets, trackballs, and touch screens) and menus and dialogues that follow standard practice for the user interface. The program itself ought to be the result of many trials with untrained users so that minor problems in interpretation of the interactive dialogues will have been eliminated. Complex dialogues will have been either subdivided into several simpler dialogues or, where the complexity is unavoidable, supported by "help" and online instructional material. If the element added to the ESS is hardware, then the user programs should already have been designed to test for the existence of the device and to be able to access it upon the request of the user.

Other Requirements

An ESS must have an extensive communication capability. It will require access to central computer facilities and to other ESSs for programs and data and for shared resources such as printers and disks. Communication capability is also needed for electronic mail—the ability of the ESS user to send messages to other users via mail or equivalent facilities is indispensable. A workstation requires several data communication tools [3]. Connection to a high-speed local area network (such as those specified in the IEE 802 standard) is needed to support communication with people on the same project or in the company [2]. At least one station on the local area network should provide a gateway to other computer networks and to computers outside networks. Network software should be integrated into the operating system, as it is in Berkeley's UNIX 4.2 [12]. The communications facility should be easy to use and as transparent as possible. A user should not need to know the location of a file to access it—a file name should suffice.

Reliability, availability, serviceability, and maintainability apply to ESSs just as much as to larger centralized computer systems. The sheer volume of units they produce should encourage ESS manufacturers to follow sound software engineering practices. An ESS user has the right to expect that such practices have been followed. Hardware bugs and software logic errors should be discovered and corrected through a careful update or re-call procedure. The problems of latent bugs and program errors that plague mainframe manufacturers selling only hundreds or perhaps thousands of units should be largely eliminated in the high-volume workstation market. Since most ESSs will be networked, they will have a greater number of re-sources available to them because there will be multiple copies of both hardware and software resources on the network. Since workstations may be dispersed around a company or city, greater attention will have to be given to maintenance. Self-diagnosis and remote diagnosis with modular replacement of major parts will be required [7].

GRAPHICS FOR THE ESS

The computer-aided engineering (CAE) area is growing in importance in an ESS environment. The computer-aided design (CAD) systems which operate on microcomputers as well as the more powerful CAD systems on minicomputers are becoming extremely useful to engineers. Improvements are needed in many aspects of CAD systems such as better three-dimensional capability and improved ease of moving design work back and forth between the micro-CAD environment and the large CAD systems.

Since engineers spend much of their time on communciation activities, presentation graphics tools are also valuable to improve the effectiveness of the engineers' presentations.

Graphics is a key part of an engineering manager's workstation that can be unique to engineering management. The graphics capability must be sufficiently powerful that the manager can participate in and review the technical work of the various engineering departments. (Graphics has the potential of becoming an extremely powerful engineering manager's tool.)

Interactive graphics adds an important new dimension to engineering training and technology transfer software. Graphics combined with expert systems and knowledge base approaches can permit engineers to utilize unstructured, simple queries and a natural problem-solving mode. Also, graphics provides trainees with the ability to manipulate and change parameters of a problem being studied.

Windowing can also provide a way for ESS users to observe the behavior of a variable in a window on a CRT screen while at the same time observing the effect of the variable on a graphical representation in another window. Engineering technology transfer will be more effective when graphics is applied to demonstrate the dynamics of a problem.

Graphics systems can be divided into four broad categories:

Turnkey design graphics ($15K to $50K per person)
Host-based graphics ($5K to $20K per person)
PC-based graphics ($3K to $10K per person)
Presentation graphics ($1K to $5K per person)

NETWORKS FOR THE ESS

The decreasing cost and increasing power of computer and communications hardware have radically enlarged the spectrum of capabilities available to workstation users via local area networks (LANs). The question is no longer whether a workstation should be connected to a local area network, but what facilities should be provided by the LAN. Basically, there are two reasons to connect a workstation to a LAN: communications and resource sharing (with some overlap in the area of shared data).

"Mail" is the most obvious communication mechanism, but access to shared resources—such as to databases for program development or management information—is another. Resource sharing includes the sharing of scarce hardware resources such as document-quality printers, high-performance graphics workstations, high-speed disks, and powerful processors, and the sharing of scarce software resources such as large common databases.

The principal issue is the features that a LAN and its associated workstation hardware and software should provide. The workstation of the near future, hereafter referred to as the "1988 workstation," will be very powerful. The network to which it will be attached will have to provide short access times to support high peer-to-peer data rates, remote file access and remote execution capability, high availability and extensibility, software protection, data integrity, and gateways to other networks. Of these features, the most important to users is, and will continue to be, high-speed/low-density performance leading to high peer-to-peer (session-to-session) data transfer rates. Existing 10M-byte CSMA/CD (Ethernet), token ring, and token bus technology will need to be replaced by 50M- to 100M-byte high-speed LANs. There will also have to be greater use of multichannel broadband and fiberoptical technologies.

The 1988 workstation will have disks, but they will not have large enough capacity to store the programs and data required by many applications. Therefore, the LAN will need two or more high-volume, low-access-time file servers. In addition to providing a large common repository, these servers will offer other advantages. They will enable many file accesses normally done locally to be offloaded from the workstation. This will lead to a smaller local storage requirement for programs and tables. Moreover, the local processing overhead for these functions will be offloaded to the server. Finally, because it is cost-effective to provide the file server with a very fast disk, remote file access can actually be faster than local access to a less expensive, slower workstation disk.

For similar reasons, the LAN and workstation must provide remote execution capability along with command interpreter support. Remote file service and file execution must be supported in as "transparent" a manner as practicable. That is, the workstation user should not know or need to know the location of files that are accessed or programs that are executed.

NETWORKING REQUIREMENTS

Because of greater availability of low-cost networking hardware and advances in communications protocols, networking is beginning to receive much-needed attention. However, few networks have been implemented to date. Consequently, it is difficult to define detailed networking requirements because most potential users are not sure what features a good network should provide. Despite this low level of user experience, we can identify at least some desirable network features. Our list will undoubtedly change as more experience is obtained.

Low Cost Per Connection

The cost per connection to a network is decreasing. The connection cost, however, depends on the requirements the network has to meet. If the network must support many data types and high transmission rates, for example, it will require coaxial cable, which is more expensive. If the network is to be used in less demanding environments, however, it will need only twisted pair cabling (existing telephone lines), which is less expensive.

Flexibility

To date it has been difficult to develop plans for networks, because rapidly changing technology makes it almost impossible to specify future requirements. It may be impossible to know exactly what types of devices will be connected to a network, which types of data it will have to transmit, what distances it will have to span, and what types of applications it will have to support. Consequently, any network plan that is developed must be flexible.

Also, if one cannot determine which type of cabling will be best, then one should install the type of cable (possibly broadband) most likely to be able to accommodate all future network requirements.

Ease of Use

Few engineers know much about networking; therefore, ease of use is an important requirement. An engineer should not be required to understand

networking concepts. Ideally, he should be able to use a single, standard
set of commands for all networks. Furthermore, he should not be expected
to use any network unable to provide a response time of less than three
seconds.

Security

Security is very important, but very little progress has been made in
maintaining security in distributed systems. There are at least two security
concerns: security of databases and security of data during transmission
For the latter, encryption techniques are required. For distributed database security, other methodologies that are more difficult to develop and
implement are needed.

Standardization

There is an urgent need to develop standard protocols for networks. In
at least one instance, rapid progress is being made; the Manufacturing Automation Protocol is being developed and approved as an international standard.
This protocol is intended for networks used in the manufacturing environment. Ideally, we would like to see only one protocol developed for this
environment; realistically, we should expect no more than two or three.
The same type of effort should be made to develop a set of standards for
the office environment. Also, as mentioned above, the network commands
that the user is required to know should be standardized.

Bridges and Gateways

Because distance can never be completely overcome, standard bridges
between networks must be developed. Because we cannot expect there to
be only one networking protocol, we need to devise a standard gateway to
allow interfacing among protocols.

   We should note that the multitasking capability of the operating system
has a role in network use. Multitasking allows the operating system to
monitor network functions and provide services such as electronic mail
while the engineer is running application programs.

ENGINEERING/SCIENTIFIC DATABASE REQUIREMENTS

A controlled database is the most essential element in the proper implementation of CAE. Ideally, the CAE database is like a well-equipped library, except that only one copy of each piece of information exists (unless it is
copied as a read-only file to a local disk for faster access), changes are
tracked; access is controlled. This ensures that all users receive identical,
accurate, and up-to-date information.

   Without a controlled database, users are limited to three basic options
for updating design data: (1) They can make a copy of the file or substructure of interest and then modify the copy, (2) they can rename the
file or substructure, or (3) they can copy the existing data to another
medium (floppy disk or magnetic tape) and then keep track of it manually.

   These operations are limiting and time-consuming and require extensive
manual bookkeeping. Moreover, having "extra" backups actually generates

a false sense of security, since one's backup floppy or tape may contain inaccuracies. And since all data, data changes, updates, and locations must be kept track of, some sort of index—on cards or in a notebook— must be used. However, a paper index of tapes and floppies cannot really be said to be a computer-based system at all!

A database with fields to show the dates and times of additions and deletions and the commands or functions involved is a better way of using the real power of a computer. Consider the example of an automated pay- roll data file containing numerous updates on thousands of entries. The most commonly sought information will consist of items added or deleted during a particular time period. Getting this information will not be a problem, however, because the computer flags and tracks the additions and deletions.

Changes to engineering data can be similarly flagged and tracked. The equation $A - B + C = D$ can be used to explain the process. A is the previous file, B represents deletions, C represents additions, and D is the current file. Any modifications can be handled as deletions-plus-additions. If fields are included to show the particular command or function used to make the change, the user has a powerful, multilevel query capability with which he can find out what was changed, when it was changed, and perhaps even why it was changed. If necessary, he can then undo the change.

The value of having this capability cannot be overstated. An example shows why. Most graphics systems include an explode or smash function which removes a reference to a subfigure and inserts (as exploded data) the contents of the subfigure into the current drawing. The value of this function lies in the fact that it allows a designer to make one-of-a-kind modifications to a standard subfigure. The danger in using it is extreme, however—later edits to the base subfigure do not propagate through the hierarchy or to previous references. Usually there is not even a record of these previous usages. Thus, the designer must manually edit each previously exploded occurrence, if he is lucky enough to remember where each is.

Despite warnings to always be careful with explode, all too frequently it happens that the need to unexplode arises. An automated CAE data- base solves this problem by maintaining information on what was exploded, making it easy to undo the operation.

"What and when" information about major operations should also be in- cluded in the database. In electronic design work, for example, major tasks that should be recorded include generation of output magtapes for photo operations, design rule checks, layer sizing, shape emerging, model extraction, and wire-list extraction. And in all databases, a major book- keeping requirement is that any off-system backup copies that may have been generated (hopefully, in an incremental, changes-only mode) be tracked.

The existence of a small amount of "what and when" information in the add and delete fields has another useful function: it makes it easier to find out what changes have been made to data between two backups (or between any two points in time). It is not necessary to perform a global explode of hierarchical data and a total graphics exclusive—OR to locate the changes. In fact, changes expressed in hierarchical form are usually more valuable than changes expressed in global, exploded formats.

This compare feature is a basic requirement for analysis of engineer- ing data. Designs by their very nature require extensive editing, and sometimes a return to "the way it was when it last worked." If the computer does not or cannot properly track engineering change data, it will be more of a burden than a help.

The engineering/scientific database system, then, must support the following operations:

Comparisons of data to determine changes made between any two
   points in time or between any two (or more) operations
The undoing of functions (especially) those that are normally one-way
   functions) and the return of data to "the way it was"
Trial operations
Automated bookkeeping
Version control, without generation of multiple copies of files
Dual edits (by the system's graphics editor or by text edits)

STANDARDIZATION OF THE ESS

Standardization of the ESS is a highly desirable goal. Incompatible hardware and software among engineering support systems will lead to fragmentation. Users will have little equipment and few programs that are interchangeable. Second- and third-tier hardware and software vendors will not develop, and ESS users will not have the benefit of their products. Standard database and file interchange formats must be developed so that text, numeric data, drawings, and parts lists can be exchanged; otherwise, each ESS will be an island and data interchange will depend on custom format conversion programs.

Lack of standardization will result in dead-end hardware and software. New hardware and software will not be downward-compatible. New peripherals from an older ESS will not be usable on a newer one. A constant complaint heard from management is, "What will we do with it when the current job is over?" Without standards, software and hardware will not easily port to other engineering support systems or computer systems. Users must insist on standard interchange formats, as there is little other incentive for manufacturers to voluntarily agree on them.

A nearly universal complaint of users is that most ESS documentation is poor. The ESS is still undergoing rapid development and manufacturers do not have time to go back and repair old problems. They are too busy building the next module. Standardization can slow this process, allowing time for the software to mature and the documentation to be improved.

Some will argue that the imposition of standards will slow the development of the ESS or that it will result in inefficiencies in execution. These predictions may both prove true. But the benefits of standardization outweigh these disadvantages. How many users find themselves with a library filled with software written in a nonstandard programming language that will not compile or run on their new computer system?

A standard can develop in many ways:

A single, powerful vendor can set the standard (a de facto standard)
A customer large enough to dictate to manufacturers can simply de-
   clare the standard

Manufacturers can agree among themselves, as they did, for example,
   in the case of disk interfaces
A standards committee or professional society can set the standard

REAL-TIME COMPUTING AND THE ENGINEERING SUPPORT SYSTEM

A workstation for industrial real-time control can be characterized as a
workstation that is connected to one or more physical processes. These
processes can be continuous or discrete in nature, and may be associated
with laboratory analysis equipment, motors and mechanical devices, robotic
arms, manufacturing assembly lines, or chemical processing units. Specialized
hardware is required to interface the workstation to the sensors that measure process variables (much as temperature, pressure, and motor speed
and position) and to the actuators and other final control elements (such
as valves, pumps, power switches, and armature voltage controllers) that
manipulate the process. As a result, the activities or tasks that the workstation performs must take place concurrently and at regular intervals, and
satisfy constraints in real time.

These characteristics demand an operating system that is multitasking,
able to schedule and prioritize tasks; and able to do so in an environment
in which events occur in real time.

The real-time workstation usually is subject to demanding time constraints that span several orders of magnitude. Even recording and data
processing for servomotor control or flight system control may be required
every millisecond or so, whereas tasks involving changes in product demands, or material availability may be required only on a once daily basis.
Other time scales of interest fall within this range, from the time it takes
a mechanical arm to transfer a machine part from a conveyor to an assembly
point to the response times of large-capacity chemical processes.

A hierarchy of activities, from direct digital control of individual
process steps up to management decisions that are based on production
rates, raw material availability, and market demands, is performed by an
engineering support system made up of several real-time and non-real-time
workstations. (In such a system, it is implicit that the non-real-time workstations become dependent on the real-time activities.) A real-time workstation can be the kernel of CAM (computer-aided manufacturing) and CIM
(computer-integrated manufacturing) systems, which coordinate all phases
of production, from the scheduling of raw material and product delivery
to the monitoring, control, and coordination of each processing step occurring within the plant.

A configuration of hardware devices representing a distributed computer control system for factory automation includes a hierarchy of master
and slave units [17]. Manufacturing processes are interfaced to microprocessor-based slave devices that communicate with a workstation. The
slave devices perform A/D (analog-to-digital) and D/A (digital-to-analog)
conversion, signal processing, and periodic sampling of each process. The
workstations, or "masters," are networked to other real-time workstations,
and to a mainframe or computing engine. The workstation has both control
of and access to the physical plant environment, as well as access to the
central computer or computing engine that provides mass data storage,
high-speed number crunching for process simulation, and a window into
non-real-time workstation networks.

CURRENT PROBLEMS

In real-time computing, the lack of implemented standards, particularly software standards, continues to be a major problem. Hardware standards that focus on the specific computing equipment used to implement the workstation are not particularly important. Also, although there are no unique process input/output standards, this lack represents no great impediment to implementation. A variety of modular hardware permits process input and output signals to be converted to a form compatible with the computer I/O interface. For example, digital outputs from a process represented as contact closures (relay contacts closed) can be easily converted to transistor-transistor logic (TTL) level signals compatible with the computer I/O equipment. Similarly, analog process output signals can be converted from any one of several commonly used current (milliampere) ranges to an appropriate input level for the system's A/D converter.

The major impediments to the development of a generally applicable workstation lie in:

> The language suitable for real-time applications
> The lack of what might be called standard interfaces between the user
>   application area and its environment

In the former category, virtually every high-level language has been adapted at one time or another to real-time applications. There have been a relatively large number of applications of the BASIC language to real time; in the past, many commercial process control languages have been founded on BASIC and, more recently, many vendors of process I/O hardware for personnal microcomputers have supplied an extended version of BASIC with I/O drivers, some scheduling capabilities, and so forth. An attempt by the International Standards Organization (ISO) to standardize a real-time version of BASIC has been in progress for several years by the International Purdue Workshop.

Fortran represents one major success story in this area. Under the leadership of the International Purdue Workshop on Industrial Computer Systems, standards for an industrial real-time Fortran had already been adopted by the ISO in the mid-1970s [18,19]. These standards, based on the Fortran-1966 standard, have been replaced recently by the Industrial Real-Time Fortran, or IRTF, standard [20], which is based on the current Fortran-77. IRTF now appears close to adoption by the ISO as ISO/DP 7846. Much more will be said about these results later in this report.

Several other high-level languages have been extended to include real-time primitives, i.e., elementary I/O and scheduling functions. Pascal is available in this form from several commercial vendors, including Digital Equipment Corp. (DEC) and Oregon Software. Modula-2, a relatively new high-level language, contains some real-time capabilities as well.

Several new languages have been specifically written to handle real-time applications: PEARL, largely used in European industrial applications, and ADA developed recently under the auspices of the U.S. Department of Defense, are prime examples. Vaughn [21] gives brief descriptions of these languages and a historical perspective as part of an extended description of ADA. Finally, virtually every assembly language has been (or can be) used for real-time applications, as can be languages closely related to the assembly level, such as C and Forth.

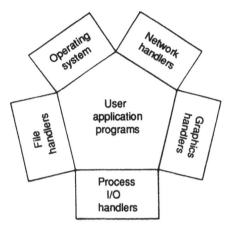

FIGURE 1 Interfaces between a user's application program and its environment.

However, to focus on the lack of nonstandard user application languages written or modified strictly for real-time purposes is to miss the key problems: the lack of a suitable model for programming real-time applications (a model that can deal with the natural parallelism in this area) and the lack of standardized interfaces to function between the user program and its environment. Figure 1 illustrates the situation with respect to interfaces.

The application program communicates exclusively with five system interfaces:

a. The operating system
b. Network handlers
c. Graphics handlers
d. File handlers
e. Process I/O handlers

If these interfaces can be "reasonably standardized," the problem of utilizing any application language will be greatly reduced. Notice that of these five software interfaces, three of them (b, c, and d) are required for any application program, and hence are not unique to real-time computing. The other two, the operating system and process I/O handler interfaces, are unique. Consequently, efforts now underway to standardize user interfaces for networks, graphics, and file handlers will benefit development of real-time workstations as well, and real-time users should concentrate on the development of interface standards suitable for the operating system and process I/O.

Within the improtant category of operating systems, one controversial attempt to standardize them—the IEE 855 Microprocessor Operating Systems Interface—is being made [22]. However, this proposed standard supplies only very primitive operators for real-time scheduling and a limited multiple task structure. Hence it offers few potential benefits to the real-time user. Although it is by no means a proposed standard, the rudimentary three-state multitasking system proposed by Heath [23] at least offers a framework for small-scale users to build on. However, it was not designed to furnish the full structure required by professional real-time system programmers. Fortunately, there is a better example of what is needed, namely the operating system interface and programming model proposed as part of the Industrial Real-Time Fortran standard. The IRTF approach is discussed in some detail in the next section as a potential general approach, one that points to a way out of the dilemma.

EXAMPLE OF A FIX: THE IRTF STANDARD

One proposed international standard for real-time extension of a general-purpose language already exists: the ISO/DP 7846i Draft Standard on Industrial Real-Time Fortran, termed IRTF for short [20]. It is expected that IRTF will become a fully accepted ISO standard in the near future, possibly in 1995.

IRTF presents a form of user interface to the operating system that also supports the important constructs of real-time multitask program execution, usually referred to as multitasking. In addition, it supplies process input/output references in the form of a set of standardized I/O calls (discussed below) along with a set of file references that eliminate (or adjudicate) contention for common bulk storage units. Since the file handling elements are similar to those used in non-real-time workstation environments, we will not discuss them further. Note that the importance and applicability of IRTF extend far beyond the Fortran language; in particular, the IRTF provisions for multitasking can be thought of as a possible model for the interface between any application language and any operating system that can support real-time multitask management.

Multitasking (or, equivalently, multitask programming) represents a way of dealing with computer processing applications that are inherently parallel in structure. Classical industrial examples are in the areas of data acquisition and control where many process elements must be observed, analyzed, and manipulated in parallel. Sometimes these operations must follow a strict progression that can be changed, however, by random process events. The idea of breaking down such complex operations into a set of single tasks, each of which can be written as a sequence of computer operations, is the essence of multitask programming. Whenever external process operations must follow a time schedule or whenever the user program must respond to process events within certain time limits (time constraints), we speak of real-time multitasking. Note that some operating systems, such as UNIX, support multitask applications but not real-time multitask applications.

Whether the multitasking is realtime or not, such software interface systems attempt to furnish the user with a high degree of parallel processing capability, and much flexibility, by separating user-related functionalities from the operating system's own handling of "internal resources"— in particular, from the allocation of the processor time during which the individual tasks are executed. Hence, the operating system interface consists, in part, of a definition of task states and specifies a scheduler that can take a given set of tasks (which have been previously prepared for execution) and allocate the system's resources to them on the basis of pre-established "rules."

The most important advantage of standardizing on a particular tasking model such as that of IRTF is that it then becomes possible to define a unified and complete set of tasking calls that can be used as the interface between any language and any operating system. Obviously, this statement implies some standardization of the stack structure used for call arguments along with an identification of the call and return address conventions.

Process I/O

Standardized calls are also needed to perform process I/O operations such as inputting measurement values from sensors and outputting control signals to actuators. Such signals may be in analog (continuous) or digital (discrete).

Although there may be arguments over the specific form of I/O calls, particularly in terms of large commercial systems with many I/O channels versus small research systems with smaller I/O facilities, the important point is that a standardized set of calls, regardless of form, will eliminate the confusion that presently exists in dealing with different hardware systems.

CONSEQUENCES OF ADOPTING STANDARDS SUCH AS IRTF

A real-time workstation is typically used to support the following real-time multitask operations:

Gathering data from a process
Performing computations and logical decisions
Outputting the results to the process in the form of control inputs
Communicating with users, operators, and supervisors
Providing a variety of graphical outputs
Sending standardized files or messages over a communications network

Furthermore, a real-time workstation should support the development and debugging of application programs.

Adoption of the IRTF standard would have several consequences for these activities. Difficult comparisons of alternative engineering workstations could be largely avoided. Real-time workstation development and modification would be simplified: real-time systems would be easier to document and easier to operate.

A user of a standardized real-time multitasking workstation will encounter networking, graphics, and file-handling standards in other professional activities. The real-time capabilities are likely to be added to, or be a subset of, an existing standard engineering workstation.

In selecting a real-time workstation, the engineer requires only a computer with processing power to migrate to improved performance while maintaining user interface and multitask standardization. The processor probably should be one of the primary de facto standard devices that have become the basis for significant hardware and software developments and improvements in the computer industry; in other words, it should be a member of a successful family of microprocessors.

Signal conditioning modules should be readily available for such de facto standard machines; note, for example, the large number of data acquisition boards that plug into the IBM PC bus. More generally, front-end interfaces that communicate through laboratory RS-232 or IEEE 488 communication ports will be available. As standards become adopted for the hardware components of the real-time workstation, the user will be able to easily configure a system that can satisfy a project's real-time needs for process input/output.

Third-party documentation of real-time applications, analogous to the texts describing spreadsheet and word processing programs on the market today, will appear. The real-time user will need a large third-party software base, including specialized software for real-time applications. (The Laboratory Notebook for the IBM PC represents a good, early example.) Greater emphasis on short courses and self-teaching tutorial material will also result from standardization. Capabilities gained from progress with artificial intelligence and expert systems will be applied to documentation and to self-teaching media. Modern techniques of data input (menus, queries, icons, etc.) will facilitate users learning how to use real-time application programs. Standard approaches such as IRTF may become easier for users to become familiar with because of their economy of concepts and generality.

A manufacturer who is a user or vendor of real-time systems will be able to rely on standard third-party systems, third-party documentation, and growing familiarity with the standards. Greater public knowledge of real-time systems will lead to a decreased tendency for users to be forced into dependence on proprietary (secret) systems. The user of real-time systems will no longer be a captive of a single manufacturer, and hence will not be forced to accept the inadequate software that is so typical of a captive market. Real-time software development and modification by a co-ordinated group of engineers will be much easier to accomplish with a standard such as IRTF.

RELATION OF THE ESS TO THE GENERAL COMPUTER FACILITY

Many organizations will continue to maintain a central computing operation whose role will be substantially expanded to support large-scale use of the ESS. The lowest level of such support involves the purchasing, installation, and maintenance of the ESS. Centralized control is essential not only for the management and operation of networks and intermachine interfaces, but also for high-level programming support of debugging activities; i.e., detecting bugs in both operating systems and utilities, reporting bugs to the appropriate vendors, and following up after the installation of each fix. These are not trivial tasks, and they may force a drastic change in the central organization's support procedures. At the next higher level, the central organization should provide services to assist engineering personnel to perform functions essential to the organization but not perceived as a part of the engineer's primary responsibility. A final, and critical, service of the central organization is to maintain (or at least provide access to) appropriate supercomputer systems to support large number-crunching tasks.

A major obstacle to complete integration of the ESS into the central facility has been the reluctance of some computing center managers to recognize the usefulness of ESS-like systems to the practicing engineer. We feel that the tendency to dismiss such systems either as "toys" or as competition for resources is waning, but that vigorous support from higher

TABLE 1 Estimated Hardware Costs of an ESS for a Secretary,
a Manager, a Low-Level Engineer, and a High-Level Engineer

Microcomputer, IBM PC/XT	$5,500
Monochrome monitor and interface	850
Modem	850
Letter-quality printer (1/3 of the cost)	800
Hardware subtotal for secretary	$7,750
High-resolution color display	$2,500
Color monitor	1,000
Low-quality color printer	600
Hardware subtotal for manager	$11,850
Memory expansion to 1M byte	1,000
Tablet	1,000
Mouse	250
Light pen	100
Additional features (unspecified here)	800
Hardware subtotal for low-level engineer	$15,000
Full-size, flat-plate electroluminescent display (36" by 48") and additional features (unspecified here)	3,000
Hardware subtotal for high-level engineer	$18,000

management is still needed to ensure cooperation. It is essential to recognize that correctly designed and configured ESS facilities complement the central organization and enhance overall productivity.

PERCEIVED OBSTACLES TO MEETING ESS USER NEEDS

Belief That an ESS is Too Expensive

Objections have been voiced that our model ESS with its standard, integrated hardware and software is too expensive. Our estimated costs for an ESS with various hardware and software illustrate the inaccuracy of this argument. Our estimates are based on an IBM PC/XT-based configuration for several user classes. Subtotals have been identified for four different categories of users, starting with a secretary and proceeding through a manager, a low-level engineer, and a high-level engineer (see Tables 1, 2, and 3). It is assumed that the more demanding categories require all the equipment of the preceding category plus some additional equipment.

Prices for personal computer operating systems and utilities have stabilized at $750 or less; further significant price erosion cannot be expected. The integration of utility programs into application programs, as

TABLE 2   Estimated Software Costs of an ESS for a Secretary,
a Manager, a Low-Level Engineer, and a High-Level Engineer

Operating systems	$300
Word processor	500
Software subtotal for secretary	$800
Database management software	$1,500
Graphics interface	500
Software subtotal for manager	$2,800
Drafting software	$1,500
Spreadsheet (integrated package)	500
Projector scheduler	500
High-quality accounting software	1,000
Software subtotal for low-level engineer	$6,300
Printed-circuit design software	$1,500 to $15,000
Software subtotal for high-level engineer	$7,800 to $21,300

done in Lotus 1-2-3 and Symphony, should continue. Bundling should reduce software costs to 25 percent of the prices shown in Table 3. Application programs are less expensive than their counterparts on mainframes, and their price should drop significantly if a broad user base is developed (something not always possible in specialized engineering areas). Consider the following software costs for an IBM PC/XT configuration.

Depending on the user and the application, software costs range from $800 for an ESS that is targeted to secretaries, to $2,800 for one aimed at managers, to between $7,800 and $21,300 for one for high-level engineers. The wide range for high-level engineers reflects their varying needs for application-specific packages.

It can be seen that the hardware costs for an initial version of our ESS—one based on the IBM PC/XT—are reasonable. Although a PC/XT

TABLE 3   Total Estimated Costs of an ESS for a Secretary,
a Manager, a Low-Level Engineer, and a High-Level Engineer

	Hardware	Software	Total
Secretary	$ 7,750	$ 800	$ 8,550
Manager	11,850	2,800	14,650
Low-level engineer	15,000	6,300	21,300
High-level engineer	18,000	7800–21,300	25,800–39,300

does not have the resolution, processing speed, or networking capabilities of a more powerful workstation such as the Apollo DN300 [24] or Sun Microsystems Sun-2 [25], its price per node, as computed above, is representative of the cost of these systems without extensive software packages. In addition, in the future, PC/XT-based workstations can be expected to offer greater performance for a given price. Costs are also reasonable for low-level ESS applications software, but may become prohibitive for specialized applications software. An optimist would suggest that costs will decline, as they have for most other software.

The expense of the workstation correlates to the level of user expertise. The capital investment tends to match the investment in personnel.

Design Obsolescences

The rapid advances in technology in the computer and communications industries, which have been driven by the "silicon revolution," plus the advances in magnetic technology tend to make ESSs obsolete almost before they reach the market. The rate of change has been greatest in microprocessors, memories, and disk drives. To slow ESS obsolescence, it is necessary to stabilize hardware and software design in the areas that are changing more slowly, and allow for upward compatibility in the areas that are changing more rapidly. Planned product introduction, transparent network components, and generation of and support for standards by professional and internationally recognized organizations are other ways to combat early obsolescence of ESSs.

Stable Hardware and Software Designs

Existing de facto hardware and software standards include the following:

> The S-100 systems currently supplied with 8-inch disk drives; these systems can handle most software and can be configured with over 800 different boards. They are mainly CP/M systems; hence, the extensive CP/M users' library is an important asset.
> The IBM PC: wide distribution and a familiar name are the PC's main assets; they protect it from early obsolescence.
> The UNIX operating system is becoming a de facto standard ESS operating system [12—14]

Planned Product Introduction

The early announcement of new products—possibly through a newsletter or an electronic bulletin board sponsored by an ESS user group or an IEEE committee—could simplify the evaluation of such products and provide a beacon for future direction. The early sales of engineering support systems would be the motivation for manufacturer compliance.

Transparent network components. Many useful schemes for interchangeable or transparent network components are, or will soon be, available. ISO OSI protocols and IEEE 802 standards should be assessed. Fiber optic-based local area networks have very attractive features (e.g., low cost, light weight, isolation, and low noise and RFI interference).

Standards and Review Organizations

IEEE, ACM, and ISO should support ESS standards and review ESS functions. The market is so vast and immediate that professional users could well benefit from such activities. Automatic bugs or needs reports, sent in regularly to a review organization, would be of great benefit.

RESULTS OF NOT MEETING ESS USER NEEDS

The absence of well-integrated ESSs, caused by the proliferation of hardware, operating systems, and applications software, is a major source of user anger and frustration. The dearth of well-designed and equipped engineering support systems in industry is the result of a biased and unreasonable trade-off between cost-effectiveness and capital investment on one hand and the productivity and well-being of the engineering staff on the other. Companies pay $600 for a typewriter and $50,000 per year (including overhead) for a secretary who is assigned to an engineer. A one-time investment of $25,000 will supply the engineer with an ESS and reduce his need for the secretary and the typewriter. This investment will also eliminate or reduce drafting costs and result in a faster response to engineering tasks. A local area network and an electronic mail system will allow the engineer to more easily maintain control of team efforts. Large companies maintain that this shift of expertise (secretarial, drafting, design, etc.) to the engineer will require him to be given specialized training. The cost of such training is difficult to capitalize, and the investment is lost if the engineer leaves the company. However, these companies must realize that if their engineers are not provided with an ESS, they will be lured away to competing companies offering such a tool.

Small companies are already investing in "turnkey" application systems that are the closest approximations to an ideal ESS now available. These companies have found that the use of interactive design and management tools results in products reaching the marketplace six months to a year ahead of their competition.

A few numbers taken from Schell [26], who discusses computer-aided very large-scale integrated (VLSI) design, point out the advantage of investing in an ESS. Product complexity is increasing by a factor of four every three years. Even with the latest ESSs and the latest CAD tools and techniques to increase the number of "drawn transistors," worker productivity is growing only by a factor of two every three years—half the needed rate. Even so, when we consider that the typical VLSI device takes six months to get to market and becomes obsolete in three to four years, supplying an engineer with an ESS and training him to use it seem mandatory.

The engineers who are valued for their creative ability and expertise will be the first to see the professional benefits of a job change. If large companies are to stem a tide of departing talent, they will be forced to provide better design tools, namely an ESS.

Poor documentation and training are other areas that engender frustration. All too often training is limited to supplying documentation that is cryptic, that describes a previous release or another version, or they may be inaccurate. The user is left with trial and error, a notoriously inefficient learning tool. Autoinstructional diskettes and videotaped lectures are acceptable substitutes for expensive training classes.

THE CONTROVERSY OVER PROVIDING ESSs

Even in the face of the advantages cited, some still question the merits of engineering support systems. In particular, the following questions persist:

Is there really a need for the ESS?
Is the ESS worth the inherent problems?

In other words, do the benefits of increased engineer productivity outweigh the costs associated with acquiring, using, and maintaining an ESS? Of even more importance, are there any significant increases in productivity achieved by setting up an ESS in an engineering organization?

In reality, much of the controversy is a disagreement about the value of an individual's time. Large corporations tend to devalue an individual's time (be it managerial, engineering, or clerical), but smaller companies (with fewer people per task type) tend to place a higher value on the individual's time. In larger companies, the "capitalization" per employee (the amount of money per employee workplace) is traded off against employee salary. For example, if an employee works at 50% efficiency without an ESS as compared with the efficiency he or she would have with one, the cost of the workstation is equal to three years' salary. Hence, the company may view the purchase of an ESS as unattractive. Moreover, some argue that training people to use an ESS is time-consuming and expensive, gives trained employees better leverage when they bargain for higher wages and improved working conditions, and may result in higher turnover as other companies seek the trained individuals.

Furthermore, larger companies often have a large computer center oriented toward maintaining its size, influence, and centralized service. This may create a bias in the company against the decentralized computing power typified by an ESS.

In smaller engineering companies and in educational institutions, where an engineer's or educator's time and productivity are precious resources, this controversy tends to be viewed differently. The improved interpersonal communication, the availability of resources, the ability to share resources, the text-processing capability, the system extensibility, and the advantages of a shared database are seen as desirable.

In addition, the human factor must be considered. Enhancing and extending an engineer's abilities by supplementing them with the capabilities of an engineering support system allows more productivity which leads to a greater feeling of self-fulfillment.

In summary, there appears to be no doubt that use of the power made available by advancing computer technology (here, the emerging engineering support systems) can lead to improved profits for industry and increased output and satisfaction for engineers.

CONCLUSIONS

Engineering workstations, or engineering support systems, are needed because of the increasing complexity of the design process, competitive pressures from abroad and from within the country, and the increasing difficulty of meeting user needs through centralized computer processing installations.

The increased complexity of the engineering process is reflected in the increased complexity of the task of managing engineers and engineering work. Traditional management functions are not eased by the new technology, and, in fact, communications problems are often aggravated by an engineering support system. The introduction of workstations may lead to changes in traditional forms of company organization; for example, there may be a change from a hierarchical organization to a matrix one, a shift which will impose new problems on engineering managers as well as on working engineers. In addition, the sense of greater personal freedom provided by an engineering support system may conflict with the larger goals of the enterprise.

The solution to these difficulties is to use the technology itself to alleviate the problems it has caused. Managers must adopt the workstation to help themselves cope with the problems it has introduced.

The users of an engineering support system are, and will continue to be, demanding. The proliferation of available computing hardware and software has greatly enhanced the productive potential of the individuals within an organization. Engineering support systems do exist and can be constructed from readily available components at moderate cost. However, ESSs are highly diversified, and they have been produced at a rapid and undirected pace. This has caused the growth and development of these systems to become bottlenecked.

The use of standard microprocessor families will allow upward migration to faster speeds, greater processing power, and more complex task handling. Faster semiconductor technologies, e.g., gallium arsenide technologies, could result in a 100-fold increase in computing speeds. Multiprocessing, incorporating multiple slave processors that operate under a real-time workstation, will permit tasks to execute truly in parallel. Vendor independence will be enhanced because process I/O hardware will function as groups of standard operations.

There are two fundamental questions that must be asked about real-time computing:

What is the potential scope and importance of real-time multitasking approaches in industry?

If a standardized approach to real-time multitasking systems could be used over a substantial portion of the time scales that are commonly encountered, how pervasive would the standard become?

A standardized approach to real-time multitasking systems such as that of IRTF may lead to both general and specialized applications. Standardization leads to mass markets and to commercial incentives to build systems in silicon, namely, silicon engines that may function as real-time coprocessors. Real-time task primitives implemented in silicon may increase the speed of execution by a factor of 1,000 or more over traditional high-level software, and may have a beneficial and perhaps unforeseen impact in industry; for example, the need to deal with interrupts at the assembly language level, as in present-day high-speed control systems such as flight control systems, may be completely eliminated. This step alone could increase the potential market of a standard real-time workstation greatly.

In short, standardized concepts, approaches, and products would augment the ability of the engineer to conceive and implement new real-time multitasking applications.

A study of the brief history of engineering workstations shows that the early requirements for success were:

A multitasking, virtual-memory operating system
Sufficient CPU power
Massive memory (disk and semiconductor)
Interactive graphics software interfaced to fast raster graphics displays

The future requirements for successful ESSs include:

Greater standardization of workstation components
More effort to make systems extensible
Better on-line training and help facilities
The availability of effective, low-cost, high-speed networks
The development of controlled scientific engineering databases

These are the steps to higher performance, lower costs, and wider acceptance throughout the design engineering community.

REFERENCES

1. L. Gomes, "Networks of Networks at Gandalf Technologies," *Solutions*, (published by Intel Corp., Santa Clara, CA), March/April (1984).
2. S. Yalamanchili, M. Malek, and J. K. Aggarwal, "Workstations in a Local Area Network Environment," *Computer*, November (1984).
3. P. L. Asmus, "Engineering Workstations—A New Approach to Engineering," presented at the Second Phoenix Conf. on Computers and Communications, March 1983.
4. R. Dhar, "A System Integrator's Guide to Selecting CAE Workstations," Mini-Micro Systems, March (1984).
5. E. Freeman, "Computer-Aided Engineering/Design Workstations," *Elec. Des. News*, May 30 (1985).
6. L. Holland, "Future Applications of a Full Capability Engineering Work Station," presented at Wescon 1982.
7. T. N. Pyke, Jr., "Assuring User Service Quality in a Distributed Computer Network," *Dig. Papers*, Compcon (1976).
8. H. J. Hinden, "Revolution Brewing in Workstation Technology," *Comput. Des.*, January (1985).
9. T. Minot, "Workstation Moves in on Mainframes, Tackling Hefty Gate Arrays," *Electr. Des.*, March 7 (1985).
10. N. Mokhoff, "Complete Systems Now Possible with 32-bit Chip Sets," *Comput. Des.*, July 1 (1985).
11. D. O. Knight, presentation at First Engineering Support System Workshop, held at College of Engineering and Applied Sciences, Arizona State University, Tempe, April 1984.
12. W. Joy, "UNIX in a Network of Personal Workstations," *Proc. Compcon*, Spring (1984).
13. M. Dubrall, "UNIX State of the Art," panel presentation at National Computer Conference, July 1984.

14. J. R. Goff, "UNIX Established a Growth Pattern," *Mini-Micro Sys.*, June (1984).

15. D. R. Cheriton and W. Zwaenepoel, "The Distributed V Kernel and Its Performance for Diskless Workstations," Proc. 9th ACM Symp. on Operating Systems Principles, October 1983.

16. W. Joy, "UNIX State of the Art," panel presentation at National Computer Conference, July 1984.

17. N. Komoda, K. Kera, and T. Kubo, "An Autonomous, Decentralized, Control System for Factory Automation," *IEEE Comput.*, December, 73–83 (1984).

18. ANS/ISA s61.1 (1976) Standard, Industrial Computer System FORTRAN Procedures for Executive Functions, Process Input-Output, and Bit Manipulation, Instrument Society of America 1976.

19. ANS/ISA s61.1 (1976) Standard, Industrial Computer System FORTRAN Procedures for File Access and the Control of File Contention, Instrument Society of America 1978.

20. Draft Standard. Industrial Real-Time FORTRAN. International Purdue Workshop, IPW/EWICS TC 1, 1/82, ISO/DP 7846 August 1982.

21. W. C. M. Vaughn, "Application of the ADA Language to Process Control," in *Chemical Process Control 2* (D. E. Seborg and T. F. Edgar, Eds.), American Institute of Chemical Engineers, New York, 1982, pp. 71–89.

22. D. L. Jackson and J. Cowan, "The Proposed IEEE 855 Microprocessor Operating Systems Interface Standard," *IEEE MICRO*, August, 63–71 (1984).

23. W. S. Heath, "A System Executive for Real-Time Microcomputer Pro Pro[Dams," *IEEE MICRO*, June, 20–32 (1984).

24. P. J. Leach et al., "The Architecture of an Integrated Local Network," *IEEE J. Selected Areas Commun.*, November (1983).

25. B. Mackinlay, "The Sun-2 Workstation," UNIX World, October (1984).

26. R. M. Schell, "The VLSI Complexity Crisis," *Solutions* (published by Intel Corp., Santa Clara, CA), March/April (1984).

27. F. A. Putnam, "New Software Tool Extends 'Lotus 1 2 3' to Handle R&D Data," *Res. Dev.*, October, 154–157 (1984).

DONALD O. KNIGHT

ENHANCED GRAPHICS: MOLECULAR MODELING*

INTRODUCTION

Molecules are the basic building blocks of all matter. Under certain circumstances they may react with each other to form new compounds. The new compound most likely will have different properties when compared with the original molecules. A detailed understanding of and control over such chemical reactions have led to a large number of manmade products that today form an integral part of our daily life. For more than a century scientists have been able to deduce the basic composition of the molecules, i.e., how the atoms were interconnected. In some cases, they even had a good understanding of the three-dimensional structure.

In nature we find a vast range of highly complex molecules such as proteins, nucleic acids, and carbohydrates. Most of these molecules perform a specific function in the living organism, without which the organism often cannot exist. Until a few decades ago, the structure of those molecules eluded biochemists, resulting in a very rudimentary understanding of why these molecules function the way they do.

In the 1950s the science of x-ray diffraction studies of target molecules started to develop rapidly, leading to the ability to construct complete three-dimensional prototype structures of proteins. Suddenly, it became possible to study minute structural details that had been completely inaccessible to scientists. In the early days of this epoch, the only way to visualize these wonderful results was to build huge models of the proteins based on x-ray data. This process was a cumbersome and time-consuming effort, often necessitating many months of work.

It was soon evident that computers and fast graphical displays had a vast potential for visualization of such molecules.

Molecular Modeling as a Tool

The molecules of major interest in medical, biological, and biotechnological research are complex macromolecules, and to facilitate the progress of the research requires viewing the molecules from various angles, for looking at special parts of the molecules, and for modifying the presentation of the molecules. This cannot be accomplished without the assistance of computers.

---

*It should be noted that the information given in this article may not be complete or even strictly correct in *all* circumstances and that it may be necessary to modify, correct, or supplement the information depending on the actual circumstances. It should likewise be noted that the products referenced in this article are mentioned for informational purposes only. Other suitable products are available in addition to those listed. Neither the authors nor the publisher endorse the purchase of specific listed products, nor can they be held responsible for errors.

Molecular modeling has the potential of substituting for time-consuming and expensive laboratory research and tests in industry, thereby reducing the costs for development of new and improved products. More complete insight into and understanding of the structure of molecules obtained by three-dimensional presentations on the computer screen gives the pharmaceutical industry the opportunity to develop useful new drugs, and in the biochemical industry, it contributes, for instance, to the development of more efficient, more specific, and more stable enzymes for applications in both industry and households.

Molecular modeling may show how to build a drug that fits more precisely to the receptor (Fig. 1) which is the target of the medication, to increase the specificity, or to modify a hormone in such a way that a more soluble product is obtained which is more readily absorbed by the body.

One class of molecules which is important in the biochemical industry is the enzymes. Enzymes are proteins that catalyze specific biochemical reactions. Some may break down starches into smaller molecules, which can be utilized in fermentations to produce alcohol, organic acids etc., others may be incorporated into washing powders to break down proteins on soiled clothing so that the dirt bound by the protein is detached from the fibers of the textile and effectively removed.

The three-dimensional structure of an enzyme is crucial for the specific action of the enzyme on the target molecule (Fig. 2). By studying this structure displayed by the computer, possible inhibiting effects of various substances may be examined. Furthermore, it may inspire the research

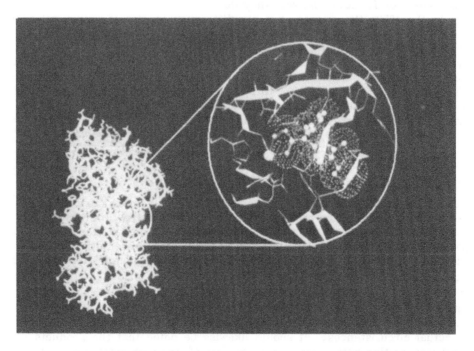

FIGURE 1   The protein thermolysin with hydroxamic acid inhibitor, showing detail of the active site, modeled using Chem-X and photographed from a Sigmex 6264 graphics terminal. (Photo courtesy of Chemical Design Ltd.)

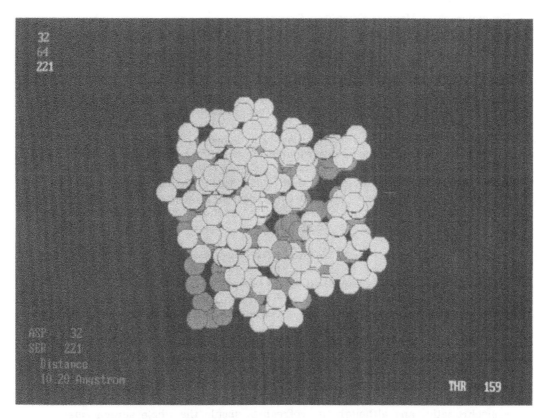

FIGURE 2 A DIST3D space-filling presentation showing the active cleft of a proteolytic enzyme from *Bacillus subtilis*.

chemist to design a modified enzyme with improved specificity or with increased stability in relation to temperature, specific chemicals, or to highly alkaline or acidic conditions.

The transformation of the design into actual molecules of the modified enzyme, which can be examined, requires of course a modification of the microorganism, or more precisely, the gene, which produces the native enzyme. And here is the most fascinating aspect of molecular biology and probably the background for the recent increased interest in molecular modeling of proteins.

In the course of this article we will show how the use of computers has led to new models or representations of molecules, and how new methods of interacting with these models have been developed. The type and size of molecules under study and the questions to be answered will dictate the approaches to be taken; inasmuch as the whole field is rapidly developing there is no way of providing comprehensive coverage of the topic within the limits of this encyclopedia. Rather, we will try to identify the general principles and then exemplify in the field of particular interest to the present authors, namely biochemistry and protein chemistry.

Development of Modern Computer Graphics

Molecular modeling on computers requires powerful multicolor computer graphics to be an efficient tool for the modeler. Today rather powerful systems for computer color graphics are available at prices so low that they were unthinkable only a few years ago. How is this possible?

Three main components constitute the modern color graphics computer system: the computer, the display controller, and the display itself. The development of the first two components is based on the technology of the integrated circuit whereas the display has its own specific technology.

Until now, the only device capable of displaying complicated color graphics fast enough was the cathode-ray tube (CRT), which also is the most prominent component of TV sets. The light-emitting particles in the display surface or screens of such CRTs emit light when they are hit by the electron beam, but only a fraction of a second later, the light emission of the particle will terminate when the energy absorbed from the beam has been re-emitted.

Consequently, adequate amounts of energy must, at short intervals, be supplied to the particles to maintain the image drawn by the electron beam. This refresh may be accomplished either by simply redrawing the image or by exposing all particles to an equally distributed flood of low-velocity electrons with an energy sufficient to maintain the emission from the light-emitting particles, but insufficient to get the other particles to emit light.

The latter principle is used in the direct view storage tube (DVST), which a decade ago was very much appreciated for displaying of graphs and for computer-assisted design (CAD) with very high resolution. A useful property of this display type is that the refresh of even the most detailed graph requires no memory, but the disadvantages are that the display is monochromatic, and although the refresh is simple the whole screen must nevertheless be erased and the image completely redrawn to make even the smallest correction.

A much more convenient display type, the vector display, was developed in the mid-1960s, strangely enough a few years before the DVST appeared. In the vector display, the image consists of a number of lines or vectors drawn by the electron beam, which is extinguished between the end of one line and the start of the next (move command). The image is generated under control of the display processor and the display buffer which contains the data as well as the commands (the program) necessary to draw the image. The display processor loops through the program to refresh the image. The refresh or display buffer of this type of display requires only a modest amount of memory, which was a very expensive commodity in the mid-1960s, but nevertheless the vector display was and is relatively expensive because the refresh demands a fast display processor, and even then flicker occurs when comprehensive images are refreshed.

The raster scan display was originally developed for use in television, in which color and intensity of all points on the screen must be specified. In television this is not a problem because the continuous flow of data is provided by a synchronous scanning of the corresponding points of the object. But when the raster scan display is used for computer graphics, all display data have to reside in the refresh buffer, and that requires substantial amounts of memory, especially in color graphics. The mass production of very large-scale integrated (VLSI) dynamic random-access memory (RAM) modules has made the application of the raster scan display for high-resolution computer graphics more attractive.

Earlier, when memory modules were much more expensive, computer users had to be satisfied with a restricted resolution and a limited range of colors in the palette. However, lately we have experienced a rapid increase in display bandwidth and scan frequency of raster scan displays and a corresponding increase in screen resolution with a parallel increase in the number of colors in the palette, which of course requires a tremendous amount of memory in the screen buffer(s). We are now talking of megabytes rather than of kilobytes. The vector graphics adapter (VGA) color graphics in resolution 640 × 480 pixels with 16 colors and two screen buffers (active and visual page) already requires 300 kb, and a resolution of 1024 × 768 pixels with 256 colors (8-bit planes) and two buffers require 1.5 Mbytes.

The rapid progress in large-scale integration, which brought large screen buffers within reach economically also made possible the design of fast processors for data processing as well as for high-resolution, multicolor image processing. It further established the basis for the application of a limited selection of processor types in a variety of designs of computer architecture, a standardization which provided the relatively inexpensive, powerful, and reliable hardware required for high-quality computer graphics.

The Age of the Personal Microcomputer

The breakthrough of the personal computer concept has accelerated the scientific applications of microcomputers and probably scientific computations in general as well. Applications which only a decade ago had to be processed on minicomputers or mainframes may today be executed on a high-performance microcomputer thereby avoiding the long turnaround times of typical computer departments.

The general acceptance of the main features of the concept and increased competition resulted in considerably reduced prices, which in concert with a rapid increase in performance matching extensive demands for fast and convenient data processing has made the personal computer a standard tool in scientific laboratories and in the research and development departments of the industry.

Contributing to this situation is the fact that the range of applications of the personal microcomputer has widened considerably, thanks to enhancement of the graphics capability whereby the needs for graphical presentations, especially in molecular modeling as well as in various design applications, have been met.

The performance of color displays has so improved in the last few years that moderately priced color displays today have a dot pitch of about 0.3 mm and a screen resolution of 640 × 480 pixels, a level which was regarded as professional only 5 years ago. Furthermore, modern multisync monitors are adaptable to a wide range of resolution standards.

With the current state of analog color displays it is possible to present a wide range of colors, and the memory necessary to obtain a palette of 256 simultaneous colors is available at a reasonable price.

MOLECULAR MODELING

In order to display a two- or three-dimensional atomic model of a molecule the three-dimensional coordinates (x, y, and z) for each atom are required, either explicitly or implicitly, for example, in the so-called Z matrix which gives a distance, an angle, and a dihedral angle for each atom relative to the preceding atom according to some sorted order.   In general, one needs at least 3N-6 independent coordinates to specify the relative positions, i.e., the structure of N atoms.   The distance matrix (see later) is another, over-determined way of specifying the same information.

Additionally, one may need information about atom types, connectivity, electron densities, and so on.   In some cases, these extra data may be derived from the coordinates.

The atomic coordinates may be obtained in various ways.   One way of obtaining approximate atomic coordinates, which is particularly useful if the molecule in question is small and simple (Fig. 3), is to calculate the positions of the atoms of the molecule from reference values of the bonding radii and bond angles of the elements constituting the molecule.   These reference values may be found in the literature or, as in the case of some commercially available modeling programs, in computer-readable datafiles.

It is, however, uncertain to what extent the model you build in some way will correspond to the structure of the real molecule.   For instance, it may be possible by rotation around a single bond to change the position of a specific group of atoms in regard to the remaining part of the molecule, but it is not possible to say which of the possible orientations will

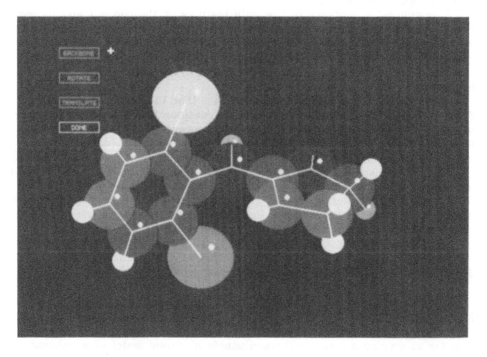

FIGURE 3   A PC-Chemmod spacefill display of Clonidin.   (Photo courtesy of U-Microcomputers Limited.)

be the one assumed by the group in the real molecule. Molecules are flexible, there is, in general, no single structure which can be considered the correct one.

This is particularly important for large molecules where many degrees of freedom (e.g., rotation around single bonds) result in a multitude of possible spatial structures.

Consider as an example a protein containing 200 bonds, about each of which there are some three rotational states of significance. The number of possible three-dimensional structures is three to the power of 200. This number is so large that it totally excludes the possibility of an exhaustive computer analysis in the forseeable future.

In such cases, experimental data (e.g., spectroscopic) may provide information on the positions of the atoms in the actual structure of the molecule. This is particularly true of proteins where the folding of the long chains of amino acids into a three-dimensional arrangement takes place in a poorly understood and hence unpredictable manner.

As a consequence, it is of the utmost importance to the understanding of the properties of the molecules to be able to visualize the structure in three dimensions.

Experimentally Obtained 3-D Coordinates

There are various experimental techniques that lead to information about the three-dimensional molecular structure.

Diffraction Techniques

Probably the most widely used method of obtaining detailed information about atomic positions in a molecule is that of x-ray crystal diffraction. This, in short, entails an analysis of crystals containing many identical molecules arranged in a lattice. X-rays of well-defined wavelength are diffracted off the crystal and their intensity is recorded. An often lengthy and seldom straightforward analysis of a large amount of such records eventually may lead to a complete set of x, y, z coordinates for every single atom that interfered measurably with the x-rays.

From high-quality data on small molecules, the precision in positions may be better than 0.001 Angstrom, whereas for larger molecules such as proteins it may be worse than 0.1 Å and the hydrogen atoms will mostly be invisible as will solvent molecules. In addition to the three positional parameters, there will often be one or more describing the thermal motion of each atom. Again, these parameters will be more poorly determined for larger molecules.

Generally, crystallographic data are published in scientific journals. Furthermore, the atomic data will be deposited in data banks. Small, organic, and organometallic structures are collected by the Cambridge structural database [1], inorganic structures in the inorganic crystallographic database [2], and large protein and nucleic acid structures are deposited in the Brookhaven Protein Data Bank [3].

Other diffraction techniques include neutron diffraction from crystals, which is comparable to x-ray diffraction, only more difficult experimentally, but it does provide better information on hydrogen atoms. Gas-phase electron diffraction has been used in the past to study volatile compounds. It has the advantage of providing information about isolated molecules, rather than in a crystal packing environment, but the accuracy is poor for all but the smallest molecules. There is no data depository.

Spectroscopic Techniques

The most important spectroscopic method is undoubtedly nuclear magnetic resonance (NMR), which is capable of giving three-dimensional information as well, but this method relies on a quite different physical principle. NMR is excellent for observing the hydrogen atoms in the molecules, and the method is capable of giving information about distances between different hydrogen atoms in the molecule. Such information has been used for determining the structure of a large number of smaller molecules as well as a growing number of smaller protein molecules. A data depository or database for these structure determinations does not exist, although one was recently proposed [4].

Mostly, the technique is applicable to molecules in rather concentrated solutions, but solid-state techniques also exist. In some cases data have been obtained about dynamic phenomena, e.g., determining kinetic and energetic parameters of structural changes.

Other spectroscopic techniques include microwave spectroscopy which only applies to small molecules in the gas phase, but then can provide highly accurate data, and infrared and Raman spectroscopy, which can be applied to liquid and solid samples. The two latter techniques are sources of vibrational data and may also provide information about energy barriers to rotation of atomic groups.

Predicting Molecular Structures

Most likely, the very molecule that you would like to work on has never been solved structurally. As mentioned before, there is one way to start doing some modeling; building the molecule from known distances and angles. This is rather tedious and results are inaccurate, particularly for larger molecules.

In order to improve the reliability one may refine the first, rough structure by various computational procedures. Molecular mechanics can optimize the positions of the atoms according to some model function, typically the strain energy. This energy function expresses the total energy of the molecule in terms of bond distances, angles, and other types of atom interactions such as electrostatic interactions. The energy function is empirical in nature, but often sufficiently accurate to provide a reasonable structure prediction.

The method may be enhanced by what is called molecular dynamics which allows for more elaborate searching of the available conformational space than does simple optimization. It may turn out that the molecule is predicted to have two equally stable conformations in equilibrium.

For larger, flexible methods, an exhaustive search is not feasible. Artificial intelligence (AI) approaches have been developed [5], which combine the molecular mechanics method with a reasoning machine for avoiding many futile calculations on improbable conformations.

Instead of building the trial structure from atoms using reference data, one may search databases for comparable molecules. If the only difference is a missing chlorine atom, it could fairly safely be built into the known structure extracted from a database. Particularly, the Cambridge Structural Database has extensive utility programs for searching molecular fragments. As far as the Brookhaven databank is concerned, such utility programs are not generally available, and are only slowly emerging from various laboratories around the world.

Finally, when one is concerned with protein molecules, a search for similar proteins could be performed on the amino acid sequence. It may be that a given protein belongs to a family of homologous proteins, one of which has been structurally studied. Even if this is not the case, the mere existence of homologous sequences may point to regions of particular importance regarding function. Thus, there are many computer programs designed for manipulation of protein and nucleic acid sequences which belong to the molecular modeling field in a broader sense.

Operations in Modeling

The modeling process can involve a host of different operations, many of which will be intimately related to the (interactive) display of atoms and molecules. The operations may range from from asking to turn the molecule a number of degrees around one of the principal axes to actually modifying the molecule at a specific location.

In a full-fledged molecular modeling system, there are probably more than a thousand different possible commands and combinations thereof. Therefore "hands on" is the only way to obtain the unbiased view on the different types of queries and their effectiveness. Here we will attempt to group the queries into the following categories:

(a) Transformations (rotations, translations, scaling)
(b) Clipping; segmentation of the displayed data (display only a slab which is parallel to the screen of the total molecule)
(c) Segmentation of the information (display only some of the atoms in the molecule)
(d) Use the color information as an additional dimension of the data representation (give all atoms of a specific type a certain color)
(e) Use labels to identify specific regions
(f) Measure a specific quantity related to two or more atoms (distance, bond angles, torsion angles) and possibly display this quantity (hydrogen bonds)
(g) Display physicochemical characteristics of the molecule (e.g., electrostatic field)
(h) Compare two molecules (how closely do they resemble each other)

The above list is far from exhaustive, but it does illustrate some basic queries that the user can perform, and since in many (but not all) cases combinations of those queries are legal as well, a seemingly unending list of possible representations of the molecule is possible.

Whether they serve their purpose or not depends on the skills of the molecular modeler. His (her) ability to isolate the important part of the total information from the less important part is vital for the success of the modeling exercise. An equally important aspect is the modeler's ability to convey the graphical message to the people with whom he or she is communicating.

Here we will illustrate the potentials of molecular modeling queries through the use of selected examples. Figure 4 is a presentation of the ion channel of gramicidin-A. Figure 5 is a presentation of the electrostatic potential of a cyclohexammonium ion with a chloride counter ion.

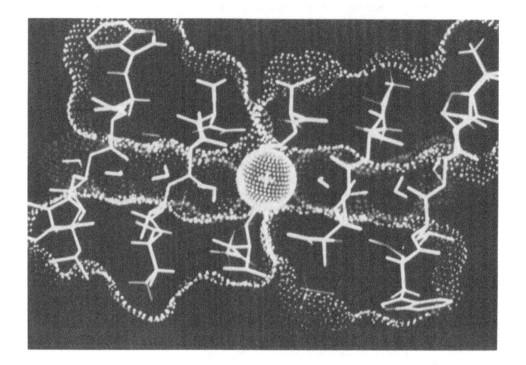

FIGURE 4 Cross-section of the ion channel, gramicidin-A, with 8 waters
and a cesium ion bound to the channel interior. This structure is a single
snapshot of a dynamics calculation performed to study the mechanism of ion
transport across membranes through peptide channels. Gramicidin-A is the
best characterized membrane-bound ion channel and as such serves as a
useful model for the general ion transport problem ubiquitous in living
systems. With molecular dynamics, one can examine the microscopic interactions and deformations which occur as a function of ion type and position
along the pore. (Photo courtesy of BIOSYM Technologies, Inc.)

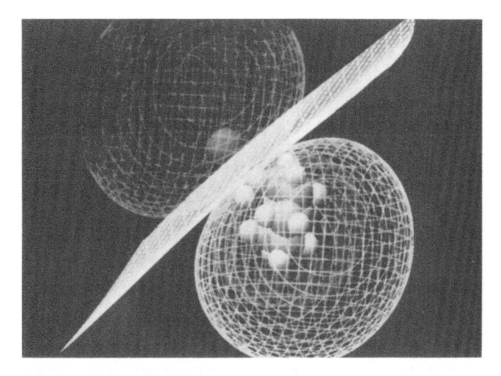

FIGURE 5 Electrostatic potential of a cyclohexanammonium ion with a chloride counter ion, modeled using Chem-X and displayed on a Graphicon high-performance raster terminal. (Photo courtesy of Chemical Design Ltd.)

3-D Presentation Types

The basic presentation in molecular modeling is a stick model which shows all the bonds in the molecule as lines between the coordinates of the atoms at the end of each bond, usually in an orthogonal projection on the screen.

The computations required to draw this type of presentation are few and simple and with a limited number of bonds it is already possible to display continuous rotations and other changes in the position or orientation of the model without too visible jumps even with such moderately fast microcomputers as the 20—25 MHz 80386-based models of the IBM PS/2 or Compaq Deskpro computers.

The presentation can be given a more interesting and nicer appearance by showing the molecule as the traditional stick and ball model or as a so-called solid model, a compact structure of spheres representing the atoms (Fig. 6).

In both of these cases, a remarkable degree of realism is achieved if the program allows for realistic illumination. This involves a complex and time-consuming calculation where one or often more light sources are simulated and the combined light intensity on any pixel in the molecule is translated into color intensity for that pixel.

The spherical shapes, be they in the stick and ball or the solid model are often modeled as three-dimensional polygons consisting of triangles. Pending the number of triangles per sphere, the calculation load will vary accordingly.

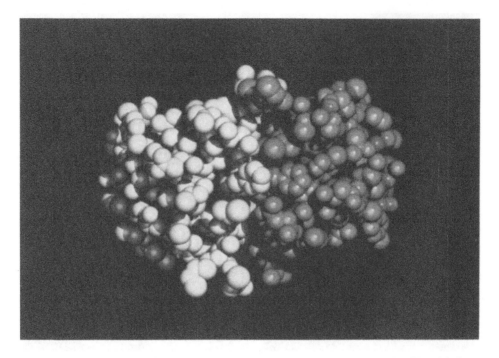

FIGURE 6 The insulin dimer as produced by the program QUANTA (Polygen Corporation) written by Dr. Rod Hubbard, University of York. This
program is among the most advanced in its league. The figure illustrates
how the ray-tracing technique helps to visualize the 3-D aspects of the
insulin dimer.

Complicated graphics as the stick and ball or the solid model presentations are very demanding in terms of computations and display activity.
Consequently, real-time modifications of the presentations (e.g., changing
the orientation of the model) require a system with fast floating-point processing as well as fast display system, and until now this has not been
available on microcomputers.

With some types of molecules, various modifications of the stick model
may be appropriate. This applies especially to protein molecules.

Proteins consist of long chains of amino acid residues folded in complicated ways to form characteristic secondary structures with helices and
other structural elements called beta-sheets and turns. To make these
structural elements more visible, a smoothing, for instance, by using a B-
spline algorithm, may be applied to the coordinates connecting the C-alpha
atoms of the residues. A smooth curve can now be drawn through the positions of the C-alpha atoms thereby highlighting the folding of the protein
(Fig. 7).

The structure may be further emphasized in a ribbon-type model where
a few curves drawn parallel to the above-mentioned curve give the impression of a flat ribbon. Alternatively, only two parallel curves are used and
the space between is filled with color to give a solid ribbon appearance.

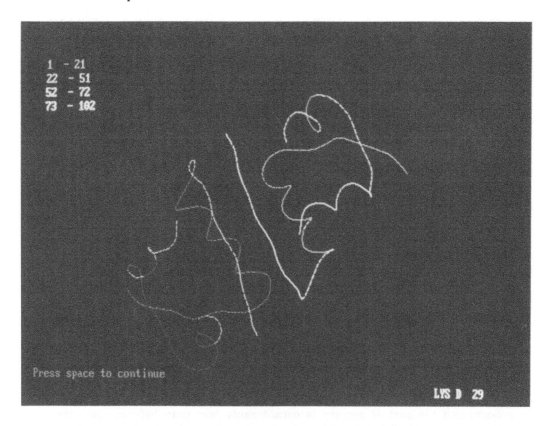

FIGURE 7 A DIST3D B-spline presentation of the four chains of a double molecule of pig insulin in the same orientation as the spacefill presentation in Figure 10.

Still other presentation types more clearly demonstrate the structural elements by showing the helices as cylinders and the beta-sheets as ribbons. In short, there are no limits to the ingenuity in regard to construction of new types of presentations.

In some types of presentations, potentials or fields may be shown as a network of lines and charges may be shown as colored points surrounding the coordinates of the atoms.

Programming Considerations

The power of microcomputer systems is rapidly approaching what a couple of years ago was considered to be available only on workstations. However, economy may still limit what is within reach of many research chemists. Therefore programs for microcomputers designed by scientists at universities or by research or data processing departments in industry as well as similar programs designed by professional software houses may cover a range from the rather sophisticated to more modest levels.

If the level of ambition is adapted to the facilities which are available, it is nevertheless possible to build modest but useful modeling programs even within the limitations of such an inexpensive computer as a Macintosh system with only 128 kbytes and a monochrome graphic display [6]. The referenced program written by E. J. Kirkland in Microsoft Macintosh BASIC has a capacity for displaying molecules with up to 600 atoms in a 3-D true perspective presentation.

In 1985, most personal computers had only a small fraction of the addressable memory installed and the Kirkland program adapts to this condition in various ways. First of all, the presentation of the molecule is simple. Each 'atom' in the molecule is shown as a shaded circle on a monochrome display and a simple hidden surface technique is used to show where an atom covers more or less of other atoms behind it, thereby giving you a primitive impression of depth. Of course, Kirkland could have written a much more sophisticated program within the memory of the Macintosh. The program is only meant as an appetizer for the readers to make them consider their own possibilities.

In this presentation of molecules, the demands for memory are modest because each atom requires only four floating-point numbers, namely, the three coordinate values x, y, and z and the size of the atom, and no specification of the bonds between the atoms is needed.

If bonds need to be displayed, connectivity information is required as well; consequently, the memory capability will need to be increased. Proteins often include several thousands of atoms, and the data storage capacity needs are more or less proportional to the number of atoms in the molecule. If additional information, such as calculations of electrostatic fields or similar calculations, are required, additional memory is necessary too.

The above mentioned smoothing to show the characteristic structural elements of the protein molecules (alpha helices, beta sheets, and turns) also results in a considerable increase in memory requirements. Fortunately, operating systems able to use one megabyte or more are becoming more common and the cost of memory is considerably less than before; also, the addressing range of todays personal computers is much larger than it was in 1985.

Sometimes two or more molecules combine to form a polymer. This multiplies the memory required to contain the coordinates by the same number as the number of molecules in the polymer, unless symmetry can be applied.

Some applications require that two or more molecules be visible simultaneously to allow the user to operate on the orientation and position of the molecules to examine the interaction and binding possibilities of the molecules. Again increased memory requirements are necessary.

One frequently used feature of molecular graphics is its ability to display a molecule in different orientations after appropriate rotations. In large systems using workstations, this manipulation is achieved with a control box connected to the computer, with a knob for control for each coordinate axis. As the knob is turned, the molecule is rotated equivalently around the corresponding axis while the molecule seen on the screen rotates synchronously with the turning of the knob. This real-time rotation is almost attainable with todays fastest and most expensive personal microcomputers such as the 20—25 MHz versions of the IBM PS/2, Models 70 and 80, and the Compaq Deskpro, but it requires a fast microprocessor assisted by a fast floating-point coprocessor as well as a fast video chip. However, it may soon be less difficult and less expensive to achieve.

Users of personal computers will probably abstain from using a control box and will instead press a key to rotate the molecule. But a mouse or other handy pointing device to select the parts of the molecule for which information is wanted is obviously adequate.

One of the more basic problems in molecular graphics is how to convey the impression that the objects presented on the flat surface of the display or plotted on paper are, in fact, three-dimensional. In architectural presentations, there is no doubt that the answer is to use true perspective. In Kirkland's previously mentioned program, the molecules are shown in true perspective because monochrome displays offer very few alternative means of giving an impression of depth.

In screen presentations of molecules, true perspective will, to some extent, provoke visual ambiguity and consequently will not be quite adequate. The reason is that the molecular presentation will not have the same references for the interpretation of the interaction between apparent size of the objects and the depth, as in a perspective presentation of a street with houses, cars, and people.

Molecules contain different types of atoms, each with a different atomic radius, and the distance between two atoms with small atomic radii will be shorter than the distance between atoms with greater atomic radii. But when molecules are shown in true perspective, it may be difficult to judge whether the distance between a pair of atoms is truly short or only appears to be short because the atoms are more remote than other parts of the molecule. Likewise, in presentations, where each atom is shown as a circle or as a ball, an apparently small atom may appear small simply because it is far away. With this in mind, it is understood that a true perspective presentation does not always provide a reliable impression of the depth of the molecule.

In fact, it is probably much more appropriate to apply an orthogonal projection of the molecule on the surface of the screen showing the size of the atoms independent of their position in relation to the axis of projection. In this way, it is always possible to distinguish between atoms of different sizes; and application of an appropriate technique to remove hidden surfaces will still allow one to see which atoms are positioned in front of others, however, to some extent, the impression of the depth of the molecule becomes obscure.

Color displays, however, can convey an impression of depth by using color for depth cueing. The trick is to simulate light coming from a point in front of the model of the molecule and to darken the colors to represent more and more distant parts of the molecule. In real life light intensity is reduced smoothly as the distance from the light source increases, and such a simulation would require a tremendous number of steps in the palette of the color display and a corresponding number of bit planes and amount of memory in the screen buffer.

Fortunately, a rather satisfactory impression of depth requires only a limited number of steps in the brightness scales of the colors. In fact, within the very limited palette of the Enhanced Graphics Adapter, a rather good impression of depth has been obtained using the high-intensity version of the colors for the atoms of the nearest half of the molecule and the low intensity version of the colors for the atoms of the other half.

Another, technically more difficult method of providing depth perception is the use of stereographics. By some means the left eye is made to see only a 'left' image and likewise for the right eye. The difference between the two images arises from applying slightly different projections equivalent to the eye separation relative to the object distance. Technical solutions to this range from simply drawing the two images side by side to the use of complicated video glasses and shutters. There is no standard yet, but the option is of great usefulness to chemists doing molecular modeling.

More demanding types of molecular presentations, such as the solid model types, in which atoms are shown as solid spheres or as spheres connected with rods, imply that light and shadows must be dealt with. This requires a much more powerful color system, especially if one aspires to satisfy the ever-increasing expectations of photographic quality graphics. In the extreme, such graphics can only be produced on expensive workstations with extra high resolution color displays. A minimum of 256 simultaneous colors and a resolution of at least 640 × 480 picture points (pixels) must be available. This corresponds to the maximum resolution of the VGA standard for color graphics of the IBM PS/2 line, but only the IBM 8514/A color graphics adapter makes the display of 256 simultaneous colors possible in this resolution.

The same color and resolution requirements were also satisfied by the now obsolete IBM Professional Graphics Display in connection with the IBM Professional Graphics Controller card. Other color graphics adapters for IBM PC/AT-compatible computers and following the IBM Professional Graphics adapter standard are produced by NEC (MVA-1024), Orchid Technology (TurboPGA), and Vermont Microsystems (IM-640). Other AT-compatible but not IBM PGA-compatible color adapters, for instance the Pepper PRO1280 card from Number Nine Computer Corp., satisfy the demand for 256 simultaneous colors at an even higher resolution. The resolution of the Pepper PRO1280 card is 1280 pixels horizontal and 960 pixels vertical.

Unfortunately, no command language is common to all color graphics cards. The instruction or command set of the color graphics adapters usually differ from one manufacturer to the other. Furthermore, such cards function as specialized computers where the command processor converts the commands to a transmission of signals to the video processor. The consequences of this are that programs are usually not portable between different adapters and the programming which is rather tedious consists of building long strings with commands for transmission to the command processor. The IBM Professional Graphics adapter is no exception.

Design of Coordinate Files

Molecular datafiles published in large databases by scientific institutions are usually rather comprehensive, because they contain supplementary information such as data source, publication and revision dates, specification of structural features, and other details. Although this additional information is negligible for large molecules compared with the amount of atomic data, it does mean that size is a matter of concern, for reasons of sheer economics.

For example, the Brookhaven Protein Data Bank contains datafiles on molecular structures of proteins and other biopolymers. In this database the file size of large molecules is frequently from 100,000 to 300,000 bytes, and the whole set of files presently amounts to some 70 megabytes. Actually, there have been some attempts at compressing these files (e.g., saving incremental coordinates) [7].

With the usually modest mass storage capacity of ordinary microcomputer systems it is, however, necessary to economize with file space. Molecular modeling programs using such files as primary source of coordinates and other data needed for the application have to store only the necessary extract of data in smaller files. If the primary database resides in a minicomputer system from which files are transmitted to the microcomputer it will only be necessary to keep a copy of the primary file on the microcomputer until the reduced datafile has been established, and if the complete file resides on a floppy disk, then the reduced file may be established on another drive directly from this disk.

In addition to the coordinates, at least the atom types have to be specified in the file. With an a priori knowledge of molecular type, this may be sufficient to tell how the atoms are interconnected, but usually it will also be necessary to specify the bonds between the atoms in order to show the structure of the molecule, especially if some of the atoms have multiple bonds to another atom.

Molecules may, as previously mentioned, be specified not by a tabulation of the atoms and their coordinates, but by simply giving the atomic structure of the substance. To show the three-dimensional structure of the molecule the program must in this case calculate the coordinates of the atoms from a tabulation of the atomic radii and the angles of the atoms involved. Subsequent adequate filing of the calculated coordinates is appropriate to eliminate unnecessary calculations in connection with future operations on the model. Hence coordinate files are necessary elements even when using building facilities in modeling programs.

As mentioned above, coordinates of molecular structures may be found in the scientific literature or you may subscribe to a public database from which you may access molecule files through your telephone connection. Circumstantially new or preliminary unpublished data from x-ray crystallography are communicated between collaborating scientists. In this case, floppy disks represent the most convenient and inexpensive medium for communicating molecular data, especially since floppy disks may have a considerable capacity. However, it will probably soon be possible to buy molecular databases on laser or WORM disks.

Mathematical Tools

Displaying three-dimensional models of molecules on the color display of a microcomputer calls for the application of a wide range of mathematical operations:

> Calculation of the atomic coordinates of the molecule after rotation around one or more of the three axes or around an arbitrary line through the molecule
>
> Removal of hidden lines or hidden surfaces
>
> Calculation of the distribution of light and shadow in solid model presentations
>
> Smoothing the backbone of a protein through the coordinates of the residues in order to display structural characteristics of the protein

Fortunately, there are a number of very good texts on the mathematics of computer graphics. Probably the best known of these are by J. D. Foley and A. Van Dam [8] and William M. Newman and Robert F. Sproull [9].

Both of these books thoroughly treat the mathematical problems relating to the various aspects of computer graphics, for instance, the application of matrix operations for geometric transformations and rotations and the application of smoothing algorithms such as spline functions for interpolations between coordinates of curves or surfaces.

Manipulation of 3-D Models

Modeling programs offer a number of very useful operations which increase the understanding of the structure of the molecule.

One of the most frequently used operations is rotation, which allows the operator to view the most interesting part of the molecule on the display. In more sophisticated professional programs it is possible to rotate around an arbitrary axis or even to let the molecule rotate continuously until a stop signal is given or controlled by turning the control knobs for the three coordinate axes. On smaller PCs the processing speed does not allow pseudo-real-time rotation, and consequently, some programs prompt the user for the rotation axis and angle. After a few rotations one will usually obtain an appropriate orientation of the molecule.

Another desirable feature is the possibility to view more than one molecule at a time, either to compare the structures or to try to find orientations in which two molecules can get in close contact with each other (docking). In such situations both 3-D rotations and translations of the two models are needed. Docking is usually a manual process, although certain programs do allow for automatic docking. Docking is a highly complex process, involving total freedom of motion for both molecules. In many aspects the problem is the same as that encountered when a spaceship is manoeuvered in space in order to dock it with a spacestation. In some programs it is possible to let the computer find the best fit by calculating the positions which minimize the sum of squares of the distances between selected atoms of the two molecules.

Many molecules are so large that some of the interesting details are obscured, if the complete molecule is to be represented by the limited number of pixels of ordinary color screens. In such cases it is useful to be able to select the part of the molecule which is of interest, and to specify an appropriately larger scale for a new presentation of this part (zooming). When the picture buffer largely exceeds what corresponds to the number of pixels on the display then the zooming mechanism will be activated almost instantaneously, and new details will be visible. But that is more likely to be a facility on workstations than on ordinary microcomputers. With less expensive equipment it will usually be necessary to let the computer draw the new presentation from scratch.

For larger molecules such as proteins and nucleic acids, it is often useful to display only a slab of the molecule. This is done by discarding all atoms which are not within a predefined range of Z values, where Z is the coordinate axis perpendicular to the display screen. Combining the scaling operation with a setting of a certain slab size and position, one can isolate a volume of the molecule for a more detailed inspection.

Likewise, one can use color to code specific parts of the molecule, such as the active site in an enzyme versus other residues in the enzyme. This is a very convenient feature, especially because such parts will be easily detectable during rotations or other transformations.

A mouse or a similar device is, as previously mentioned, a necessary interface between the operator and the presentation on the display to permit pointing at single atoms of the molecule for which information on atom type, position in the molecule, or other data is wanted. Another application is to select pairs of atoms in the molecule to have atom types, positions, and interatomic distances printed on the screen. Finally, it is often used for picking menu commands or options.

Modifications Applied to the Models

In the preceding section only such operations were mentioned which preserve the structure of the models. The molecular modeler may, however, often need the option to modify the structure, and to some extent, calculate the consequences of such modifications.

Modifications may include substitution, insertion, or deletion of a part of the molecule, for instance atoms, groups, or fragments, with other atoms, groups, or fragments.

Other possible modifications may be to break or establish bonds or to alter torsion angles and to calculate the resulting change in potential energy.

Hardware Requirements for Selected Programs

Modeling programs, whether they are designed by professional software houses or by individual scientists, differ very much with respect to the hardware required. Needless to say, the higher your aspirations are to the power and sophistication of the software the more you will have to invest in hardware.

The most powerful modeling systems providing very sophisticated presentations (Figs. 1, 4, 5) still require a DEC VAX computer or similar processing units. For instance, the program INSIGHT from BIOSYM Technologies, Inc., runs on a VAX minicomputer as a host and on an Evans & Sutherland PS300 graphics display for the graphics. It also runs on UNIX-based workstations with fast RISC-type processors, such as the Silicon Graphics workstations.

The "Chem-X" molecular modeling system from Chemical Design Ltd. runs only under the DEC VMS operating system and requires at least a DEC MicroVAX 2000 or a VAXstation 2000 and a high-performance raster terminal, e.g., the Graphicon terminal or terminals from Sigmex or Tektronix, for displaying the graphics.

Chem-X consists of 9 modules: ChemCore (build and display), Chem-Guide (menu interface), ChemModel (comparison and analysis), ChemMovie (display interfacing), ChemQM (quantum mechanics), ChemDBS-1 (database), ChemLib (library and data interface), ChemProtein (protein modeling), ChemStat (structure/activity module). Some modules are optional and may be added later as needed. Chem-X is probably the most widely distributed molecular modeling software system (Figs. 1 and 5 show Chem-X graphics).

Still other computer modeling systems require some sort of workstation. The "Molecular Advanced Design" (MAD) modeling system by R. Lahana of the Centre de Recherche Pierre Fabre, which was initially conceived on an IBM 5080 graphics processing unit connected to a VM/CMS mainframe, is applicable on all PHIGS-compatible graphic workstations. It is especially compatible with the UNIX operating system and claims to be compatible with any other operating system. Today, it is still not adapted to IBM PC or IBM PS/2 compatible computers, but it can be installed on an IBM RT 6150 RISC computer with an IBM 5080 graphics systems.

MAD handles input from and output to Brookhaven PDB files, Polygen ChemNote files, and Tripos SYBYL files, as well as various other general file formats. Figure 8 shows a presentation of the solvent surfaces of a small molecule as an example of MAD graphics.

Table 1 is a summary of suppliers, prices, and hardware requirements of terminal and workstation-based molecular modeling programs.

TABLE 1   Terminal and Workstation-Based Molecular Modeling

Product name and supplier	Cost	Processing unit	Additional hardware etc.
BIOGRAF, BioDesign, Inc.	100,000	VAX, Silicon Graphics 4D, Ardent Titan workstation	Evans & Sutherland PS300 vector display
Chem-X, Chemical Design Ltd.	50,000– 120,000	VAX VAXStation	Hi-Res Sigmex or Tektronix display
Chemmod U-Microcomputers Ltd.	24,000 includes workstation	U-MICRO Chemmod system	
HYDRA, Polygen Corporation	Academic institute free	VAX or Silicon Graphics workstation	Evans & Sutherland PS300 vector display
INSIGHT, BIOSYM Technologies, Inc.	25,000	VAX or Silicon Graphics 4D	Evans & Sutherland PS300 vector display
MAD AQUITAINES Systemes	25,000 Academic institute 3,300	IBM 6150 or other PHIGS compatable workstation	IBM 5080 Graphics System and display
QUANTA, Polygen Corporation	25,000	Silicon Graphics, Stellar workstation	
SYBYL, Tripos Associates	100,000	VAX or Silicon Graphics workstation	Evans & Sutherland PS300 vector display

Prices are not necessarily comparable, and discounts are common for academic users.

At this moment the boundary between workstations and personal computers becomes more and more diffuse. Personal computers become more and more powerful due to the continuing increase in power of the microprocessors and floating-point coprocessors and to the advent of accelerator boards with the Inmos 'transputer' parallel processor system, while the price of workstations is decreasing thanks to such developments as SMD technology and to application of robots in production which, in combination, increases the competition. Quite a few companies are launching or plan to launch low-priced workstations, partly based on new RISC processors or on parallel processing. Even the manufacturer of home computers, ATARI, has already introduced a low-cost workstation.

The problem is that software development has difficulties keeping pace with hardware development, and interested buyers must always investigate carefully which combination of microcomputing system and modeling software will be most profitable. Any attempt to give specific advice in this matter would probably be outdated by the time of publication.

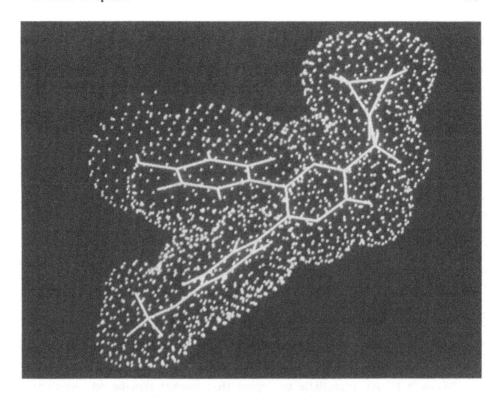

FIGURE 8 MAD presentation of the solvent surface of a small molecule. (Photo courtesy of Centre de Recherche Pierre Fabre.)

However, some general guidelines with respect to the capacity of the hardware may be given.

As regards available memory, the requirements will undoubtedly increase in the future since new systems will seek to let as much as possible of the program be memory resident in an attempt to increase the rate of processing. Some operations require an expansive memory as well. The most obvious examples of this are smoothing, where arrays with smoothed coordinates hold five or more times as much memory as the original coordinates; building solid models with light and shadow; removal of hidden lines and hidden surfaces; or sorting with respect to the Z axis for hidden surface removal.

As mentioned, some modeling programs require only a limited amount of memory, for instance, the Academic Press 'PCMODEL' program by F. H. Clarke and J. G. Henkel, which, with a memory requirement of only 192 kbytes, is able to build graphic representations of molecules with as many as 999 atoms.

Usually, however, molecular modeling programs require more memory, even in excess of the 640 kbytes, which up to version 4.0 was the maximum of memory that could be utilized under the IBM DOS operating system. Narrow memory limitations like this often seem to place unpleasant restrictions upon the design of programs with memory requiring resident data.

Dividing the program into a number of chaining modules is one way to reduce memory requirements, but only by sacrificing fast processing.

Fortunately, new versions of DOS and new operating systems for personal microcomputers are about to eliminate this 640 kbyte restriction. This is one reason why the memory requirement of modeling programs is expected to increase.

Next, but of nearly equal importance as memory requirements, are the requirements for capacity and speed of the mass storage of the microcomputer. Again, the most modest types of programs require only a couple of drives for floppy disks or even a single drive, but usually a hard disk is required, or at least recommended. Often a rather high capacity hard disk with short access time will be a must if your collection of molecular data is comprehensive and flexible switching between various molecule files is required.

It is a bitter experience to wait for a slow build-up of color graphics on an expensive, high-resolution color display. The performance of the display processing system is of the utmost importance for fast generation of the presentation on the screen, especially if real-time rotations are desirable.

Here the latest developments offer good news. Several chip manufacturers are developing more and more powerful video processors. Texas Instruments, whose graphics microprocessor TMS34010 is highly esteemed and consequently is incorporated in many high-performance graphics adapters, has developed a new version, the TMS34020 chip, which depending on the instruction mix, is between 6 and 50 times faster than the TMS34010.

Hence it is not unrealistic to expect that workstation-based molecular modeling programs will soon be adapted to personal microcomputers with high-performance color systems, which within a couple of years, will replace less powerful systems as a very important tool in biotechnological research.

The quality of color graphics depends primarily on screen resolution and on the number of simultaneously available colors. To obtain the necessary details and a not too grainy appearance, a resolution of at least 640 pixels horizontal by 480 pixels vertical is required. Consequently, the cathode ray tube has to have high precision and the bandwidth must be at least 32 MHz or higher. These requirements result in high production costs and the price of this category of color displays has only recently been reduced to a moderate level. We expect that it will be possible to buy acceptably priced color displays of even higher resolution within the next few years.

A high number of simultaneous colors is a prerequisite for displaying complex color graphics such as color presentations of macromolecules. The development of analog RGB color displays has been a significant contribution in this context, and the low price of dynamic memory chips permits establishment of screen buffers of the size necessary to represent the color indices of the pixels at reasonable cost. Nevertheless, in resolution 640 by 480 pixels, only 16 simultaneous colors, much less than the highly desirable 256 colors, is the VGA standard of the IBM PS/2 line of personal microcomputers. At present this can only be obtained with the IBM 8514/A adapter. However, it probably will become the next standard.

Some professional modeling programs for the IBM personal computers require special graphics processor boards and extra-high-quality color displays.

Converting Large Commercial Programs to PC Level:
Problems and Possibilities

There are several reasons why many commercial programs for molecular modeling have so far been designed for minicomputers and workstations. First, they must cover as many as possible of the operations and calculations needed by the modelers to make the critically minded, professional customers find the acquisition of the program profitable, especially since the price of such programs must be relatively high due to a rather limited market.

Furthermore, the modeling system must be powerful, and able to execute as fast as possible so that the program does not become a nuisance to the modeler by delaying the work.

A couple of points in which minicomputers and workstations differ from the personal microcomputers are processing speed and virtually addressable memory. In these respects minicomputers and workstations still rank well above today's personal microcomputers.

To speed up processing, the producers of workstations (and minicomputers) design their systems with high-speed and sometimes proprietary CPUs. But if they are to remain competitive, producers of inexpensive personal microcomputers cannot include such fast processors because they require equivalently fast and expensive memory.

However, the general trend in the development of personal microcomputer architecture is to substitute yesterday's 16-bit standard for microprocessors with 32-bit processors and to increase the clock rate from 10 Mhz to 20–30 MHz or more, and to increase memory performance correspondingly. New and faster versions of the 32-bit Motorola 68000 microprocessor, the chip which was some time ago acceptable in workstations, are more and more often included in high-end personal computers. High clock rate versions of the Intel 80386 32-bit microprocessor have recently given the Motorola chips competition in the same class of personal microcomputers.

Other means for increasing processing speed are parallel processing as found in the Inmos Transputer, high-performance RISC processors, and the Weitek series floating-point coprocessor boards or other floating-point coprocessors.

In sophisticated molecular modeling programs designed for workstations, processing is often performed with multitasking and the total memory requirements of the active modules exceed the amount of memory actually available. Of course, this requires a virtual memory system, and to accelerate processing, this system is implemented in hardware which makes such workstations more expensive. It is unlikely that this approach will find its way into ordinary personal microcomputers in the near future. Consequently, adapting such a modeling system to a personal microcomputer means sacrificing some workstation speed or part of the convenience of the workstation version.

Virtual memory processing also means a considerable amount of saving and loading which requires high-capacity, powerful and fast storage devices that so far have not been available at a reasonable price with personal microcomputers. Here, there is perhaps more reason for optimism, especially because fundamentally new technology is emerging.

Another main problem in the adaptation of large, workstation-based commercial modeling programs is the implementation on the less expensive personal microcomputers of sophisticated color graphics, which are primarily characterized by the application of a multitude of simultaneous colors and by a resolution which is somewhat higher than that of the VGA.

The many simultaneous colors are especially desirable for making solid type models look realistic. The application of light and shadow in the presentations requires fine gradation in the brightness of colors, and combined with the request for color coding of various characteristics of the molecule it requires a high number of bits for each pixel. This high number of pixels due to the high resolution again means that the screen buffer requires extensive memory.

When working with computer graphics, it is usually preferable to have two screen buffers, so that work can be started on a new screen image while the other screen page is displayed. This of course doubles the amount of memory required. Furthermore, supplementary data is required to support certain graphical techniques, e.g., removal of hidden surfaces, again further increasing memory requirements. In the Silicon Graphics 4D workstation the buffers which support the color screen with a resolution of 1280 × 1024 pixels and 8 bit planes for each of the three primary colors have a total of 15 Mbytes.

To transmit such vast amounts of information to the display with satisfactory speed requires a high-speed videoprocessor which is rather expensive. But there is more to the requirement of a videoprocessor.

As mentioned, it is desirable to be able to perform continuous so-called real-time rotations of the model during the screen display. This is not really possible if the necessary computations have to be done by the program. To get acceptable performance of this as well as of some other operations such as zooming, these operations must be implemented in the hardware of the videoprocessor and be activated through the command or instruction set of the videoprocessor, which again means that the operations must be programmed in the command language of the videoprocessor. This contributes to the costliness of developing such modeling programs, even for personal microcomputer versions.

However, the implications of the graphical requirements of large commercial modeling programs are merely that a standard personal microcomputer must be equipped with additional hardware for graphics to be able to render acceptable performance with modeling programs converted to PC level.

One possible approach is to install in one of the expansion slots of the PC a graphics adapter card with similar characteristics as the graphics controller of the workstation. Alternatively, one can install a graphics controller and adjust the program to this controller, possibly using an interface program module which transforms the graphical instructions of the modeling program into equivalent commands for the controller card.

Such interface programs to be used in connection with widely applied software systems requiring high-performance graphics are occasionally provided by producers of high-performance graphics cards in order to stimulate sales.

If it is not possible to install an adequate graphics controller in the computer, another approach is to let the computer transmit the graphical data to a separate graphics processor system which controls the color display.

This is the solution chosen by U-Microcomputer for the PC-Chemmod modeling program which requires the U-Micro Vector Graphics Processor as a controller for the Chemmod color display, the same Vector Graphics which is used in the Chemmod workstation.

SMALL MOLECULE MODELING

The modeling of small molecules does not present major graphical problems. The amount of structural data for the molecule is limited and coordinates may, with reasonable precision, be obtained from tabulated values of atomic radii and bond angles of the atoms in the molecule.

As long as the modeler has to deal with the small molecule only and not with the environment with which it may have to interact, he will not encounter major problems in the presentation of the molecule on the color display. However, if detailed calculations of molecular properties such as electron distribution are to be performed, severe demands suddenly emerge even for such simple molecules.

The number of details to be shown in the presentation is small, and consequently, the limited resolution of an ordinary display on a personal microcomputer will usually be sufficient.

Furthermore, there will be few restrictions and many possibilities for including refinements in the design of the program.

The limited amount of data in the model makes near real-time update of the screen possible. On the other hand, it must be remembered that molecular modeling of small molecules is of interest to a large number of users.

Available Programs and Databases

Practically all modeling systems may be used for modeling of small molecules. In fact, several large modeling systems such as Chem-X (ChemProtein) and SYBYL started out as programs for small molecule modeling. The price of the large modeling systems may, however, prohibit this application when the economy of a project is limited and the system is not available for other reasons.

In such situations a number of smaller, inexpensive programs, e.g., those intended for design of drugs may be considered. The Academic Press program PCMODEL and some programs from the Swiss company Etronics AG may be mentioned as examples.

The Quantum Chemistry Program Exchange (QCPE) of the University of Indiana is a source of many programs available at nominal cost. Originally, QECP programs were almost exclusively made for mainframe computers, but lately a large number of programs intended for the IBM PC and the Apple Macintosh have appeared [10].

Coordinate sets for various small molecules are, as mentioned in the section on Diffraction Techniques, deposited in the Cambridge Structural Database.

MACROMOLECULE MODELING

In principle, macromolecules are simply large molecules (i.e., molecules with many atoms). Macromolecules will obviously be more complicated to study and understand than small molecules. There are three important categories of macromolecules in scientific research and in industrial research and development

    Proteins
    Nucleic acids
    Polysaccharides

All three are polymers, that is they are composed of repeated chemical units (i.e., amino acids, nucleic acids, and saccharides). The linking of the units in general produces a linear graph (connectivity), or in the case of polysaccharides, a tree structure. This feature in combination with the fact that the molecules are large is the reason behind a need for software dedicated to macromolecule modeling.

Modeling Programs for the Personal Computer

If you are looking for commercial standalone programs for the modeling of macromolecules on an IBM PC-compatible computer or on an IBM PS/2 computer, you will not have a large number to choose from.

A few programs, among them the NITRO program from TRIPOS Associates and the ChemNote program from Polygen, use the personal microcomputer as an intelligent terminal to a minicomputer host, which is equipped with large volumes of disk storage for a molecule database and performs fast and heavy computations.

One standalone modeling program for the PC, the U-MICRO program PC-Chemod, is a downgraded version of a workstation-based program Chemmod. The program even exists in a transputer version for the Chemmod workstation equipped with a transputer board.

Below are short descriptions of the PC version of the program and a few other modeling programs for the IBM PC and the IBM PS/2 microcomputers.

The DIST3D Program

The program DIST3D (developed at NOVO by one of the authors) requires an IBM PC/AT equipped with an Enhanced Graphics Adapter board with 256 kbytes RAM or an IBM PS/2. The display must be an EGA-compatible color display. The program requires a Microsoft Mouse pointing device. The program is still being improved. A higher resolution VGA version is to be prepared.

The program is designed for graphic representations of proteins. From files with protein coordinate data in Brookhaven Protein Data Bank (.PDB) file format, the program has facilities for conversion of the c-alpha structure data in the .PDB file to a smaller file in a format especially designed for the operation of the program. With a text editor the user has the option to modify this file or to create a file in the same format with new C-alpha coordinate data.

The program has two types of presentations:

1. A distance map or DISTANCE MATRIX, in which the color of each point indicates the distance between the two residues with residue numbers corresponding to the abscissa and the ordinate of the point. A color scale to the left of the diagram shows the distance intervals corresponding to each of the 16 colors of the distance diagram. A photograph of a distance matrix diagram of an enzyme is shown in Figure 9.

2. Presentations of the spatial structure of the proteins either as stick models or as spacefill models. In both of these types of presentations you have the option to color code five different types of residues or groups of residue types. In the same way, it is possible to show where up to five selected single residues or intervals of residue numbers are located in the structure. Optionally only color-coded fragments are shown. In the spacefill model, the successive display of the atoms of the molecule according to their

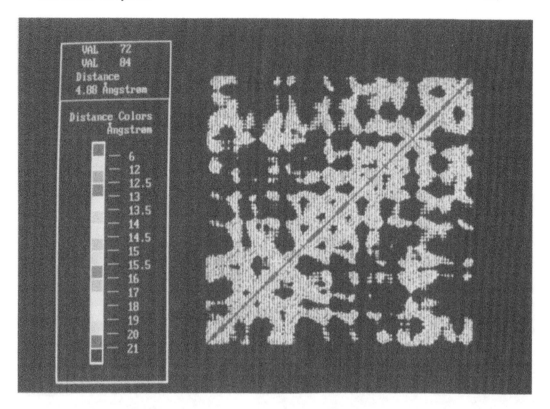

FIGURE 9 A DIST3D distance matrix diagram of the same *Bacillus subtilis* enzyme as in Figure 2.

Z coordinates may be halted to allow inspection at various sections perpendicular to the Z axis.

The stick models may be either simple stick models or they may be displayed after a B-spline smoothing. The molecule may be viewed from different directions after user-specified rotations around the coordinate axes.

In the distance matrix plot as well as in the spacefill presentations, the mouse may be used to get a screen printout of the residue types, chain identifiers, and sequence numbers of selected pairs of residues and of the distance between these residues.

Figure 2 of a spacefill presentation shows the active cleft of an enzyme. Figure 10, a spacefill presentation and Figure 7, a B-spline presentation, both show the 4 chains of a double-molecule of pig insulin.

The PCMODEL Program

The PCMODEL program from Academic Press requires only an IBM PC-compatible microcomputer with a CGA-compatible graphics adapter and a color monitor. With DOS 2.0 or higher and 192 kbytes of memory, the program has a capacity for 999 atoms and 999 bonds. An Apple version requires an Apple II-type microcomputer with 64 kbytes or more. With 64 kbytes the capacity is 600 atoms and 600 bonds.

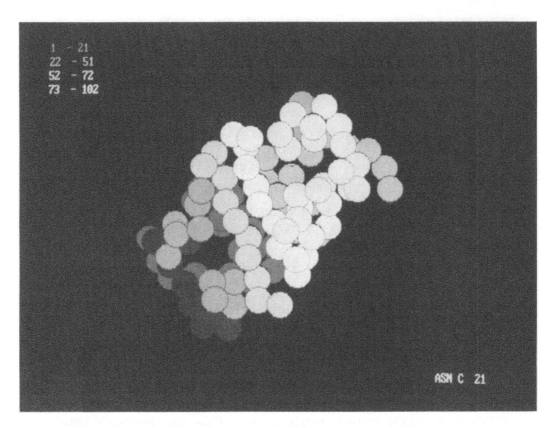

FIGURE 10   A DIST3D spacefill presentation showing the four chains of a
double molecule of pig insulin.

The user-created coordinate files contain specifications of the number
of atoms and the number of bonds, and for each of the atoms a record with
the coordinates of the atom and an identifier of 1—8 characters.   Following
the coordinate records, there is a connectivity table specifying the pairs
of atoms for each bond.

The program shows the molecules as stick models optionally with circles
around the coordinates to simulate a stick and ball presentation.   Three steps
of depth cueing are applied, and the model may be rotated around one of
the coordinate axes or around a bond.   Two molecules may be shown simultaneously and moved independently to allow "docking."   The program has
facilities for calculating interatomic distances, bond angles, and torsion
angles.   Furthermore, it has an edit option for modification of the models
and the modified models may be saved on disk.

The ALCHEMY Program

The ALCHEMY program from Tripos Associates, Inc. requires an IBM PC,
IBM XT, IBM AT, or IBM PS/2 or a compatible computer with minimum 512
kbytes of memory, one 1.2 Mbyte floppy disk drive or two 360 kbytes

drives, an Enhanced Graphics Adapter (EGA) with 256 kbytes of graphics memory, an EGA-compatible color monitor and a mouse. A hard disk drive and a floating-point coprocessor are recommended. For hard copies, the configuration requires a serially connected plotter compatible with the HPGL standard from Hewlett-Packard.

The modeler may use ALCHEMY to examine steric similarities, differences, and interactions among sets of molecules in a three-dimensional, real-time environment. The program has facilities to

Construct three-dimensional molecules by combination of molecular fragments

Obtain reasonable molecular conformations with an energy minimization procedure

Use a least-squares routine to fit series of molecules to one another and to compare molecular geometries

Use colors to differentiate atom types in space-filling representations of single molecules

Generate space-filling images of sets of molecules, where each molecule has its own color

Modify molecules and determine inter- and intramolecular distances

Rotate molecules interactively, move one molecule relative to another and manually execute "docking"

Display representations as side-by-side stereoscopic images

ALCHEMY has options to read and write files in the format used by the Tripos minicomputer modeling program SYBYL.

The Promodeler I Program

The Promodeler I program from New England BioGraphics requires the following hardware:

An IBM PC/AT-compatible computer with minimum 512 kbytes of memory, one 5.25" diskette drive and a hard disk

An 80287 or 80387 floating-point coprocessor

An IBM PGA-compatible graphics adapter

An IBM PGA-compatible color display

A Microsoft-compatible mouse for selecting atoms and menu items

With 512 kbytes of memory, approximately 2500 atoms may be displayed. With 640 kbytes, which is recommended, about 5000 atoms can be displayed and manipulated simultaneously in any representation.

The Promodeler I capabilities include large molecule support, interactive rotations, translations and zooming, interactive side chain substitutions, shaded, colored space filling, bond and backbone representations, and stereo viewing. In bond and backbone representations stepwise rotations, translations, and scaling may be performed at a rate of 1–3 s/position.

More than one molecule may be displayed simultaneously, and each molecule may be moved independently or "docked" with another molecule as in Figure 11, which shows a space-filled model of the dimer of the repressor I434 bound to a DNA protein.

The program has facilities for measurement of distances and angles and for specific coloring of atom types, residue types, and residue ranges.

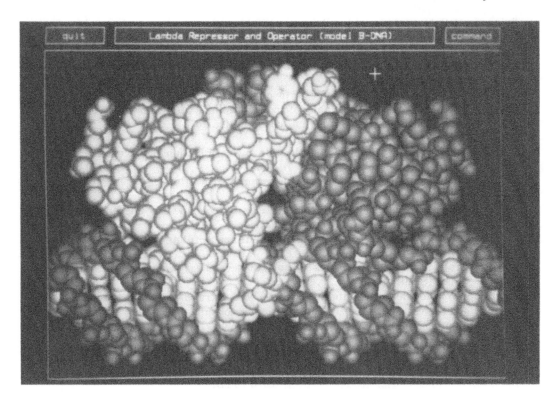

FIGURE 11 A Promodeler I presentation of the dimer of repressor I434 bound to a DNA protein, modeled from coordinates supplied by Steve Harrison of Harvard University. (Photo courtesy of New England BioGraphics.)

Input from Brookhaven Protein Data Bank files as well as from various other file formats is supported. Internally a high-speed, compact file format is applied for interactive sessions.

The PC-Chemmod Program

The PC-Chemmod program from U-Microcomputers Limited is a downgraded version of the same company's Chemmod package, which requires a Motorola 68000-based Chemmod workstation.

The PC-Chemmod package consists of the following four programs:

CHEM: the main program with Build, Manipulate, and Display facilities
CHEMMIN: a module for obtaining an energy minimum conformation of the structure of the molecule
DELRE: the charge distribution program
CONTOUR: a program for redisplaying Ramachandran maps

The hardware requirements of the PC-Chemmod program are:

The Chemmod Vector Graphics Processor and compatible high-resolution color display plus an appropriate optical mouse

      An IBM PC-, PC/AT-, or IBM PS/2-compatible computer with 640 kbytes
          of memory, hard disk, an 8087 or 80287 floating-point coprocessor
          and a free serial port
      A keyboard and a (monochrome) monitor as text screen
      A Canon inkjet printer for hard copy of the graphics in color
      The add-on hardware will take up one expansion slot in the personal
          microcomputer

The resolution of the Chemmod color display is 512×512 pixels in 64 colors. The capacity of PC-Chemmod is about 1000 atoms.

PC-Chemmod has libraries with predefined ring types and atom types. Molecular structures are saved in files with unit cell parameters, number of atoms, atomic coordinates, and a connectivity table. When they are loaded the structures are immediately displayed as stick models. Single as well as multiple molecular structures may be loaded.

With the Build and Edit facilities molecular structures may be built from individual atoms or predefined rings as well as by adding molecules or fragments by elimination of hydrogen atoms, and the structure may be modified by changing atom types, bond angles, and lengths and torsion angles or by changing charges.

The Display options allow spacefill display of structures (see Fig. 3) with options to draw backbone, rotate, or translate the structure, as well as to display the structure with color coding of atoms, atom types, or structures, or to display charge information as color codes. The display options also include displaying Ramachandran maps, automatic superimposition of multiple structures for comparing, and red-green stereoscopic presentations.

With the Manipulation facilities, the structures may be translated along a coordinate axis or be rotated about one of the coordinate axes or about an arbitrary axis between two atoms. Other options are to increase or decrease the scaling of the representations or to display a close-up of a part of the structure or to perform Z-clipping gradually from the front of the structure. Depth cueing as well as display of hydrogen atoms are optional.

The ChemNote Program

The ChemNote program from Polygen Corporation is a PC-based molecular construction program which also provides an interface to the CHARMM and HYDRA molecular modeling programs that are distributed by Polygen as well for use on high-performance workstations and minicomputers. It may be used as a standalone program (in fact, it is callable from within QUANTA on the Unix workstations) for building molecules from two-dimensional sketches and converting into three-dimensional models. It also has provisions for building protein sequences by naming amino acids and applying various link operations. The display facilities of the program are rather rudimentary.

The CAMSEQ Program

This program from AIMS (Grayslake, IL) was originally developed for mainframe computers. The PC version of the program requires an IBM PC/XT/ AT or PS/2-compatible computer with a minimum of 640 kbytes RAM and a floppy and a hard disk, a CGA. EGA, VGA, or Hercules graphics adapter and equivalent display.

In addition to proprietary files it also supports MDL and SYBYL file formats. The system comprises a "librarian" for handling molecular data-files, a "sketchpad" for drawing, building, and modifying molecular models, and facilities for obtaining minimum energy conformations. It also offers the usual facilities for determination of distances and angles and for stick, stick and ball, and spacefill models. Stereoscopic presentations with adjustable separation are also possible.

The Desktop Molecular Modeller

This program, which is distributed by Oxford University Press, requires a computer compatible with IBM PC, XT or AT, or IBM PS/2 with one or two floppy disk drives and at least 512 kbytes RAM, a CGA, EGA, VGA, or Hercules graphics adapter and equivalent display.

Coordinate and connectivity data for a number of molecules and fragments are distributed with the program which can handle structures comprising up to 1500 atoms and bonds. It will also read externally generated coordinate files. In addition to various options for displaying, manipulating, and editing and for calculation of distances and angles, the program has facilities for energy minimization and for compressed storage of screen images.

Table 2 is a summary of suppliers, prices, and hardware requirements of PC-based molecular modeling programs.

TABLE 2   Modeling on Personal Computers

Product name and supplier	Cost	Processing unit	Additional hardware etc.
ALCHEMY, Tripos Associates	875	IBM PC/XT/AT or IBM PS/2 Apple Mac II	
CAMSEQ, AIMS	790	IBM PC/XT/AT IBM PS/2	EGA, CGA, VGA or Hercules adapter and display
Desktop Molecular Modeller, Oxford University Press	525	IBM PC/XT/AT IBM PS/2	EGA, CGA, VGA or Hercules adapter and display
DIST3D, Novo Research Institute	Free for research use	IBM PC/AT or IBM PS/2	EGA, VGA
PC-Chemmod, U-Microcomputers Ltd.	13,000 includes Vector Graphics	IBM PC, PC/AT IBM PS/2	Chemmod vector graphics processor, and compatible display, optical mouse
PC-MODEL, Academic Press	150	IBM PC or Apple II	CGA
Promodeler I, New England Biographics	750	IBM PC/AT	Professinal Graphics Adapter and Display or compatibles

Databases and Interface

The molecular modeling activity is often aimed at evaluating consequences of a modification of a known structure (e.g., of a protein). In almost all such cases, the three-dimensional structure of the modified protein is not known. The molecular modeler can now either rely on his intuition or better try to validate his predictions for the modified structure. If he can find an analogous situation in another protein, one can claim that other structures contain the same motif. This seems like a very simple and straightforward process, but so far very few researchers have had access to tools which allowed them to make such an inquiry for proteins. A typical example that may illustrate the above is the following: let us assume that for some reason we would like to increase the number of amino acids sitting in a loop connecting two alpha helices in a given protein. It is very easy to build something which on the display looks rather plausible, but usually we have no idea a priori whether nature has created something similar in other proteins for which we do know the structure. The basic issue is therefore how do we ask this very relevant question?

As previously mentioned, all publicly available protein structures are compiled in the Brookhaven Protein Data Bank (PDB). These data can be obtained at a marginal cost. The data are provided as a list of the coordinates of the thousands of atoms present in each protein plus a few other pieces of information. Although the data in principle is there, it is not trivial to ask a question like "find all alpha helices." The raw data in PDB must be processed in a way that prepares them for typical queries and still allows the questioner the liberty of designing more elaborate questions. The most substantial activity addressing these issues has been undertaken by Professor Jane Thornton and her group at Birckbeck College in London. They have built a relational database on the raw PDB data files which allows the user to ask questions very similar to the example above. We are informed that a version of this database will soon be available on PCs [11].

CONCLUSION

From its origin as a comparatively primitive tool the PC has grown up to become a highly sophisticated aid with a wide range of applications. Molecular modeling is only one. The current CPU performance and average graphical capabilities have shown tremendous development over the past decade. There is little doubt that this trend will continue, although the current bottleneck seems to be appropriate software for the wonders currently emerging on the hardware market. Given the sophistication of the hardware, it is becoming ever more important that the user interface must be very accommodating even for newcomers. This is easier said than done. Even if it could be done, the user may complain that there seems to be no universally accepted command design. Why on earth can people not agree on certain simple function key assignments. We can come up with a thousand good manufacturers' reasons, but the end user could not care less. We anticipate that more elaborate but more user-friendly interfaces will be developed as a vital aspect of the software diffusion. It should also be noted that the so-called ToolBox on the Macintosh forces programs (programmers) to use a rather uniform user interface. It is uncertain whether the Presentation Manager of IBM's OS/2 will do the same.

The hardware will become much faster, especially through the use of parallel processing. We anticipate that we will see at least a 10-fold increase in the price performance ratio over the next five years. In addition, the high performance of special add-ons such as floating-point coprocesors will further improve the mathematical performance of the PC in the years ahead. Today's fastest PC models show performances aproaching that of a VAX 780 minicomputer (introduced in 1977). Maybe a good PC in five years time can be compared similarly with today's low-end CRAY.

Given the above circumstances, it appears that almost all of the calculations that today seem to hinder the PC in performing as well as the so-called professional modeling workstation will be gone. Future products will most likely be attractive to the chemist or biochemist, who cannot afford a price tag of $100,000; the time seems near when he or she will be able to perform all applications without paying more for the hardware than what he or she is paying for a high-quality PC today. This PC of the near future will be capable of interactive dynamics calculations of limited size, as well as real-time rotations of several thousands of atoms with perhaps 256 simultaneous colors in high resolution, probably 2000 × 1500 pixels.

The conclusion must be that we can expect the arrival of high-quality, PC-based, molecular modeling on the research scientists desk in just a few years time. For the companies that are currently selling the high-priced, high-performance systems, this will become a problem over the next few years; for the software houses a quite similar problem will arise. Few individuals, let alone companies, will be willing to pay prices currently being requested for full-fledged molecular modeling systems. Industrial companies will probably want to distribute this technology to more of their scientists instead of reserving it for the few selected modelers. Dedicated experts will, as always be in demand, but as a tool, molecular modeling will be available for the many, not just the few. A quite promising future to which we all will have to adjust.

REFERENCES

1. F. H. Allen, S. Bellard, M. D. Brice, A. Doubleday, H. Higgs, T. Hummelink, B. G. Hummelink-Peters, O. Kennard, W. D. S. Motherwell, J. R. Rodgers, and D. G. Watson, "The Cambridge Crystallographic Data Centre: Computer Based Search, Retrieval, Analysis and Display of Information," *Acta Crystallogr. Sect. B*, *35*, 2331 (1979).

2. G. Bergerhoff, R. Hundt, R. Sievers, and I. D. Brown, "The Inorganic Crystal Structure Database," *J. Chem. Inf. Comput. Sci.*, *23*, 66—69 (1983).

3. F. C. Bernstein, T. F. Koetzle, G. J. B. Williams, E. F. Meyer Jr., M. D. Brice, J. R. Rodgers, O. Kennard, T. Shimanouchi, and M. Tasumi, "The Protein Data Bank; A Computer Based Archival File for Macromolecule Structures," *J. Mol. Biol.*, *112*, 535—542 (1977).

4. E. L. Ulrich, J. L. Markly, and Y. Kyogoku, "Creation of a Nuclear Magnetic Resonance Data Repository and Literature Database," *Protein Seq. Data Anal.*, *2*, 23—37 (1989).

5. D. P. Dolata and R. E. Carter, "WIZARD: Applications of Expert System Techniques to Conformational Analysis," *J. Chem. Inf. Comput. Sci.*, *27*, 36—47 (1987).

6. E. J. Kirkland, "Viewing Molecules with the Macintosh," *BYTE*, February, 251—258 (1985).

7. A. M. Lesk, "A Toolkit for Computational Molecular Biology I; Packing and Unpacking of Protein Coordinate Sets," *J. Mol. Graph.*, *1*, 118—121 (1983).

8. J. D. Foley and A Van Dam, *Fundamentals of Interactive Computer Graphics*, Addison-Wesley Publishing Company, Reading, MA.

9. W. M. Newman and Robert F. Sproull, *Principles of Interactive Computer Graphics*, McGraw-Hill, New York.

10. QCPE Catalogue, Quantum Chemistry Program Exchange, Department of Chemistry, Indiana University, Bloomington, IN 47405 (1988).

11. D. Akrigg, A. J. Bleasby, N. I. M. Dix, J. B. C. Findlay, A. C. T. North, D. Parry-Smith, J. C. Wootton, T. L. Blundell, S. P. Gardner, F. Hayes, S. Islam, M. J. E. Sternberg, J. M. Thornton, and I. J. Tickle, "A Protein Sequence/Structure Database," *Nature*, *335*, 745–746 (1988).

Additional Reading

For further study interested readers are referred to the following journals:

Journal of Molecular Graphics, Butterworth Publishers, Reed Publishing, Inc.
Journal of Chemical Information and Computer Sciences, American Chemical Society

Referenced Companies

Academic Press, Inc., Harcourt Brace Jovanovich, Publishers, 1250 Sixth Avenue, San Diego, CA 92101-9665

AIMS, P.O. Box 646, Grayslake, IL 60030

AQUITAINE SYSTEMES, Department Scientifique, Tour ELF, 2 place de la Coupole, Cedex 45 92078 Paris La Defense, France

BioDesign, Inc., 199 S. Los Robles Avenue, Suite 270, Pasadena, CA 91101

BIOSYM Technologies, Inc., 10065A Barnes Canyon Road, San Diego, CA 92121

Chemical Design Ltd., Unit 12, 7 West Way, Oxford OX2 OJB, England

Etronics AG, St. Niklausstrasse 1, Postfach 23, 8103 Unterengstringen, Switzerland

Evans & Sutherland, Gallop House, Hasler's Lane, Great Dunmow, Essex CM16 1XS, England

New England BioGraphics, P.O. Box 24, Peachham, VT 05862

Oxford Electronic Publishing, Oxford University Press, Walton Street, Oxford OX2 6DP, England

Polygen Corporation, 200 Fifth Avenue, Waltham, MA 02254

Silicon Graphics Computer Systems, 2011 Stierlin Road, Mountain View, CA 94043

TRIPOS Associates, Inc., 6548 Clayton Road, St. Louis, MO 63117

U-Microcomputers Limited, 12 Chetham Court, Calver Road, Winwick Quay, Warrington, Cheshire WA2 8RF, England

CURT GISTRUP
LEIF NØRSKOV-LAURITSEN
STEFFEN B. PETERSEN

EPIDEMIOLOGY AND MICROCOMPUTERS

INTRODUCTION

Epidemiology, the study of "the distribution and determinants of disease in populations," became a science rather suddenly around 1850, when Dr. John Snow [1], a London physician, studied cholera cases and their water sources and concluded that specific water supplies were associated with disease. His removal of the handle on the Broad Street pump, an implicated water source, has been a model of effective disease control efforts for 140 years.

In contrast to other health sciences, epidemiology focuses on populations rather than individuals and uses rates and other statistics as a principal tool. Careful counting of cases and of "exposed" persons is the basis of epidemiologic methods.

"Cases" are defined as persons in a given population having particular diagnoses, symptoms, laboratory findings, or other characteristics describing their state of health over a defined time period. "Exposed" persons are those with defined personal, temporal, and geographic characteristics considered to have possible influences on disease rates. Exposure variables may include food intake, use of drugs or devices, sexual practices, presence in a particular place, work history, genetic type, or other factors that may be associated with an increased risk of disease. Other variables that define populations with different rates of both disease and exposure are called "confounding variables," and these are also, of necessity, the subject of epidemiologic study, since they can cause incorrect results if not controlled for in the analysis.

Most epidemiologic studies are based on comparison of exposure in ill and non-ill people (a case-control study), or on comparison of illness rates in exposed and unexposed persons (a cohort study). Studies that compare two groups in this way are called analytic studies. Descriptive studies, which describe characteristics of only a single group of ill or exposed persons, are also frequently performed, sometimes to generate hypotheses before an analytic study is undertaken.

In the physical sciences, units of measurement tend to be continuous variables like mass, distance, and time. Epidemiology, like the social sciences, deals more frequently with categorical data such as sex (M/F), baked ham consumption (Yes/No), income category (1–5), age group (by 5 or 10 years), or illness (Yes/No).

Sometimes the categories are ordered (ordinal) as in age groups, sometimes not, as in race. Statistical methods to deal with categorical data are different from those for continuous variables, and epidemiologists have their own favorite procedures for statistical analysis that differ in emphasis, name, and application from those in other sciences. Computer statistics packages for general use often contain abundant resources for analysis of continuous data, but lack such epidemiologic staples as the Mantel–Haenszel

Submitted: March 1988.

analysis for stratified tables, the Fisher exact test for 2-by-2 tables, and logistic regression. They usually do contain chi-square tests, which are much used in epidemiology. In a later section on investigative epidemiology, we will mention the common procedures for categorical data analysis and several microcomputer packages that are designed specifically for epidemiologic work.

Epidemiology can be divided into at least two broad areas, which we will call "inductive" and "deductive" epidemiology. Public health investigation and public health research usually begin with data gathered about a population and proceed to form conceptual models which are compared with the actual situation to test hypotheses. This can be considered inductive (or investigative) epidemiology.

"Deductive" epidemiology, or mathematical modeling, constructs a hypothetical population from assumptions about its members, and then describes the consequences of a disease or exposure having defined characteristics. The model is sometimes tested for validity by comparing the results with data from real populations.

Both approaches use mathematical models to describe disease and risk factors in a population. The investigative method begins with data on a particular population and extracts rates or fits curves. The deductive method produces a hypothetical population and a mathematical model, and does not necessarily involve data from an actual situation, although this is often done for validation purposes.

INDUCTIVE EPIDEMIOLOGY: EXTRACTING MODELS FROM NATURAL POPULATIONS

Although within epidemiology "epidemic modeling" is often taken to mean the study of theoretical populations as described in the section of deductive models, it also applies in a broad sense to the construction of models, however simple, from populations as found in nature, using classification, counting, arithmetic, and sometimes more sophisticated statistics. Most epidemiologic investigations start with an affected population, attempt to count persons with and without exposure and disease, and then use statistics to examine possible associations. All of these processes can be assisted and made more accurate by computers. Many textbooks of epidemiology [2–4] and of epidemiologic statistics [5–9] are available.

In doing an epidemiologic study, the first step is to verify that the problem being studied actually exists and that the numbers of cases or exposures are truly in excess of what is expected for the population. The epidemiologist then performs the all-important political/administrative step of establishing contact with appropriate authorities and enlisting cooperation in performing a study. He or she then decides *what information to collect* by defining hypotheses, *from whom to collect it* by developing a study design, and *how many persons to study* by deciding on a sample size.

Often a questionnaire is developed to collect and organize the appropriate information. Collection of data usually is through telephone, mail, or face-to-face interviews or abstraction of information from medical records.

The data records are "cleaned up" by verifying, selecting, and recoding. Analysis is performed manually or on a calculator, microcomputer, large computer, or by a combination of means. In some cases, more than one study is performed simultaneously, or a descriptive study is performed to generate hypotheses followed by an analytic study to test these hypotheses. When conclusions have been reached about the associations observed, control measures are instituted and a written report is prepared.

All of the processes can be assisted by computer programs that provide access to information or provide methods for manipulating data or textual material. Most available programs focus on analytic procedures and provide a variety of statistical procedures used in epidemiology, but computers can be used for many other steps in an investigation—either through specialized programs like the two "expert systems" described later or through creative use of spreadsheets and word processing programs.

Hypothesis Generation and Literature Searching

The early stages of epidemiologic investigation involve a quick review of the problem, perhaps through a descriptive study as described later, and then the generation of hypotheses through knowledge of the subject matter and/ or searching the scientific literature. In their simplest form, these steps may be performed by public health workers, practicing physicians, citizens, or parents in communities, hospitals, industries, or schools. One or more cases of illness with known cause are questioned about contacts or recent exposures, a conclusion is reached, and appropriate action is taken. Any statistics can usually be done on the fingers of one hand, and the need for computer assistance lies in the realm of record keeping and access to medical information.

Descriptions of common infectious diseases and public health responses are found in *Control of Communicable Diseases in Man* [10], a printed handbook of information for public health use. For more comprehensive assistance in hypothesis generation, the National Library of Medicine MEDLARS system provides an on-line database of over six million reference citations to to journal articles, books, and audiovisual materials, that can be accessed through major telecommunciations networks, using a terminal or a microcomputer.

Grateful Med [11] is a user-friendly front-end program for MEDLARS which runs on IBM PC-compatible microcomputers and makes searches easy for persons without library training. Grateful Med is available from the National Technical Information Service, Washington, D.C.; the user must apply for an account with MEDLARS to use the service. A number of other commercial bibliographic services such as Paper Chase, Dialog, and BRS Colleague, offer access to MEDLARS, usually at higher cost.

Gathering and Quality Control of Data

Data for epidemiologic studies must meet several requirements not necessary for individual patient records. For a sample to be useful, it must bear a known relationship to the population being sampled, as either a random or a systematic sample. For an analytic study of ill people, the population of non-ill people must also be represented. Studies of exposed and unexposed persons must include both populations. Distortions of results caused by uncertain relationship of the sample to the denominator population are called "selection bias." Other types of bias are caused by inconsistent or inaccurate data collection, errors in data entry, laboratory inaccuracies, misdiagnosis, and other difficulties that can influence the accuracy of results. Much of the epidemiologist's work is in recognizing and minimizing various types of bias.

A major limitation in epidemiologic studies is the difficulty in obtaining data from defined populations. Information about ill persons and their exposures or risk factors (the two terms are used interchangeably) is still obtained largely from face-to-face interviews or from visual review of medical records. Large computerized databases such as death certificate files, insurance claim records, and computerized hospital records are useful for obtaining overall frequencies or trends, but are often disappointing inaccurate or incomplete for purposes other than those originally intended.

The diversity and lack of standardization of both medical services and medical records in most settings requires abstraction of data from handwritten records or oral interviews into a form useful for study. In-patient records in the United States—even laboratory data, consisting primarily of numbers—are recorded in hundreds of formats in different institutions. Patient identification numbers usually apply to a person only within a single institution and sometimes only for a single hospital stay. Billing records may describe families without distinguishing individuals. Computerized medical databases useful for epidemiology are found only in a few isolated institutions, and often do not relate to a population defined more precisely than as members of the institution's clientele.

In an epidemic, many ill persons may not visit a physician or they may visit many different physicians and so must be interviewed or examined or have their records abstracted uniformly to permit epidemiologic study. A portable microcomputer can be used to enter questionnaire information directly or to transfer the information from a paper record to the computer. Data entry may be done in a statistics or database program, or in a dedicated data entry and file creation program.

Analytic packages with specific epidemiologic features and data entry capability include (in alphabetical order) CRISP, Epi Info, EpiLog, Epistat, and True Epistat. Other more general packages are SPSS, SAS, and dBADE III and III Plus. Not all handle nonnumeric data equally well, and one should evaluate this as well as program size, price, and compatibility with other programs before deciding which one to use.

It is important in field investigations to use software that the investigator can operate comfortably and has employed for a similar purpose in the past. Unfamiliar computer programs have a way of consuming time unexpectedly, and learning time is at a premium in many epidemic investigations, particularly if one epidemiologist is doing the investigation and also trying to operate the computer. The ease of setting up or changing a questionnaire in the system is important, since investigations of acute problems often have to be done in a hurry, and hypotheses may change after even a few hours in the field.

Skilled programmers or those planning long-term studies may want to write dedicated data entry programs in BASIC, Pascal, or other languages, but this is seldom necessary, since several of the statistics packages allow data entry to be programmed with considerable specificity, and most packages provide means to transfer files to other formats.

More than 40 epidemiologists from the Centers for Disease Control assigned to work in states have been provided with portable IBM PC-compatible microcomputers to assist in epidemic investigations. They and a number of other epidemiologists now routinely enter data into microcomputers while in the field. Some use portable computers in hospital record rooms to abstract records without using an intervening paper form.

Data entry programs that incorporate range checking and other types of error prevention can play a useful role in providing accurate data for large studies where time permits setting up the necessary error checking. Software packages that permit rapid analysis of data can be used to screen for errors by producing tables showing extreme values and illogical conditions (e.g., male pregnancies), while they can still be corrected from the original data source.

Large research studies such as those assessing the effect of risk factors on cardiovascular disease, spend millions of dollars on carefully controlled interviews and examinations of defined populations so that accurate data can be stored for comparison with future disease rates. One study of risk factors for atherosclerosis funded by the National Heart, Lung, and Blood Institute uses microcomputers for data collection in centers in four different cities [12]. Each examination center has a number of microcomputers for entry of data as a study participant is interviewed and examined. The subject carries his own floppy disk from station to station, and paper forms are not used. Customized data entry programs provide error checking and formatting of the data so that ambiguities can be resolved while the subject is still present. At intervals the records are sent to a national center for processing on a mainframe computer. Coordination between centers is assisted by a microcomputer bulletin board accessed daily by each of the four centers.

Study Design

Most investigations involve careful collection of data from which a mathematical model is constructed of an ill or exposed population and possibly of a non-ill or nonexposed population. If a single group of ill or exposed persons is involved, the study is "descriptive." Adding a comparison group produces either a case-control study (ill versus non-ill) or a cohort study (exposed versus nonexposed). The four major types of epidemiologic study are shown in Table 1.

Another type of study, called the cross-sectional study, begins with an entire population, such as persons who attended a particular banquet, or were included in a survey. Conceptually, however, the information is analyzed as either a case-control or a cohort study, depending on how the problem is viewed.

The most common model employed for analysis of case-control or cohort studies is the 2-by-2 table, often set up as follows:

		Illness	
		+	−
Exposure	+	A	B
	−	C	D

Each letter represents the number of persons having the characteristics in the margin. Thus, C is the number of ill persons who were not exposed to the factor under study.

For case-control studies, the odds ratio AD/BC is used to reflect the degree of association between illness and the specified exposure. Counts

TABLE 1   Types of Epidemiologic Studies

Starting point	Descriptive study	Analytic study
Ill persons	Describe illness and exposure in the ill population (Case series)	Case-control study: Com Compare Ill and well persons with respect to exposure
Exposed persons	Describe exposure and illness in the exposed population	Cohort study: Compare exposed and unexposed persons with respect to illness

in the A and D cells support the hypothesis of association: those in B and C weaken it. If the sick are exposed and the well are not the association is supported. The chi-square test and an associated p (probability) value are often used to test for association, sometimes with a correction for small numbers (Yates' correction). Methods for calculating confidence limits provide a range of values of the odds ratio which are consistent with the data. The confidence interval may also be used as a test of significance. If the confidence limit includes 1.0, the level reflecting no association, the association is considered "not significant."

The measure of association most used in exposure-based (cohort) studies is relative risk, which is the proportion of illness in exposed persons, divided by the proportion of illness in the unexposed

$$\text{Relative Risk} = \frac{\dfrac{A}{A + B}}{\dfrac{C}{C + D}}$$

Chi-square tests, p-values, and confidence intervals can also be calculated for relative risks.

This simple model would be sufficient if the illness and a single type of exposure were the only differences between cases and controls. Except in carefully matched studies, this is rarely true. Suppose that 2-by-2 tables show associations between the rate of illness and the eating of three foods—ham, mustard, and raisin sauce, and also with age (adult versus child). In the study of any one of these factors the others are potential *confounding factors*, since they are associated both with disease and with exposure. It is easy to postulate that adults ate ham in preference to hot dogs, and that ham eaters were more likely to use mustard and raisin sauce; in fact, it may be hard to find either ill or well ham eaters who did *not* use mustard or raisin sauce.

One way of evaluating the significance of cases' consumption of ham alone is to choose matched controls who have the same age/mustard/raisin sauce values. This would require a separate study for each factor being considered, and is generally impractical because of the limited number of attendees at the event who can be used as controls. Matching for common confounding variables, such as age and sex, with 1, 2, 3, or 4 comparison subjects per case or exposed person is often used in research studies, however.

If cases and controls are not matched for confounding variable status, the fair way to study the association of disease with ham is to choose groups with the same mustard-sauce-age group and study ham within each group. This splitting into subgroups is called "stratification." Mantel and Haenszel [13] showed how to combine the results from each stratum into an overall estimate of the odds ratio, and this procedure is still the recommended way to begin an analysis of several categorical variables in epidemiology.

If the case rate in ham eaters differs with age, sauce, or mustard, one or more of the factors would be said to *interact* with ham eating.

Interaction is usually handled in epidemiology by statistical modeling, which will be described in the next section. There is not universal agreement on the definition of interaction, since there are two kinds (additive and multiplicative) [14], and factors may interact in one model and not in the other. Asbestos exposure and smoking are known to interact strongly in producing lung cancer in an additive model, but the interaction is minimal or absent in a multiplicative model.

Multivariate Regression Analysis

In regression analysis, an equation containing variables and constants is "fitted" to the data describing disease and exposure in a population. The process involves finding the values of constants or "coefficients" that give the best fit, a task that is usually practical only when done on a computer.

Experts say that this is one area where a little knowledge is a dangerous thing, and that regression analysis, like French cookery, requires more than a recipe for its successful performance and interpretation. Determining which data sets should be used for regression, and exactly how to proceed with analysis and interpretation, is an area requiring statistical judgment. Although it seems to be an ideal area for development of an "expert system," no one appears to have reported such a development in the medical literature. General strategies and a flow chart for doing the analysis have been published [15].

Some of the problems involved in using regression models have been discussed by Vanderbroucke [16], who raises the question, for the sake of argument, of abandoning regression models altogether. He concludes that results of regression modeling should at least be checked against those of stratificiation with the Mantel-Haenszel analysis discussed above. Rothman in his textbook on epidemiology, expresses the same view by saying, "The epidemiologist is better off to rely primarily on the more straightforward procedures of stratified analysis whenever possible, since these procedures engender greater familiarity with the data for both the investigator and the reader" [17].

A form of regression often used in epidemiology is logistic regression, which fits an equation of the following form to the data.

$$\text{Probability of disease} = 1/\{1 + \exp[-(a + \beta_1 \cdot x_1 + \ldots + \beta_j \cdot x_j)]\}$$

Disease must have values of 0 and 1 (binary outcome). The x values represent individual risk factors, x_1 being the exposure under study, and the other x's either risk factors or confounding variables, since both are treated as confounding variables in this analysis. An x term may be replaced by the product of two risk factors thought to interact, such as $\beta_6 x_1 x_2$. One of the goals of the analysis is to choose the minimal number of such terms that will produce a good "fit" to the data.

In performing logistic regression, information on disease outcome and individual risk factors for a number of individuals is fed to the computer. Two methods of calculation are available—conditional and unconditional logistic regression. Conditional logistic regression is more accurate for studies with small numbers of subjects, but consumes more computer resources. The results of interest are the beta coefficients and the odds ratios and confidence limits that may be derived from them. An odds ratio of 2 for the risk factor *smoking* in a study of myocardial infarction would mean that smokers were twice as likely as nonsmokers to have myocardial infarctions, with all other risk factors and confounding variables (e.g., cholesterol, blood pressure, exercise, age, sex) held constant. If interaction terms are included, their values must be specified in the results, since the odds ratio changes with different values of the interacting terms.

Multivariate Poisson regression is used for grouped data in diseases of low frequency, and survival analysis is used to study deaths or other events in exposed and unexposed groups over a defined period of follow-up. Computer programs for doing many of these procedures are available on microcomputers, and all are parts of mainframe packages such as SAS, BMDP, and SPSS.

LOGRESS [18] is a public domain program for logistic regression on IBM PC-compatible microcomputers, written in FORTRAN and assembly language. Data values to be input from a file or the keyboard include the names of variables, codes for missing values, and frequencies for each category of each variable. LOGRESS then produces odds ratios and 95% confidence limits associated with each risk factor. An odds ratio of 1.4 for "smoking (yes/no)" suggests that smokers have a 40% greater frequency of disease than nonsmokers who are otherwise similar in all respects entered into the model. Other statistics, such as beta coefficients, standard errors, and "z" scores are also given.

Loglinear modeling is another technique used in epidemiology for analysis of several variables. In logistic regression, the outcome variable, such as disease (ill/well), must have only two values, but loglinear methods allow more than two categories of outcome. Koepsel [19] describes a BASIC program called LOLA which does loglinear modeling on microcomputers.

A program called PC Fit for fitting a variety of functions to observed data points has been described by Smith [20]. Like LOGRESS, it uses the method of maximum likelihood estimation. Wallenstein and Bodian [21] have recently provided methods for using weighted least-squares analysis rather than maximum likelihood estimation for multivariate analysis. The calculations can be performed with current microcomputer versions of SAS and SPSS.

Cyrus Mehta and colleagues [22] have developed network algorithms for calculation of exact confidence limits on the odds ratio, a procedure which was formerly practical only on mainframe computers. Extension of similar methods to logistic regression analysis is under way in Dr. Mehta's group.

Other Programs for Epidemiologic Statistics

A description of 18 "free or inexpensive" programs for performing epidemiologic work has been published [23]. Most of the programs perform statistical operations. One should assume that they are not all of equal quality in terms of the user interface and documentation.

A public domain program for performing nutritional surveys has been produced by the Division of Nutrition at the Centers for Disease Control, Atlanta, Georgia. Known as CASP, it compares height, weight, and age measurements with appropriate standards and also tabulates results for a population.

"Expert Systems" for Epidemiologic Work

Epi Info and EPIAID form an experimental microcomputer system for epidemiologic field investigations developed at the Centers for Disease Control [24]. It uses interactive word processing to assist the investigator in drafting a report of an investigation. The programs contribute sentences or phrases to the report and then prompt the user to add words or sentences describing the current investigation. The result is a series of text summaries which form the introduction, methods, discussion of hypotheses, results, tables, references, and sample-size calculations for the written report of the investigation. The data handling and statistics package in Epi Info is being used in many epidemiologic settings.

Another application of "expert system" methods to epidemiology in Italy has been described by DeRosis, Pizzutilo, and Greco [25]. Their MICRO-IDEA system provides assistance in selecting correct methods for analysis of data. It uses decision trees to arrive at appropriate statistical methods and then performs the necessary calculations. MICRO-IDEA was written in compiled BASIC on an IBM PC-compatible microcomputer.

Disease Surveillance Systems

In the United States, a number of lcoal health departments and the majority of state health departments now maintain records of "reportable" diseases on microcomputers. Almost any file-handling or database system, including a spreadsheet program, can be used at the local level. In January 1990, 31 state health departments were using the program called Epi Info, developed at the Centers for Disease Control, for maintaining reports of disease. Others use dBASE III or other database systems on computers of all sizes.

PUBLIC HEALTH COMMUNICATION

A public health network administered by the Public Health Foundation, Washington, D.C., on a commercial telecommunication network has (January 1990) 783 users, including most state health departments. All 50 states send weekly disease reports to the Centers for Disease Control in Atlanta in the form of electronic mail messages containing structured data records.

Microcomputers are used in state health departments for maintaining records on sexually transmitted disease, acquired immunodeficiency syndrome

(AIDS), immunization, and random telephone surveys of chronic disease risk factors. Each of these programs is coordinated nationally, and records are sent from microcomputers at the state level to the Centers for Disease Control, where the files are merged and then processed on a mainframe computer.

Mapping of Disease

Mapping of disease cases and disease rates has been performed on mainframe computers for many years. Commercial microcomputer programs such as Mapmaster and Atlas AMP produce maps of the United States down to zip code level, and of other countries in less detail. Producing maps other than those supplied as options with the programs is not yet convenient, and files containing detailed coordinates are often expensive.

DEDUCTIVE OR A PRIORI MODEL BUILDING: CONSTRUCTING A WORLD AND THEN A MODEL

Mathematical models of communicable disease in hypothetical populations were pioneered by Sir Ronald Ross for malaria in 1909 and are the topic of hundreds of articles and at least ten books. Reviews of the subject have been published by Fine [26], Bailey [27], and others [28, 29].

Models of infectious disease begin with assumptions about the source, route, and probability of infection. Most models assume infection from human cases, as in influenza, a popular subject for modeling. "Mass-action" models assume that risk of infection is proportional to the product of the number of active cases and the number of susceptible persions, much as in models of chemical reactions. The Reed—Frost model gives similar results if the population is large and the cases are widely scattered, but it also adjusts for multiple exposures (only one of which can be effective) in populations of smaller size. Programs incorporating the Reed—Frost model for calculators [30] and for IBM PC-compatible microcomputers [31] have been described.

Models assuming society to be a series of cases, susceptibles, and immunes bouncing off each other randomly, like molecules of a gas, have clear limitations. A series of Reed—Frost models with increasing flexibility for compartmentalization of subpopulations and inclusion of multiple risk factors has been developed by Ackerman et al. [32]. The "Resource for Simulation of Stochastic Micropopulation Models" at the University of Minnesota offers collaborative research facilities for those wishing to explore particular models on a minicomputer within this framework.

The term "stochastic" refers to the use of random events generated by the comptuer to simulate the real world. If the probability of an event is 0.70, for example, a random number is generated between 0 and 1.0. If it falls in the range 0 to 0.70, the event "occurs"; otherwise, it does not. This type of simulation requires the generation of many epidemics—often 100—to describe the range of statistical possibilities that can occur. More computer time is likely to be needed for these models than for "deterministic" models in which a series of equations is solved, although this depends on the methods used for their solution.

Time is handled differently in different models. "Discrete-time" models use slices of time, calculating all the nececessary results for a finite period such as an hour or a day. Calculations for the next interval are based on these results, each cycle being the basis for giving the model another "crank" for the next time period. Continuous-time models use differential calculus to work with changes in rates at each point on a curve. Theoretically, the results of discrete-time models should approach those of continuous-time models as the intervals used become smaller.

We have briefly described models of society as random individuals arranged in family, school, or work groups. A variant on compartmentalized groups occurs when the groups are different cities and the determinant of contact is the amount of air traffic between the infected and uninfected cities. A microcomputer model of this type has been described by Longini, Fine, and Thacker [33].

Airborne and close-contact infection are the easiest situations to model. Epidemics of foodborne disease do not appear to have been the subject of deductive modeling, since they arise through a series of rare events (e.g., slicing the cooked turkey on the same cutting board used for raw turkey, followed by storing it several hours at the wrong temperature), and the microscopic components of those events usually can only be imagined. It is rare that uniform mixing of the food vehicle occurs to allow necessary assumptions about dose.

Malaria has been extensively modeled since 1909. Bailey's book on the subject [34] concludes with pleas for field validation of mathematical models and comments that "It may well be that genuinely new and useful applications of malaria biomathematics will only be effectively fostered and promoted by carrying them directly into the areas where their contribution to the alleviation of human suffering will be most keenly appreciated." In other words, improved health is the real test, one that has not yet produced a good score for mathematical modeling in the malaria field, despite the large amount of thought which has been stimulated by the process.

AIDS is a problem of immense concern to world health that appears to offer several favorable features for modeling. A number of modeling groups have begun to work on this important problem. The difficulties, as pointed out by May and Anderson [35], lie in the lack of data to describe the behavior of the causative virus in even one population, since studies have not continued long enough to discover the 10-year outcome of infection, for example. The results of infection may vary by route of infection, genetic background, or other factors. Data collection is impaired by the fact that major risk factors, such as homosexuality and intravenous drug use, are difficult to monitor accurately.

Modeling of Chronic Disease

Many chronic illnesses such as heart disease and cancer can be measured through their effect on mortality, which is comprehensively (although crudely) reflected in the death certificates kept by every state health department. Surveys of the prevalence of risk factors such as smoking, hypertension, obesity, and lack of exercise are also commonly available [36]. Rice and Hodgson et al. [37] have combined these and other types of information into an estimate of "attributable risk," or the fraction of disease attributable to smoking. Shultz [38] has incorporated these models into spreadsheets for IBM PC-compatible computers, and they have been used in a number of states to estimate the fraction of illness attributable to smoking for use in public policy decisions.

Models for Teaching

Simulation offers obvious advantages for teaching epidemiology, particularly for illustrating the results of random sampling. Bland [39] has used microcomputers to simulate a cancer treatment trial in classes of medical students. An interactive microcomputer program for teaching simple epidemiologic concepts has been developed by Pastides et al. [40].

The potential exists for realistic simulation of epidemics using computers to present illnesses, interviews, and other factors that could be sampled randomly by each member of a class. Video disc technology has been used in clinical teaching of medicine [41], but apparently the first epidemic on a computer-controlled video disk has not yet appeared.

Evaluation of Epidemic Models

Most mathematical models, if they have been evaluated against the real world at all, have been compared with data sets from past epidemics, often from isolated populations such as those of Iceland or Tristan da Cunha. Even if such epidemics fit the model within, say, 95% confidence limits, the value of a single epidemic for such validation is limited, as is any other sample of one in the statistical world. Assuming that epidemics are driven by random processes (as most models assume), one would expect natural epidemics to match the central tendencies of models very seldom; in fact, it would be very surprising to see an exact match. There is no way of knowing whether the epidemic observed came from the right tail, the left tail, or the center of nature's normal curve, and the same is true of individual elements that were measured to form the basis for the model. Only when numbers are very large does randomness begin to approach some kind of predictability. With large populations, frequent, detailed observations of sick and well people are not affordable—throwing a kind of uncertainty principle in the way of deductive epidemiological modeling.

Mathematical modeling played a substantial role in planning the World Health Organization's unsuccessful worldwide malaria eradication compaign of the 1950s and 1960s, a major example of unsatisfactory forecasting. Empirical discoveries on vaccination strategy, not modeling, were the basis for the successful worldwide smallpox eradication which began in 1966 [42]. The "swine flu affair" [43] of 1976—1977 in the United States arose from predictions of a worldwide epidemic of influenza, in a field that had been the subject of numerous mathematical models. The shortcoming is usually not in the model, but in the information which is available to feed into the model, for example, the infectivity of a new strain of virus in human populations, or political and economic factors which affect health programs. Other predictions based on modeling have been more accurate, such as those of Hethcote on measles and rubella trends in the United States [44].

It appears that deductive modeling has raised interesting questions, contributed to teaching and understanding of epidemic processes, and given rise to hundreds of articles and books. It has not yet become a regular part of disease control programs. Fine, an expert in the field, says, "An enterprise cannot survive on potential alone, and one may well question to what extent the large literature on mathematical models has lived up to any potential usefulness. It is probably correct to say that it has not . . . " [45]. Nevertheless, contributions of mathematical modeling to teaching and statistical analysis of disease patterns remain, and probably will increase if microcomputers make modeling available to a wider audience at lower cost.

FUTURE POSSIBILITIES FOR MICROCOMPUTERS IN EPIDEMIOLOGY

Neural Network Models

Computer hardware and software patterned after networks of neurons in the central nervous system has lately become a subject of intense interest in artificial intelligence circles [46]. A neural network is built of "neurons," each of which has many inputs and usually a single output. The output is a function, such as summation, of the inputs, and each of the inputs can have a weight or more complex function attached to it. Unlike a sequential processor, the "program" is embodied in the connections between elements and the weights assigned to each connection. Neural networks are particularly adapted to optimization and equilibrium problems and to "learning" from repeated exposure to similar patterns. They function by parallel rather than sequential processing, and work largely with analog rather than digital variables. "Neurons" can be constructed in hardware form or simulated in software on a conventional computer. Neural network programs are available for both the Macintosh [47] and IBM PC-compatible microcomputer [48].

In epidemiology, illness (or lack of illness) might be viewed as the sum of a complex series of risk factors. It might be possible to represent society as a collection of "neurons" representing persons, and infection as the propagation of impulses from one neuron to another. If suitable time delays could be introduced, such a system might offer an alternative format for modeling human disease in a population, although connecting the model with the real world would present the same challenge as it does with present models.

The ability of neural networks to learn by incorporating new data to change the strength of connections between elements might be used for disease surveillance. A disease surveillance system in a public health department someday might consist of a neural network model of society, updated daily by births, deaths, and illness information obtained from the real world. The model would remain as imperfect as our data and our knowledge of the causes of disease, but constructing it would at least pose some interesting questions.

Expanded Role of Microcomputers

Microcomputers are already being used to collect and process data from outbreak investigations and to maintain surveillance records for selected diseases. It is practical to handle files of 100,000 or 200,000 modest-sized records on an IBM-compatible computer. Larger files are usually handled on mini- or mainframe computers. The level at which this crossover occurs will undoubtedly rise as processors become faster and disc capacity grows larger and cheaper.

At present speeds, microcomputers can handle files containing *samples* of larger files adequate for most analytic purposes. Given a file of many million Medicare records, for example, a sample of the file can be selected and downloaded to a microcomputer for analysis. Considering the inaccuracies in the original data due to sampling, data input, and provider bias, there seems to be little reason to process the entire file. Since samples of a few thousand records often represent a population quite well, the actual processing now falls within the capabilities of microcomputers, making such data handling technically possible for persons outside the mainframe world.

Clearly, this expanded access to processing of larger data sets invites the inexperienced user to make mistakes, but it also expands the epidemiologic community's pool of experienced "data crunchers." In developing countries, where mainframe computers are in short supply, microcomputers potentially can make even larger contributions to epidemiology.

Improved Data Collection

Computerized epidemiologic data files are almost all created by manual typing of information from other sources. This has advantages in condensing and cleaning up the data, but essentially limits epidemiologic studies to situations in which a commitment has been made to do a special study, or to use large data files collected for other purposes. Medical records are not currently accessible in machine-readable form from most general hospitals and clinics.

A medical record is often several inches thick, the equivalent of a megabyte of information (300 pages × 3,000 characters per page = 900k). On some of today's microcomputers and workstations, it would be possible to manipulate such a document, extract information, and produce a standardized record—perhaps on optical storage media—which could be used for clinical, archival, and epidemiologic purposes. Although research on methods of extracting useful information from the free-flowing form of most medical records has begun [49], the task of producing and using records in machine-readable form is a major obstacle. Voice-input dictation and improved text and cursive-handwriting scanners will probably be needed to carry this effort to the practical stage.

The next decade will produce the necessary technical tools for making medical records machine readable and available for epidemiologic analysis. Radical changes in medical practice and new approaches to maintaining both confidentiality and useful access to records will be needed before epidemiologic work can benefit from these advances. Many legal and political problems will have to be solved to provide for adequate systematic sampling of computerized medical records for public health purposes.

SUMMARY

During the past decade, microcomputers have come into routine, but not universal, use for data collection and processing in epidemiology. Two experimental "expert systems" have been developed for epidemiologic work. A variety of microcomputer programs for data entry and statistical processing are available, several of which are designed specifically for the categorical data analysis frequently used in epidemiology.

Advances in computer technology over the past few years have allowed tasks formerly confined to mainframe computers to be done on microcomputers, and many epidemiologists now make extensive use of microcomputers. A major advance in public health surveillance and epidemiologic study can be expected if patient medical records become routinely available in machine-readable form, and if epidemiologic analysis of national or other population-based samples of such records becomes possible. Microcomputers alone or connected with larger computers will play an increasing role in medical record keeping and in collection and analysis of epidemiologic data.

REFERENCES

1. J. Snow, *Snow on Cholera*, The Commonwealth Fund, New York, 1936.
2. J. P. Fox, C. E. Hall, and L. R. Elveback, *Epidemiology: Man & Disease*, Macmillan, New York, 1970.
3. G. D. Friedman, *Primer of Epidemiology*, 2nd ed., McGraw Hill, New York, 1979.
4. A. M. Lilienfeld and D. E. Lilienfeld, *Foundations of Epidemiology*, 2nd ed., Oxford University Press, New York, 1980.
5. J. L. Fleiss, *Statistical Methods for Rates and Proportions*, 2nd ed., John Wiley, New York, 1981.
6. J. J. Schlesselman, *Case-Control Studies*, Oxford University Press, New York, 1982.
7. N. E. Breslow and N. E. Day, *Statistical Methods in Cancer Research*, Volume 1, *The Analysis of Case-Control Studies*, International Agency for Research on Cancer, Lyon, France, 1980.
8. D. G. Kleinbaum, L. L. Kupper, and H. Morgenstern, *Epidemiologic Research*, Lifetime Learning Publications, Belmont, CA, 1982.
9. B. Rosner, *Fundamentals of Biostatistics*, Duxbury Press, Boston, 1982.
10. A. S. Benenson, *Control of Communicable Diseases in Man*, American Public Health Association, Washington, DC, 1985.
11. H. M. Schoolman, "The Physician and the Medical Literature. From Index Medicus to MEDLARS to GRATEFUL MED and Beyond," *Arch. Dermatol.*, *122*(8), 875–876 (1986).
12. A. L. Dannenberg, Personal communication, 1987.
13. N. Mantel and W. Haenszel, "Statistical Aspects of the Analysis of Data from Retrospective Studies of Disease," *J. Nat. Cancer Inst.*, *22*, 719–748 (1959).
14. D. G. Kleinbaum, L. L. Kupper, and H. Morgenstern, *Epidemiologic Research*, Lifetime Learning Publications, Belmont, CA, 1982, pp. 403–418.
15. D. G. Kleinbaum, L. L. Kupper, and H. Morgenstern, *Epidemiologic Research*, Lifetime Learning Publications, Belmont, CA, 1982, pp. 447–456.
16. J. P. Vandenbroucke, "Should We Abandon Statistical Modeling Altogether?," *Am. J. Epidemiol.*, *126*, 10–13 (1987).
17. K. J. Rothman, *Modern Epidemiology*, Little, Brown, Boston, 1986, p. 284.
18. D. L. McGee, "A Program for Logistic Regression on the IBM PC," *Am. J. Epidemiol.*, *124*, 702–705 (1986).
19. T. D. Koepsell, "Loglinear Modeling with Inexpensive Computing Equipment," *Am. J. Epidemiol.*, *120*, 777–787 (1984).
20. W. P. Smith, "PC FIT: A Distribution Fitting Program," *Am. Statist.*, *39*, 141 (1985).

21. S. Wallenstein and C. Bodian, "Inferences on Odds Ratios, Relative Risks, and Risk Differences Based on Standard Regression Programs," *Am. J. Epidemiol., 126*, 346–355 (1987).

22. C. R. Mehta, N. R. Patel, and R. Gray, "Computing an Exact Confidence Interval for the Common Odds Ratio in Several 2 × 2 Contingency Tables," *J. Am. Statis. Assoc., 80*, 969–973 (1985).

23. "Inventory of Free or Inexpensive IBM-PC Compatible Software for Epidemiologists," *Epidemiol. Mon., 8*, 1–8 (1987).

24. A. G. Dean, "EPIAID," *Byte*, October, 225–231 (1985).

25. F. DeRosis, S. Pizzutilo, and D. Greco, "MICRO-IDEA: Improving Decisions in Epidemiological Analysis by a Microcomputer," *Med. Inform., 11*, 225–236 (1986).

26. P. Fine, "Applications of Mathematical Models to the Epidemiology of Influenza: A Critique," in *Influenza Models: Prospects for Development and Use* (P. Selby, Ed.), MTP Press, Hingham, MA, 1982, pp. 15–85.

27. N. T. J. Bailey, *The Mathematical Theory of Infectious Diseases and Its Applications*, Hafner, New York, 1975.

28. K. Dietz and D. Schenzle, "Mathematical Models for Infectious Disease Statistics," in *A Celebration of Statistics: The ISI Centenary Volume* (A. C. Atkinson and S. E. Fienberg, Eds.), Springer-Verlag, New York, 1985, pp. 167–203.

29. N. Becker, "The Uses of Epidemic Models," *Biometrics, 35*, 295–305 (1979).

30. E. L. Franco and A. R. Simons, "Simple Algorithms for the Representation of Deterministic and Stochastic Versions of the Reed-Frost Epidemic Model Using a Programmable Calculator," *Am. J. Epidemiol., 123*, 905–915 (1986).

31. "Inventory of Free or Inexpensive IBM-PC Compatible Software for Epidemiologists," *Epidemiol. Mon., 8*, 1–8 (1987).

32. E. Ackerman, L. R. Elveback, and J. P. Fox, *Simulation of Infectious Disease Epidemics*, Charles C. Thomas, Springfield, IL, 1984.

33. I. M. Longini, P. E. M. Fine, and S. B. Thacker, "Predicting the Global Spread of New Infectious Agents," *Am. J. Epidemiol., 123*, 383–391 (1986).

34. N. T. J. Bailey, *The Biomathematics of Malaria*, Charles Griffin, London, 1982.

35. R. M. May and R. M. Anderson, "Transmission Dynamics of HIV Infection," *Nature, 326*, 137–142 (1987).

36. E. M. Gentry, W. D. Kalsbeek, G. C. Hogelin, et al., "The Behavioral Risk Factor Surveys: II. Design, Methods, and Estimates from Combined State Data," *Am. J. Prevent. Med., 1*, 9–14 (1985).

37. D. P. Rice, T. A. Hodgson, P. Sinsheimer, et al., "The Economic Costs of the Health Effects of Smoking, 1984," *Milbank Memorial Fund Q., 64*, 489–547 (1986).

38. J. M. Shultz, SAMMEC: Smoking-Attributable Mortality, Morbidity, and Economic Costs (Computer Software and Documentation), Minnesota Department of Health, Minneapolis, MN, 1986.

39. J. M. Bland, "Computer Simulation of a Clinical Trial as an Aid to Teaching the Concept of Statistical Significance," *Statis. Med., 5*, 193–197 (1986).

40. H. Pastides, K. A. Mundt, and C. B. MacKnight, "Microcomputer-Based Instruction: Applications in Epidemiology," Program and Abstracts, American Public Health Association 115th Annual Meeting, New Orleans, October 18–22, 1987, session #2118, APHA, Washington, DC, 1987.

41. W. G. Harless, M. A. Zier, and R. C. Duncan, "A Voice-Activated, Interactive Videodisc Case Study for Use in the Medical School Classroom," *J. Med. Educ.*, *61*, 913–915 (1986).

42. The Global Eradication of Smallpox: Final Report of the Global Commission of the Certification of Smallpox Eradication, Geneva, December 1979, World Health Organization, Geneva, 1980.

43. R. E. Neustadt and H. Y. Fineberg, *The Swine Flu Affair*, Washington, U.S.D.H.E.W., Government Printing Office, Washington, DC, 1978.

44. H. W. Hethcote, "Measles and Rubella in the United States," *Am. J. Epidemiol.*, *117*, 2–13 (1983).

45. P. Fine, "Applications of Mathematical Models to the Epidemiology of Influenza: A Critique," in *Influenza Models: Prospects for Development and Use* (P. Selby, Ed.), MTP Press, Hingham, MA, 1982, p. 31.

46. M. Gaudill, "Neural Networks Primer, Part 1," *AI Expert*, *2*, 46–52, (1987).

47. *McBrain: Neural Network Simulation System, User's Manual*, Neuronics, Cambridge, MA, 1987.

48. "Hecht-Nielsen's ANZA," *IEEE Expert*, Winter, p. 92 (1987).

49. S. M. Downs, M. G. Walker, and R. L. Blum, "Automated Summarization of On-Line Medical Records," in *MEDINFO 86, Proceedings of the 5th Conference on Medical Informatics*, Washington, October, 26–30, 1986 (R. Salamon, B. Blum, and M. Jorgensen, Eds.), Elsevier Science Publishers, Amsterdam, 1986, pp. 800–804.

ANDREW G. DEAN

EPROM

An EPROM (Eraseable Programmable Read-Only Memory) is one of several types of semiconductor memory integrated circuits (ICs). An EPROM is a *nonvolatile* memory. This means that the memory contents are not lost when power is removed from the device. A traditional random access memory (RAM) will 'forget' the contents when power is turned off. The most common types of EPROM ICs have several address inputs and eight data outputs, and a few control pins. The address inputs select one location in an internal memory array. The eight bits of the memory location are then output to the data pins. Unlike a traditional fuse-link PROM (see the explanation at the end of this article), the EPROM may be erased and re-used. EPROMs were originally created for use in developing programs for new products, but they have fallen in price enough that they are often used for production quantities as well. All microcomputer systems need some type of nonvolatile memory in order to know what to do when the power is turned on. This memory, often an EPROM, contains the program that tells the computer what to do up to the time that it loads an operating system from disk or tape.

The most common use of an EPROM is to hold a computer program. The program that a computer executes after it is turned on, but before it reads anything from disk, is often stored in an EPROM. Computer-based products that do not have any type of mass storage will often hold the entire operating program in one or more EPROMs.

When the microprocessor wants to read data from an EPROM, it selects the desired EPROM (there are frequently more than one in a system), and provides the EPROM with an *address* for the location that it wishes to read. The EPROM can produce one output for every unique address. That is, if the EPROM is 1 k × 8, it contains 1024 8-bit bytes. For a 1 k EPROM, 10 unique address lines are required to access all of the locations. The common sizes for EPROMs are: 2 k × 8, 4 k × 8, 8 k × 8, 16 k × 8, 32 k × 8, and 64 k × 8. There are EPROMs that contain more locations, but they are, at the present, less common.

Most EPROMs produce data 8 bits at a time. This is primarily because the early microprocessors were 8-bits wide, and the fact that the 8-bit format fits neatly into the commonly available IC packages. More bits would require larger devices, with more connecting pins.

Early EPROMs were quite expensive and could not survive many program/erase cycles. Programs were tested using EPROMs, but the production machines used mask read-only memory (ROMs) or fuse PROMs. EPROMs have since become inexpensive enough that they are often used in production as well as for development processes. After a program is stored in an EPROM, the combination is usually called *Firmware*.

Today, EPROMs are commonly constructed with negative or complementary metal oxide semiconductor (NMOS or CMOS) technology. Internally, each bit of each location in the EPROM contains a *memory cell*. The state of this cell determines whether that bit will be a one or a zero when its location is accessed. The memory cell of an EPROM contains an electronic mechanism called a *floating gate*. This is a transistor with a control element that is electrically insulated from the surrounding circuitry. This device has the capability to store an electrical charge. When the EPROM is exposed to ultraviolet (UV) light, the charge is removed from the gate, and the associated transistor will not conduct current, producing a given output when it is selected. When the bit is programmed, a charge is added to the gate, which will cause the transistor to conduct when selected, and the output will then be the opposite of the erased state. Most EPROMs produce an output of all ones when erased, and the bits to be zero are programmed with a charge on the floating gate. The EPROM has a transparent window, usually quartz, to allow the UV light to erase the device. Because of the requirement to bond the window to the device package in varying temperature conditions, most EPROMs are packaged in ceramic, as opposed to plastic.

The EPROM is programmed with data using a *PROM programmer*. Say a programmer develops a program that is to become a permanent part of the computer system. The finished program is converted to some type of machine-readable format and sent to the PROM programmer. The PROM programmer will program the EPROM with data. The EPROM is plugged into the machine for use. If the program does not work, or needs to be changed, the EPROM can be erased and reprogrammed. Most commercially available programmers will check the EPROM before programming to insure that it is blank, and verify the data after programming. Nearly all commercially available programmers today use a microprocessor that executes a program stored in EPROM.

If the programmed EPROM will be required to retain the data for a long time, the quartz window is usually covered with an opaque label to prevent stray ultraviolet light from inadvertently erasing the device. Most EPROMs will hold the data programmed into them for more than 10 years, but they can be erased by fluorescent room lighting in as little as two years, and by exposure to the sun in a few days.

One problem that occurred about the time that the 8 k × 8 EPROMs were introduced was that of programming time. The early EPROMs required .05 seconds for each location to be programmed. For a 4 k part, this was only 204 seconds, or about 3 1/2 minutes. For a 64 k part, this time stretches out to nearly an hour. For this reason, the EPROM manufacturers introduced fast programming algorithms that program the device in much less time. Most manufacturers make EPROM programmers that can program a single EPROM, and also make so-called 'gang' programmers that program multiple EPROMs at one time, for production use.

Manufacturers of EPROMs include Intel, Motorola, Advanced Micro Devices, Signetics, NEC, Toshiba, Fujitsu, and Texas Instruments. Manufacturers of EPROM programming equipment include Data I/O Corp, GTEK, and Prolog.

OTHER TYPES OF NONVOLATILE MEMORIES

The EPROM is one of many types of nonvolatile memories. Others include:
    OTP (One Time Programmable) EPROMS: These are like ordinary EPROMs, except that they are housed in a plastic package and do not have the window on top. Since there is no window, there is no way to erase

the device, so they can only be programmed once. OTP PROMS are less expensive than the ordinary ceramic EPROMs, and so are used in production environments where the program is not expected to change, or where the old EPROMs will be discarded if the program does change.

Mask ROMs: These are very cheap ROMs. The mask ROM is programmed by the chip manufacturer by adding a semiconductor mask over the basic ROM die. These are the lowest priced ROMs available, but the extremely high cost of designing the programming mask (thousands of dollars) precludes their use in any product that will not have sufficient production volume to recover the upfront costs.

Fuse PROMs: These, like the OTP PROMs, are intended to be discarded if the program that they contain needs to be changed. The memory cells of the fuse PROM contain tiny semiconductor fuses that are blown open at programming time. There is no way to reconnect a blown fuse, so the parts can be used only once. Fuse PROMs are usually very fast, so they find use in specialized, high-speed applications.

Nonvolatile RAMs: These devices are low-power RAM components (usually CMOS) that have their contents maintained by a battery. The battery may be external to the RAM itself, or it may be contained in the RAM package. These devices are more expensive than an equivalent EPROM, and are used where the contents need to be changed without difficulty. NVRAMs sometimes contain a real-time clock chip inside the package, integrating memory and timekeeping functions in one IC.

EEPROMs (Electrically Eraseable PROM): The EEPROM is a fairly recent development. The EEPROM can be reprogrammed like the EPROM, but does not need exposure to UV light in order to be erased. Most modern EEPROMs can be randomly written, like a RAM, but the write cycle is several milliseconds long. EEPROMs are limited as to the number of write cycles that they can withstand, but this number is usually greater than 10,000 cycles. In addition, while the read access time is comparable to a RAM, the write time is more like that of an EPROM, several milliseconds. For these reasons, EEPROMs are used in applications where the contents need to change, but are not constantly rewritten. EEPROMs are currently more expensive than EPROMs, but several manufacturers are attempting to reduce the cost to the point where EEPROMs can directly compete with EPROMs.

Core Memory: This is a nearly obsolete technology. Core memories store information by magnetizing tiny ferromagnetic beads. The information storage is nearly indefinite, but the access time is slow, usually several microseconds. Early minicomputers often used core as the only RAM in the system. The low density and slow speed of core memory have nearly made it obsolete but it still finds occasional application where environmental conditions preclude the use of conventional memories.

Serial Memories: These are just special packaging configurations of standard memories, usually EEPROMs. The serial EEPROM will accept an address input, usually as a serial bit stream, and output data as a serial bit stream. These devices are fairly low density ($<$ 1 k bits), and are used where a small amount of memory is adequate, but where the designer of the circuit does not want to use any of the microprocessor's memory space. Serial memory will include internal shift registers for the address inputs and data outputs.

STUART R. BALL

EPSON CORPORATION

Epson's roots date from the 1964 Olympics held in Japan. the International Organizational Committee (IOC) chose The Seiko Group, long a world leader in the manufacturing of watches, to create a small portable timing device to be used to clock athletic events.

The member of The Seiko Group selected to handle this assignment was Suwa Seikosha, a manufacturing company located in the Suwa region of Japan. Like the other member companies within Seiko, Suwa Seikosha had long been associated with the art of fine watch making. The first company in the group, originally called K. Hattori & Co., had been founded in Tokyo in 1881 by Kintaro Hattori, grandfather of the family members who run it today. At that time, it operated as a trading company which imported Swiss-made watches.

To service the watches the company sold throughout the Orient, K. Hattori set up a parts and service business and, later, a full-line manufacturing company which he named Seikosha ("seiko" means "precision" in Japanese; "sha" means "company"). Still later, the company founded two additional manufacturing units, Daini Seikosha and Suwa Seikosha.

Over time, the large trading group and its three manufacturing units have grown to be the largest watch and clock manufacturing company in the world and one of Japan's largest and oldest family-run industrial empires. Sales in 1985 topped $3.5 billion.

From the start, one of the tenets of growth within Seiko has been vertical integration. The company makes everything, from the smallest component to finished product. As a result, investment in research in technologies basic to its primary line of business has always been substantial, leading to many discoveries and innovations. Seiko soon earned a reputation as a company which has achieved many firsts in watch manufacturing.

It was this technical leadership that prompted Japan's Olympic Committee to invite The Seiko Group to develop something special—and special it was. Working long hours in a research laboratory, Suwa Seikosha engineer S. Aizawa developed a new type of clock using a highly reliable new material, quartz crystals, for the moving parts. The resulting "quartz watch" revolutionized watch making worldwide.

But this was not enough. Suwa Seikosha wanted the timing device to provide instant print outs of the results; Aizawa's addition of a small printing device was also to cause a revolution, this time in a new industry.

After the Olympics, the printing device was initially marketed by Shinshu Seiki, a subsidiary of Suwa Seikosha, as a miniature printer mechanism, the EP-101, which helped pave the way for development of pocket-sized calculators and smaller, more compact cash registers. This innovation earned for Shinshu Seiki, later known as Epson Corporation, a leadership

---

Trademarks and Register information available upon request.

position in the printer mechanism market; a position the company still maintains. After further development, this device became the world's first dot-matrix printer, marketed under the name "Epson," or "son" of EP-101 for "prosperous heir."

Along the way, however, Shinshu Seiki had discovered that the existing distribution and marketing network for watches was inadequate for the company's new marketing thrust into the microcomputer industry. In the early 1970s, the decision was made to set up a new worldwide marketing and distribution organization under the name Epson. This commenced with the establishment of Epson America, Inc. in Torrance, California in 1975.

Initially, the U.S. company sold only to original equipment manufacturers (OEMs) who used Shishu Seiki's component parts to manufacture brand name products of their own. In 1978, however, the first dot-matrix printer (the TX-80) was ready, and Shinshu Seiki brought it out under the Epson brand name. The world's first reliable microcomputer printer, selling for roughly half of the industry price for printers, achieved 60 percent of the worldwide market share within just six months.

Since the introduction of their first printer product, Epson has developed a full line of dot-matrix, daisy wheel, ink-jet, and thermal printers, compatible with Epson, Apple, IBM, Commodore, Atari, and most popular personal and home computer brands. More innovations were to follow.

In 1982, Epson introduced the world's first notebook-sized computer, the HX-20. This unique portable was small enough to fit in a briefcase, yet incorporated all the features of a full-scale personal computer, including a complete keyboard and a digital readout display. Two more Epson portables followed, making new inroads into a new market segment.

In 1983, Epson unveiled its first line of personal computers, the QX series, which featured one of the industry's first integrated software packages. A second line, the IBM-compatible Equity series, was introduced in 1985. Offering high-performance 16-bit power and complete compatibility with all MS-DOS software, the Equity line offered users upgrade options and complete modularity.

As Epson and other Hattori company products began to achieve worldwide success, particularly in the American market, management began to reorganize its manufacturing into product groups and to update company names to capitalize on its two primary and most visible brand names.

The original trading company has become Hattori Seiko Co., Ltd., and still handles the marketing and distribution of watches, clocks, and consumer electronics products for all three of the large manufacturing companies and their subsidiaries through traditional jewelry stores, department stores, mass merchandisers, and chains. As new products are developed by its subsidiaries, Hattori Seiko's product line is diversifying.

Seikosha, the first manufacturing unit to be established after the trading company, today concentrates not only on the manufacture of clocks and clock parts, but has diversified into computers and computer peripherals for small and medium-size businesses.

The second manufacturing unit, Daini Seikosha, which changed its name to Seiko Instruments and Electronics Ltd. in 1984, manufactures both men's and women's watches. This group has also diversified into electronic devices, scientific intruments, and CAD/CAM systems.

Suwa Seikosha, recognizing the great contributions of Epson brand products, first changed the name of its Shinshu Seiki subsidiary to Epson Corporation in 1982. In 1985, the two companies merged, forming Seiko

Epson Corporation. Watches manufactured by Seiko Epson Corporation plants and factories are distributed through the trading company. Liquid crystal displays (LCD), integrated circuits (IC), small industrial products and other electronic devices, floppy disk drives, print mechanisms, and all Epson brand consumer products are distributed worldwide by Seiko Epson Corporation's marketing and distributing subsidiaries.

Collectively, these diverse companies, still owned principally by Hattori family members, are called The Seiko Group.

COMPUTER PRODUCTS DIVISION

The Computer Products Division (CPD) is a complete marketing and distribution organization. In late 1984, rapid product and sales expansion prompted the division of CPD into three product groups: Computer Peripherals, Computer Systems, and Consumer Electronics.

Computer Peripherals

Epson is a full-line supplier of single and multicolor correspondence and letter-quality dot-matrix, daisy wheel, and ink-jet printers and plotters.

Printer Line

LQ-800. 80-column, 24-pin dot-matrix printer, 180 cps (counts per second) draft and 60 cps letter-quality, 7 KB buffer, friction paper feed, parallel and serial interfaces. Features IBM ProPrinter or Diablo 630 emulation through unique Personality Cartridges, smaller wire diameter printhead, front panel-controlled letter-quality and draft modes, and built-in fonts (draft, letter-quality, proportional).

LQ-1000. 136-column, 24-pin dot-matrix printer provides 180 cps draft, 60 cps letter-quality and 7 KB buffer memory. Features friction paper feed, parallel and serial interfaces, IBM ProPrinter or Diablo 630 emulation through Personality Cartridges, smaller wire diameter printhead, front panel-controlled letter-quality and draft modes, and buil-in fonts (draft, letter-quality, proportional).

DX-10. 82-column daisy wheel printer, 10 cps, friction feed, bidirectional logic-seeking printing, Diablo 96 petal print wheel, pica and elite character sets, Olivetti ET-121 ribbon, dip switch for international character sets.

DX-20. 110-column daisy wheel printer, 20 cps, 1 KB buffer (expandable to 7 KB), pica, elite, or 15, proportional and N/120" character sets, bidirectional logic-seeking printing, Diablo API interface, Diablo 96 character print wheel, Olivetti ET-121 ribbon cartridge, dip switch for international character sets.

DX-35. 110-column daisy wheel printer, 35 cps, 1 KB buffer (expandable to 7 KB), pica, elite, proportional, and N/120" character sets, Diablo API interface, bidirectional logic-seeking printing, Diablo 96 petal print wheel, Olivetti ET-121 ribbon cartridge, dip switch for international character sets.

AP-80. 80-column dot-matrix printer featuring single switch-selectable draft (75 cps) and near-letter quality (15 cps) printing modes, plug compatible and fully supports all Apple ImageWriter text and graphics software for Apple IIc, IIe, and Macintosh computers.

Spectrum LX-80. 80-column dot-matrix printer with both draft (100 cps) and near-letter quality (16 cps) modes. SelecType feature offering 160 type styles.

FX-85. 80-column dot-matrix with both draft (160 cps) and near-letter-quality (32 cps) print modes, built-in IBM character sets, 8 KB print buffer, bidirectional printing, SelecType feature giving a panel selection of nine different type styles and two utility features.

FX-286. 136-column dot-matrix with both draft (200 cps) and near-letter-quality (40 cps) print modes, built-in IBM character sets. 8 KB print buffer, bidirectional printing, SelecType feature giving a panel selection of nine different type styles and two utility features.

JX-80. 80-column, 7-color dot-matrix with speed of 160 cps, 128 type styles, full descenders, capacity to download additional fonts, one-to-one graphics ratio, and SelecType feature for altering print mode without software control.

LQ-1500. 136-column, 24-pin dot-matrix printer featuring draft, NLQ, and graphics modes at speeds up to 200 cps.

HS-80 LetterJet. 80-column, portable (4 lbs), nine-nozzle ink-jet printer with both draft (160 cps) and near-letter-quality (32 cps) modes, friction feed, nickel cadmium rechargeable batteries, unique ink-injector/ink-filling system.

SQ-2000. 136-column, 24-nozzle ink-jet printer with both draft (176 cps) and letter-quality (106 cps) modes, exclusive printhead cleaning system to prevent clogging, 9-bit image graphic modes with densities from 60 to 240 DPI.

420i. 136-column, dot-matrix printer with draft (420 cps) and NLQ (104 cps) modes, 18 KB print buffer. Features emulation of Epson FX-series and IBM graphics printers, tractor feed, and serial and parallel interfaces.

HI-80 Plotter. Epson's 4-pen color plotter supports most major lines of business computers, including IBM and Apple. Features 42 intelligent commands, a snap-in pen cassette, printer emulation, and a parallel interface, which can be converted to serial.

Computer Systems

Personal Computer Line

Equity I. Epson's first entry in the IBM PC-compatible market. A high-performance, 16-bit desktop computer, available in three factory-built configurations: a single floppy disk drive, dual floppy disks, or a single floppy with a 20 megabyte (MB) internal hard disk. The base configuration comes standard with an 8088 microprocessor, 256 KB of random access memory, 360 KB, 5.25" half-height floppy disk drive, and RS-232C serial port, an 8-bit parallel printer port, three full-size IBM PC-compatible expansion slots, an internal speaker, and an IBM AT-type detachable keyboard.

Equity II. Features IBM XT compatibility, dual speed operation with the NEC V30 microprocessor (8086 compatible), power-on control by switch, timer, or ring-detect, and power-off control by switch or software. Available in two basic configurations: a single floppy disk drive or a single floppy and a 20-Mb internal hard disk. The base configuration comes standard with 640 KB RAM, 360 KB, 5.25" half-height floppy disk drive, an RS-232C serial port, an 8-bit parallel printer port, five full-size IBM PC-compatible expansion slots, an adjustable volume, internal speaker, real-time clock, calendar, and 3.1 version of MS-DOS.

Equity III. Provides IBM AT compatibility for multitasking or multi-user functions. Features and 80286 microprocessor, 6 MHz clock speed, 640 KB RAM, 5.25" floppy disk drive with 1.2 MB storage capacity, and RS-232C serial port, an 8-bit parallel printer port, eight expansion slots (six with 16-bit bus and two with 8-bit bus), an internal speaker and real-time clock, and calendar with battery back up. Available in four configurations: one 5.25" half-height 360 KB floppy disk drive, a half-height 5.25" 20 Mb internal hard disk, or a full height 40 Mb internal hard disk drive. Equity III comes with the 3.1 version of MS-DOS.

QX-11. Designed exclusively for the value-added reseller (VAR) market. Expandable, versatile desktop computer featuring 8088 16-bit central processing unit (CPU), MS-DOS 2.11 (read-only memory ROM), 256 KB RAM (expandable to 512 KB), two 3.5-inch 360 KB double-sided, double-density disk drives, ROM cartridge slot, RS-232C serial and Centronics-compatible parallel interfaces, Texas Intruments 3-channel sound chip, compact IBM Selectric type keyboard, 12-inch high-resolution (640 × 400 pixels), green monochrome monitor, two joystick ports. Enable and DDD Business Graphics (with 512 KB RAM only) software is included. Optional hardware includes 256 KB RAM memory expansion, full-size IBM Selectric type keyboard, 5" high-resolution (640 × 400 pixels) monochrome monitor, IBM video emulation board, 10-Mb hard disk (external), RS-232C and RS-422 serial interface boards, RF modulator, and 300-baud direct connect modem (internal).

QX-16 Personal Computer. A powerful computer that features a 16-bit processor with an MS-DOS operating system and an 8-bit processor with a CP/M-80 operating system. These twin capabilities permit the QX-16 to run a wide range of MS-DOS and CP/M programs. Standard features include 512 KB RAM, Valdocs 2/ integrated software package, and a dual 5-1/4" disk drive.

QX-10 Personal Computer. World's easiest to use personal computer, with English-language function keys, 256 KB memory, 8-bit CP/M-80-compatible operating system, and optional 16-bit MS-DOS board, including 192 KB additional memory expandable to 512 KB. Standard Valdocs software includes word processing, graphics, scheduling, calculating, and electronic mail. Can be operated either at novice, advanced, or expert level.

Portable Computer/Printer Line

Geneva. 4-pound, notebook size, with standard CP/M operating system, 64 KB RAM, 32 KB ROM, and three standard "diskless" MicroPro programs on ROM capsules for word processing, spreadsheet, and scheduling. 8-line by 80-character, high-resolution liquid crystal display (LCD), with full-size ASCII keyboard, numeric keypad, and microcassette storage. Optional peripherals include 3-1/2" floppy disk drive, direct connect modem, up to 184 KB RAM expansion, and thermal printers.

HX-20 Notebook Computer. Notebook size (8-1/2" × 11') with 16 KB RAM and ROM, expandable to 64 KB. Standard features include 4-line by 20-character LCD display, SkiWriter word processing software, serial communications port, built-in printer, and full-size typewriter keyboard.

HX-40. Designed exclusively for the value-added reseller (VAR) market. 3.5 lb, notebook size, with extended CP/M operating system, 32 K ROM, 64 K RAM, enhanced Microsoft Basic and a microcassette drive. Features 40 characters by 8 lines pop-up high-resolution LCD display with full-size typewriter keyboard. Optional peripherals include RAM and ROM cartridges, digital multimeter cartridge, N-164 cartridge printer, PF-10 portable floppy, TF-20 dual-terminal floppy, and CX-20 acoustic coupler. Parallel interface.

P-80X Portable Printer. 24-pin, thermal transfer printer designed specifically for use with Epson Geneva portable computer. Features 40 cps draft, 22 cps letter-quality, and 80 column width. Battery-operated.

Consumer Electronics

Established in 1984 with the introduction of the Elf ET-10, the world's first flat-screen LCD color television. In 1985, the Elf ET-12, a new pocket-sized color LCD set, and the Elf ET-20, one of the smallest black and white televisions available, were introduced.

Elf ET-10. The world's first flat-screen LCD color television, measures 3.15 inches high by 6.3 inches long by 1.22 inches in depth, and weighs just over a pound. A high-resolution color image is produced on a 2-inch diagonal screen. Runs on any of four power sources: five AA flashlight batteries or nickel cadmium batteries, a rechargeable battery pack, a car battery adapter, or an AC power adapter.

Elf ET-12. Pocket-sized LCD color television with a built-in backlight. Has a 2-inch diagonal screen size and measures 3.15 inches high by 6.3 inches long by 1.22 inches in depth. Improved horizontal synchronization makes reception, even under weak signal conditions, very sharp. Weighs slightly more than a pound and runs on any of four power sources: five AA flashlight batteries or nickel cadmium batteries, a rechargeable battery pack, a car battery adapter, or an AC power adapter. Accessory kit is available and includes power adapter, rechargeable battery pack, and screen magnifier.

Elf ET-20. One of the cmallest black and white LCD television sets available. Provides a high-resolution picture on a 2-inch diagonal screen. Measures 2.85 inches wide by 4.70 inches high by .81 inches deep, and weighs only 7 ounces, including batteries. Runs for 10 hours on two AA batteries.

DOUGLAS KLINE

EQUIPMENT AND SOFTWARE MAINTENANCE

INTRODUCTION

Maintenance is defined here as the tasks and effort to support microcomputer hardware and software in an acceptable operational state. The standard of acceptability varies by organization and function being performed. The long useful life of microcomputers combined with user dependence make maintenance a major issue and concern in systems support. Since microcomputers are employed for various purposes by a wide variety of managers and staff members in an organization, there is a need to recognize that there are different levels of acceptable maintenance and performance. Maintenance here is also taken to include fixing or repairing systems, improving performance, and enhancing systems to add greater capabilities.

There are several quantitative measures associated with maintenance that are derived from reliability theory for hardware and structures. Some of these are:

Mean time between failure: This is the average time between successive failures of a system. A variation is the mean time until failure.

Mean time to diagnose: This is the average time needed to identify the problem after work has begun.

Mean time to repair: This is the average time between when a problem is reported and when repairs are completed.

These measures are used in microcomputer maintenance as part of outside contracts with service companies and for agreements between users and internal support groups within the organization. The goal of maintenance in terms of repair is to minimize the likelihood of failure, and if failure occurs, to minimize the time to repair and maximize the likelihood that repair was successful. For changes to the system, the objective is to minimize the time and effort for enhancement and to provide for the longer term evolution of the system.

Hardware maintenance differs considerably from software maintenance. In hardware maintenance it is possible to perform periodic preventive maintenance to reduce the likelihood of failure. Hardware maintenance for most microcomputer components involves the replacement of the failed part by new or reconditioned parts as opposed to repair. In hardware maintenance most of the repair time is consumed in diagnosing the problem as opposed to replacement. Newer hardware requires less maintenance effort since it is improved in design, there are fewer parts, and the parts are more modular—leading to simpler replacement.

Software maintenance depends on the type of software being considered. Software tools and packages that are obtained from suppliers are maintained and updated by the suppliers. Software applications built upon the tools are created by the organization. Since the packages are not within the control of the organization directly, the focus here will be on applications software.

In applications software both the diagnostic time and the repair time can be substantial. The repair time may include making a number of changes and then testing the changes. Debugging on microcomputers for large applications can take as much time as that for systems on mainframe computers. The steps involved are very similar. Preventive maintenance for applications software exists through taking regular backups of data and programs.

THE MAINTENANCE PROCESS

In order to provide for maintenance of hardware and software, an organized approach is needed. This involves:

A formal method for reporting and recording problems and requests
An information system for tracking reported problems and requests
A stepwise approach for diagnosing and resolving problems
A testing and quality assurance procedure to ensure that the problem
    has been corrected or the request has been satisfied

Without a maintenance process and approach, users are forced to fend for themselves. Some will obtain their own maintenance contracts and support. This is expensive because there is no economies of scale of support reaped. Other users may ignore the maintenance issue until failure occurs. This usually means loss of a substantial amount of data. The lack of maintenance is typically correlated with the lack of backup and recovery procedures. Thus, when failure occurs, the effects are compounded.

In terms of frequency of failure, the most likely sources of concern are subsystems that have mechanical components. Examples are printers, disk drives, diskette drives, and tape backup units. Of these the failure of a hard disk typically makes the disk drive unusable. Recovery of data is often not possible.

Resources that will perform maintenance activities have to be identified. These are listed in Figure 1 for hardware, software packages, and applications software. How some of these resources apply to maintenance will now be examined.

Hardware testing and diagnostic tools includes software programs for performing testing as well as hardware test tools. As microcomputers have grown in power, their diagnostic support internally has improved. Many machines now are equipped with internal error checking which is performed when the computer power is turned on. The growth of local area networks (LANs) has increased the need for network diagnostic tools.

Hardware maintenance agreements may be available from the manufacturer as well as from third-party suppliers. The cost of the maintenance program depends on the hardware and software, the level of service desired, and the extent to which replacement components are included. Maintenance often must be contracted for when the computer is initially sold. While take-in service is less expensive, it also has several disadvantages. First, the computer may be unavailable for days while repairs are being made. Using a replacement computer may be infeasible if the data files needed are on the failed unit.

Hardware

Internal systems staff
Maintenance contract and vendor
Inventory of spare parts and components
Hardware diagnostic and testing tools

Software packages

Software vendor hot line
Software product upgrades
Software fixes available by mail or by electronic
    mail through an electronic bulletin board
Software product upgrade and maintenance

Applications software

Key software support staff member
Documentation of the applications software
Test data and files
Internal program documentation
Software tools
Backup and recovery procedures

General

Configuration management for both hardware
    and software
Project management
Inventory database
User database
Problem and incident database
Operations procedures
Change control process

FIGURE 1   Resources Associated with Maintenance

Software packages are more complex as the developers attempt to
supply more capabilities and higher performance. It is impossible, due to
the complexity of most major software products to expect that the developers
can identify and fix all errors. To address this situation, software suppliers have often adopted several approaches.

After a product is initially available for sale, reported errors and
work-around solutions may be obtained from the supplier directly or through
an electronic bulletin board service. This provides immediate help in dealing with a problem.

Another approach is to release a version of the product in which some
of the fixes to problems have been included. The user can often recognize
when this is occurring by the numbering system associated with the release.
For example, if the initial product is 1.00, then an initial repaired version
may be issued within six months numbered 1.01. This usually fixes only
some of the major problems that have been reported repeatedly. A later
version of the product may incorporate these repairs and include additional
new features. A release that offers some new features may be numbered

1.1, while a major new release may be numbered 2.00. In the latter case, there may be many new features and changes to build a relationship with customers and to distribute the new versions, a software supplier may offer an upgrade option agreement, trade-in allowance for the old version, or even a free upgrade to registered owners of the software.

In most cases, a software application is programmed using a software package. An example might be a spreadsheet or database application which draws on the underlying spreadsheet or database management system. The applications software may be developed within a user department or by the information systems organization. A fundamental problem with many applications developed in an organization is the lack of standards and documentation. A key person may have developed the application. This key person will often inherit the maintenance burden after the application has been developed. When the key person leaves or is no longer available, the application may fall into disuse due to lack of support.

It is recommended that since applications are often critical to a department or group, that some minimal level of documentation and procedures be supplied. A backup person should be identified for the key person. This is important for applications that run in a local area network environment where failure can affect everyone on the network as well as the users of the application system. One approach that is sometimes employed is to classify application systems as to their importance by levels. Applications at level 1 may not have any requirements whatsoever. Level 5 application systems may have documentation, testing, and other requirements. Levels in between have degrees of support.

Configuration management is the tracking and verification of the various hardware and software components of microcomputer systems. This can be maintained by a central support group. Configuration management serves a number of purposes. First, it provides the basis for tracking problems and identifying all components of the same type. Second, when new software releases are available, configuration management can identify who should receive the upgrade. Third, the data on configurations can be used to analyze alternative modernization and replacement strategies. In local area networks this is often easier to do, since the files on the file server and other network resources can be accessed by a network coordinator.

Project management is the formal approach for carrying out tasks. Major enhancements and upgrades involving many different users, need a formal project plan with schedules, resources, and tasks identified.

The inventory database can be considered to be part of configuration management. It consists of part numbers and other characteristics for all hardware and software. The inventory database is useful since it has software serial numbers for upgrades and hardware serial numbers. In the event of theft or loss, the database will likely be important for insurance purposes. The inventory database is updated by the entry of new equipment and software as well as by periodic data collection and verification. Some components are obtained without going through standard purchasing due to their low cost.

A user database is employed by some organizations as a means of providing improved support. The database can contain information on training that the user has had, level of proficiency in computing, past contacts, and other information.

The problem or incident database allows the users to report a problem in a structured approach. The software for the database then can track the problem until it is resolved. This database can also serve as a basis for identifying problems that may occur with several users over an extended period of time.

Linking these databases together provides better service since the user does not have to supply basic information on configuration, their use, etc. on a repetitive basis. This suggests that the databases should be designed and constructed together.

Change control is the process of managing and directing changes to the hardware and software configuration. In the past, it was not necessary to have a formal change control process since there were few microcomputers in the organization. This has changed with the growth and evolution of technology. At any given time there may be five or more different hardware vendors or models. Adding multiple versions of software packages makes the process of changing systems very expensive and time consuming. The need for change control will also grow with the spread of local and wide area networks. Users in a department who are sharing the same software have to be assured of a common software base and compatible hardware. In some organizations, there is a lack of modernization of system because there is no formal change control process.

PLANNING AND MANAGEMENT OF MAINTENANCE

The above discussion of resources and tools to support maintenance has provided suggestions for tactical support of maintenance to address specific tasks. With this background, the overall management of maintenance can be addressed. Figure 2 provides a schematic view of maintenance. In this figure three levels of maintenance have been identified for the resources shown in the third dimension.

On the left are internal factors within the organization that maintenance management and planning must accommodate. Some of these internal factors are:

> Existing base of hardware, software, and networks installed. Size and growth point to a need for strategic management of support.
> Extent to which the user areas are automated. Increased automation means greater dependence and, hence, the need for an overall plan for maintenance.
> Access to mainframe and minicomputer systems. Microcomputers and local area networks are often tied to larger computers to allow users to access data, input transactions, and perform other functions.
> Need for appropriate audit controls.

Factors external to the organization that impact maintenance include the following:

> Competitive pressure that increases the drive for efficiency and automation
> Changing technology which encourages an organized approach for technology transfer and support
> Growing need for information access within and external to the organization

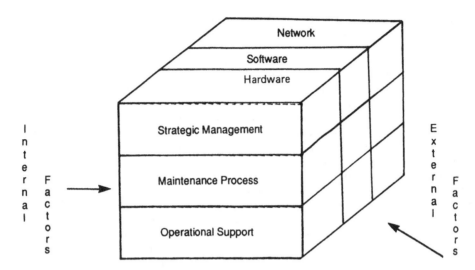

FIGURE 2   Management view of maintenance.

All of these factors encourage a more strategic view of maintenance and support. On a strategic level, a key decision is to identify the level of importance of maintenance to the organization. This can be done directly by estimating benefits from having high reliability or indirectly by assuming that a certain number of failures or problems will occur and then estimating the costs and impacts of these problems. The level of importance associated with maintenance will translate into resources.

A separate management issue is to plan for the process of maintenance. This includes the process of change control, the method of tracking and tactically managing maintenance, and how to cope with an evolving techno-logical hardware and software base. An early model of this was the estab-lishment of an end-user computing function. This group would often pro-vide training as well as maintenance support. As users became more expert in the use of the systems or as more had prior training and experience, the need for the group changed or diminished. Today some organizations have disbanded their support groups. Users have sometimes been assigned direct responsibility for support maintenance.

The increase in local area networks has been spurred by several factors that impact maintenance. First, some hardware components are still quite expensive so that hardware sharing of printers, modems, and disk drives can be economically justified. Second, the rising capabilities of the software and hardware together with increased dependence on the systems by users makes a network more attractive for support. Third, users are increasingly using networks for data and file sharing. Fourth, the technology associated with local area networks has improved rapidly over the past few years.

The above factors support the establishment of a central support group that is quite different from the end-user computing group. As opposed to supporting individual user tools, the support function focuses on networked and shared resources. There is a greater need for support given the increased dependence. There is also an opportunity for economies of scale of support.

A maintenance long range plan should address the areas identified in Figure 3. The first section addresses the issues relating to maintenance in the current environment. This may include the mixture of equipment and software, types of applications, and existing maintenance issues.

The future environment includes the business and technology products and factors that are projected in the future as well as the estimated pace of change. Since microcomputers are part of the entire computing and communications fabric of the organization, it is also important to address the mainframe, minicomputer, and general network requirements. Maintenance objectives often include the following:

Service level objective for hardware
Targets for conversions, introduction of new technology, and enhancements
Cost objectives as percent of total systems costs, cost per employee, cost per workstation
Support of the information systems architecture

The last objective is aimed at steps that will be taken to move the computer systems toward the desired and specified architecture of the information systems organization. Note that these objectives should address maintenance in its broadest sense.

The constraints that restrict the short-term attainment of the objectives should also be identified in this section. Obvious constraints are available resources. However, there are a number of constraints that should be specified. Several might include:

Gaps in technology that prevent an immediate improvement in a maintenance situation. An example here is a lack of software for a specific interface or that a particular software package does not support a given printer.
Difficulties of users in migrating to more maintainable systems. Users may have become so enmeshed in the current software that they do not wish to move to new systems.

1. Summary of current environment and issues

2. Scenario for future environment
   Anticipated user requirements
   Projected technology base in the future
   Mainframe, minicomputer, and networking
   requirements

3. Maintenance and support objectives and constraints

4. Systems strategies

5. Operational support of maintenance

6. Measurement of maintenance

7. Implementation strategy

FIGURE 3 Components of a maintenance long range plan.

Limited available testing and diagnostic tools. While the new technology has improved reliability, there are still a restricted number of testing tools.

Limitations of current software packages and incompatibility between systems. Incompatibilities may exist to prevent file sharing and communications.

Geographic dispersion of installed user base. Multiple locations typically involve more support time and effort along with greater coordination.

To achieve the objectives in maintenance, a series of strategies are needed. One strategy should address how maintenance will be tracked and controlled. Another strategy will likely relate to the method of allocating resources between competing requirements. A third strategy should be to identify methods for getting the most out of the resources through cross-training, tools, and methods. Examples of strategies by area are listed in Figure 4.

The strategies should map to the objectives and should adhere to the constraints that were identified. It is clear that maintenance should pro-actively support the technology and systems in place. In the past, many strategies were reactive. That is, a strategy would be to achieve a specific level of response for classes of reported problems. However, it should also be noted that when a technology is to be replaced, maintenance support should be reduced.

Once the strategies associated with maintenance have been defined, the next step is to identify specific actions that can be taken to implement the strategies. This is part of the implementation part of the plan. An example follows. If, for example, an objective was to achieve greater economies of scale of support, then a strategy might be to adopt certain technologies as part of a technology backbone. An action that could be taken in support of the strategy and objective is to restrict the extent of support for specific technologies that are not in the backbone.

Support greater self-sufficiency of users with respect to hardware

Restrict support to only certain technology hardware and software products

Minimize the requirement for internal (or external) resources

Ensure that maintenance costs are included as part of the justification for the new computer systems

Implement a career path for maintenance and support staff

Ensure that an adequate supply of spares and duplicate items are stocked

Implement a network testing capability to ensure the reliability of local area networks

FIGURE 4 Possible strategies for maintenance.

Number of requests by user

Resolution distribution of requests by
source of problem

Number of requests by type of equipment

Repair time per request

Backup effort

Parts cost and distribution of parts

Categorization of request by type:
enhancement, repair, etc.

New equipment installations supported

Upgrades and enhancements supported

Maintenance costs

FIGURE 5 List of maintenance-related data for collection.

The approach for maintenance operations support should be detailed in
the form of easy to follow procedures. An appeal process should be specified in the event of a high priority problem. Operations support procedures
should include handling of requests for support, the maintenance process,
security and backup, and daily operations procedures.

The objectives of maintenance impact how maintenance can be measured.
A specific level of mean time to failure or mean time to repair naturally
leads to measurement methods of maintenance. It is appropriate here to
consider a more general structure for measuring maintenance. A list of
some of the data that can be collected is given in Figure 5. Note that the
data identified is both quantitative and qualitative. Quantitative measurements includes what can be collected without ambiguity or opinion. The
qualitative data is aimed at measuring the opinion of users and managers
regarding maintenance.

Ratio of number of users to maintenance staff

Ratio of number of devices to maintenance staff

Distribution of requests by equipment type

Ratio of number of requests to number of users

Maintenance cost per unit

Maintenance cost per device

Distribution of maintenance effort by type of activity

Effect of aging of hardware on extent of maintenance

Distribution of maintenance effort over time

Trend in extent of maintenance by equipment type

FIGURE 6 Measures of maintenance.

Based on the data collected in Figure 5, analysis can be performed to develop the measures in Figure 6. Note that some of these are first-order results, calculated directly from the data. Others require more in-depth analysis. For each measure actually used, it is advisable to develop a description of what the measure means and how it is to be used.

SPECIFIC ISSUES IN MAINTENANCE

Handling a multiple vendor and product environment is one of the most common and complex issues within maintenance. For example, a local area network could have three different makes of workstations, a cabling supplier, local area network software, and several software vendors. The number of vendors could then be ten or more. When a problem occurs, a common source is that several software packages may require the same area of memory in the computer. The result is a deadlock. The system freezes up and failure occurs.

Several steps can be taken to minimize the likelihood of problems such as the one mentioned above. One approach is to have a set of equipment and software that is typical of the user environment. This will support the replication of the reported problem. The network hardware and software are sufficiently similar that the problem can be recreated and analyzed. This approach works if the range of equipment and software is narrow so that a single network can be modified to fit different situations. If there is a broad range of systems, this is impossible since not all systems can be duplicated within a budget.

Another step is to implement the capability to support users remotely over communications lines. In this situation, when a problem is reported, a network control center has the ability to seize control of the remote site and to do testing, backup, and recovery. This approach will have success if the file server or network gateway is still functioning. If the network interface fails, then a separate link needs to be established. Under remote control, the system can be tested using network-based software. This principle of remote support is common with distributed networks that are being implemented by IBM Corporation under the Systems Application Architecture (SAA) and a similar architecture by Digital Equipment Corporation (DEC).

A third step is to implement more testing and diagnostic software at the user level. In this approach, local users may have periodic backups made routinely without user intervention. The theory here is that the more automated the process, the lower the manual involvement and the greater the chance of recovery.

In organizations with large installed bases of microcomputers and local area networks, a combination of the above methods may be needed to ensure a satisfactory level of availability and reliability. Note that the alternative of additional staffing is not proposed. The current budgets for support in information systems are typically not sufficient to accommodate hiring additional staff in a support capacity.

Another common issue in maintenance is the support requirements for a new, but acceptable technology. Here it will consume more resources to learn the new technology and provide support. This learning curve and effort is independent of the number of users to some extent. This means that to recover the initial costs of support, there should be many new users and applications of the technology. It should be kept in mind that the effort to learn the technology to perform maintenance and support is substantially greater than that to be able to use the system. Learning a new technology or system is not merely understanding how it works, it is also understanding technical interfaces, performance, and technical gaps that are promised to be closed in later releases of the software. Generally, the effort to understand the system rises more rapidly than the increase in complexity. As an example, if the complexity doubles, then the effort to master the system more than doubles.

Another maintenance issue is that of overbuilding the system. This may occur when the user is satisfied with the system and now seeks to enhance the system over a period of years. The total investment over several years may exceed the cost of the original system by a factor of two or three. This leads to the subject of replacement.

SYSTEM REPLACEMENT

System replacement is the process of replacing a computer system with another system that is newer and typically is more maintainable and has additional capabilities. In the microcomputer area, companies are now beginning to face the problem of replacement.

The problem of replacement is made more complex since system failure is not involved. Instead, the computer still functions. New software, however, cannot be processed on the existing hardware and requires greater speed, memory, or disk. The system has not failed, but its usefulness is ending. This planned obsolescence by the hardware and software vendors may not seem desirable, but it is inevitable as technology progresses.

The issue of replacement is then to develop an overall strategy to deal with the problem. One approach is to develop a method for migrating in an organized manner hardware and software from more sophisticated to less sophisticated and experienced users. The computer may be reconditioned and have software upgrades in the process of transition. There are some subjects that should be monitored in the process. First, to control support costs the range of software across new and old hardware platforms cannot be too wide. Otherwise, incompatibility will give rise to interface problems. Moreover, the training cost for multiple packages in the same area may be prohibitive.

There is no optimal replacement strategy, since the approach depends on the characteristics of the individual company. Included are the number of microcomputers, the volume of workstations involved in transition over a period of several years, the ability to modernize older systems, and the capability to interface files between the old and new systems.

BENNET P. LIENTZ

EQUIPMENT LIFE CYCLE MANAGEMENT THROUGH MICROCOMPUTERS

Equipment management consists of four distinct activity modules; the identification module (ID), procurement module (PM), support module (SM), and the disposition module (DM). Each of these modules in turn may consist of one or more internal processes, acting upon and being acted upon by other processes, within and without the four individual modules. The functions of the modules remain the same regardless of the type of equipment management system used.

Processes within the individual modules are initiated and controlled by personnel, equipment, calendar, or situation. Each module requires an input to achieve result. Input can be originated by formal management decisions or by machine-, time-, or situation-generated processes.

Through all levels of equipment management systems (EMS) the range of interaction between the modules, as illustrated in Figure 1, remains the same. This process of cradle-to-grave equipment management is called life cycle management (LCM).

Simply stated, life cycle management is a series of controlled processes which begin when a need is recognized and ends when the need and the item that satisfied that need no longer exist.

It is difficult to identify a beginning or end in any LCM system. Each module within the LCM system feeds information to and receives data from the other modules. It is this mutual interactive relationship that validates results within the LCM process. However, for this discussion we will trace activities from left to right as noted in Figure 2.

In this case, the switch that initiates the life cycle management process is found in module one, the identification module (ID).

This switch can consist of internal or external activities ranging from a simple mechanical go—no—go flag to a complex series of high-level, interactive logical decision-making processes. The basic requirement for all LCM processes is that they complement the function of the parent module. Therefore, all of the processes within the ID module must be directed toward selecting the correct item needed to satisfy a recognized need within the organization.

The second module in the life cycle management process is the procurement module (PM). This module converts the requirement identified in the ID module into an on-hand inventoried asset. Additional activities within this module may be dictated if the item being procured requires logistic support of its own. In this case not only must the item be procured, but plans must be incorporated into the procurement action which will guarantee that a full range of logistic support activity is in place prior to induction of the item into inventory. Spare parts, support equipment, special environmental conditions, and training for service personnel are just some of the logistic concerns which must be considered during the PM.

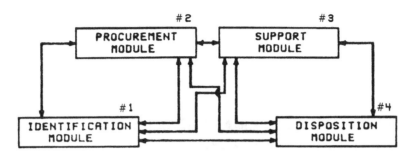

INTERACTIVE MODULES

FIGURE 1 Life cycle management interactive modules.

The third module within the life cycle management process is the support module (SM). Although the most often discussed process within LCM, the SM actually requires the least amount of management effort to accomplish. Simple, straightforward, repetitive equipment management processes such as warehousing, inventory control, and maintenance are some of the individual activities falling within the SM module. Because of the routine nature of activities within the SM module, it is the best candidate for any computer-based equipment management system. The primary task of the SM is simply to ensure that the inventory item is operational and available when and where required.

The fourth and final module is the disposition module (DM). If an item is procured, it must eventually be disposed of. During its lifetime, something must inevitably happen to each item of inventory. It will either be used, sold, discarded, or lost. The DM module is the least understood and most commonly ignored of all. However, without appropriate feedback from the DM to the ID module the ID module may not trigger the LCM system, and a replacement item may never be identified. Without accurate and timely interaction between the DM and the other LCM modules serious logis-

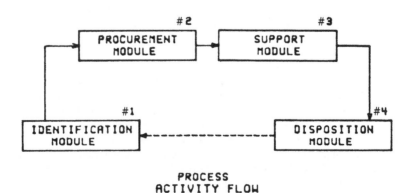

PROCESS
ACTIVITY FLOW

FIGURE 2 Life cycle management activity flow.

tic problems will arise.   Processes occurring within the DM ensure that all logistic aspects of support and replacement are considered during disposal.

There are life cycle management systems which provide equipment management support for all levels.   At each level, however, it is the inter- action between the LCM modules which guarantees effective, timely, and accurate results.   A good example of a simple LCM process initiated by a situation-generated input is the process by which spare parts are made available to service technicians working at a small electronics repair shop.

Ten-megohm resistors are a commonly used part in the repair of a particular brand of car stereo.   The stock room has a stack of these resis- tors vacuum sealed on rectangular pieces of cardboard in a bin.   Bench technicians draw from this supply on an as-needed basis.   Once the supply of resistors reaches a lower limit a bright orange flag becomes visible.   The stock clerk, making his regular rounds of the supply room, notices the orange flag and initiates action to reorder a supply of ten-megohm resistors. Once the resistors are received he then adds them to the stack of replace- ment resistors remaining in the bin.

Every action within this scenario is a process within one of the four LCM modules.   This simple LCM system is identical in concept to every other LCM system including those used in the most complicated equipment management evolution.   An increased number of inventory items or the need for more information will obviously increase the complexity of the LCM sys- tem.   However, the basic concept remains the same.

Even in this very simple example, the process interaction within the ID module is much more intricate than it would appear.   The orange flag displayed at the depleted ten-megohm resistor bin is the output of the ID module.   However, the preliminary or hidden processes within the ID module which must occur prior to the display of the flag require difficult analysis to insure accurate results.

For example, in order for the stock clerk to be able to order replace- ment resistors of the correct size, type, wattage, and tolerance rating, several preliminary information gathering and evaluating processes were needed.   During these preliminary processes data on stock number, cost, availability, and vendors were gathered.   Once this information was analyzed, evaluated, and what-if situations considered, a prioritized list of potential suppliers was developed.   Then, when the flag signals that a procurement action is necessary, the supply clerk already has the information needed to reorder the correct resistor.   The flag said, "order parts."   But the pre- liminary processes within the ID module provided the information that guaranteed the right parts from the right vendors at the right price.

Once the item has been identified, the procurement module comes into play.   In this example, all of the actions of the stock clerk after he was triggered into action and before he received the resistors are processes with- in the PM module.   The ID module output flag triggered the action of the supply clerk by giving him the signal to restock a bin of repair parts.   The preliminary processes within the ID module provided the information needed to insure the right part is ordered.   The final output of the PM is the actual process of procuring a supply of ten-megohm resistors.

Just as the simple output of the ID module hides a set of intricate internal processes, so to, does the output of the PM module.   There are several preliminary processes which are necessary to guarantee the correct output action of the PM.   In this case the supply clerk must be trained to

respond correctly to the ID module output. He must know format and procurement techniques and methodologies. Procurement forms must be available
(an LCM process all by itself). Communication procedures required by the
procurement action must be known. The stock clerk must also be taught
how to respond correctly to what-if situations that were not considered as
part of the ID module. All of these are integral parts of the PM module.

The SM module in this scenario is the actual process of inducting the
resistors into inventory, following up on all of the procurement administrative
duties, then insuring that the resistors are stacked, sealed, and available
in the correct bin within the store room. In more complex LCM situations
not only must the item be available, it must also receive some level of in-
house support such as maintenance, inventory control, and monitoring.

The final module in the LCM process is the disposition module (DM).
In this example, the technicians drawing resistors from bench stock becomes
the DM.

In this life cycle management scenario neither electronic data processing
(EDP) or automated LCM systems were used to improve support. The only
mechanical device used is the mechanism which causes the orange flag to be
displayed when a certain number of ten-megohm resistors are used. Some
mention is made of the hidden or preliminary processes involved, but again
they can be manually accomplished using a notebook or set of 3 × 5 cards.
The manual system described in this example is probably one of the most
familiar LCM systems and has successfully met the demands of business and
industry for quite some time.

Within the last few years, however, a revolution has occurred in LCM
methodologies and techniques. The function of the four basic LCM modules
has remained the same. But information processing techniques within the
modules have changed significantly.

Until recently there were essentially two tiers of LCM systems. An
organization may be able to satisfy all LCM requirements through the use of
a simple and inexpensive wall chart or notebook. If necessary, and if
funding is available, a large organization may use a set of programmed
instructions designed to be run on a mainframe computer as a LCM system.

Inventory size, the complexity of logistic support requirements, cost
factors, and query response time are four of the most obvious determining
factors in deciding the tier or type of LCM system. If an organization is
responsible for a small number of inventory items or if the nature of the
inventory items indicate that complex data elements are not necessary or if
LCM responses are not time-critical, a simple, inexpensive manual LCM
system is usually all that is used.

Several of these manual systems have been on the market for quite
some time. Most logisticians and managers may not call them LCM systems
or tools, but that is exactly what they are. The Wheel-Book familiar to
every veteran is an LCM tool. The old-fashioned chalkboard lined off in
rows and columns and faithfully filled in at the end of each reporting period
is another simple LCM system. The trusty old oak box filled with ink-
stained, dog-eared 3 × 5 cards on the foreman's desk is a LCM system.
And the most commonly used but least recognized LCM tool of all is the
corporate memory of the spit-and-whittle crowd resident in every company
or business organization. All of these manual LCM systems have been providing LCM support for years.

In a large organization or one required to monitor several interdepen-
dent LCM functions or in situations where time-sensitive responses are

necessary, a mainframe computer is used. Some organizations have their own on-site mainframe computer serviced by a group of nearly invisible COBOL programmers under the control of an equally invisible and almost inaccessible EDP department head. EDP resources available to assist in designing and developing software programs for equipment management support are, in most instances, limited. Usually the routine nature of equipment management requirements is considered below the esoteric talents of the mainframe COBOL programmers. The old saying "If it isn't broke, don't fix it" goes a long way toward limiting innovation within EDP support groups and insuring a status quo situation throughout the equipment LCM industry.

If the equipment or inventory control manager did have access to a computer he probably approached such support with a pronounced feeling of apprehension. He would gather up his supply of ancient 3 × 5 cards filled with vital inventory or logistic support information and pass them through a slot in a wall to a room lined with stange consoles of blinking lights and whirling spools of tape. He would see his cards snatched up by a grim-faced operator who would coldly calculate their fate and then slap them down on the narrow desk of another cold, uncaring human automaton hopelessly mesmerized by row after row of letters and numbers scrolling up a small green and white TV monitor. As he left he would probably be laying odds on whether his information would be lost or merely entered into the wrong database this time.

Assuming the information was entered into the correct database, the manager was again at the mercy of the EDP department to provide him with status reports, simple tracking information, and trend analysis on how best to manage his inventory. Most of the programs written by EDP personnel for the equipment management tasks were usually limited to rewrites of existing software which could easily be modified to provide the minimum level of support. The equipment manager was often made to feel as if even these miniuscule scraps of EDP support were above and beyond the call of duty.

In some other instances the organization would use a distant mainframe computer through a time-sharing arrangement. This meant that vital LCM management data may not only be outside the control of individuals within the logistic support department, but could now be outside the city, county, or state as well. The equipment manager would then be faced with the possibility that the data may not only be lost within the on-site computer but now could possibly be incorporated into data files for a different or perhaps even competitive organization. Both of these situations could lead to interesting and in some instances embarrassing results.

The recent emphasis on the importance of LCM and information processing in general has resulted in the introduction of several new equipment life cycle management tools.

The new manual systems consist, in most cases, of redesigned or restructured forms marketed to be generic in nature so that they may be easily modified to satisfy several different types of businesses. Some of these have taken advantage of emerging hardcopy technology. The result has been a new and improved data storage media. In these the blackboard and wheel book have been replaced by wall charts and desk pads laid out in neat rows and columns with boxes of multicolored felt or, in some cases magnetic, color-coded flags to help identify equipment status and location.

In all of these systems, however, the tracking process has remained manual in nature and still demands individual item manipulation. The systems still produce black-on-white hard copy data lists, which must be manually manipulated, stored, copied, analyzed, and disbursed.

These systems are designed to be effective LCM tools for managing a limited amount of information on a small number of inventory items. They are most effective when managing equipment which does not require frequent information updating. Because of the physical limitation of space they are also not designed to monitor LCM processes involving more than a few items of inventory. They are simply not capable of satisfying complex LCM requirements.

Advances have also been made in application programming developed for equipment life cycle management systems designed for existing mainframe computers. These packages provide a broad range of LCM support. Most are sold in modules which can be modified to meet customer requirements. They are geared to large complex inventories where massive data manipulation is expected on a day-to-day basis.

The introduction of the latest families of super-minicomputers has made available another type of LCM management tool. These systems can handle large amounts of data very rapidly. Query response time is calculated in nanoseconds while complex sort, select, and search routines seldom require more than a few seconds to complete.

Both the advances in mainframe LCM packages and those designed for the new group of superminis are welcome additions to the growing number of management tools available within the field of logistic or equipment management. However, both of these advances have the same disadvantages. They are very expensive. They are difficult to convert to specific requirements, and they still need the assistance of the, no less invisible, EDP professional to install, support and customize to local LCM conventions and reporting norms.

There is, however, an alternative to both the new generation of manual LCM systems and the expensive mainframe- and minicomputer-based packages.

The data explosion of recent years has left most of us wondering what happened. Many of us have been reluctantly dragged into the computer age. We have been forced to use the new generation of data processing hardware and software just to maintain our own position within the work place.

In most areas of the country local education governing bodies have realized the importance of developing a learning environment that makes computer literacy as important as history and economics. School children are becoming acquainted with basic computer principles early in their education. Some, even as early as kindergarten, have been introduced to the world of electronic data processing through microcomputers in their classroom. A decade ago, Sesame Street was the focus of preschool education, now it is the rapidly developing potential of interactive video learning games programmed for home microcomputers.

Many of us are concerned and frightened about the growing number of human/computer interfaces and wonder how to react to a chattering automated teller machine or a gossiping grocery checkout cash register. However, we must realize that consumer-related EDP progress has been dramatic and will continue to dominate our lives. The computer along with all of its potential and flaws has arrived. We must now learn to bring this enormously powerful tool under our control.

Big government, big business, and big industry have already tapped the potential of the large computer systems costing million of dollars and requiring a cadre of stalwart custodians to tend. What remains is the equally powerful, yet relatively untapped, potential of the microcomputer.

There are basic similarities between the large mainframe computer and the small desktop micro. Both are clever at solving routine problems involving repetitive manipulation of strings of data. Both consume verbal abuse with equal nonconcern, and both are inanimate. Major differences between the two are measured in degrees of processing speed and magnitude of data storage available. A mainframe computer is capable of manipulating a large amount of information in a very short period of time. A microcomputer will handle a lesser amount of data at a slower rate of speed. Large systems are built to satisfy massive information thruput while the small micros are designed to accommodate a smaller quantity at a slower rate.

There are other similarities as well. Just as the large EDP systems require operating systems and programs to function, so do the various types of microcomputers. An operating system is basically a set of internal instructions which pre-establish processes within the computer. Necessary housekeeping functions are performed under the operating system which insure that the computer is capable of performing as it should.

A good example of a non-EDP operating system is the action of the involuntary muscle system within the human body. These life-sustaining functions were preprogrammed through a natural operating system activated or turned on at conception and remaining engaged throughout our lifetime. Heart beat, respiration, and the blinking of an eye are all part of the human body's preprogrammed set of operating instructions. Without these processes the body could not survive nor would it be prepared to accept other instructions such as walking, speaking, or driving a golf ball 250 yards down a fairway. These activities are, in essence, application programs we write for ourselves for specific voluntary functions.

A computer, be it one of the most advanced supercomputers capable of 250 million calculations a second or the one sitting on your desk at home used to track a household budget, would be equally helpless if it didn't have an operating system. There are several operating systems available. Each has its own attributes and limitations. However since the introduction of the first IBM microsystem a few years ago, the operating system of choice for most large organizations which use micros seems to be the one associated with IBM, PC/DOS; or its clone counterpart MS/DOS.

An operating system will prepare the computer to perform an action. However it cannot by itself do more than that. Programs or software provide exact instructions to perform a specific task. Some of the most popular types of programs designed for microcomputers are word processing, database management, and spread sheets. Each of these perform specific types of data manipulation based on a set of programmed instructions. Graphics and desktop publishing are also becoming available as packaged programs available for microcomputers. Recent innovations in communication technology, massive data storage devices, and local area networking have also increased the potential for microcomputers. Equipment LCM, like word processing, is a specific function capable of being supported by microcomputer technology.

The key to successfully managing equipment through a microcomputer is timely, accurate, and verifiable information. Information within the EDP environment is maintained within a database.

Most people think of a database as a collection of information stored on a computer. In the data processing world, a database is defined as a collection of identified relationships driven by a database manager. A database manager is a piece of software that allows the data to be stored, entered, retrieved, and manipulated by an operator.

Physically speaking, a database consists of files. Logically speaking, a database is a group of records and the relationships that tie those records together.

There are two ways of managing data. One is the traditional data management system and the other is the database manager. The traditional data management system stores data redundantly and uses a very structured system. A database manager stores data in a nonredundant manner and allows much more functionality and versatility.

A relational database, driven by a database manager, is viewed as one of rectangular tables consisting of rows and columns. Each of these tables contain several relationships. The rows are called records and the columns are called fields. Each record is assigned a number (record number) and each field will have a field number or name. A relational database provides the ability to cross reference between relationships.

A relational database controlled by a database manager allows data to be stored in a nonredundant manner. This means that a given data item appears only once, thus using less space on the storage media and maximizing sort, search, and select functions. Additionally, nonredundant data simplifies updates, eliminates data pollution caused by duplicate data entries, and allows for more secure access, control, and protection of data.

Security and integrity are more easily maintained using a database manager. Certain data files within the database can be restricted to read-only access. Others can be restricted by the use of passwords. The ultimate security is the ability to remove your database from your machine and take it home with you at night.

A relational database and a database manager resident on a microcomputer can be a powerful equipment LCM tool. Through a system like this, personnel from bench technician to facility manager can have access to an on-line query and response management tool capable of satisfying even the most difficult equipment management problems. A microcomputer system physically capable of supporting the database manager and the database itself provides two thirds of a total turnkey equipment management system. The remaining third is an intelligent identification system which will provide accurate and easily definable asset identification.

A key to any equipment management system, be it a manual, mainframe-based, or one designed to run on a local microcomputer is item identification. Once an item of equipment is identified in the identification module, it must be able to be referenced to that number throughout its lifespan. The equipment management community has a need for a short yet intelligent method of absolute item identification to complete the triad of equipment management requirements.

The advantages are obvious.

1. Standardization of model/part number and nomenclature
2. Prevention of misidentification and duplication of inventory items
3. Rapid, accurate, and convenient retrieval of inventory, scheduling, and historical data
4. Easy interface with other compatible management information systems

There is also a requirement to make the equipment identification number more than a license plate. Several organizations, including several departments within the federal government have taken the lead in developing identification numbers with some level of intelligence built in.

The intelligence that is present in these types of identification numbers may be no more than an indication of type, style, size, or location. Others may contain sophisticated parametric data capable of isolating specific equipment and identifying facility capability and capacity.

For instance, an oscilloscope used in maintaining military radar systems may be coded with an identification number that would provide clues as to its capability as well as location and manufacturer. That could evolve into an identification number that would look something like this: 7904-28480-B3-5667-OSO-3-8-6-A-Y.

This number may appear cumbersome, however, it contains the equivalent amount of information as would several standard text lines. It also has one more major advantage over straight text. It can be manipulated using a simple microcomputer.

For example, the first four digits in the code equate to the model number of the piece of equipment. The next five digits equate to the manufacturer. B3 places the item at a specific location for inventory control. The last four numbers (5667) refer to the serial number. OSO-3-8-6-A-Y provides technical and parametric information about the number.

An example of a successful intelligent item identification number system that has been in operation for a number of years is the Unique Number Identification System (UNI-NUMBER) developed by DALFI, Inc. and in use throughout the United States Navy Metrology Community since 1981.

In this system the DALFI, Inc. UNI-Number of ten alphanumeric characters is capable of providing some level of intelligence as well as a cradle-to-grave tracking with positive identification for over 1.7 million items.

An additional benefit brought about by the acceptance of the DALFI, Inc. UNI-Number is the assurance that all facilities in the USN Metrology Community are using one set of naming conventions for all items in inventory. A calibration lab in Diego Garcia will be able to communicate requests for logistic support to a group in Washington, D.C. and be assured that both are referring to the same item.

This type of uniformity also makes data transfer between users very easy. It helps in tracking equipment through the various levels of calibration and repair. It facilitates like-item replacement and ensures parameter for parameter substitution.

Every organization can develop a UNI-Number approach to meet its own management requirements. Every organization has different demands as far as item identification is concerned. However, each of these facilities has the identical need which is to be able to monitor, track, and report on equipment. An identification number with some level of built-in intelligence will provide all levels of equipment management an important tool to assist in this endeavor.

Most manual LCM equipment management systems would be unable to handle coded information such as the example. Yet a microcomputer could contain thousands of items of inventory in just such a system. The combination of the latest high-speed microprocessor, relational database system with a powerful database manager and a UNI-Number identification system would be one of the powerful equipment management tools available.

BIBLIOGRAPHY

"And Now the Megaflops Barrier...," *Aviat. Week Space Technol.*, July (1986).

DALFI, Inc., "Micro Inventory Control System (MICS)," 1984.

DALFI, Inc., "Unique Number Identifier (UNI-NUMBER)," 1981.

dBase ii, Version 1.1, Ashton Tate, 1984.

Hessinger, P. R., "DBMS: Adding Value to Vanilla," *Datamation*, March (1987).

James, P. N., "What is the User Interface?," *J. Inform. Sys. Mgt.*, 3(2) (1986).

Martin, J., *Strategic Data-Planning Methodologies*, Prentice Hall, Inc., Englewood Cliffs, NJ, 1982.

Merrett, T. H., *Relational Information Systems*, Reston Publishing Company, Reston, VA, 1984.

"Networking Key to Computer Use," *Aviat. Week Space Technol.*, July (1986).

Oracle Corporation, *Oracle Relational Data Base Management System*, 1986.

"Software: Problem, Opportunity or Solution," *Aviat. Week Space Technol.*, July (1986).

Stephanou, S. E., *Management Technology, Innovation and Engineering*, Daniel Spencer Publishers, Malibu, CA, 1980.

Van Winkle, C. T. and L. Wyrick, "Understanding Microcomputer Relational Data Bases that Use Bar Code with Intelligence as the Key to Establish an Industry Standard for Equipment Management," National Conference of Standards Laboratories, Gaithersburg, MD, 1985.

Van Winkle, C. T. and L. Wyrick, "Equipment Management Through Microcomputers," Measurement Science Conference, Irvine, CA, 1986.

VAX-11 DBMS, *Data Base Administration Student Handbook*, Digital Equipment Corporation, 1983.

Wyrick, L., "Bar Code: A Tool for Equipment Identification and Tracking," Measurement Science Conference, Irvine, CA, 1985.

MICHAEL J. BENNETT

ERGONOMIC ASPECTS OF COMPUTER USE

INTRODUCTION

Ergonomics, deriving from the Greek word "ergon" work is now mainly considered to mean "the science of designing machines and environments that are most suited to the efficiency, comfort, safety and peace of mind of those working with them" (see Armbruster, 1983). The widespread introduction of computer technology into the working environment of those who have had little previous exposure to working with machines (librarians and information professionals, managers, clerks, and typists), has led to increased interest in the subject of ergonomics. In particular, individuals are concerned that the use of computers not pose new health hazards in the workplace. Ergonomics goes beyond the prevention of health hazards, it aims to optimize the coexistence between people and technology within the working environment. As such, it sees the potential positive contribution that technology can make to the health of people in the workplace. This is pertinent if one considers that the World Health Organization defines health as being a state of complete physical, mental, and social well-being not merely the absence of disease and infirmity.

In the broad sense of the word, ergonomics includes all the physical, social, and psychological aspects of work and workplace design. It is important in all types of work environments, however this article will concentrate on computer-based work. Paying due attention to ergonomics can benefit everyone in the workplace. The employee can be physically and psychologically more comfortable, thus more likely to work more effectively. The organization can benefit in terms of reduced absenteeism, improved morale, and greater job satisfaction, which ultimately should be reflected in better performance and, in the case of private sector, increased profits.

In considering how the introduction of new computer technology can be ergonomically sound, it is necessary to look at four different elements:

> Machine design
> The physical design of the workplace
> Software
> Job design and work organization

Before considering each aspect, however, a brief review of some of the health concerns in relation to the use of computers will be given.

COMPUTERS AT WORK

Computer technology, specifically the use of visual display units (VDUs) has been implicated in a number of reports as causing a variety of medical complaints, from adverse reproductive outcomes to eyestrain, skin rashes to stress. It will be seen that many of the problems mentioned can, and indeed should, be avoided by the adoption of sensible policies for the use of computers at work, including proper attention to ergonomic considerations. However, it is worth bearing in mind that even if all the "ergonomic problems" have been sorted out, there may still be some complaints about the use of computers. The reason may well be that health issues are seen as a legitimate area of work that people can complain about—concern about health can often mask a deeper concern and fear about the introduction of technology in general, and the ability of the individual to cope with it.

The most pervasive type of computer technology used at work is the VDU. The video display unit is basically a screen-based device with a keyboard. Currently most of these screens are based on cathode ray tube (CRT) technology which enables text, numbers, graphics, and in some cases, images to be represented electronically onscreen. Keyboards tend to follow the standard QWERTY layout sometimes with the addition of a pointing device or "mouse." While all VDUs share these same basic components the same is not true of the jobs for which they are used. Computers can be used for a wide variety of tasks from programming to word processing, on-line searching to data entry. Thus tasks can vary dramatically and differ along such dimensions as:

> Skills required
> Visual emphasis of the task
> Pace of work
> Length of time spent at the machine
> Control which an individual has over the work being done

Each of these factors is important in influencing the extent to which an individual feels "healthy" at work. The point to note is that many of the problems reported to be associated with the use of computers arise not from the machines themselves, but from the nature of the jobs for which they are used.

HEALTH ISSUES ASSOCIATED WITH THE USE OF COMPUTERS

The most discussed health issues relating to the use of computers at work come under the following categories:

> Adverse pregnancy outcomes and the related question of radiation
>   emissions from VDUs
> Eye strain and visual fatigue
> Migraine headache
> Photosensitive epilepsy
> Muscle pain, aches and strains
> Skin rashes
> Stress

Each of these will now be considered.

PREGNANCY

One of the most controversial issues raised in relation to the use of computers at work has been the question of the effect of VDUs on pregnancy outcome. Reports of "clusters" of miscarriages and birth defects occurring among groups of female VDU operators led to fears that VDUs are in some way connected with adverse pregnancy outcomes, and that the link may be a causal one. This raised several important issues. First is the need to thoroughly investigate this "health hazard" to determine if such a link exists. No one could justify allowing women to face a possible health risk to themselves and/or their unborn children, nor is it desirable that they endure increased anxiety and insecurity as a result of doubts as to the safety of their using a computer at work. On the other hand, the wholesale "banning" of pregnant women from VDU work, a proposition some would favor, is not an attractive prospect since it would make the already considerable difficulties which many women face in obtaining high echelon employment even more insurmountable. What is needed is an evaluation of the research already conducted to establish whether risks are indeed present.

Some reports of "clusters" of miscarriages and birth defects among VDU workers suggest that the use of the VDU was responsible for these adverse outcomes and that a high proportion of pregnant VDU workers had such experiences. The question here is one of establishing whether such conclusions are justified. As with any particular group of workers experiencing ill health, it is first necessary to determine whether the cause was an occupational one. This is usually done by comparing the incidence of ill health in an occupational group, in this case VDU workers, with the incidence in the general population. If it is then found that the rate of ill health in the occupational group is significantly greater than that in the general population, then the cause of that ill health is usually thought to be an occupationally related one.

In relation to adverse pregnancy outcomes among VDU workers, such comparisons have proved difficult to undertake. Problems of definition arise, for example, who is to be considered a VDU worker? Should we include all individuals who use a VDU however infrequently? Should we include those who work within the vicinity of the machines? Indeed what is an adverse pregnancy outcome? These can range from:

Spontaneous abortions or miscarriages
Birth defects
Low birth weight
Still birth

A third problem lies in establishing the control group; should this include all women of reproductive age or only working women? The only baseline figures available for adverse pregnancy outcomes against which the experiences of VDU workers can be assessed relate to all women, not only those in the workforce. They show that pregnancy is a hazardous affair in its own right, with 15—20% of all known pregnancies resulting in miscarriage; 3—4% of all births producing a child weighing 4 lbs or less; 2.5% of all babies being malformed.

The current known occupational risks to pregnancy are:

Exposure to radiation
Exposure to chemical and biological agents

However, a number of well known other risks to pregnancy include:

Maternal age: miscarriages are more common among the under 20 and
   over 30 age groups
Maternal abnormality and disease
Number of pregnancies; the likelihood of miscarriage increases with
   the number of pregnancies
Socioeconomic class
Exposure to infectious agents
Provision and quality of antenatal care
Delivery methods
Smoking and alcohol

To establish whether adverse pregnancy outcomes had an occupational cause, all such other causes would have to be eliminated.

A further problem in evaluating the evidence relates to the methodology of the study in question. Some studies on "clusters" of miscarriages have dealt with sample sizes which are too small to be valid statistically. Doctors at the Occupation and Health Unit at Toronto University estimate that in order to evaluate a "cluster" and to avoid statistical coincidence it would be necessary to study 12,000 working women over a two-year period; half of whom used VDUs in their work and half who did not. Since the distribution of adverse pregnancy outcomes in the population will follow the normal bell-shaped distribution curve, and given the ever wider usage of VDUs by women of reproductive age, together with the well-established risk of miscarriage in early pregnancy, it is thought that many "clusters" are to be expected on the basis of chance alone.

One recent well-constructed study of the effect of VDUs on pregnant women was conducted by the National Board of Occupational Safety and Health and the National Social Welfare Board in Sweden. This study is using the Swedish Miscarriage register to examine pregnancy outcome in occupational groups which have a low, medium, and high exposure to VDUs. Their preliminary findings do not indicate that there is a relationship between the use of VDUs and adverse pregnancy outcomes.

In the United Kingdom, the Health and Safety Executive reports that none of the three reliable epidemiological studies which have compared the reproductive outcome in VDU workers against non-VDU workers has indicated an excess rate of adverse pregnancy outcomes among the former.

Concern over adverse pregnancy outcomes arose because of the fact that computers give off radiation, which is known to have adverse effects on health. It is true that VDUs emit radiation, but so do microwave ovens, televisions, the sun, and nuclear explosions. Radiation is an emotive term and it is important to realize that there are a number of forms of radiation, not all of which are harmful. Broadly, radiation comes in two types: ionizing and nonionizing. It is generally accepted that while VDUs do emit some ionizing radiation, it is well below background levels. The Health and Safety Executive in the United Kingdom reports that in the case of ionizing radiation:

1. The level of x-ray emissions found from VDUs are substantially
    below background level and do not add significantly to the latter.

2. In relation to ultraviolet emissions, only UVA-type emissions have been detected from VDUs. UVA can be hazardous, but only in very large quantities. Such quantities are not found to be emitted from VDUs.

On the question of nonionizing radiation emissions from VDUs, there are of three types: visible light, microwaves, and electromagnetic emissions. Visible light must be emitted from a VDU in order for it to function. However, with a full screen of characters and at maximum brightness, the light emitted from a VDU has been found to be of negligible risk to the eye. With regard to microwave emissions, the National Radiological Protection Board in the United Kingdom has found such emissions from VDUs to be barely detectable and not hazardous to health.

Any residual concern about radiation in relation to VDUs has centered on a discussion of the effects of low-frequency electromagnetic emissions. Such electric and magnetic fields can be detected in the vicinity of a computer or indeed from any electrically powered device such as a hair dryer or shaver. Such fields are difficult to measure, but are thought to be well below levels thought to be hazardous. VDUs also emit VLF (very low frequency) and ELF (extremely low frequency) electromagnetic emissions. It is agreed that these do occur; where scientists differ is as to whether such radiowaves cause changes in the human body. A study by Delgado generated concern when he claimed that chicken embryos exposed to such emissions had changed. A number of studies are attempting to repeat Delgado's work on chicken and mice embryos. Initial reports suggest that his findings cannot be replicated, and therefore cannot be substantiated. Still other research suggests that the type of emissions used by Delgado are not similar to those from a VDU.

The widely accepted consensus, therefore, on the subject of radiation and VDUs is that there is no evidence to suggest that the radiation levels emitted by a VDU pose a health hazard. This is supported, for example, by both the Health and Safety Executive and the National Radiological Protection Board in the United Kingdom. To summarize the issues of adverse pregnancy outcomes and the use of computers we can say:

1. VDUs do not appear to emit levels of radiation likely to adversely effect the outcome of a pregnancy
2. None of the reliable studies conducted on pregnancy and VDU work has demonstrated any link between such work and adverse pregnancy outcomes

One other point remains to be made on this subject. Anxiety and stress resulting from uncertainty about the health hazards of VDUs can of itself be inimical to a successful pregnancy. Making women aware of the reliable evidence on the subject can allay such fears. However, it is not unreasonable to suggest that some women, despite available reliable information, will retain their fears. For that reason many employers now offer pregnant women the option of transferring off VDU work for the duration of their pregnancy, and many trade unions include this stipulation in their contract negotiations.

While adverse pregnancy outcome is the most emotive health issue raised in relation to the use of computers at work, it is not the most common or frequently raised one. Complaints of eye strain or muscle fatigue are far more usual. These are discussed below.

EYE STRAIN AND VISUAL FATIGUE

The introduction of computers in the workplace has raised questions about the effect of screen-based work on eyesight. For example, in November 1985, the results of a survey of computer terminal users were published in *Health and Safety at Work*. The study found that 70% of respondents experienced eyestrain and 34% reported blurred vision. It is important in this context to distinguish between eye damage and dysfunction and eye-strain. Medical evidence suggests that screen-based work does not damage eyesight nor aggravate existing eye problems. There is evidence, though to support the suggestion that it can lead to short-term visual discomfort or visual fatigue, that is eye strain. Such a conclusion is hardly surprising when we see the type of work which some people are asked to do on a com-puter and the environmental conditions within which the machines are operated.

Eyestrain and visual fatigue are largely preventable if attention is paid to the visual environment within which the computer user works. The most common source of eyestrain comes from glare; glare from the screen itself, the lighting in the room, both artificial and daylight, and from the room surfaces. Reducing or eliminating glare via the proper positioning of the VDU unit and the provision of appropriate lighting can go a long way toward reducing visual discomfort. Traditional office lighting was designed for desk work, and is generally too bright for reading characters on a reflect-ing vertical surface, which computer-based work requires.

The quality, as well as the quantity, of lighting is also important; certain types of lighting are more restful than others. Further factors influencing the extent to which visual fatigue is experienced by the computer user are the screen display, its color, contrast, and stability; the length of time that people work on the machine without a break; and the type of work which they do. The eye like any other muscle will tire if held in the same position for long periods of time.

It should also be remembered that eyestrain is not a new phenomenon brought about by computer-based work. Many other industrial and clerical tasks make similar visual demands upon individuals. People who wear glasses can experience particular difficulties when using computers, especially those whose glasses are designed for a narrow range of reading distance or who wear multifocal lens glasses. Such glasses are not designed to cope with work involving varying visual distances such as VDU work. Such problems can be easily overcome by modifications to their prescription, and a consultation with an optician before starting screen-based work can sort this out.

On the question of eye testing in general for computer users, there are differing viewpoints. Many trade unions recommend that members have eye tests before starting such work, with regular follow up examinations there-after so that any deterioration can be monitored. On the other hand, bodies such as the Health and Safety Executive do not feel that wholesale pre-employment testing of eyesight of VDU users and its subsequent reassess-ment is really justified. It should be remembered that individuals may have eye defects of which they are currently unaware, but which could be aggra-vated by VDU use, because such work presents different and often new visual demands on the user. Therefore, consultation with a qualified prac-titioner is a sensible precaution to take before embarking on computer-based work. Screen design and visual environment factors need to be taken into account when introducing computers to the workplace so as to avoid visual fatigue and these are discussed later.

MIGRAINE

There is some concern that screen-based work can be particularly aggravating to migraine sufferers. More specifically, it is speculated that the screen light/flicker might trigger attacks. This is difficult to prove or disprove, as the term migraine is generic, covering a wide range of symptoms. Its known causes range from factors as diverse as specific foods (e.g., chocolate or red wine), to low blood sugar, fatigue, or even light patterns. The cause of migraine even in particular individuals is difficult to isolate. However, consideration of the visual environment of the computer user can probably go a long way toward avoiding computer use from becoming the triggering mechanism of such attacks.

PHOTOSENSITIVE EPILEPSY

A final issue relating to the visual demands of screen-based computer work and health concerns photosensitive epilepsy. Use of computers does not cause epilepsy. However, some people suffer from a comparatively rare form of epilepsy known as photosensitive epilepsy, and may be at risk of provoking an attack when using a VDU, as seizures in this form of the condition can be triggered by a flickering light source, or in some cases, from viewing striped light patterns. The onset of this type of epilepsy is most likely to occur between 10 and 14 years of age, with most first attacks occurring before age 20. Therefore, the likelihood of someone experiencing an attack for the first time while using a computer is extremely low.

Doctors have found that word processing presents little or no hazard, but graphic displays could in theory be a problem. Professor Lee states that the physical features of the stimulus of VDU work such as brightness, size of screen, frequency of picture repetition, and viewing distance make it unlikely that work with VDUs will provoke an attack. However, it is wise to consult a doctor before commencing computer-based work.

MUSCLE AND BODY PAIN

A study by the Swedish Board of Occupational Safety and Health of operators engaged in full-time sedentary VDU work revealed the following results:

    55% felt discomfort in their backs and shoulders
    32% felt discomfort in their head and neck
    25% felt discomfort in their arms and wrists
    15% felt discomfort in their legs

Similarly, in Britain, the results of the *Health and Safety at Work* survey showed that 53% of VDU users experienced pain in the neck or shoulders, 43% suffered some degree of back pain, 14% got hand cramps, and 58% said they experienced general fatigue. Such findings indicate that muscular fatigue can be a problem for some computer users.

Two factors influence the extent to which muscular fatigue is experienced in computer work. The first relates to the demands of the job itself: does this require the computer user to sit or stand over prolonged periods of time, possibly repeating the same movement over and over again?

The second relates to the type of office furniture used with a computer, in particular the chair and desk.

Normal muscular work requires the alternate contraction and relaxation of the muscle. This increases the rate of blood flow, which easily removes the waste products (lactic acid) which cause muscle fatigue. When a muscle is, for example, held in one position over a period of time it remains contracted, receives little blood, and tires easily as the waste products are not removed. People carrying out repeated movements over and over again, such as keyboarding, filing, sitting, or standing for long periods, and in one position, are therefore likely to experience such muscle fatigue.

Since the late 19th century, information-oriented occupations (largely office based) have been sedentary in nature, often entailing a person to adopt a stooping posture with the head advanced and the back curved. When working in such a position the stomach is often compressed against the desk which is bad for posture and the lungs, and interferes with normal abdominal movements. Badly designed chairs and prolonged sitting can also lead to swollen feet and ankles. Uncomfortable and poorly designed chairs contribute to the problem.

The design and selection of office furniture with which computers are used is therefore a vital factor in preventing muscular aches and pains for computer users. The physical dimensions of chairs and desks are very important, since they affect the posture adopted and ease of work. Any posture which is maintained over long periods creates a "static" load on the body which is much more tiring than the load created by movement. Therefore, chairs which permit shifts in posture so that the load is spread to different parts of the skeletal and muscular systems are desirable.

Highly repetitious jobs requiring people to remain in fixed postures for long periods of time or those entailing fast repetitive movements of the hands and wrists are more likely to give rise to fatigue and pain than jobs where a number of different tasks are performed and the individuals concerned have to move around in the course of their work. Paying attention to ergonomic factors, therefore, in the computer user's workplace can prevent muscle fatigue and aches and pains.

Less common and less likely to be found among computer users are chronic musculoskeletal complaints referred to as "repetitive strain injury" (fondly known in Australia as kangeroo paw). Strictly speaking, such conditions should be known as occupationally related upper limb disorders and they include such things as tenosynovitis, writer's cramp, and carpal tunnel syndrome. Repetition of movement is not necessarily sufficient nor the only cause of such conditions. These are medically recognized complaints and should be distinguished from short-term muscular discomfort. Again, attention to the ergonomics of the workplace should avoid the development of such complaints.

SKIN RASHES

Some computer users have reported experiencing facial skin complaints ranging from itchiness to redness to distinct rashes. As yet, no direct link with the use of VDUs has been established. The cause is thought to be more indirect, and due to either excess static in the work environment and/or low humidity. Computers, give off heat and therefore can increase the static in the atmosphere and reduce humidity. Overall, the number of individuals affected by skin complaints as a result of using computers is low, and their problems have been resolved by either reducing the static or raising the humidity levels by such measures as treating the carpets with antistatic fluids, improving ventilation to avoid buildup of particle deposition, and introducing plants to increase humidity levels.

STRESS

Stress is a complex issue with which to deal, and certainly stress and related illnesses are to be found in many occupations other than computer users. The physical and mental symptoms associated with stress are numerous and can vary considerably from person to person, so too can the degree of stress tolerance. While occasional stress can be conducive to good work, prolonged stress is not.

The introduction of new computer technology into the workplace, especially when those using it have no previous experience of computers or perhaps of changes in working practices, can be stressful. Lack of proper training can exacerbate the situation. In a Labour Reserach Department survey covering 17,000 workers, a third of the respondents found that using computers in their job was more stress inducing than their previous working situation.

Several other factors in the work situation can contribute to stress. A lack of sufficient physical space in which to work comfortably can generate stress. Computers are often "added on" to an existing work environment and equipment without any extra space being allocated for them. Poor lighting, excessive noise, inadequate heating systems, and "inhuman" surroundings can further contribute to stress. The type of computer equipment used, its design, response time, reliability, and the ease of use of the software are all factors influencing stress levels of users.

The jobs people are asked to do, specifically the extent of task variety, use of skills, level of concentration required, and the physical effort involved in the job are other factors which can contribute to stress. Finally, the way work is organized, including such things as the standards required, the type of supervision provided, the training undertaken, and the extent to which an individual feels in control of their work situation can influence the degree of stress experienced. Care in selecting computer equipment and software, designing work environments and jobs, and implementing technology is necessary if undue stress is to be avoided.

Computers, as seen from the above, have been implicated in a range of medical complaints. It is the contention of the author, however, that some of these problems can be avoided if sound and intelligent ergonomic practices are employed when computer technology is introduced to the workplace. The remainder of this article provides ergonomic guidelines for the use of computers at work and provides a list of suggested reading on the subject for interested readers. It should be remembered that the aim of ergonomics is a positive one; not merely to avoid hazards at work but to improve the efficiency, comfort, and safety of employees, which in turn, should lead to positive benefits in terms of their effectiveness and, indeed, health. Applying ergonomic principles to the use of computers can add to the costs associated with their introduction to the workplace, especially where major changes to the environment are concerned. It also requires that considerable time be spent planning and implementing their introduction. Some argue against this trouble and expense. Others feel that the fuss

about adverse health effects of computers is a short-term reaction to technological change which, if left to itself, will peter out.

Such attitudes are short sighted and misguided. The health hazards
are apparent and very real. Unless the equipment is properly designed,
installed, and used, many more people will suffer ill effects as the use of
computers increases. What of the costs of ill health such as increased
absenteeism, people operating below capacity, low morale? Such costs are
not so easily quantified, but they too are real. Many experts writing on
the benefits of computer technology feel that computers can only improve
productivity significantly if people use the equipment creatively—they are
unlikely to do so if the equipment makes them sick.

Many of the ergonomic practices recommended below have applicability
to noncomputer work also. The increasing use of computer technology is
highlighting the fact that many working environments are less than adequate
from the point of view of health (in the broadest sense) and that many jobs
are not "designed" at all, but rather evolve, often in a haphazard way.
Applying ergonomic principles then can benefit all workers.

There are many checklists available of ergonomic standards for visual
display units. Indeed, some countries such as Sweden and West Germany,
have compulsory standards to which VDUs must conform. A common problem with standards though is their use of technical language which can be
confusing to the layperson. These checklists can be helpful when choosing
a VDU, as the manufacturer's specification can be checked against the
recommended standards. Furthermore, they can be of assistance in negotiations about the use of new technology. The danger though is of getting
absorbed in the detail of the standard/checklist and neglecting its intention—
at the least, that computers be introduced in such a way as to ensure
hazards are avoided and at best that their introduction leads to positive
enhancements in jobs and the working environment.

For these reasons, the recommendations cited here are in nontechnical
language and concentrate on what the author considers to be the most
important ergonomic factors to bear in mind when selecting and implementing
computer technology at work. The recommendations are in several parts.
First, the computer with its components of screen and keyboard is discussed.
The key features to consider for these are highlighted, together with an
explanation as to why such features are important from an ergonomic point
of view. Then the immediate workplace within which the computer system
is sited, together with the general work environment, comes under scrutiny.
This is followed by a section on software ergonomics and job design, both
of which contribute to the physical and psychological well-being of the
computer user. Finally, there is a section on managing the introduction of
new technology to the workplace with special emphasis on the role of
training.

SCREENS AND KEYBOARDS

The characteristics of the screen used with a computer system will have an
important influence on whether users suffer from eyestrain and visual
fatigue. Fundamental to the screen design is the idea of adjustability; the
person should be able to adapt the technology to meet his or her visual
requirements and not vice versa. One aspect of adjustability concerns
screen position. It should be easy to swivel the screen left and right and

to tilt it up and down to the most comfortable position for the user. Ideally, the screen should be positioned at or below eye level to avoid muscle strain caused by constantly looking up at it. Antireflection treatments or the provision of an antiglare filter on the screen can cut glare, and thus reduce possible eyestrain. Another aspect of adjustability concerns screen image. There should be easily accessible controls to adjust brightness and contrast. Furthermore, users should be shown how to adjust settings on the screen (there are many anecdotes of computer users working with badly contrasted screens for many months because they didn't know that the contrast could be adjusted).

The color of the screen is largely a matter of personal preference, and it is hard to be dogmatic about this. Increasingly, color monitors are becoming standard on many computer systems. White, yellow, amber, or green characters on a neutral background are generally considered most restful to the eye. More important for avoiding eyestrain are the display characters and image stability. All computer screens flicker to some extent, but there seem to be differences between individuals as to their threshold of awareness of any flicker. When selecting computer equipment it is important to observe the screen under actual operating conditions to look for signs of flicker. The characters on the screen need to be of adequate size and of good presentation. They should be easy to read, clearly formed, and well defined. Some screens have poor definitions whereby Bs can look like 8s, U like V, and 5 like S, such displays make proofreading onscreen very difficult and fatigueing for the user.

Keyboards are a very important part of a computer system, providing the dominant form of person—machine interaction. Keyboards should be detached from the screen, thus allowing the user to adjust their position on the desktop. They should be stable and well balanced so no movement occurs even when the keys are pounded. A shallow sloped and thin keyboard (thin refers to the height of the keyboard above the desktop) reduces the likelihood of excessive loads being placed on the hands and arm, thus muscle ache or strain is prevented. Unnecessarily wide keyboards should be avoided as these can lead to fatiguing of the neck—torso should the user reach for paper/books lying on the desk beside it.

Ease of use of the keyboard is affected by layout. The alphabetic keys should follow the standard QWERTY positions familiar to most users. If the task requires substantial entry of numeric information, a separate numeric pad, adjacent to the keyboard (either to the left or right of the alphabetic keys depending on whether the user is left or right handed), should be available. Function keys, those that perform specific tasks, are useful on the keyboard but they should be clearly differentiated from the alphanumeric keys either by size/color or location.

The keys themselves should help aid accurate location by the finger tip. Square keys with a concave (dished) top are ideal for this purpose. The legends, that is, what is printed on the key, should be easily legible and moulded onto the key surface to resist wear and abrasion. A maximum of two legends per key is a useful guide; more legends will only confuse the user as to the key's function.

Keyboard surfaces of matte finish with keys having low reflectivity, can reduce glare in the vicinity of the computer user. The act of keyboarding is a complex process whereby the movement of the hands and fingers is activated and controlled by signals from the brain responding to a variety of stimuli. Some kind of feedback from the keying-in process is

necessary to inform the operator that the intended action has been taken
and to aid in the detection of errors. Keyboards should therefore provide
some kind of auditory and/or tactile feedback to the user.

Selecting computer screens and keyboards of good design incorporating
the features outlined above can reduce the likelihood of the computer user
experiencing eyestrain and/or muscle fatigue. Good design of screens and
keyboards can also contribute positively to the psychological satisfaction
derived from computer-based work, and so reduce stress.

SITING THE COMPUTER: PERIPHERALS
AND FURNITURE

The immediate working environment will influence the degree of comfort
computer users experience at work and thus affect their efficiency at performing work tasks. The screen and keyboard, together with peripherals
such as disk drives and printers, take up a lot of room—they are usually
an addition to existing equipment rather than a substitute for it. Extra
space in the immediate work environment may be necessary to accommodate
the computer system. All items should be positioned for the users' convenience and in such a way as to avoid unnecessary stretching and possible
strains when users seek out frequently used materials.

Printers can pose a particular problem as the noise they generate can
break concentration and increase stress, not only of the computer user,
but of those working in the vicinity, especially if large amounts of printing
are undertaken. Acoustic hoods, set on top of the printer are vital unless
printing is infrequent and lasts for very short periods of time. If an
acoustic hood cannot be used, then the printer should be sited away from
the immediate work environment; in situations where printers are used as
a shared resource among a number of computer users, this is most desirable.
The provision of a simple document holder can greatly ease input of material
to the computer and avoid strain to the neck—torso, which can occur when
users read input documents from the desktop. These holders should be
nonreflective and matte paper should be used, again to cut down on glare.

The desk should, ideally, be adjustable so that users can position the
computer and themselves at the correct height for working. A lower desk
height is required for keyboarding than for writing. There needs to be
adequate knee clearnace beneath the desk and users of short height should
be provided with a foot rest. Desk tops should be matte so as to cut
down on glare.

Chairs are perhaps the single most important item in the prevention of
back pain, one of the most frequent complaints of computer users. The
best type of chair is a swivel one with a stable base and an adjustable seat
height. When seated at the computer, the user's feet should be firmly on
the floor (or footrest). The chair must adequately support the spine, with
a backrest which supports at least the lumbar region of the back (the lower
back). This backrest should also be adjustable both for height and for
moving backward and forward. It should be curved so as to avoid catching
on the shoulder blades. Again, users need to be shown how to adjust this
furniture so as to take advantage of its flexibility.

Two other points about the immediate working environment of the
computer user need to be made. The first concerns wiring and safety.
Computers seem to spawn a spaghetti-like mess of wires. These should not

be allowed to trail or hang where they may cause accidents. Power points should not be overloaded, and the use of extension boards is to be avoided if at all possible, as they add to the proliferation of wires. Some newer desk furniture for computer work contains channels along which wires can be run to keep them from getting in the way of the user. Such furniture, though, can be expensive. The second point concerns the level of concentration required for some types of computer work. If it is very high, the user may require high levels of visual and auditory privacy. This can be achieved by giving them a separate office or, in open-plan layouts, by the use of partitions to deaden sound and provide visual privacy.

THE AMBIENT WORK ENVIRONMENT

The main point about the ambient environment (sound, light, temperature, and air quality) for computer and other forms of sedentary work is that the environment should be a draught-free one with a comfortable and stable temperature, high-quality lighting, and no intrusive noise. Like other types of machinery, computers generate heat and particularly in warm weather, where several computers are operating, this can cause problems of excessive temperatures which can lead to drowsiness or irritability on the part of users. To avoid such problems, adequate ventilation and reasonable humidity must be provided. The latter is necessary to avoid skin itchiness and possibly rashes or facial dermatitis and dryness/irritation of the eyes. Generally, most offices are too dry rather than too moist. Humidification and adequate ventilation will also reduce static in the environment. Excessive static has been implicated in facial rashes as well as causing unpleasant "shocks" to individuals. Antistatic treatment of carpets in rooms with VDUs can further reduce this problem.

One of the most significant contributing factors to eyestrain in computer users is the visual environment. Desk illumination for computer work should be below that of a normal office environment to cut down glare. However, some local task lighting in the vicinity of the machine may be necessary to facilitate the reading of source documents. Quality as well as quantity of light is important. Artificial lighting in the form of a totally illuminated ceiling where the lighting is diffused to reduce glare is suitable for computer work, as is the use of "up lighters" which bounce the light up off the ceiling. Lighting should also be adjustable so that individuals can set their own desired level of illumination. The position of the computer in relation to the light source is also important. To avoid glare, computers should be placed between, rather than under, rows of lighting with the line of sight parallel to the light fittings. Computers should also be placed parallel to windows to avoid reflection in the screen. Glare from windows can be further reduced by the use of blinds, curtains, or even light-absorbing film. Where possible, nonreflective surfaces should be used throughout the environment where computers are in place. Muted matte colorings on the walls can reduce glare and provide a restful work environment.

SOFTWARE ERGONOMICS AND JOB DESIGN

Computer jobs involve the user in interaction with software. In fact, software is at the heart of computer-based work—it commands the users' immediate attention and is at the forefront of their consciousness. This cognitive interface can determine how individuals react to working with a computer and, in particular, the degree of stress they experience. Software ergonomics covers such things as the presentation of information on the screen, the way information is input to the system, the task sequence or actions required of the user to manipulate the system, error messages and help facilities, etc. Poorly designed software can frustrate the user, lead to increased training time, increased error rates, and even to abuse of systems. "User-friendly" is a much maligned term with regard to descriptions of software. As one computer user put it, software can be about as user friendly as a cornered rat!

The level of experience of the user is also an important factor influencing the response to software. Novice users may, for example, welcome step by step menus, experienced computer users may find such an approach tedious and time consuming, as they already know precisely what they wish to do. Some software is flexible enough to allow different levels of users to choose their mode of operation, other packages do not have this flexibility.

Ideally, the applications software chosen/written should be specific for the type of tasks the user wishes to undertake. It should have a good screen format and presentation which enable the user to see at a glance what is going on. In some software packages the screen is cluttered, in others, especially where color is used, the information content is obscured through poorly designed screen displays. Software should be transparent in that it should allow the user to focus on the work itself rather than on manipulating the interface with the computer. Ideally, it should be natural to the user in the sense that the actions required to do a task are similar to those with which the user is familiar. It should have predictable responses and provide feedback to the user on his or her actions.

Software should be relatively easy to learn and use, though the two are not necessarily always compatible. Those very features which make a package easy to learn can become frustrating once the user has gained the skills necessary to manipulate it. Easy to learn does not obviate the need for proper training either. While self-teaching can be a useful method for some, it is not always efficient either in terms of the time taken, or, more importantly, the kind of understanding and methods of use of the package which the user ends up with. Error messages are another important feature of any software package. They should be intelligible, in a form that users can understand, and informative, ideally explaining why the error occurred and how the user can correct it.

Manuals can be a help or hinderance in the use of computer systems and software packages. They should be well written, avoiding jargon as much as possible, with comprehensive indexes and quick reference sections. The sheer bulk of many manuals is enough to put many users off! Finally, the response time and mode of the system is important. For many users it is not the length of time that it takes for the computer to do something that they find frustrating (and this if often dependent on the hardware), it is not knowing what is going on. Software which provides messages to the user, even is only to alert them to the fact that something is happening (e.g., PROCESSING PLEASE WAIT) is infinitely preferable to those that provide no messages at all.

As the use of computers spreads, so too does concern over the nature of computer-based work. A common distinction which is made is between those jobs where people work with computers—where the computer is just another tool to help in the task of performing a job function, and jobs where people work at computers—where the operation of the machine seems to be the end in itself and the user is paced and controlled by it. There can be an important difference in attitude between those who use a VDU out of choice and those who "have to." Acting as a terminal minder can be as boring as working on a production line. There is also considerable evidence accumulating to indicate that people who work at computers are more likely to suffer from physical complaints and mental stress in their job than those who work with them.

Whether a person works at or with the machine is largely a question of how a particular job has been designed and the extent to which the person feels in control of the work situation. In considering the design of jobs involving the use of computers, the following factors are useful to bear in mind.

First there should be a mix of work, some computer-based, some not, and preferably some which enables the person to get up and move around thus avoiding muscle and eye fatigue. The content, frequency, and sequence of the tasks done on a computer need to be considered. Doing many boring repetitive things is likely to be just as stressful and frustrating as doing one task over and over again. Jobs should contain some variety, a variety which enables the individual to use different skills and acquire new ones. The introduction of computers often provides opportunities for job enrichment, enlargement, and rotation, all of which should be considered. The level of concentration and physical effort involved in the job need to be taken into account, so a change of routine or rest breaks can be instituted if necessary during the day. Finally, jobs should provide some potential for self-development and job satisfaction, and these obviously will depend on the individual's own preferences and needs, which should also be considered.

MANAGING THE INTRODUCTION OF COMPUTERS: TRAINING

Computers can inspire fear; fear of job loss, deskilling, inability to cope, loss of status are commonly found among those using computers for the first time and among all levels of the organization hierarchy. How computers are introduced is as important as what is being introduced. The process of change, as well as the product, requires preparation and planning. Ergonomic considerations are just some of a myriad of factors to take into account.

In general, a participative approach to the introduction of computers will do much to alleviate fears and inspire confidence. Individuals need to be informed at an early stage about plans and how the change will affect them. There should be opportunities for people to discuss any proposals, to air their fears and grievances, and to make their suggestions known, especially in the area of job design. For many, new technology is synonymous with redundancy and there may be misconceptions about what the technology does, as well as what it is unable to do. Changes in job content and working practices can seem threatening, and time is needed to allow people to become accustomed to the new arrangements. Changing technology is as much about changing attitudes as it is about selecting computer hardware and software.

Education and training play vital roles in the successful implementation of computer systems. Education about why the change is necessary is as important as education about the capabilities and limitations of the system being used. Training in specific machines and software will help to ensure that computers are used effectively and user satisfaction obtained. Too often people are given a manual and told "get on with it" or sent on intensive two-day courses and expected on their return to be experts. This can be extremely stressful and can color attitudes toward new technology.

Ideally, training should be job related so that the benefits from using the computer can be made apparent in the context of the user's own work. Training should also be phased, with time between sessions to allow for the consolidation of the material learned before moving to progressively more difficult aspects of the machine and software use. Health and safety matters and good ergonomic practice relating to computer use should be incorporated into the training, not only so that users can avoid the "health hazards," but so that they learn how to maximize their interactions with the machines so as to increase their own comfort and efficiency.

CONCLUSIONS

Applying good ergonomic practice intelligently in respect of computers is a prerequisite for their effective use. Such practices may not always be cheap to apply, but neither are the costs of ignoring them. The justifiable concern about the "health hazards" of computer technology is unlikely to abate, and indeed may increase as their use widens. Applying ergonomic principles such as those outlined here makes economic and social sense. Technology can enable us to advance, but only if it is applied wisely. If computers are used to improve the quality of working life and make positive impact on the health of users, then indeed they can be seen as revolutionary in nature.

BIBLIOGRAPHY

Armbruster, A., "Ergonomic Reguirements," in *New Office Technologies: Human and Organizational Requirements*, M. Peltu and H. Otway (eds.), Francis Pinter, London, 1984.

Bird, J., *Ergonomics of VDU Installation*, NCC Publications, Manchester, 1985.

Craig, M., *The Office Worker's Survival Handbook*, BSSRS Publications, London, 1981.

Dainoff, M. J. and Dainoff, M. H., *A Manager's Guide to Ergonomics in the Electronic Office*, John Wiley, Chichester, 1987.

Department of Employment and Industrial Relations, Working Environment Branch, "VDU's at Work," Occupational Safety and Health: Working Environment Series Number 13, Australian Government Publishing Service, Canberra, 1983.

"Ergonomics: People and Systems in Dialogue," *Bus. Sys. Equip.*, May 1985.

Labour Research Department. *VDU's, Health and Jobs*, LRD Publications, London, 1985.

Lee, W. R., "Working with Visual Display Units," *Br. Med. J.*, *291*(6501) (1985).

MacKay, C., "Human Factors Aspects of Visual Display Unit Operation," *Health and Safety Research Paper, 10,* 1980.

NALGO, "The Health and Safety Aspects of VDU Work," Health and Safety Briefing, Nalgo, London, 1986.

Pearce, B., *The Contribution of Software Ergonomics and Job Design to the Avoidance of VDU Health Problems,* Humane Technology Ltd, Leicestershire, 1986.

Pearce, B. (ed.). *Health Hazards of VDT's,* John Wiley, Chichester, 1984.

Pearson, W., "Taking Precautions," *Pers. Comput. World,* March (1986).

"Visual Display Units," *Health and Safety Executive,* 1983.

"Working with VDU's," *Health and Safety Executive,* 1985.

NOREEN MAC MORROW

ERROR DETECTION AND CORRECTION

INTRODUCTION

Error detection is the detection, but not correction, of an error in transmission at the receiving end. Error correction is the detection and correction of an error in transmission at the receiving end. The theory of error detection and correction is the theory of the transmission of data in a noisy environment. Redundancy measures are used to detect and correct the occurrence of errors in the transmission of the data codes, the errors being caused by noise in the transmission medium (channel). The detection of errors is the recognition that an error occurred without the ability to correct the error at the receiving device. In this case, correction is obtained by requesting retransmission of the message. Error correction is the use of a code that is able to detect, then correct, the error or errors involved in transmission. No retransmission is involved; hence, the technique or techniques used are referred to as "forward error correction," techniques applied on the receiving rather than the sending end.

THE COMMUNICATION MODEL

The communication model is the model of a sender of a message, a receiver of the message, and a channel between (connecting) the two (Fig. 1).

The encoding mechanism is not always explicitly represented in the model, but it is implicitly present. The message, being initiated with the sender, is encoded for transmission across the medium to the receiver (Fig. 2).

The message sent, m(S), is encoded, E, for transmission across the medium, C, then decoded, D, at the receiving end, for consumption/comprehension, m(R), by the receiver. Encoding is a transformation, t(m(S)) = c, that is reversible, t'(c') = m(R), where c = the encoded message, m(t) in the diagram, as sent by the transmitter, and c' = the encoded message as received by the decoder, and c = c' in a noiseless environment (Fig. 3).

The transmitted message, "hello," is encoded into the ASCII code, which is a shorthand for the binary signals sent (68 = 0110 1000, 68 is hexadecimal), then transmitted and received, m(r), then decoded, ASCII to character representation (68-->h). The code of Figure 3 would be implemented by a table look up of letters/ASCII and ASCII/letter pairs, imple-

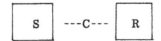

FIGURE 1

343

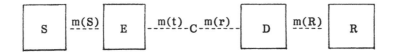

FIGURE 2

mented in software (a data dictionary) or hardware (a decoder or hard-wired data dictionary). Alternative codes can be developed using computational schemes (Fig. 4).

The initial code, h = 68, a table lookup, is transformed by the computation, code = original + 1, into the transmitted message, i f m m p, or 69 66 6D 6D 70 (Fig. 4a), then the computation is reversed (Fig. 4b), original = code − 1, to obtain the original message, 68 65 6C 6C 6F, or "hello," from the received message, 69 66 6D 6D 70. The latter codes are often used in encrypting data [1]. They can be studied for their own sake. The focus here, however, will be on the transmission of the messages (encrypted or nonencrypted) and the use of coding schemes to detect and correct errors (noise) in the data transmission. A binary transmission mechanism will be assumed.

ERROR DETECTION

An example of error detection is the simple parity bit (Fig. 5).

A parity (redundant) bit is affixed to each code value (0110 1000 --> 0110 1000-1). The parity is selected so as to make the total number of bits

m(S)	m(t)	m(r)	m(R)
hello	68 65 6C 6C 6F	68 65 6C 6C 6F	hello

hello

h -->68
e -->65
l -->6C
l -->6C
o -->6F

transmission: 68 65 6C 6C 6F

reception: 68 65 6C 6C 6F

decode

68 --->h
65 --->e
6C --->l
6C --->l
6F --->o

FIGURE 3

```
h  =  68
e  =  65
l  =  6C
l  =  6C
o  =  6F

code = original + 1:  69 66 6D 6D 70
                       i  f  m  m  p
```

(a)

```
original = code − 1

    69 66 6D 6D 70
     i  f  m  m  p
    68 65 6C 6C 6F
     h  e  l  l  o
```

(b)

FIGURE 4

(not the code value) even or odd. In the example shown, the parity is even: all transmitted codes have an even number of 1 bits (bits "on").

If a single error occurs in transmission it will be detected (Fig. 6).

The number of 1 bits received is not even. Hence, the transmission is in error.

While, in this case, the error may be correctable in terms of English, it is not correctable in terms of the transmitted message (Fig. 7).

The codes are a distance of one part; that is, they differ from one another, at least in some cases, by a single bit. Hence, the reversal (0-->1, 1-->0) of a single bit in a valid code results in another valid code. This can be seen by considering the codes for b and c:

```
b  62  0110  0010
c  63  0110  0011
```

The reversal of the rightmost bit of the b results in the code for c, and vice versa. The code "in error" is indistiguishable from a valid transmitted (sent) code.

hello

```
68              65              6C              6C              6F
0110 1000       0110 0101       0110 1100       0110 1100       0110 1111
0110 1000-1     0110 0101-0     0110 1100-0     0110 1100-0     0110 1111-0
```

FIGURE 5

sent:

hello	68	65	6C	6C	6F
	0110 1000	0110 0101	0110 1100	0110 1100	0110 1111
	0110 1000-1	0110 0101-0	0110 1100-0	0110 1100-0	0110 1111-0

received:

iello	69	65	6C	6C	6F
	x				
	0110 1001	0110 0101	0110 1100	0110 1100	0110 1111
	0110 1001-1	0110 0101-0	0110 1100-0	0110 1100-0	0110 1111-0

FIGURE 6

THE HAMMING DISTANCE

Successful encoding of a set of messages requires a distance of one among all code values. This is shown in Figure 8 for a set of 8 code and message values.

The set of code values differ from one another in at least one bit across all code values $[(x,y)(x,y \; C)(x<>y)(d(<x,y>) \geqslant 1))$ or (x,y) $(x,y \; C) \; (x<>y \; --> d(<x,y>) \geqslant 1)]$.

The Hamming distance is the number of bit positions in which two code values differ. It is one for a and b, b and c, and a and c. It is two for a and d:

```
000
011
```

A distance of one is required for unique encodability and reversability (a 1—1 correspondence between message values and code values). A distance of two is required for single error detection and a distance of three for single error correction [2, 3].

A distance of two among all code values is necessary for error detection. This is illustrated in Figure 9 for a set of four messages and code values.

The code values in Figure 9 differ from one another in at least two bit positions, taking all pairs of codes (Fig. 10).

a	61	0110 0001
b	62	0110 0010
c	63	0110 0011
d	64	0110 0100
e	65	0110 0101
		.
		.
		.

FIGURE 7

```
a   000 (0)
b   001 (1)
c   010 (2)
d   011 (3)
e   100 (4)
f   101 (5)
g   110 (6)
h   111 (7)
```

FIGURE 8

The number of messages that can be sent is now reduced (halved). The distance of two requires that not all valid code values (000–111) be used.

The parity bit insures the distance of two. All code values of Figure 9 (00 = a, 01 = b, 10 = c, 11 = d) have an even parity bit attached. An alternative set of code values would be 001 = a (1), 010 = b (2), 100 = c (4) and 111 = d (7) (Fig. 11).

The code values of Figure 11 have odd parity. The use of the four basic code (message) values:

```
00 = a
01 = b
10 = c
11 = d
```

with even parity:

```
000 = a
011 = b
101 = c
110 = d
```

or odd:

```
001 = a
010 = b
100 = c
111 = d
```

insures a distance of two among all codes. The original (message) code values (00, 01, 10, and 11) differ in one position. The addition (concatenation) of the parity increases the distance by one.

```
a   000 (0)
b   011 (3)
c   101 (5)
d   110 (6)
```

FIGURE 9

```
a   b   000   011   d=2
    c   000   101   d=2
    d   000   110   d=2
b   c   011   101   d=2
    d   011   110   d=2
c   d   101   110   d=2
```

FIGURE 10

The use of a distance of two insures single error detection. A distance of three insures single error correction. This is illustrated in Figure 12 for a set of two messages, each code value differing from the other in three bit positions with four possible coding schemes (codes or mappings).

There are now only two ($2^{**}3/2^{**}2$ or $2^{**}n/2^{**}p$, where n = the number of bit poisitions, p = the number of parity bits) message values:

```
0 = a
1 = b
```

The two additional bit positions are both parity bit positions. They insure single-error correction as well as detection (Fig. 13). The message received, 010, is closer to the message sent (000) than to the alternative valid code (111). This allows for the single error correction (i.e., error correction assuming that a single bit has changed).

A distance of two does not allow for error correction, although it does allow for single error detection. This is illustrated in Figure 14 for the code (mapping) of Figure 9.

The sending of the message a:

```
000
```

may be received as:

```
010
```

This is an invalid code.

The code received can be recognized as incorrect. The code value 010 is an invalid value. It cannot, however, be corrected. The value 010 is equidistant from 000 (a), 011 (b) and 110 (d). It could have been generated by a single error in the transmission of any one of these valid code values (000, 011, 110).

```
a   001 (1)
b   010 (2)
c   100 (4)
d   111 (7)
```

FIGURE 11

000 (0)
111 (7)

001 (1)
110 (6)

010 (2)
101 (5)

011 (3)
100 (4)

FIGURE 12

A distance of one is required to create a unique code (Fig. 15).

The code is ambiguous. While both the a and the b can be uniquely encoded, they cannot be uniquely decoded [4].

A distance of two insures single error (parity) detection. A distance of three insures single error detection and correction, referred to simply as a single error (forward error) correction.

ERROR CORRECTION

Error correction is the detection and correction of one or more errors on the receiving end. Retransmission is not required.

This is illustrated in Figure 13. The code of Figure 13 (a = 000 (0), b = 111 (7) or a = 010 (2), b = 101 (5) (Fig. 12), . . .) is an example of a majority code. It is also an example of a Hamming code.

THE HAMMING SYNDROME

The most efficient code from the point of view of the number of parity bits sent per information bits sent is the Hamming code [2], which uses a syndrome (bit pattern) to identify a single bit in error. This is illustrated in Figure 16 for a three message (bit) code with three parity bit positions.

The message bits are bit positions 6, 5, and 3. The parity bit positions are 1, 2, and 4.

The parity bit positions follow the powers of two (1, 2, 4; 1, 2, 4, 8; . . .) for as many parity bit positions as are necessary. The number of message bit positions is derived from the number of possible message values to be sent (Fig. 17).

sent:

000

received:

x
010

FIGURE 13

```
a 000 (0)
b 011 (3)
c 101 (5)
d 110 (6)

sent:        000
              x
received:    010
```

FIGURE 14

The number of message values (possible) determines the number of message bit positions in a fixed-length binary code [2, 5]. For four messages this is 2**n, with n = 2. For eight messages this is 2**n, with n = 3, where n = the number of message bit positions. The number of messages (unique message values) is referred to as the alphabet size [6, 7].

The number of parity bits required is derived from the number of message bits. This is the calculation:

$$2**p \geqslant p + n + 1$$

for the Hamming code. The variable p is the number of parity bit positions; the variable n is the number of information (message) bit positions. The constant one is derived from the message "no bit in error" or correct transmission. This is shown in Figure 18.

The syndrome gives the number of the bit in error (bit 1 in error, bit 2 in error, . . . , bit n + p in error, where n + p = the total number of bits sent, 6 in the example) and the message "no bit in error" (correct transmission). This is a total of n + p (information plus parity bits) plus one.

The calculation:

$$2**p \geqslant n + p + 1$$

is solved by trial and error, i.e., by successively substituting values for p in the relationship for a given n (Fig. 19).

The number of parity bits must "cover," i.e., be greater than or equal to, the number of error messages necessary. This is the number of bits sent (n + p) plus one.

The number of message bits, n, is derived from the number of possible messages:

n = ln (base 2) of a

```
a = 000
b = 000
```

FIGURE 15

parity bit positions

$\overline{6}$ $\overline{5}$ $\overline{4}$ $\overline{3}$ $\overline{2}$ $\overline{1}$

```
4:  4, 5, 6
2:  2, 3, 6
1:  1, 3, 5
```

FIGURE 16

where a = the alphabet size or

$a \leqslant 2**n$

where n = the number of information bits for a given alphabet size, a. The number of parity bits is derived from the same calculation with a = n + p + 1:

$n + p + 1 \leqslant 2**p$

or:

$2**p \geqslant n + p + 1$

The variable p appears on both sides of the relationship because it determines both the number of bits sent (n + p) and the number of messages (error messages) that can be carried by the parity bits:

$2**p$

The number of messages (2**p) carried by the parity bits must "cover" (>) the number of bits sent (n + p) plus the correct transmission ("all ok") message.

The message bits carry the information conveyed [m(S), m(R)]. The parity bits carry the information about the bits (in error or not). This is shown in Figure 20 for a three bit message code (n) with three parity bits. The three parity bits are derived from the calculation:

$2**p \geqslant n + p + 1$

$2**3 \geqslant 3 + 3 + 1 = 7$

```
000 = Happy Birthday
001 = Happy Anniversary
010 =        •
011 =        •
100 =        •
101 =        •
110 =        •
111 =        •
```

FIGURE 17

```
                        syndrome value
                        |
nothing wrong:          0
1 bit in error:         1:  bit 1 in error
                        2:  bit 2 in error
                        3:  bit 3 in error
                        .
                        .
                        .
                        n + p:  bit n + p in error
```

FIGURE 18

$$2**1 \geqslant 2$$
$$2**2 \geqslant 4$$
$$2**3 \geqslant 8$$
$$\cdot \qquad \cdot$$
$$\cdot \qquad \cdot$$
$$\cdot \qquad \cdot$$
$$2**p \geqslant n + p + 1$$

FIGURE 19

```
6 5 4 3 2 1

0 0   1
— — — — —
i i p i p p
```

Happy Anniversary = 001

FIGURE 20

```
0 0   1
— — — — —
6 5 4 3 2 1

4:  4, 5, 6
2:  2, 3, 6
1:  1, 3, 5

(a)

6 o 5 o 4 = 0 o 0 o 0 = 0 (4)
6 o 3 o 2 = 0 o 1 o 1 = 0 (2)
5 o 3 o 1 = 0 o 1 o 1 = 0 (1)

(b)
```

FIGURE 21

where three parity bits can carry up to four (n = 4) message bits (2**3 ⩾ 4 + 3 + 1).

The message is Happy Anniversary (Fig. 17). The message is selected from the set of available messages. The information bits are 6, 5, and 3. The message is 001.

The information bits are placed in the appropriate bit positions (Fig. 20), and the parities are calculated from these (Fig. 21).

The information bits are placed in the appropriate positions and the parity bits are calculated from these (Fig. 21a). The calculation is made from the bit positions shown in the syndrome (Fig. 21a). The calculation is the exclusive OR (o = the exclusive OR).

The parity shown is even. Bits 4, 5, and 6 are used in calculating the parity value for parity bit 4. Bits 2, 3, and 6 are used in calculating the value for parity bit 2 and bits 1, 3, and 5 are used in calculating the parity value for bit position 1 (Fig. 22).

The calculations of the parities (even parity) is made according to the scheme shown in Figure 23.

The bit names of all bits (4,5,6; 2,3,6; 1,3,5, Fig. 23a) are placed on the lines representing the binary bit position values (1 to m, where m = the total number of bit positions, $1 \leqslant m \leqslant n + p$) used in calculating their values (e.g., 6 = 4 + 2, Fig. 23b, hence appears on "rows" 4 and 2, Fig. 23a; 5 = 4 + 1, hence appears on rows 4 and 1). The scheme will, when used to "set" the parity bits at the sending end and "test" (or check) them at the receiving end indicate whether or not an error (single error) has occurred in transmission (calculation of the parity "syndrome" value = 0 = no error, non-zero = error), and, if an error has occurred (single error), will identify the bit in error by "name" (1 through 6). This is indicated in Figure 24.

The message sent (encoded message) is 000111. The message received is 100111. It is unknown whether or not the message received is correct (that transmitted) or not.

The parities are calculated on the receiving end (Fig. 24c), and two bits are found to be in error (Fig. 24c and d). The diagnosis is that "bit 6 is in error" (Fig. 24d and e). The bit is "corrected" (1 to 0, 0 to 1, whichever is the case) (Fig. 24e and f), and the correct message extracted (Fig. 24f).

The Hamming syndrome (pattern) identifies the bit in error by name. It does so through the calculation (binary) of the value of the bit. Each bit position, 1 to n + p, is involved in the calculation of the parity values used to calculate that number in the binary number/numeral system. This is 4 + 2 for bit 6. If a bit is in error, single error assumed, it will trigger all parities calculated with that bit position (4, 2 for bit position 6). These

```
6 5 4 3 2 1

0 0 0 1 1 1
- - - - - -
i i p i p p
```

Happy Anniversary = 001

FIGURE 22

```
4:   4, 5, 6
2:   2, 3, 6
1:   1, 3, 5
```

(a)

```
6 = 4 + 2
5 = 4 + 1
4 = 4
3 = 2 + 1
2 = 2
1 = 1
```

(b)

FIGURE 23

Message sent: 000111 (Happy Anniversary)
Message received: 100111 (?)

(a)

```
4:   6, 5, 4
2:   6, 3, 2
1:   5, 3, 1
```

Hamming syndrome

(b)

```
6 o 5 o 4 = 1 o 0 o 0 = 1 (4)
6 o 3 o 2 = 1 o 1 o 1 = 1 (2)
5 o 3 o 1 = 0 o 1 o 1 = 0 (1)
```

(c)

Bit in error = 4 + 2

```
            1 1 0
            − − −
            4 2 1
```

(d)

Message received: 100111
Diagnosis: bit 6 in error
Corrected message: 000111

(e)

Extracted message: 0 0 1
                     − − −
                     6 5 3   --> Happy Anniversary

(f)

FIGURE 24

"error bits" (parities) can be read as 1's in the binary number system (Fig. 24d). The error is corrected on the receiving end (Fig. 24e). Retransmission is not necessary. Hence, the technique is referred to as "forward error correction." The use of the binary number scheme insures that the identification of the bit (in error) is sufficient to correct the error (0 to 1, 1 to 0).

The Hamming syndrome (pattern) relies on the binary number system for its values. Each parity bit $(1, 2, 4, \ldots, 2^{**}p$, where p = the total number of parities derived from the calculation $2^{**}p \geqslant n + p + 1$, and $n + p$ = the total number of bits sent) is "set" and "tested" by the values of the binary digits (bit position names, 1 through $n + p$) involving that parity value in the binary representation of the bit position name. This isures that the single error will trigger the positions necessary to identify the (single) bit in error.

The Hamming syndrome can correct a single error that occurs in transmission (on the receiving end). A correct transmission will result in no bit in error or a Hamming "syndrome" of zero (bits in error). This is illustrated in Figure 25.

Message sent: 000111 (Happy Anniversary)
Message received: 000111 (?)

(a)

4:   6, 5, 4
2:   6, 3, 2
1:   5, 3, 1

Hamming syndrome

(b)

6 o 5 o 4 = 0 o 0 o 0 = 0 (4)
6 o 3 o 2 = 0 o 1 o 1 = 0 (2)
5 o 3 o 1 = 0 o 1 o 1 = 0 (1)

(c)

Bit in error: 0 0 0 = "none" (transmission correct)
                — — —
                4 2 1

(d)

Message received: 000111
Diagnosis: correct transmission
Corrected message: 000111

(e)

Message extracted: 0 0 1
                     — — —
                     6 5 3   --> Happy Anniversary

(f)

FIGURE 25

```
Message sent:   000111 (Happy Anniversary)
Message received:   000100 (?)
```

(a)

```
4:  6, 5, 4
2:  6, 3, 2
1:  5, 3, 1
```

Hamming syndrome

(b)

```
6 o 5 o 4 = 0 o 0 o 0 = 0 (4)
6 o 3 o 2 = 0 o 1 o 0 = 1 (2)
5 o 3 o 1 = 0 o 1 o 0 = 1 (1)
```

(c)

```
Bit in error = 2 + 1

               0 1 1
               - - -
               4 2 1
```

(d)

```
Message received:  000100
Diagnosis:  bit 3 in error
Corrected message:  000000
```

(e)

```
Extracted message:  0 0 0
                    - - -
                    6 5 3  --> Happy Birthday
```

(f)

FIGURE 26

    The message received is the message sent. No bit is in error (Fig. 25c and d). The message extracted is the transmitted message (Fig. 25e and f).

    The Hamming syndrome assumes a single error in transmission. A double error will result in an incorrect diagnosis (Fig. 26).

    The message sent is the message 001, or 000111, with the parities set. The message received is 000100, with two bits in error (0001XX). The Hamming syndrome gives the diagnosis of bit 3 in error (Fig. 26d and e).

    The Hamming syndrome triggers an incorrect diagnosis if more than a single error occurs, e.g., bits 6 and 5 in error will trigger the diagnosis "bit three in error." Parity bit 4 will be "ok," with offsetting (an even number of) errors; bits 2 and 1 will be triggered by the 6 and 5, respectively. For this reason a parity bit (to detect the double error) is often affixed to the "syndrome" message [2] (Fig. 27).

Message sent: 000111-1 (Happy Anniversary)

(a)

```
4:  6, 5, 4
2:  6, 3, 2
1:  5, 3, 1
```

Hamming syndrome

(b)

```
6 o 5 o 4 = 0 o 0 o 0 = 0 (4)
6 o 3 o 2 = 0 o 1 o 1 = 0 (2)
5 o 3 o 1 = 0 o 1 o 1 = 0 (1)
```

Syndrome parity bits

(c)

Overall parity bit: 000111-1

(d)

FIGURE 27

An overall parity is affixed to the syndrome and message (000111, syndrome and message, 000111-1, overall parity). The overall parity is even. The message sent is 001 and the parities are as before

```
00-0-1-11
ii p i pp
```

The overall parity bit will, however, detect a double error. The analysis is shown in Figure 28.

If a single error occurs in transmission, the syndrome will be non-zero, as before, and the single parity bit will be odd. This is the second case in Figure 28. The correction is made as before.

If a double error occurs, the syndrome will be non-zero and the parity (even) will be "correct," case three in Figure 28. This can be recognized by the "correct" (even) overall parity as a double error and an incorrect syndrome. The message must be retransmitted (Fig. 29).

The message (transmission) is received incorrectly (0001XX-1) as before (Fig. 26). However, in this case, the incorrect diagnosis is avoided

syndrome	overall parity	diagnosis
ok	ok	no error (correct transmission)
non-zero	odd	single error
non-zero	even	double error
zero	odd	error in the overall parity, no correction necessary, syndrome ok

FIGURE 28

Message sent: 000111-1 (Happy Anniversary)
Message received: 000100-1 (?)

(a)

4:   6, 5, 4
2:   6, 3, 2
1:   5, 3, 1

Hamming syndrome

(b)

6 o 5 o 4 = 0 o 0 o 0 = 0 (4)
6 o 3 o 2 = 0 o 1 o 0 = 1 (2)
5 o 3 o 1 = 0 o 1 o 0 = 1 (1)

(c)

Bit in error = 2 + 1

            0 1 1
            – – –
            4 2 1

(d)

Overall parity: 000100-1 (correct)

(e)

Message received: 000100-1
Diagnosis: double error, syndrome incorrect
Corrected message: none

(f)

Extracted message: none
                     – – –
                     6 5 3

(g)

FIGURE 29

by the use of the second (overall) parity bit (Fig. 29e and f). The diagnosis, syndrome in error, parity "ok" is recognized as a double (or quadruple) error (Figs. 28 and 29f). Retransmission is requested.

A correct transmission will be recognized by a zero syndrome and a correct parity (Fig. 28, case one). The last case, overall parity in error and syndrome ok is the case of a correct transmission of the message bits and the syndrome with the overall parity bit in error (Fig. 30).

The message sent is 000111-1. The message received is 000111-0. The information (message) and the syndrome are correct. This is indicated by the zero syndrome. The parity bit (overall parity) is in error. It need not be retransmitted. The message is extracted and received (m(R)).

Message sent: 000111-1 (Happy Anniversary)
Message received: 000111-0 (?)
                          X

(a)

4: 6, 5, 4
2: 6, 3, 2
1: 5, 3, 1

Hamming syndrome

(b)

6 o 5 o 4 = 0 o 0 o 0 = 0 (4)
6 o 3 o 2 = 0 o 1 o 1 = 0 (2)
5 o 3 o 1 = 0 o 1 o 1 = 0 (1)

(c)

Bit in error: 0 0 0 = "none" (transmission of syndrome correct)
               — — —
               4 2 1

(d)

Overall parity: 000111-0 (odd)

(d)

Message received: 000111-0
Diagnosis: correct transmission of message
Corrected message: 000111-1

(e)

Message extracted: 0 0 1
                    — — —
                    6 5 3 --> Happy Anniversary

(f)

FIGURE 30

The efficiency of the Hamming scheme can be recognized by comparing it with other schemes of single error correction. These are the majority code, the rectangular code, and the triangular code in the common schemes [2, 3, 5].

The majority code is the repetition of the message three times (Fig. 31).

The message may be repeated three times (Fig. 31b), or the bit configuration (in this case the single bit, 0) repeated three times (Fig. 31a). If an error occurs, 0X0, X00, or 00X, the correct message can be recognized by the "majority" of the bits (or messages) received. This assumes a single error in transmission.

000

(a)

Hello Hello Hello

(b)

FIGURE 31

A doubling of the message results in error detection, but not correction (Fig. 32).

The occurrence of a single error, in this case 00-->01 or 00-->10, is detectable by the distinction in the bits (or messages) received. It is, however, not correctable. The correct bit cannot be isolated, despite the assumption of the single error in transmission. This is due to the distance of one between the received code (01 or 10 in the case of a single error in the double transmission) and the two valid codes (00 and 11 in duplicate transmission). Retransmission is required.

The majority code is two thirds redundant (two parity bits or messages sent for each information bit or message sent) in the case of the correction scheme. It is fifty percent redundant [1p/(1p + 1n)] for the error detection, but not correction, scheme. Other codes have been developed to accomplish the same objective, single error correction, with fewer parity bits per information bit sent. Two of these are the rectangular or square code and the triangular code (or coding scheme).

THE RECTANGULAR CODE

The rectangular code uses a scheme such as that shown in Figure 33.

There are 16 information bits, arranged in a rectangular array. These bits are augmented by a parity bit, one for each row and one for each column and the corner bit. These are filled in according to even or odd parity, with even being the more common [2]. This is shown in Figure 34.

A single error in the transmission of the message can be detected and corrected by the intersection of the row and column parity bits affected (Fig. 35).

Sent:

00

(a)

Received:

01

(b)

FIGURE 32

```
0 1 0 1 _
1 1 0 1 _
0 0 1 0 _
0 1 0 1 _
_ _ _ _ _
```

FIGURE 33

The single error has occurred in row three, column three (one based counting, top down, left to right). The error has affected both the x (column) and y (row) parities set with this bit.

Each bit (information or message bit) is involved in the calculation of two parity values, the row and the column parities involving that bit. If a single bit is in error it will "trigger" both parities. These give the "x" and "y" coordinates (indices) of the bit in error. It is at the intersection of the two affected parity positions, looked at as the coordinates of or indices into (pointers) the rectangular array.

The single error can be corrected by simply reversing the value of the bit in error. This recovers the original portion of the message.

If an error occurs in a parity bit, it will affect only that column and row or row and column (unless it is the corner bit) (Fig. 36).

The occurrence of the error in the row parity (y) (Fig. 36a), has affected only the parity column. The occurrence of an error in the column parity (x) (Fig. 36b), affects only the parity row. Neither situation need be corrected.

An error occurring in the corner bit will affect both the parity column and parity row, but the information parities are correct, hence the message may be extracted (Fig. 37).

The message is placed conceptually in the form of a rectangle or a square. It is, however, simply a linear array of bits:

0101 1101 0010 0101

It may be transmitted in any fashion (serially). Only the location of the parity bits and the information bits need be known in order to perform the requisite calculations.

The rectangular code uses n + m + 1 parity bits for an n × m array of information bits, in this case (Fig. 33) nine. The minimum number of bits (perimeter) is achieved in a square array (n + n + 1 parity bits for an array of n × n information bits) if the number of information bits lends itself to this configuration (n × n).

```
0 1 0 1 0
1 1 0 1 1
0 0 1 0 1
0 1 0 1 0
1 1 1 1 0
```

FIGURE 34

```
0 1 0 1 0
1 1 0 1 1
0 0 0 0 1 y
0 1 0 1 0
1 1 1 1 0
        x
```

FIGURE 35

THE TRIANGULAR CODE

The triangular code is a variation of the rectangular code in which the information bits are arranged in a triangle with the first row having one information bit (n) and each succeeding row having an additional bit. The triangle may be organized as shown in Figure 38 or in the opposite direction (1 bit on top, with each succeeding row growing downward).

Parity bits are placed alongside each row and under the leftmost column (Fig. 39).

The parity bits are calculated in a manner different from that of the rectangular or square configuration (Figs. 40 and 41).

The parity bit values for the topmost row and the leftmost column are calculated from that row and column only (Fig. 40a). This is 1 and 1 for the example shown (10101-1, top row, 11001-1, leftmost column) (Fig. 40b).

Parity values for the remaining positions are calculated from both a row and a column component (Fig. 41).

The parity for row two, column five is computed from the bits in this column (five) and row (two). This is 1100 (row) and 1 (column) for row two, column five, or 1 for that parity position (Fig. 41).

The remaining parities are calculated in the same fashion (011, row three, 00, column four, for the intersection of row three and column four, or 0 for the parity value: 01, row four, 101, column three, or 1 for the intersection of those two vectors (parity bit 4, 3); finally, row 5, column 2, has a parity of 0). Figure 42 shows a filled-in version.

```
0 1 0 1 0
1 1 0 1 0 y
0 0 1 0 1
0 1 0 1 0
1 1 1 1 0
```

(a)

```
0 1 0 1 0
1 1 0 1 1
0 0 1 0 1
0 1 0 1 0
1 1 0 1 0
        x
```

(b)

FIGURE 36

```
0 1 0 1 0
1 1 0 1 1
0 0 1 0 1
0 1 0 1 0
1 1 1 1 1
```

FIGURE 37

```
10101
1100
011
01
1
```

FIGURE 38

```
10101_
1100_
011_
01_
1_
_
```

FIGURE 39

```
10101_   <--
1100_
011_
01_
1_
_
^
|
(a)

101011   <--
1100_
011_
01_
1_
1
^
|
(b)
```

FIGURE 40

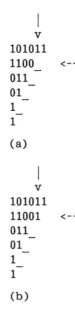

```
        |
        v
  101011
  1100_      <--
  011_
  01_
  1_
  1
```

(a)

```
        |
        v
  101011
  11001     <--
  011_
  01_
  1_
  1
```

(b)

FIGURE 41

An error (single error) occurring in transmission is diagnosed as shown in Figures 43 and 44.

An error has occurred in row two, column four, which will affect both parities calculated with these columns or rows. This is shown in Figure 44.

The parity for column five, row two (horizontal arrow) is incorrect. So, too, is the parity for column four, row three (vertical arrow). The intersection of these two parities (arrows), row two, column four is the incorrect bit (horizontal arrow gives the row, vertical arrow gives the column). It can simply be reversed.

PERFORMANCE ANALYSIS

The performance of the four coding schemes (single error correction schemes) is in the order:

```
  101011
  11001
  0110
  011
  10
  1
```

FIGURE 42

```
101011
11011
0110
011
10
1
```

FIGURE 43

Majority
Rectangular
Triangular
Hamming

with the more redundant (least efficient) codes listed first. (Fig. 45).

The majority code is (constantly) two thirds redundant. The rectangular code is less redundant as the blocks get longer (message "block" or message code lengths increase), as are the triangular and the Hamming codes. The brackets in the Hamming code calculation represent the "ceiling," the next larger integer ($\geqslant$) than the log to the base 2 of $(n + p + 1)$.

DERIVATION OF THE RATIOS

The derivation of the majority code ratio is derived from the nature (repetition) of the code. There are two parity bits (p) for each information bit (n) sent. The ratio gives the ratio of the parities (p) to the total number of bits sent $(n + p)$, the redundancy ratio (p over $p + n$). This is $2n/3n$ or $2/3$, constant, for the majority code.

The ratio for the rectangular code is derived from the nature of the configuration. There are n row parity bits and m column parity bits for an $n \times m$ information bit configuration (array), plus the corner bit. This is:

$$\frac{n + m + 1}{nm + (n + m + 1)}$$

for the rectangular array and reduces to:

$$\frac{n + n + 1}{nn + (n + n + 1)}$$

```
101011
11011  <--
0110
011^
10  |
1
```

FIGURE 44

Majority code: $2n/3n = 2/3$

Rectangular code: $\dfrac{n + m + 1}{nm + (n + m + 1)} = \dfrac{n + n + 1}{n^{**}2 + 2n + 1}$ for a square code

Triangular code: $\dfrac{n + 1}{n(n + 1)/2 + (n + 1)} = \dfrac{2(n + 1)}{(n + 1)(n + 2)} = \dfrac{2}{(n + 2)}$

Hamming code: $\dfrac{[\ln\ (\text{base } 2)\ (n + p + 1)]}{n + p}$

FIGURE 45

or:

$$\dfrac{2n + 1}{(n + 1)(n + 1)}$$

for a square array. This is approximately $2/(n + 1)$.

The triangular computation is also derived from the nature of the physical configuration. There are n rows of information bits. This is $n(n + 1)/2$, the sum of the integers from 1 to n [8], information bits. There are $n + 1$ parities [one for each row, one for the leftmost column (one extra row)] for these n rows. This is:

$$\dfrac{(n + 1)}{n(n + 1)/2 + (n + 1)} \quad \begin{array}{l} \text{parities} \\ \text{information + parities} \end{array}$$

for the redundancy ratio [p over $(m + p)$ with $p = (n + 1)$ ($n =$ the number of rows) and $m = (n(n + 1)/2$ for the sum of the integers from 1 to n]. This reduces to:

$$\dfrac{(n + 1)}{(n(n + 1) + 2(n + 1))/2}$$

or:

$$\dfrac{2*(n + 1)}{(n + 1)(n + 2)}$$

or $2/(n + 2)$. The redundancy proportion obviously decreases as n increases, being a function of n alone.

The redundancy ratio depends only on the number of rows for the triangular array. This is illustrated in Figure 46.

The redundancy ratio (proportion) decreases as the block size [i, $n(n + 1)/2$, or n, the number of rows)] increases. The limiting case (zero) is unacheivable. This is shown in Figure 47.

The redundancy ratio approaches zero asymptotically as n, the number of rows, increases.

There is a trade off in the transmission of information. The redundancy ratio (proportion of parity bits sent to total bits, information and parity, sent) decreases as the block size (i, information bits, or n, the

n	n(n + 1)/2 (i)	n + 1 (p)	p/(i + p)	
1	1	2	2/3	(.67)
2	3	3	3/6 = 1/2	(.50)
3	6	4	4/10 = 2/5	(.40)
4	10	5	5/15 = 1/3	(.33)
5	15	6	6/21 = 2/7	(.29)
6	21	7	7/28 = 1/4	(.25)
.	.	.	.	.
.	.	.	.	.
.	.	.	.	.
10	55	11	11/66 = 1/6	(.17)
.	.	.	.	.
.	.	.	.	.
.	.	.	.	.
100	5050	101	101/5050 = 1/50	(.02)

FIGURE 46

number of rows in the triangular and rectangular schemes) increases. The likelihood of error also increases (Fig. 48).

The analysis of Figure 48 is made with the binomial distribution [independent errors, error (p) or no error (q)] [9–11]. It may or may not be applicable to a given data transmission (nonindependent or dependent, i.e., burst, errors). It will, however, give a conservative estimate of the likelihood of one or more errors since the likelihood of more than one error increases for dependent errors [2,12,13].

The likelihood of error (p, 1/10) is chosen as a representative example. This value is usually lower in real cases [13,14]. It is, however, illustrative of the effect of block size on the likelihood of one or more errors.

The probability of a single error (p) is the probability of one error occurring. The probability of the transmission of the single bit being correctly is q (1 − p). The probability of two or more errors occurring is approximately np, where n = the block size (number of bits sent, i.e.,

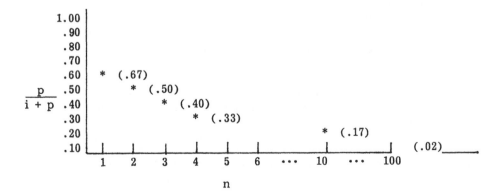

FIGURE 47

p	n	np	q**n
1/10	1	1/10	(.9)
	2	2/10	(.9)**2
	3	3/10	(.9)**3
	4	4/10	(.9)**4
	.	.	.
	.	.	.
	.	.	.
	10 <	10/10	(.9)**10

FIGURE 48

total number of bits sent, parity plus message) (the symbol < in the last line, np < 10/10, indicates "approximately" np). The probability of a correct transmission, q**n, is exact. This is .66 for n = 4 and p = 1/10. It is .43 for n = 8 and .35 or 3 chances in 10 for n = 10 at that (inflated) error rate. This indicates that the likelihood of error (one or more) increases as the block size (n) increases (np, approximately, or 1 − q**n, for independent errors).

The performance of the triangular and the rectangular codes are similar, 2/(n + 2) for the triangular, approximately 2/(n + 1) for the rectangular. The calculation for the Hamming code is made for:

$$\frac{[\ln \text{ (base 2) } (n + p + 1)]}{n + p}$$

where [ln (base 2) (n + p + 1)] is the number of parity bits sent and n + p is the total number of bits sent (n + [ln (base 2) (n + p + 1)]) (Fig. 49).

The Hamming calculation is from the number of parity bits (lg, base 2, of n + p + 1, where the notation lg is introduced as the log to the base 2) to information (n) plus parity (p) bits sent (p/n + p). This is calculated as shown in Figure 49 and decreases as n increases.

The Hamming code is the most efficient of the four codes. It increases in efficiency (decreasing proportion of redundancy) as n increases. Some representative values are given in Figure 49. These indicate that the redundancy approaches 1 percent as the block size (n, information bits) approaches 1024 (2**10 ⩾ n + p + 1 = 1024, the last line of the table).

For purposes of comparison, a 9 bit "block" code of information (bits) could be sent with a 3 × 3 rectangular array and (3 + 3 + 1)/(3 × 3 + 2 × 3 + 1) or 7/16 redundancy ratio. A block of 10 information bits could be sent in a 4 (n) row triangular array with 2/(2 + n) or 2/6 redundancy. The triangular array gives slightly better performance than the rectangular, though not significantly for large n (2/(n + 2), 2/(n + 1), approximately for the rectangular).

The performance increases (redundancy ratio decreases) for all but the majority code as the "block" size (number of information bits) increases. There is, however, a trade off, since the likelihood of error increases with the block size. It also increases with the occurrence of errors for dependent ("burst") errors.

n	p	n + p + 1	2**p	n + p	p/(n + p)
1	2	4	4	3	2/3
2	3	6	8	5	3/5
3		7		6	3/6
4		8		7	3/7
5	4	10	16	9	4/9
•				•	•
•				•	•
•				•	•
11		16		15	4/15
248	9	258	512	257	9/257
•				•	•
•				•	•
•				•	•
502	9	512	512	511	9/511
503	10	514	1024	513	10/513
•				•	•
•				•	•
•				•	•
1013	10	1024	1024	1023	10/1023

FIGURE 49

BURSTS OF ERROR

The codes developed so far have been developed to detect (distance of two) or correct (distance of three) a single error (assumed in data transmission. This assumption, single error in transmission, is not always valid. There are cases, e.g., in data transmission (communication) where bursts of error are to be expected [2, 13]. This is due to the disturbance (noise) on the line lasting for more than a single bit "frame" (duration) (Fig. 50).

The message is Fall 1980 [2]. The message is encoded in the binary (ASCII) [12, 15] coding scheme. The code is given to the right of the hexadecimal representation of the ASCII characters for the message [m(S)] sent [m(s) or m(t)].

A check digit (character) is appended to the message. This is the BEL in the example (ASCII 07, a control character that rings the bell if sent to the terminal) [12, 16, 17].

The check digit is computed by computing the XOR for each column. This results in the calculation 0000 0111 for the eight vertical columns (the BEL). The scheme will catch bursts of error up to eight digits (bits) (one character) long (Fig. 51).

A burst of errors eight bits long has occurred. This will affect the parity value (incorrect value for a single error in that column) for each vertical column. This is shown in detail in Figure 52.

The received message is Fal??1980. These are the characters Fal-13h-A0h-1980 in the hexadecimal representation of the code. The hexadecimal 13 is a control character (DC3, Data Control 3) [16] and the A0 is undefined in standard ASCII [15]. The check digit (character), F8, is also undefined in standard ASCII. It is, however, non-zero. This indicates an error in the transmission (burst of errors ≤ 8, the data length (character) of the code). This is illustrated in Figure 53.

Fall 1980

(a)

message	hex	binary (burst)
F	46	0100 0110
a	61	0110 0001
l	6C	0110 1100
l	6C	0110 1100
sp	20	0010 0000
1	31	0011 0001
9	39	0011 1001
8	38	0011 1000
0	30	0011 0000

		0000 0111 = BEL

(b)

FIGURE 50

The message sent and received is Fall 1980BEL. The "block" check character is generated on the transmitting end and received on the receiving end. It is included in the calculation of the parity values on the receiving end. This is indicated in Figure 53 by the inclusion of the BEL in the calculation.

The calculation of the parity is zero. This is indicated in Figure 53 by the calculation including the BEL and summarized in Figure 54.

The computed parity, 0000 0111 (07), represents the summation of the bits (Fall 1980) sent. It is also the received parity (BEL + BEL or Fall 1980 + Fall 1980, 0000 0111 or 07 + 07). By summing the message (Fall

Fall 1980

(a)

message	hex	binary (burst)
F	46	0100 0110
a	61	0110 0001
l	6C	0110 1100
l	6C	0xxx xxxx
sp	20	x010 0000
1	31	0011 0001
9	31	0011 1001
8	38	0011 1000
0	30	0011 0000
		----------
		xxxx xxxx = ?

(b)

FIGURE 51

Sent:

Fall 1980

(a)

Received:

Fal??1980

(b)

message	hex	binary (burst)
F	46	0100 0110
a	61	0110 0001
l	6C	0110 1100
l	13	0001 0011
sp	A0	1010 0000
1	31	0011 0001
9	39	0011 1001
8	38	0011 1000
0	30	0011 0000

		1111 1000 = ?

(c)

FIGURE 52

Sent:

Fall 1980BEL

(a)

Received:

Fall 1980BEL

(b)

message	hex	binary (burst)
F	46	0100 0110
a	61	0110 0001
l	6C	0110 1100
l	6C	0110 1100
sp	20	0010 0000
1	31	0011 0001
9	39	0011 1001
8	38	0011 1000
0	30	0011 0000
BEL	07	0000 0111

		0000 0000 = zero wrong correct transmission

(c)

FIGURE 53

```
         computed parity:  BEL   07   0000 0111
         received parity:  BEL   07   0000 0111
                                ------------------
         XOR                           00   0000 0000
```

FIGURE 54

1980 or BEL) with the check character (BEL) (XOR), the result (correct transmission) is zero (Fig. 54).

The calculation of the parity (XOR) is the summation (exclusive or) of the bits in the original message (XOR 1 o 1 o 1 o 1 o 0 o 0 o 0 o 0 o 0 = 0 for column two in the original message (Fig. 50), 1 o 0 o 1 o 1 o 0 o 0 o 0 o 0 o 0 = 1 for column six, one-based counting, left to right in Fig. 50). The parity is "set" by this summation (XOR Fall 1980 = BEL). When the received parity (BEL) is XOR'ed with itself (Fall 1980 = BEL) the result is zero (0 XOR 0 = 0, 1 XOR 1 = 0 or x XOR x = 0).

The scheme shown will detect error bursts up to ($\leqslant$) eight bits (one character) long [2]. It will, in fact, detect bursts up to 16 bits long [2 × L, where L = the length of the code (burst)], since at least one column will be non-zero for all double (column) errors up to 16. This is shown in Figures 55 and 56.

Sent:

Fall 1980BEL

(a)

Received:

Fal??1980-?

(b)

message	hex	binary (burst)
F	46	0100 0110
a	61	0110 0001
l	6C	0110 1100
l	6C	0xxx xxxx
sp	20	xxxx xxxx
1	31	0011 0001
9	39	0011 1001
8	38	0011 1000
0	30	0011 0000

```
                           ---------
                           x000 0111 = ?
                           1000 0111 = 87 hex = undefined
```

(c)

FIGURE 55

Sent:

Fall 1980BEL

(a)

Received:

Fal???980BEL

(b)

message	hex	binary (burst)
F	46	0100 0110
a	61	0110 0001
l	6C	0110 1100
l	6C	0xxx xxxx
sp	20	xxxx xxxx
1	31	x011 0001
9	39	0011 1001
8	38	0011 1000
0	30	0011 0000

		0000 0111 = BEL

(c)

FIGURE 56

Figure 55 shows a burst of 15 bits. The parity values for all columns (bit positions of the burst length) are correct except for the first column (offsetting double errors in columns 2 through 8). The message will be recognized as incorrect.

Figure 56 shows a burst of exactly 16 bits. The message (BEL, check character) will be accepted.

There are offsetting double errors in each column [18]. The transmission will be accepted despite the error.

The error detection and correction schemes cannot detect or correct all errors to be detected [2, 18].

The scheme of figures 50 through 56 will accept bursts of length $m \times L$, where m is an integral multiple of the burst length, L. This is eight in the example and can be set to detect bursts of any length ($m \times L < n < (m + 1) \times L$, m = 0,x).

The burst scheme is developed to detect "bursts" (more than one or "dependent" errors). It is common in data communications where disturbances on the line often cause more than a single (parity bit) error. It is useful in situations where the binomial [independent errors, p = the probability of error, q = the probability of a correct transmission ($1 - p$, per bit)] is inapplicable [9, 10].

HUMAN ERROR

The codes in use so far were developed to detect or correct machine errors, i.e., errors that occur in the transmission of data across data communica-

0-87835-145-0 (ISBN)

(a)

	sum	sum of sums
0	0	0
8	8	8
7	15	23
8	23	46
3	26	72
5	31	103
1	32	135
4	36	171
5	41	212

$$(41 + x) \quad 212 + (41 + x) = 11 \times m$$
$$253 + x = 11 \times m$$
$$253 + x = 11 \times 23$$
$$x = 0$$

0

(b)

FIGURE 57

tion lines (channels), within a computer system or other mechanical/elec-
tronic devices (e.g., the disk). Codes (coding schemes) have also been
developed to detect (and/or correct) human errors in data transcription
or transmission [19] (Fig. 57).

The ISBN (International Standard Book Number/Code) is a block code.
Each portion of the code means something [20]. The first digit is a group
identifier, which is 0 or 1 for most English-speaking countries, 2 for
France, 3 for Germany, and 90 for The Netherlands. The second group of
five digits is the publisher identification number. The third group of
digits (145 in the example) is the title or edition identifier [20], e.g., the
number 0-85139-836-7 stands for Britain (English-speaking country) (0),
Architecture Press (85139), title *Furniture Designed by Architects* (836).
The last digit, 0 in Figure 57, in the prior example, is the check-digit.
It is used to detect human errors in the transcription of the message (e.g.,
keying errors) [21].

The check digit is computed by computing the sum and the sum of
sums. This weights each digit by the coefficients $10 \times x1$, . . ., $1 \times x10$
[2] for the ten-digit ISBN code. This is illustrated in Figure 58.

Each code value (xi, $i = 1$, n, the length of the code) is included in
a sum (the parenthesized expressions, $x1$, $(x1 + x2)$, . . . , $(x1 + x2 +$
. . . $+ x10))$ and a sum of sums (the sum of these terms). This includes
the first term, $x1$, in ten sums ($10 \times x1$ or $n \times x1$, where n = the length
of the code), the second in nine ($n - 1$) sums ($9 \times x2$), and so on. Figure 58 gives the entire tree for the ten-digit ISBN code. The pattern is:

```
 1                          x1
 2                        x1 + x2
 3                      x1 + x2 + x3
 4                    x1 + x2 + x3 + x4
 5                  x1 + x2 + x3 + x4 + x5
 6                x1 + x2 + x3 + x4 + x5 + x6
 7              x1 + x2 + x3 + x4 + x5 + x6 + x7
 8            x1 + x2 + x3 + x4 + x5 + x6 + x7 + x8
 9          x1 + x2 + x3 + x4 + x5 + x6 + x7 + x8 + x9
10        x1 + x2 + x3 + x4 + x5 + x6 + x7 + x8 + x9 + x10
```

(a)

x1 + (x1 + x2) + (x1 + x2 + x3) + . . . + (x1 + x2 + . . . + x10) =
          10*x1 + 9*x2 + . . . + 1*x10

(b)

FIGURE 58

```
        x1
      x1 + x2
         •
         •
         •
  x1 + . . . + xn
```

where n = the number of the row (hence sum and sum of sums), n = 1 through 10 for the example, n = 1 to the number of digits in the code in the general case and the final sum of sums expression is $n \times x1 + (n - 1) \times x2 + . . . + 1 \times xn$ [2].

Pragmatically, one starts with the first digit (value), 0 on line one of Figure 57, and computes the sum and the sum of sums for this digit, then one adds the next digit to the sum (sum = sum + xi, i = 2, d, d = the total number of digits in the code) and that value (the sum) to the running total of the sum of sums (ss = ss + sum(i), i = 2, d). This results in an exact calculation for all but the check digit:

0-87835-145-x

In calculating Figure 57b, the last sum (ninth sum) calculated is 41 and the last sum of sums is 212. The next sum (41 + x) will include the check digit and the next sum of sums (212 + (41 + x) or 253 + x) will also include the check digit. This, 253 + x, the final sum of sums, is intended to be zero modulo (remainder) some number system, eleven in the case of the ISBN. The modulus is selected from the number of unique symbols (11 in the ISBN, 0–9, X) in the code [2, 22]. This is indicated in Figure 57 by the comparison:

253 + x = 11 × m

where m is an integral number. This is 253 (11 × 23) for the given cal-culation, hence the check digit (x) is zero and the sum (41 + x) and sum

```
0-85139-836-7

(a)

            sum      sum of sums

0        0                  0
8        8                  8
5       13                 21
1       14                 35
3       17                 52
9       26                 78
8       34                112
3       37                149
6       43                192
       (43 + x)    192 + (43 + x) = 11 × m
                   235 + x = 11 × m
                   235 + x = 242
                   235 + x = 11 × 22
                        x = 7

7

(b)
```

FIGURE 59

of sums (212 + (41 + x)) are 41 + 0 and 212 + (41 + 0) or 253 + 0, respectively. Another example is given in Figure 59. It is the calculation for the check digit in the code:

0-85139-836-7

The sum and sum of sums is calculated as before. This results in the relationship:

(43 + x) = sum

and:

192 + (43 + x) = 11 × m

for the sum of sums. This must be an integral multiple of the modulus, 11:

235 + x = 11 × m

This is 11 × 22 = 242 for the example shown:

235 + x = 11 × 22
235 + x = 242

Thus, x = 7 (235 + x = 242). This is the check digit for the code value (ISBN number, identification part):

0-85139-836-x

or:

0-85139-836-7

The ISBN, or International Standard Book Number [20,23], is used to refer to books in a unique (identification) way (country, publisher, and title or edition). The code shown in Figure 57 is that for the text by Malcolm G. Lane [24]. The code for the second book is the code for the title given [20].

The check digit is used to detect transcription (of the wrong digit), transposition (of two digits), random and other errors that tend to be committed by humans [2,21] (Fig. 60).

The code is:

0-85139-836-7

The transcribed (keyed or otherwise) transmission is (Fig. 60b):

0-85135-836-7

The incorrect transcription (5 for 9 in the sixth digit, one-based counting, left to right) is detected by the non-zero modulus 11 check digit.

A non-zero (modulus the code size, eleven in the example) answer indicates an error. A correct "transmission" (transcription) would give a zero result (Fig. 61).

The calculation of a correct transmission results in a zero result modulus some number system, eleven in this case [2]. The ISBN is an eleven-

0-85139-836-7

(a)

0-85135-836-7

(b)

	sum	sum of sums
0	0	0
8	8	8
5	13	21
1	14	35
3	17	52
5	22	74
8	30	104
3	33	137
6	39	176
7	46	222

222 mod 11 = 2

(c)

FIGURE 60

0-85139-836-7

(a)

0-85139-836-7

(b)

	sum	sum of sums
0	0	0
8	8	8
5	13	21
1	14	35
3	17	52
9	26	78
8	34	112
3	37	149
6	43	192
7	50	242

242 mod 11 = 0

(c)

FIGURE 61

-digit code. The check digit is calculated modulus 11 (0—10, remainders), hence there are 11 possible digit values. The value X (capital X) is used for ten [2, 20].

Other moduli are possible. For example, a code used with text (alphabet, 26 letters, and space) and numerals (10 digits, decimal number system) is modulus 37 (Fig. 62) [2].

A6 7 — x

(a)

symbol	value	sum	sum of sums
A	10	10	10
6	6	16	26
sp	36	52	78
7	7	59	137
		(59 + x)	$137 + (59 + x) = 37 \times m$
			$196 + x = 37 \times m$
			$196 + x = 222$
			$196 + x = 37 \times 6$
			$x = 26 = Q$

Q

(b)

FIGURE 62

$$0 = 0$$

·

·

·

$$9 = 9$$
$$A = 10$$
$$B = 11$$

·

·

·

$$Z = 35$$
$$sp = 36$$

FIGURE 63

    The check digit is calculated as before. The code values are, how-ever, as shown in Figure 63.

    There are 37 code values, the upper case letters (A . . . Z, 10—35, and the space (sp), 36) and the ten numerals (retaining their own values, 0—9). This results in a code modulus 37 (36 + 1 + 10). Values are assigned as in Figure 63.

    The calculation of the check digit for the message: A6 7 — x is Q (x = 26).

    Several "human error" detecting codes have been developed. For ex-ample, the SOUNDEX code facilitates voice (aural) encoding of messages. It is illustrated in Figure 64.

    SOUNDEX is not strictly an "error-detecting" or "correcting" code. It is developed to aid in the human identification of codes by phonetic char-acteristics [21, 25—27]. It was developed by the Bureau of the Census in the nineteenth century to search for names in the census files [26, 28, 30]. It is, however, a good example of a code developed with human (aural) characteristics in mind [31, 32].

    The code is developed according to the characteristics outlined in Figure 64. The initial letter, B in the example [21, 25, 33, 34], is retained. The remaining letters (R, C) after the vowels and the H have been removed are assigned the values of their phonetic code group (6, 2, respectively). The code is then "adjusted" to fixed length (B620) and the file (physical) accessed through this code (alphabetic and numerical order). Errors are detected by "no name found" (Name not in file or coding incorrect).

    The development of human encoding schemes, error detection (check digit) or other (SOUNDEX), is a development of human factors research as well as coding theory [31, 35]. Error detection (validation) is the more common scheme. Error correction is accomplished by "retransmission" (re-keying or retranscribing). The original data (document) is retained until the coding is complete, although the SOUNDEX system can be used in "real time" (vocal) transmission, e.g., telephone communication (queries).

CYCLIC REDUNDANCY CHECK

The cyclic redundancy check is a block check code used in data communica-tions. An example is given in Figure 65.

Birch

(a)

B620

(b)

1. Retain the first letter of the word and drop all occurrences of vowels and H, W, Y in the other positions

2. Assign the following numbers to the remaining letters after the first

B,	F,	P,	V		1
C,	G,	J,	K,	Q,	
S,	X,	Z			2
D,	T				3
L					4
M,	N				5
R					6

3. If two or more letters with the same code (not necessarily the same letter) are adjacent in the original word, omit all but the first

4. Convert to the form (fixed length code) letter, digit, digit, digit by adding trailing zeroes, if there are less than three digits, and truncating the rightmost digits, if there are more than three digits

(c)

FIGURE 64

The cyclic redundancy check (CRC) (01110) or block check character (BCC) is generated from the message bits (1010001101). It is then affixed (concatenated) to the message (1010001101-01110) to form the transmitted code. If the received "transmitted message" is the same as the transmitted code, there will be a zero result. This is due to the XOR of the message (1010001101 = 01110) with itself (BCC = 01110) (Fig. 66).

The principle is the same as that for the burst detecting code discussed above: the XOR of a bit, x, with itself, x o x, is zero (0 XOR 0 = 0, 1 XOR 1 = 0 [18, 36, 37]. Hence, if all bits in the received transmission are the same as those sent, the result (XOR) will be zero.

The method of generating the code is, however, distinct (Fig. 67).

The message (information) bits: 1010001101 are represented as a polynomial: $x^9 + x^7 + x^3 + x^2 + x^0$ (Fig. 67). The method of representation is to use a "dummy" variable x and include each binary value as the coefficient of the value (exponent) of x that represents that bit position (x^{**b}, $0 \leqslant b \leqslant (d - 1)$, d = the total number of information bits transmitted, ten in the example) [18]. This is:

message: 1010001101
CRC code: 01110
transmitted code: 1010001101 | 01110

FIGURE 65

```
transmitted code:  1010001101 | 01110
received code:      1010001101 | 01110
                    ----------   -----
                    0000000000   00000
```

FIGURE 66

$$1 \times x9 + 0 \times x8 + 1 \times x7 + 0 \times x6 + 0 \times x5 + 0 \times x4 + 1 \times x3 + 1$$
$$\times x2 + 0 \times x1 + 1 \times x0$$

for the example (1010001101) shown [18]. This simplifies to x9 + x7 + x3 + x2 + x0, where the exponents are represented as x9, x7, . . . , x0 (= 1) for convenience of representation. The correspondence between the polynomial in x:

$$1 \times x9 + 0 \times x8 + 1 \times x7 + 0 \times x6 + 0 \times x5 + 0 \times x4 + 1 \times x3 + 1$$
$$\times x2 + 0 \times x1 + 1 \times x0$$

and the message: 1010001101 can be seen by placing the two in juxtaposition:

$$1 \times x9 + 0 \times x8 + 1 \times x7 + 0 \times x6 + 0 \times x5 + 0 \times x4 + 1 \times x3 + 1$$
$$\quad 1 \qquad 0 \qquad 1 \qquad 0 \qquad 0 \qquad 0 \qquad 1 \qquad 1$$
$$\times x2 + 0 \times x1 + 1 \times x0$$
$$\quad 0 \qquad 1$$

The zero terms drop out, $1 \times x9 + 1 \times x7 + 1 \times x3 + 1 \times x2 + 1 \times x0$, or x9 + x7 + x3 + x2 + x0. This is, for all intents and purposes, the number under the division sign in Figure 67 (dividend).

A divisor is selected (in accord with the type of errors to be detected) and this is used to divide the message numerically, according to polynomial division [38]. This is: x5 + x4 + x2 + x0 or: $1 \times x5 + 1 \times x4 + 0 \times x3 + 1 \times x2 + 0 \times x1 + 1 \times x0$ for the example [14, 18, 39].

The division is handled like all division of polynomials (Fig. 67), with the exception that the partial products are handled through the XOR [18]. This is shown in Figure 68.

The polynomial (x14 + . . .) is divided by the highest power of the divisor (x5 + . . .). This results in the partial quotient x9 (Fig. 68), and the partial product x14 + x13 + x11 + x9 (x9(x5 + x4 + x2 + x0)), where the terms of the partial product are written in the appropriate bit position (exponent, x**b) to facilitate subtraction (addition) (addition = subtraction in XOR).

The dividend is obtained by multiplying the original message: x9 + x7 + x3 + x2 + x0 by the high order term in the divisor. This is shown in Figure 69.

The message, x9 + x7 + x3 + x2 + x0, is multiplied by the high order (exponent) of the divisor. This results in zero coefficients in the five (0−4) low order positions:

$$x14 + x12 + x8 + x7 + x5 + 0 \times x4 + 0 \times x3 + 0 \times x2 + 0 \times x1 + 0 \times x0$$

```
message:  1010001101
polynomial representation:  x9 + x7 + x3 + x2 + x0

divisor:  110101
polynomial representation:  x5 + x4 + x2 + x0

(a)

polynomial division:

                                              x9 +x8 +     x6 +     x4 +     x2 + x1
                     ______________________________________________________________
x5 + x4 + x2 + x0 / x14        x12 +                x8 + x7 +    x5 +
                    x14 + x13 +     x11 +     x9
                    --------------------------------
                         x13 + x12 + x11 +    x9 + x8
                         x13 + x12 +     x10 +   x8
                         --------------------------------
                                   x11 + x10 + x9 +    x7 +
                                   x11 + x10 +    x8 +    x6
                                   -----------------------------
                                              x9 + x8 + x7 + x6 + x5
                                              x9 + x8 +    x6 +   + x4
                                              ----------------------------
                                                       x7 +    x5 + x4
                                                       x7 + x6 +    x4 +     x2
                                                       ----------------------------
                                                            x6 + x5 +        x2 +
                                                            x6 + x5 +    x3 +     x1
                                                            ----------------------------
                                                                         x3 + x2 + x1

binary representation of the remainder:  0 × x4 + 1 × x3 + 1 × x2 + 1 × x1 + 0 × x0 =
                                         0        1        1        1        0

(b)
```

FIGURE 67

```
                                                x9 +
                                       _____
x5 + x4 + x2 + x0 / x14 +        x12 +               x8 + x7 +   x5 +
                    x14 + x13 +        x11 +   x9
                    ------------------------------
                          x13 + x12 + x11 +   x9
```

(a)

```
                                                x9 + x8 +
                                       _____
x5 + x4 + x2 + x0 / x14 +        x12 +           + x8 + x7 +   x5 +
                    x14 + x13 +        x11 +   x9
                    ------------------------------
                          x13 + x12 + x11 +   x9 + x8
```

(b)

FIGURE 68

or:

$$1 \times x14 + 0 \times x13 + 1 \times x12 + 0 \times x11 + 0 \times x10 + 0 \times x9 + 1 \times x8 + 1$$
$$\times x7 + 0 \times x6 + 1 \times x5 + 0 \times x4 + 0 \times x3 + 10 \times x2 + 0 \times x1 + 0$$
$$\times x0$$

in the full representation. This is the dividend (Figs. 67b and 68).

The dividend is divided by the divisor according to long division (Fig. 67), with the exception that addition modulo 2 (like terms drop out, the same effect as subtraction with like coefficients) replaces the conventional subtraction (with coefficients unrestrained to 0 and 1, binary))(Figs. 68 and 67). This is shown in full in Figure 67b and in part, the partial product (Fig. 68a), and the bringing down of the next term (Fig. 68b). The number of terms necessary for the next partial division depends on the number of terms (at least one, but sometimes more, e.g., x13 and x12, Fig. 67b) that "cancel" (coincide, $1 \times x13$ and $1 \times x13$, $1 \times x12$ and $1 \times x12$). The partial dividend needs at least six (the size of the divisor) terms in the next iteration, hence x7, and x6, if it existed ($1 \times x6$) would be brought down (Fig. 67b).

The remainder (Fig. 67b), is the parity check (set of check digits). This is: x3 + x2 + x1 or: 01110

$$0 \times x4 + 1 \times x3 + 1 \times x2 + 1 \times x1 + 0 \times x0$$

```
                x9 + x7 + x3 + x2 + x0
                            x5
-------------------------------------------------
x14 + x12 +                 x8 + x7 +   x5 +
```

FIGURE 69

for the example shown. These are appended to the message:
1010001101-01110 (Fig. 65).

The transmitted message is:

$$x14 + x12 + \quad x8 + x7 + \quad x5 + \quad x3 + x2 + x1$$

If the received message is the same (no transmission errors) the polynomial
division will result in a zero remainder. This is shown in Figure 70.

The remainder is zero. This is the indication of a correct message or
an undetectable error [2, 18].

The appending of the digits (bits) has resulted in making the polynomial:

$$x14 + \quad x12 + \quad x8 + x7 + \quad x5 + \quad x3 + x2 + x1$$

divisible by the divisor:

$$x5 + x4 + x2 + x0$$

$$(x14 + x12 + x8 + x7 + x5 + x3 + x2 + x1) =$$

$$(x5 + x4 + x2 + x0) \times (x9 + x8 + x6 + x4 + x2 + x1)$$

This results in a zero (integral division) remainder:

$$x6 + x5 + \quad x3 + \quad x1$$
$$x6 + x5 + \quad x3 + \quad x1$$
$$\text{------------------------}$$

when the polynomial calculation is performed on the received message (Fig.
70).

The process of long division and the polynomial representation is an
aid to understanding the method of generating the "sent" (remainder plus
message, sent as message followed by remainder) message [18, 39]. The
theoretical basis of the process is shown in Figure 71.

The adjusted message, $M'(x)$, is divided by the polynomial, $P(x)$
(Fig. 71). This results in a quotient and a remainder:

$$Q(x) + \frac{R(x)}{P(x)}$$

These are:

$$x14 + x12 + x8 + x7 + x5$$

$$x5 + x4 + x2 + x0$$

$$x9 + x8 + x6 + x4 + x2 + x1$$

and:

$$x3 + x2 + x1$$

```
                                                  x9 + x8 +    x6 +    x4 +    x2 + x1
                                                       + x8 + x7 + x5 + x3 + x2 + x1
                         _____
x5 + x4 + x2 + x0  )  x14 +    x12 +                   x9 + x8 +    x6 +    x4 +    x2 + x1
                      x14 + x13 +    x11 +        x9 + x8 + x7 + x5 + x3 + x2 + x1
                      ----------------------------------
                      x13 + x12 + x11 +    x9 + x8
                      x13 + x12 +    x10 +    x8
                      ----------------------------------
                             x11 + x10 + x9 +    x7 +
                             x11 + x10 +    x8
                             -----------------------------
                                   x9 + x8 + x7 + x6 + x5
                                   x9 + x8 +    x6 +    x4
                                   -----------------------------
                                              x7 +              x5 + x4 + x3 + x2
                                              x7 + x6 +              x4 +    x2
                                              -----------------------------
                                                   x6 + x5 +    x3 +    x1
                                                   x6 + x5 + x3 +    x1
                                                   ----------------------------
```

FIGURE 70

$M'(x)$: $\quad$ x14 + x12 + x8 + x7 + x5
$P(x)$: $\quad$ x5 + x4 + x2 + x0

$$\frac{M'(x)}{P(x)} = Q(x) + \frac{R(x)}{P(x)}$$

$Q(x)$: $\quad$ x9 + x8 + x6 + x4 + x2 + x1
$R(x)$: $\quad$ x3 + x2 + x1

(a)

$M'(x) = P(x)Q(x) + R(x)$
$T'(x) = M'(x) + R(x)$
$\quad\quad = P(x)Q(x) + (R(x) + R(x))$
$\quad\quad = P(x)Q'(x) + R'(x)$
$\quad\quad = P(x)Q(x)$

$Q'(x) = $ x9 + x8 + x6 + x4 + x2 + x1 $= Q(x)$
$R'(x) = R'(x) = (Rx) + R(x)) = 0$
$T'(x)$: $\quad$ x14 + c12 + x8 + x7 + x5 + x3 + x2 + x1
$T'(x) = P(x)Q'(x) = $ (x5 + x4 + x2 + x0)(x9 + x8 + x6 + x4 + x2 + x1) $= P(x)Q(x)$

(b)

FIGURE 71

in the example:

(x14 + x12 + x8 + x7 + x5)/(x5 + x4 + x2 + x0)

$$= (x9 + x8 + x6 + x4 + x2 + x1) + \frac{(x3 + x2 + x1)}{(x5 + x4 + x2 + x0)}$$

or:

(x14 + x12 + x8 + x7 + x5) = (x5 + x4 + x2 + x0)*(x9 + x8 + x6 + x4 + x2

+ x1) + (x3 + x2 + x1)

The formula:

$$\frac{M'(x)}{P(x)} = Q(x) + \frac{R(x)}{P(x)}$$

is manipulated to place the remainder on one side:

M'(x) = P(x)Q(x) + R(x)

This is M'(x):

M'(x) = P(x)Q(x) + R(x)

The remainder is then added to this:

M'(x) + R(x)

This results in the calculation: M'(x) + R(x) + R(x), where R(x) + R(x) =0 modulo 2 (XOR). This results in the transmitted message, T'(x), being an integral multiple, Q'(x) = Q(x), of the divisor (Fig. 71).

The addition of the remainder: R(x) + R(x) results in a zero (remainder) result modulo 2. This is the key to the redundancy check calculation [18]. It is, however, implemented without long division [13, 18, 24, 40]. This is shown in Figure 72.

The implementation of the cyclic (code) redundancy check is with shift registers and feedback mechanisms. This is indicated in Figure 72 by the "dashed" lines (shift registers) and the vertical lines (XOR gates) [18, 36, 37, 43].

The input message, M'(x), is in the rightmost column (1010001101-00000), where the last five zeroes represent the multiplying (shift) by x5 [shift left 5 bits = 0(x4) + . . . + 0(x0)]. This is fed into the shift registers at each time period, 1—15. The state of the registers is indicated on line n and the resulting state (after the input) is on line n + 1. Hence, the state of the system (five shift register bits and the input data line) is shown on line 1 and the resulting set of register values (after the shift) is shown on line 2 (all shifts are left shifts).

The vertical lines represent XOR gates. These are placed between shift registers A and B, C and D, and E and the input line. These represent the feedback mechanism from register A.

The XOR gates are triggered if there is a 1 (feedback) out of register A. This is fed back to positions x4, x2 and x0 (B, D and input, respec-

```
--------------------------
|A   |B  C |D  E |input |
--------------------------
|0   |0  0 |0  0 |1     |   1
----/---/--/---/--/--------
|0   |0  0 |0  1 |0     |   2
----/---/--/---/--/--------
|0   |0  0 |1  0 |1     |   3
----/---/--/---/--/--------
|0   |0  1 |0  1 |0     |   4
----/---/--/---/--/--------
|0   |1  0 |1  0 |0     |   5
----/---/--/---/--/--------
|1   |0  1 |0  0 |0     |   6
----/---/--/---/--/--------
|1   |1  1 |0  1 |1     |   7
----/---/--/---/--/--------
|0   |1  1 |1  0 |1     |   8
----/---/--/---/--/--------
|1   |1  1 |0  1 |0     |   9
----/---/--/---/--/--------
|0   |1  1 |1  1 |1     |  10
----/---/--/---/--/--------
|1   |1  1 |1  1 |0     |  11
----/---/--/---/--/--------
|0   |1  0 |1  1 |0     |  12
----/---/--/---/--/--------
|1   |0  1 |1  0 |0     |  13
----/---/--/---/--/--------
|1   |1  0 |0  1 |0     |  14
----/---/--/---/--/--------
|0   |0  1 |1  1 |0     |  15
----/---/--/---/--/--------
|0   |1  1 |1  0 |      |  16
----/---/--/---/--/--------
```

FIGURE 72

tively). These represent the terms: $x4 + x2 + 1$ in the divisor polynomial: $x5 + x4 + x2 + 1$. The polynomial (divisor) always matches in the first position ($x5$) of the partial products (Fig. 67b). It will match in the next position only if these positions represent a 1 in the polynomial divisor: 110101 or:

$$1(x5) + 1(x4) + 9(x3) + 1(x2) + 0(x1) + 1(x0)$$

and are divided. These are the bit positions B ($x4$), D ($x2$), and input ($x0$).

The XOR gates are placed with respect to the polynomial chosen as the divisor. This is $x5 + x4 + x2 + 1$ or:

$$A \text{ (output)}, B (x4), D (x2) \text{ and input } (x0 \text{ or } 1)$$

for the polynomial $x5 + x4 + x2 + 1$.

The XORs are not triggered by a zero out of gate (flip flop) A (these represent a missing exponent in the polynomial, hence a lack of division; the zero shifts correspond to the "bringing down (shifting over)" of terms (Figs. 67b and 68b).

The initial five shifts (1—2, 2—3, 3—4, 4—5 and 5—6) represent the shifting into the register (s) of the first five bits (10100) of the input message. The next bit of the message (0) is fed in, line 6. The result is line 7, 111011. This represents the division of $x14 + x12$ by the divisor $x5 + x4 + x2 + 1$ (Fig. 67b). The quotient is $x9$ (this is discarded); the message bit is $x14$ (this is transmitted out of line A) and the partial product is $x9*(x5 + x4 + x2 + 1)$ or: $x14 + x13 + x11 + x9$. The $x9$ represents the (1) input bit (after the XOR, line 6 to 7, 0 XOR 1 --> 1, line 7).

This is the computation:

```
x14 +         x12 +             x8 + x7 +    x5 +
x14 + x13 +           x11 + x9
--------------------------
        x13 + x12 + x11 + x9 + x8
```

before the bringing down of the $x8$ in Figure 67b with the result:

```
x13 + x12 + x11 +     x9 + x8
```

on line 7: 1 1 1 0 1 1.

The procedure continues for 15 (message bits, 10, and parity bits, 5) time periods, lines 1—15. The final result, the remainder, is on line 16. This is transmitted as the check character (digit) in the last five positions of the transmitted code, T'(x), replacing the five zeroes:

```
1010001101 - 00000
1010001101 - 01110
```

The message (five zeroes) is delayed to perform (XOR) the concatenation.

The delay can be avoided using a distinct technology [18].

Cyclic redundancy codes can be implemented quite easily with a set of shift registers and XOR gates. The XOR gates serve to "create" the bits that are necessary for the partial products. The technique is, however, independent of the polynomials, except with regard to the generation (creation) of the procedure [18].

Cyclic redundancy codes are used in the transmission of synchronous data. Large blocks of data (the message, M(x), before adjustment, M'(x), after the multiplication by the divisor, high order (power) in the polynomial representation of the bit (shift left five bits or (n-k) bits, where n-k is the number of bits in the parity check)) are transmitted followed by a cyclic redundancy check (CRC) character [13, 24, 39, 40]. This is, typically, 16 bits long (CRC-16, CRC-CCITT), although 12-bit CRC's (CRC-12) have been produced. The check character (s) is twice the size of a character in the code [12 for 6-bit codes, e.g., Binary-Coded Decimal (BCD) [13, 41—43, 43a], 16 for 8-bit (byte) codes (ASCII, EBCDIC, other)].

The divisors used in practice are:

```
x16 + x15 + x2 + 1
x16 + x12 + x5 + 1
x12 + x11 + x3 + x2 + x1 + 1
```

```
H    ....
E    .
L    ._..
L    ._..
O    ___
```

FIGURE 73

The divisor x16 + x15 + x2 + 1 (CRC-16) is used with eight bit codes as is x16 + x12 + x5 + 1 (CRC-CCITT). The divisor x12 + x11 + x3 + x2 + 1 is used with 6-bit codes [13, 14, 24, 39, 40].

Cyclic redundancy checks (codes) are used to detect and correct errors. Given a suitable divisor, the codes generated by the polynomial "division" or shift register encoding mechanism can detect all single, double, and triple errors (random errors) and bursts of length b, where b $\leq$ (n-k) and n is the size of the transmitted message, k is the number of information bits and (n-k) is the number of parity bits (five in the example). This is shown in the original article [18].

CYCLIC CODES

Cyclic codes [43b—45] are codes that result in a valid code value if one code value (e.g., 1101000) is shifted 1 bit (right in this example, 0110100, 0011010, and 0001101) [37]. They are popular for their ability to detect and correct both multiple errors (random or burst) and dependent (burst) errors. Peterson and Brown and others have shown that cyclic redundancy codes of a special type (irreducible polynomials) generate codes that are the equivalent of Hamming single error correction and Hamming single error correction, double error detection (syndrome plus overall parity bit) codes as a special class [18].

VARIABLE LENGTH CODES

The codes developed so far have been fixed length (n, the total "block" size, information and parity bits) codes [46—50]. There are also variable length codes. An example is given in Figure 73.

The Morse code is a three value (dot, dash, separator) code [2, 51]. It assigns the shorter codes to the more frequently occurring letters (E = ., Z = __.., J = .___).

HUFFMAN CODES

A variable length code common in information theory [2, 32, 52] is the Huffman code. This is illustrated in Figure 74 for a four message (alphabet) code.

The Huffman code is derived according to a preset scheme. This is shown in Figure 75 for the code (alphabet) of Figure 74.

The code values [A, B, C, D for the source messages, m(S)] are grouped according to their probabilities. This is shown in Figure 76 for the grouping of Figures 74 and 75.

Messages	Probability of message	Code Value
A	1/2	0
B	1/4	10
C	1/8	110
D	1/8	111

FIGURE 74

The code (message) values have the probabilities 1/2, 1/4, 1/8, 1/8 (Fig. 74), or .5, . . . (Fig. 76). These are grouped according to the lowest pair of probabilities extant at each stage of the process [2, 5].

In the code shown, the values C and D have the two lowest probabilities (1/8, 1/8, conveniently chosen as powers of two in the example). These are grouped to form one "code value" group, indicated by a leading 11:

    11_
    11_

The code values within the group:

    110 = C
    111 = D

are distinguished by the third letter (bit in the binary code).

These two code values (C, D) then function as a single group, with probability 1/8 + 1/8 (mutually exclusive messages), or 1/4 (Fig. 76). They (or another probability or group of probabilities) are then combined with the next lowest probability group, the group consisting of B alone in Figure 76. This forms the group beginning with a leading 1:

    10 = B
    11_ = C or D

This is then combined with A to form the final (four value) code:

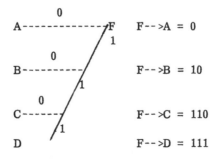

FIGURE 75

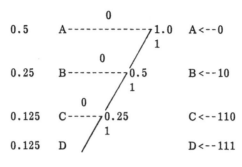

```
                         0
0.5        A-------------71.0    A<--0
                                1

                     0
0.25       B---------70.5        B<--10
                        1

                 0
0.125      C-----70.25           C<--110
                 1

0.125      D     /               D<--111
```

FIGURE 76

0 = A
1 = B or C or D

The actual (manual) procedure shown is to group the codes as indicated, placing a triangular pair of lines between the code values in the group and placing the binary value 0 on the top line, 1 on the bottom line. This procedure is repeated for all code values (Fig. 76) then the code read "back" from the finish point (F) (Figs. 75 or 76). This results in the code:

0 = A
10 = B
110 = C
111 = D

(Fig. 74). The codes may have to be moved during the process ("merge") [2].

The code groups (0 = {A}, 1 = {B, C or D}; 10 = {B}, 11_ = {C or D}; 110 = {C}, 111 = {D}) are distinguished by the leading bit (0 or 1) at each stage of the process. This is illustrated in Figure 77.

Figure 77 represents the decoding mechanism (0-->A, 1-->B, C or D; 10-->B, 11-->C or D; 110-->C, 111-->D). Each code (value) is recognized by the presence of a 0 (0 = A, 10 = B) or the code length (110 = C, 111 = D). This is known as a comma code [5]. It is also known as a "prefix code" because no code value (binary) is the prefix (first part of) another code value.

The prefix code is useful in error detection and self correction. This is illustrated in Figure 78.

```
        0 A
      .<              0 B
      1 B,C,D       .<              0 C
                    1 C,D         .<
                                  1 D

      bit 1         bit 2         bit 3
```

FIGURE 77

```
| the | man | sells | the | house |
  1    001   00000   1     00011

| to | the | man | the | horse | ...
 011   1    001    1    00001   ...
```

(a)

```
| the | man |  | likes | man | the |
              00010   001    1

| to | the | man | the | horse | ...
 011   1    001    1    00001   ...
```

(b)

FIGURE 78

The code is developed as shown in Figure 79, with the same algorithm as the code of Figure 74, with a more complicated code value (message) structure (frequencies).

The message sent is:

the man sells the house
to the man the horse ...

(Fig. 78a) [5]. The assumption is that the transmission is interrupted (lost data) for the first six bits. Hence, the decoder begins the process at the point shown in Figure 78b.

The first few bits of the message are misinterpreted:

```
| likes | man | the |
 00010   001    1
```

However, after the decoding of the word the (code value 1, Fig. 78b, first line) the decoder recovers. The decoding of the word "the" (line 1, Fig. 78b, last code value) is incorrect. However, the decoding ends on a correct word demarcation:

word	p	code	code length
the	.50	1	1
man	.15	001	3
to	.12	011	3
runs	.10	010	3
house	.04	00011	5
likes	.04	00010	5
horse	.03	00001	5
sells	.02	00000	5

FIGURE 79

| the | man | sells | the | house |
| 1 | 001 | 00000 | 1 | 00011 |

| the | man | likes | man | the |
| | 00010 | 001 | 1 | |

Hence, the remainder of the message will be decoded correctly [5].

The prefix code lends itself to self correction: a correct word (code value) boundary will eventually be used (interpreted as a code value boundary). From that point, until another disturbance, the code interpretation (decoding) will be correct:

| to | the | man | the | horse | ... |
| 011 | 1 | 001 | 1 | 00001 | |

The Huffman code is an optimal code [2, 3, 5, 53]. It will, given the techniques used, create a code the average word (code) length of which is optimal from an information theoretic point of view [5, 51, 53]. This is illustrated in the code of Figure 74 (and the code of Fig. 79).

The code of Figure 74 has an average code ("block", variable length "blocks") length of 1 6/8 or 1.75 bits (binary digits) per code value (message sent, m(S), m(t)]. This is shown in Figures 80 and 81.

If one computes an expected value [9, 10, 11] on the (individual) code lengths of Figure 80, it will calculate an average code (block) length of 1 6/8 bits per message (value) or code (value) sent. This is shwon in Figure 81.

The individual code lengths (1) are multiplied by their probability of occurrence (p), column five. This is then summed. This is the calculation Sum(i) p(i)*v(i) with v(i) (value) being the individual code length (1 in Fig. 81) and p(i) being the probability (frequency) of occurrence of that code value in the set of messages (alphabet context) (p in Fig. 81). This is 1 6/8 bit per message sent (in Fig. 81).

The expected value is a mean [9]. No code value is 1 6/8 bits long [5]. It (1 6/8 bit/message) is the average number of bits sent (1 for A, 2 for B, ...) over the "long range." It is, in this case, the optimal number of bits per message sent, on average. This is shown in Figure 82.

Figure 82 shows the Shannon/Hartley/Nyquist measure of information [51, 54—56].

The average amount of information per message (average H) is calculated from the probabilities of the messages as taken over the entire alphabet size [57]. The calculation is −(p log p), or −p log p, summed (expected value) over the entire alphabet (message set). The value log p (bits per message sent) is taken from the probability of that message value (log to

word	p	code	code length
A	1/2	0	1
B	1/4	10	2
C	1/8	110	3
D	1/8	111	3

FIGURE 80

word	p	code	code length (1)	p*1
A	1/2	0	1	1/2
B	1/4	10	2	1/2
C	1/8	110	3	3/8
D	1/8	111	3	3/8
				-------
				1 6/8

FIGURE 81

the base 2) (p, column 2, Fig. 82), column three. This is weighted by its probability (p, p log p), column four, to obtain the expected value (summation over column four or column five). In this case (the derived code of Fig. 74) the average H (average amount of information, in bits per message) is the same as the average number of bits sent for the variable length code (Fig. 81). This is a function of the example, but it indicates the optimality of the Huffman code [2].

Both the Huffman and the Hamming codes (coding schemes) are based on the Shannon/Hartley (for the discrete, binary code case) measure of information [5, 51, 56].

The Hamming code sends the optimal number of bits (for a fixed length code) to carry the alphabet (set of error messages, n + p + 1 messages, n + p bits and the "all ok" message (1)), assuming equiprobability of errors. This is shown in Figure 83 for a code (alphabet) size of eight (n + p + 1)).

The alphabet size, n + p + 1, where the alphabet is the set of error messages (including the "a-ok," correct transmission, message) is eight for a seven bit (n + p) code (n = 4, information bits, p = 3, parity (code) bits, Figure 49 and Figure 83). This results in a code (p, log (base 2) of a, the alphabet size, a = n + p + 1, p = the code size, Fig. 49) size, in bits (binary digits), of three (for a fixed length, p = 3 for all code values, n = 4, n + p = 7, fixed length code (block)) for the error message code (alphabet), if the errors (and correct transmission) are assumed equiprobable. This assumption is not always justified in data communication [2, 13]. However, it is assumed to simplify (fixed length) the encoding process [2]. This is the minimal (in number of bits per message sent) number of bits sent in the equiprobable case [2, 5]. The Huffman code reduces to —log (1/n) (log to the base 2) for the equiprobable case. This is shown in Figure 84.

message	probability	log p	p log p	—p log p (H)
A	1/2	—1	—1/2	1/2
B	1/4	—2	—1/2	1/2
C	1/8	—3	—3/8	3/8
D	1/8	—3	—3/8	3/8
			Average H:	1 6/8

FIGURE 82

message	p	log p	p log p	−p log p (H)
correct transmission	1/8	−3	−3/8	3/8
bit 1 in error	1/8	−3	−3/8	3/8
bit 2 in error	1/8	−3	−3/8	3/8
bit 3 in error	1/8	−3	−3/8	3/8
bit 4 in error	1/8	−3	−3/8	3/8
bit 5 in error	1/8	−3	−3/8	3/8
bit 6 in error	1/8	−3	−3/8	3/8
bit 7 in error	1/8	−3	−3/8	3/8

$$
\begin{aligned}
\text{Average H:} \quad &= \ 8 \times 3/8 \ \text{bits/message} \\
&= \ \log \ (\text{base 2}) \ 8 \\
&= \ -\log \ (\text{base 2}) \ (1/n) \\
&= \ 3
\end{aligned}
$$

FIGURE 83

The code (alphabet) breaks into two equiprobable blocks, {A,B} and {C,D}, of probability 1/2 or .5 each (.25 + .25). This results in the code of Figures 84 and 85.

The code reduces to a fixed length code (A = 00, B = 01, C = 10, D = 11) in the equiprobable case [2, 5, 51]. This is shown from an information theoretic reference point in Figure 86.

The average H is 2 bits per message (value) sent, calculated as shown in Figure 82.

The entropy (H) of the message, is maximized for the equiprobable case [2, 5, 51], shown in Figure 86 by the calculation of the expected value (average H) and is derived in Figure 87.

The calculation of the average amount of information sent reduces to −log (1/n) in the equiprobable case. The weights of the individual messages are all equal in the equiprobable case (1/n). Hence, they may be factored out:

$$[1/n \times \log(1/n) + 1/n \times \log(1/n) + \ . \ . \ . \ + 1/n \times \log(1/n)]$$

$$= n \ \times \ [(1/n)\log(1/n)]$$

$$= [\log(1/n)]$$

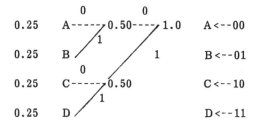

FIGURE 84

Message	Probability of message	Code value
A	1/4	00
B	1/4	01
C	1/4	10
D	1/4	11

FIGURE 85

This results in the simplification in Figure 87. The negative sign is immaterial.

The Huffman code optimizes the average length of the (transmitted) code. This is indicated in Figures 82 and 81 by the average H (average amount of information per message) (in bits) and the average code size (length, in bits). The code (Figs. 74 and 81) cannot have fewer bits (physical) than information (conceptual or logical).

The logical [Sum(i) p(i) log p(i)] amount of information is based on the probabilities in the alphabet set [2, 51, 58]. It is found by calculating the expected value, which is maximized for the equiprobable case [2, 5, 51].

The equiprobable case represents the case of maximum uncertainty (H) with respect to the message set. All messages are equally likely [51].

The average amount of information in a message is related to the uncertainty (H) with respect to the message set [a, the alphabet, size (number of messages) and probability (frequency of transmission)]. This is reduced for a set of messages that includes redundancy (predictability). This is shown by comparing Figures 82 and 86.

The messages of Figure 82 exhibit redundancy (predictability). This is indicated by the nonequiprobable (nonequal n's, 1/n(i)] of the message set (p(i) <> p(j) for all (i,j), hence v(i) = log p(i) <> v(j) = log p(j) for the set (i <> j)).

The introduction of redundancy, predictability, reduces the uncertainty (average H) with respect to the message set (a). One can predict, with some success, the messages sent. This is not true of the equiprobable (equal n's, 1/n(i)) case. This is illustrated in Figure 88.

One can, in message set A) p(A) = 1/2, p(B) = 1/4, . . .) predict the message sent (A, the most probable message) given no other information about the message (complete uncertainty about the message sent other than the probability or frequency of occurrence of the different message values). One is correct fifty percent of the time [5, 51]. This is not true in message set B.

message	probability	log p	p log p	$-$p log p (H)
A	1/4	-2	$-1/2$	1/2
B	1/4	-2	$-1/2$	1/2
C	1/4	-2	$-1/2$	1/2
D	1/4	-2	$-1/2$	1/2
			Average H:	2

FIGURE 86

$$\text{Sum(i) } p(i) \times v(i) =$$
$$\text{Sum(i) } p(i) \times (\log (1/n)) =$$
$$\text{Sum(i) } (1/n) \times (\log (1/n)) =$$
$$n(1/n) \times (\log (1/n)) =$$
$$(\log (1/n))$$

FIGURE 87

Message set B exhibits no redundancy (predictability). One will, given no other information about the message sent (other than the probabilities), be unable to guess with success greater than $1/n$ the identity of the message sent.

The calculation of the amount of information (H') is with respect to the uncertainty (H) of the message sent. This is maximum for the equally likely case [2, 5, 51].

The Huffman code minimizes the number of bits sent per message sent (average L, the average length of the code size) with respect to the average number of bits (binary code) sent per message (information, in the message). This is illustrated in Figures 81 and 82 by the congruence of the average amount of information (H or H', H = H') in the set (ensemble) of messages and the average code length (L, L = H, in this case).

The Huffman code optimizes the average length of the transmitted code. This is indicated in Figures 82 and 81 by the average H (average amount of information per message) (in bits) and the average code size (length, in bits). The code cannot have fewer bits (physical) than information (conceptual or logical). It can, however, be minimal [comparison of Figures 81 and 82, average code length, L, $\geq$ average amount of information, H, per message, = in this, the optimal (optimal = "="), case]. It is impossible for a code length (average length per message value sent) to be less than the average amount of information (in bits) carried per message [2, 5, 51]. It can, however, approach this limit arbitrarily closely. This is shown in Figure 89.

The average number of bits sent (8.5 ninths) is less than 1. The average code length (17/9) is per code pair. Each code pair contains two (independent) messages. The message (code) is comprised of two or more (independent) messages (information). The use of such schemes ("block" or "pair"/tuple encoding) is referred to as an "extension" [2]. The extension increases the variability (variance) in the codes, which increases the efficiency of the variable length (Huffman) code [2]. This is the basis of claiming that the Huffman code can approach the information threshold (lower threshold on the code length) arbitrarily closely for arbitrarily long codes (again, the likelihood of error increases with arbitrarily long codes,

	A			B
A	1/2		A	1/4
B	1/4		B	1/4
C	1/8		C	1/4
D	1/8		D	1/4

FIGURE 88

message	p	fixed length code
A	1/3	0
B	2/3	1

(a)

message	p	code	code length (1)	p × 1
AA	1/9	111	3	3/9
AB	2/9	110	3	6/9
BA	2/9	10	2	4/9
BB	4/9	0	1	4/9
	9/9	Average length per code pair		17/9

Average code per character (letter) transmitted $(17/9)/2 = 8.5/9 < 1$

FIGURE 89

requiring retransmission of the message (if they cannot be corrected), hence reducing the efficiency obtained in the encoding process; a trade off occurs).

The treatment of Hamming and Huffman codes completes the theory of error detection and correction with respect to the codes derived from information theory [5, 51, 53, 59]. Other codes (Shannon/Fano) exist [2] and are derived from information theory [60—62]. The Hamming (effectiveness, i.e., getting the message across) and Huffman (efficiency, minimizing the number of bits sent per message value sent) codes are more well-known and more closely tied to the information theory [2, 5, 51, 60, 63—65].

The Hamming code refers to code protection [redundancy or safety (detection/correction)] in getting the message across; the syndrome indicates whether the message is correct or not and corrects if not (single error). The Huffman code refers to the efficiency [of code length per information (bit) carried] with respect to the codes derived from information theory [2, 5, 51, 53]. The code of Figure 89 is derived as shown in Figure 90.

The arrangement of the code values reflects the decreasing order of probability of the code "pairs" (extension, of two). The tree is then built and the codes read off.

Information theory is the mathematical theory of communication [66, 67]. It is based on the calculation Sum(i) (p(i) log (pi)) or Sum(i) (−p(i) log(p(i)) for the discrete (binary) case [2, 5, 51, 53, 55, 56].

OTHER CODES

Other codes, e.g., the Gray code and the 2-of-5 code [41, 42] have been developed both for error detection and correction, as well as to suit the

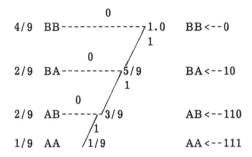

FIGURE 90

physical characteristics of the device (e.g., the Gray code). The Gray code is used to minimize the number of errors in reading (or writing) the disk. It is a code in which only 1 bit value changes per incrementation (of the number or the physical space). This is shown in Figure 91.

The Gray code represents consecutive "numbers" (sectors or other physical unit identifier) by codes that differ in one position, columns 1 and 2. The code "moves" from (2) (Gray value two) to three (3) (Gray value three) by moving from 0011 to 0010. Similarly for the other codes: the distance (Hamming distance) from code n to code n + 1 or n − 1 is always (constant) one. The corresponding binary code is given to the right of the Gray code in both decimal and hexadecimal for purposes of comparison.

The Gray code is translated into a binary value by the calculation:

Bit N(1) = Bit N(0) + Bit (N + 1)(1)

where the '+' is the exclusive OR [42]. The subscripts, Bit N(1), Bit N(0), Bit (N + 1)(1), refer to the condition/state of the code (values) before (0)

Code	Gray	Binary	
		Dec	Hex
0000	(0)	(0)	(0)
0001	(1)	(1)	(1)
0011	(2)	(3)	(3)
0010	(3)	(2)	(2)
0110	(4)	(6)	(6)
0111	(5)	(7)	(7)
0101	(6)	(5)	(5)
0100	(7)	(4)	(4)
1100	(8)	(12)	(C)
1101	(9)	(13)	(D)
1111	(10)	(15)	(F)
1110	(11)	(14)	(E)
1010	(12)	(10)	(A)
1011	(13)	(11)	(B)
1001	(14)	(9)	(9)
1000	(15)	(8)	(8)

FIGURE 91

```
ABCD        ABCD        ABCD        ABCD
0011 (3)    0110 (6)    0101 (5)    1100 (12)    (Gray)
0010 (2)    0100 (4)    0110 (6)    1000 (8)     (binary)
```

FIGURE 92

and after conversion (1). The conversion proceeds left to right, with bit N(1) = bit N(0) for the leftmost (most significant) bit. This is illustrated in Figure 92, where the binary interpretation of the Gray codes is given.

The leftmost bit of the binary code (bottom row) after the conversion (bit A in the example) [42] equals the Gray code value (top row) before conversion:

Bit N(1) = Bit N(0)

where Bit N(1) indicates Bit N after (1) the conversion (the result) and Bit N(0) equals the input (Gray code) to the conversion (Bit N(1) <-- Bit N(0)). This is 0 for the leftmost bit of the conversion (3-->2, Fig. 92), or binary = Gray, for the most significant bit (MSB). The next most significant bit [Bit (N − 1) in an n-bit code] is set by the XOR of A (the n-th or MS bit) (after conversion, i.e., the binary) with the (n-th − 1) bit before (Gray code) conversion. This is 0 (top row, second bit from the left, Gray code) XOR 0 (bottom row, leftmost bit (after conversion), binary code) for the conversion (3) to (2) (Gray to binary). The process proceeds left to right:

```
0   0   1   1
|  /|  /|  /|
v/ v/ v/ v
0   0   1   0
```

for 3(Gray) to 2 (binary) ((3), top row, to (2), bottom row, in the diagram). This is illustrated in Figure 93.

Bit A is set by the Gray code alone (a). Bit B is set by the Gray code (B or Bit B(0)) XOR the binary (Bit N + 1 (1) or A for bit B). This process continues according to the formula Bit N(1) = Bit N(0) o Bit (N + 1)(1) (e) or Bit N(1) = Bit (N + 1)(1) o Bit (N)(0).

The Gray code is devised to avoid electronic (timing) errors in reading addresses (0000, 0001, 0011, . . . , 1000, for a 16-value, 2**4-bit code). The 2-out-of-5 code is a code for error detection. This is illsutrated in Figure 94 [2].

The 2-out-of-5 code is a representation in which (exactly) two bits are set ("on") in each code value, Figure 94. An error is detected by more or less than two bits on [14].

There are ten possible (5 things taken 2 at a time) values in the 2-out-of-5 code (0−9). The digit 0 (ten) is represented by 4 + 7 (Fig. 94 [2]). All other codes are represented by their combination (addition) in the number (0, 1, 2, 4, 7) system [2].

The codes represented here are representative of the codes used.

```
A B C D
1 1 0 0 (12) Bit A(1) = Bit A(0)    (0 = before,
1                                     1 = after)
```

(a)

```
A B C D
1 1 0 0        Bit B(1) = Bit B(0) o Bit A(1) (o = XOR)
1 0
```

(b)

```
A B C D
1 1 0 0        Bit C(1) = Bit C(0) o Bit B(1)
1 0 0
```

(c)

```
A B C D
1 1 0 0 (12) Bit D(1) = Bit D(0) o Bit C(1)
1 0 0 0 (8)
```

(d)

```
              Bit N(1) = Bit N(0) o Bit (N + 1)(1)
```

(e)

FIGURE 93

SUMMARY

The theory of error detection and error correction is one of creating codes that detect and correct errors in transmission [2, 5, 18, 44, 51, 59]. These are errors caused by disturbances in a transmission line [13] or equipment malfunction (e.g., in a computer or a mechanical system). The errors are detected or corrected by adding redundancy (parity checks or parity check characters (CRC, BCC)) to the messages sent (information bits). The information bits are derived from the messages to be sent (the alphabet),

0 1 2 4 7	Decimal	Bits set
1 1 0 0 0	1	0 + 1
1 0 1 0 0	2	0 + 2
0 1 1 0 0	3	1 + 2
1 0 0 1 0	4	0 + 4
0 1 0 1 0	5	1 + 4
0 0 1 1 0	6	2 + 4
1 0 0 0 1	7	0 + 7
0 1 0 0 1	8	1 + 7
0 0 1 0 1	9	2 + 7
0 0 0 1 1	0	4 + 7

FIGURE 94

fixed length, e.g., Hamming codes or cyclic redundancy check (or ASCII), or variable length, e.g., Huffman and Morse codes.

The errors occur at random (independent errors) or dependently (bursts). Distinct codes are developed for each type [2, 18, 68].

The redundancy in the code (messages) (transmission) reduces the number of information (meaningful) bits that may be sent, but it increases the likelihood that the message will be received correctly or be recognized as incorrect if an error occurs (and corrected or retransmission requested). The redundancy is itself meaningful; it is a message about the message rather than a message about another domain [the alphabet], to the receiver [m(S), m(R)].

REFERENCES

1. F. Pratt, *Secret and Urgent*, Bobbs-Merril Co., Indianapolis, 1939.
2. R. W. Hamming, *Coding and Information Theory*, Prentice-Hall, Inc., Englewood Cliffs, NJ, 1980.
3. J. Singh, *Great Ideas in Information Theory, Language and Cybernetics*, Dover Publications, Inc., New York, 1966.
4. H. H. Clark and E. V. Clark, *Psychology and Language: An Introduction to Linguistics*, Harcourt Brace Jovanovich, New York, 1977.
5. J. R. Pierce, *Symbols, Signals and Noise*, Harper and Row, New York, 1961.
6. C. E. Shannon, "A Mathematical Theory of Communication," *Bell System Techn. J.*, 27(3), 379–423 (1948).
7. C. E. Shannon, A Mathematical Theory of Communication (Continued), *Bell System Techn. J.*, 27(4), 623–656 (1948).
8. B. Bols and A. Wayne, *Number Systems*, American Book Company, New York, 1972.
9. D. L. Harnett, *Introduction to Statistical Methods*, Addison-Wesley Publishing Company, Reading, MA, 1975.
10. H. Bierman, C. P. Bonini, and W. H. Hausman, *Quantitative Analysis for Business Decisions*, Richard D. Irwin, Inc., Homewood, IL, 1973.
11. J. Singh, *Great Ideas in Operations Research*, Dover Publications, Inc., New York, 1972.
12. T. Housley, *Data Communications and Teleprocessing Systems*, Prentice-Hall, Inc., Englewood Cliffs, NJ, 1979.
13. J. E. McNamara, *Technical Aspects of Data Communication*, Digital Press, Bedford, MA, 1977.
14. J. Martin, *Teleprocessing Network Organization*, Prentice-Hall, Inc., Englewood Cliffs, NJ, 1970.
15. S. Baase, *Vax-11 Assembly Language Programming*, Prentice-Hall, Inc., Englewood Cliffs, NJ, 1983.
16. W. D. Skees, *Computer Software for Data Communications*, Lifetime Learning Publications, Belmont, CA, 1981.
17. H. M. Levy and R. H. Eckhouse, *Computer Programming and Architecture: the VAX-11*, Digital Press, Bedford, MA, 1980.
18. W. W. Peterson, and D. T. Brown, "Cyclic Codes for Error Detection," *Proc. IRE*, 49(1), 228–235 (1961).
19. R. R. Flynn, *An Introduction to Information Science*, Marcel Dekker, Inc., New York, 1987.

20. *British Books in Print 1987: The Reference Catalogue of Current Literature in Four Volumes, Volume 1, Author, Title & Subject Index A—D,* J. Whitaker & Sons, LTD., London, 1987.

21. J. G. Burch, F. R. Strater, and G. Grudnitski, *Information Systems: Theory and Practice,* John Wiley & Sons, New York, 1983.

22. C. H. Denbow and V. Goedicke, *Foundations of Mathematics,* Harper & Brothers Publishers, New York, 1959.

23. *Books in Print 1988—89,* Volume 1, *Authors A—F,* R. R. Bowker, New York, 1988.

24. M. G. Lane, *Data Communications Software Design,* Boyd & Fraser, Boston, 1985.

25. M. J. Coe, "Mechanization of Library Procedures in the Medium-sized Medical Library: X. Uniqueness of Compression Codes for Bibliographic Retrieval," *Bull. Med. Lib. Assoc.,* 58(4), 587—597 (1970).

26. K. G. Roughton and D. A. Tyckoson, "Browsing with Sound: Sound-Based Codes and Automated Authority Control," *Inform. Technol. Libr.,* 4(2), 130—136 (1985).

27. R. H. Greenfield, "An Experiment to Measure the Performance of Phonetic Key Compression Retrieval Schemes," *Meth. Inform. Med.,* 16(4), 230—233 (1977).

28. B. Perelman and L. Calmus, "Soundex or S532," *Ashton-Tate Q.,* April/May/June, 7—10 (1982).

29. D. E. Knuth, *The Art of Computer Programming, Volume 1, Fundamental Algorithms,* Addison-Wesley, Reading, MA, 1969.

30. D. E. Knuth, *The Art of Computer Programming, Volume 3, Sorting and Searching,* Addison-Wesley, Reading, MA, 1973.

31. E. J. McCormick, *Human Factors in Engineering and Design,* McGraw-Hill, New York, 1976.

32. C. Cherry, *On Human Communication,* MIT Press, Cambridge, MA, 1966.

33. *Progressive Indexing and Filing,* Management Controls Division, Remington Rand Inc., New York, 1950.

34. "Soundex: Foolproof Filing System for Finding any Name in the File," Remington Rand Brochure LVB 809, see Ref. *21.*

35. H. P. Van Cott and R. G. Kincaid (Eds.), *Human Engineering Guide to Equipment Design,* American Institutes for Research (Sponsored by Joint Army-Navy-Air Force Steering Committee, Washington, D.C., 1972), McGraw-Hill, New York, 1963.

36. W. W. Peterson, *Error-Correcting Codes,* MIT Press, Cambridge, MA, 1961.

37. W. W. Peterson and E. J. Weldon, Jr., *Error-Correcting Codes,* MIT Press, Cambridge, MA, 1972.

38. M. P. Dolciani, (and others), *Algebra: Structure and Method,* Houghton Mifflin, Boston, 1976.

39. A. S. Tanenbaum, *Computer Networks,* Prentice-Hall, Englewood Cliffs, NJ, 1988.

40. W. Stallings, *Data and Computer Communications,* Macmillan, New York, 1988.

41. M. E. Sloan, *Computer Hardware Organization,* Science Research Associates, Inc., Chicago, 1983.

42. J. L. Hughes, Design Engineer, *Computer Lab Workbook,* Digital Equipment Corporation, Maynard, MA, 1968.

43a. W. C. Gear, *Computer Organization and Programming*, McGraw-Hill, New York, 1969.

43b. E. Prange, "Cyclic Error-Correcting Codes in Two Symbols," Air Force Cambridge Research Center, Bedford, MA, Tech. Note AFCRC-TN-57-103, September, 1957.

44. E. Prange, "Some Cyclic Error-Correcting Codes with Simple Decoding Algorithms," Air Force Cambridge Research Center, Bedford, MA, Tech. Note AFCRC-TN-58-156, April, 1958.

45. E. Prange, "The Role of Coset Equivalence in the Analysis of Decoding of Group Codes," Air Force Cambridge Research Center, Bedford, MA, Tech. Note AFCRC-TN-59-164, June, 1959.

46. T. G. Lewis and M. Z. Smith, *Applying Data Structures*, Houghton Mifflin, Boston, 1976.

47. G. Wiederhold, *File Organization for Database Design*, McGraw-Hill, New York, 1987.

48. A. Ralston, *Introduction to Programming and Computer Science*, McGraw-Hill, New York, 1971.

49. A. T. Berztiss, *Data Structures: Theory and Practice*, Academic Press, New York, 1971.

50. A. M. Tenenbaum and M. J. Augenstein, *Data Structures Using Pascal*, Prentice-Hall, Inc., Englewood Cliffs, NJ, 1981.

51. C. E. Shannon and W. Weaver, *The Mathematical Theory of Communication*, University of Illinois Press, Urbana, IL, 1972.

52. C. E. Shannon, "The Mathematical Theory of Communciation," *Bell System Techn. J.*, July, October, 1948, as reprinted in C. E. Shannon, and W. Weaver, *The Mathematical Theory of Communication*, University of Illinois Press, Urbana, IL, 1972 (reprint of the 1949 edition).

53. D. A. Huffman, "A Method for the Construction of Minimum-Redundancy Codes," *Proc. IRE*, 40(9), 1098−1101 (1952).

54. H. Nyquist, "Certain Factors Affecting Telegraph Speed," *Bell System Tech. J.*, 3(2), 324−346 (1924).

55. H. Nyquist, "Certain Topics In Telegraph Transmission Theory," *AIEE Trans.*, 7(2), 617−644 (1928).

56. R. V. L. Hartley, "Transmission of Information," *Bell System Tech. J.*, 7(3), 535−563 (1928).

57. R. R. Flynn, in preparation, 1989.

58. C. E. Shannon, "Prediction and Entropy of Printed English," in *Bell System Tech. J.*, 30(1), 50−64 (1951).

59. R. W. Hamming, "Error Detecting and Error Correcting Codes," *Bell System Tech. J.*, 29(2) (1950).

60. R. M. Fano, *Transmission of Information: A Statistical Theory of Communications*, MIT Press, Cambridge, 1961.

61. R. M. Fano, "A Heuristic Discussion for Probabilistic Decoding," *IEEE Trans.*, IT-9, 64−74 (1963).

62. B. M. Oliver, "Efficient Coding," *Bell System Tech. J.*, 31(4), 724−750 (1952).

63. C. E. Shannon, "General Treatment of the Problem of Coding," *IRE*, *P.G. Inform. Theory*, 1, 102−104 (1953).

64. E. R. Berlekamp, *Algebraic Coding Theory*, McGraw-Hill, New York, 1968.

65. E. R. Berlekamp (Ed.), *Key Papers in the Development of Coding Theory*, Institute of Electrical and Electronics Engineers, New York, 1974.

66. C. E. Shannon, "Communication Theory—Exposition of Fundamentals," *IRE, P.G. Inform. Theory, 1*, 44—47 (1953).

67. E. C. Cherry, "A History of the Theory of Information," *IRE, P.G. Information Theory, 1*, 22—43 (1953).

68. C. M. Melas, "A New Group of Codes for Correction for Dependent Errors in Data Transmission," *IBM J. Res. Dev., 4*(1), 58—65 (1960).

ROGER R. FLYNN

EVALUATION OF SOFTWARE — See Application Software: Evaluation and Selection

EVALUATION OF SOFTWARE: MICROSOFT WORD VERSION 4.0

INTRODUCTION

Evaluating top-of-the-line word processing programs has never been an easy task. Once beyond the basics of editing and printing documents, the best programs provide so many different features that it is difficult to do an evaluation that adequately compares and contrasts their strengths and weaknesses versus their competition's. The reviewer's job has unfortunately become increasingly difficult as the programs have become more complex and provide more power to the user.

Microsoft *Word* Version 4.0 typifies this problem. The latest version of Microsoft's word processor represents a major improvement in both speed and functionality. Several of the weaknesses exhibited in previous versions of this product have been corrected and many new and powerful features have been added. Microsoft *Word* Version 4.0 further blurs the distinction between word processing and desktop publishing programs (and consequently makes the reviewer's job even more difficult.) *Word* provides enough power for the vast majority of projects for which most people buy a desktop publishing program while still retaining the basic straightforwardness of a word processor.

MICROSOFT WORD: THE WORD PROCESSOR

Microsoft *Word* Version 4.0 is a big program. It requires a minimum of 320K of memory and DOS 3.1 or higher. Although the program can be used on a machine with two floppy disk drives, it works best on a computer equipped with a hard disk. Microsoft *Word* supports all of the common graphics standards, including IBM's new VGA standard for the PS/2 series. As with other Microsoft programs, *Word* supports the Microsoft Mouse. Virtually all printers, including Postscript output devices are supported.

From version 1.0 on, Microsoft *Word* has approached word processing in a manner different from the other programs in its class. *Word* looks at the printed word from the point of view of the printed page. It is set up more like a typesetter than a word processor. *Word's* competitors view the printed word as a part of a long character string that will ultimately be formatted and printed according to some set of formatting instructions. Formatting, instead of being an integral part of the process of writing, is treated almost as an afterthought that can be dealt with after the document has been created. This very important difference in approach makes *Word* a different breed of word processor and has, for the longest time, been a contributing factor to many reviews (including mine) that were critical of the product. *Word* Version 4.0 represents a major step forward in some areas, but this reviewer is still less than enthusiastic about it. There are still some things that make the product a less than perfect choice for a word processor.

INSTALLING *WORD*

Microsoft *Word* Version 4.0 maintains the long tradition of excellence in this area. The installation process is straightforward, well explained, and well prompted. No hidden traps were found for the user to stumble into and there was no difficulty in getting started, even for real beginners.

LEARNING *WORD*

One outstanding feature of Microsoft *Word* is the Computer-Based Training (CBT) program that is provided with the product. Two versions are available: one for use with systems equipped with the Microsoft Mouse, and one for those systems that operate without a rodent. The training program is excellent, well thought out, and can take a person from a no-knowledge state to a level of acceptable proficiency with the product.

For those who have need for an office word processing system, Microsoft *Word's* CBT program can be personalized for each student and is complete enough for an office training program. As subjects are covered, a check mark is placed in the program menu, so that a training supervisor can determine exactly how far a person has gone in their studies.

Microsoft's CBT is an outstanding training program, but its usefulness is doubled because it also serves as the ultimate context-sensitive help utility when using the program. The operator with a question can actually summon the appropriate section of the CBT program, run through a practice session (if available for that particular subject), and then go back to where he or she was in the program and continue with his or her work. This provides immediate on-line access to one of the most complete help facilities that this reviewer has ever seen for any program.

The manuals (five in number: the Reference, Printer, User's Guide, Pocket Guide, and Sampler) reflect a lot of work and are a distinct improvement over the previous documentation. Some sections, however, are not too well organized and entailed looking through the index several times to find out what was wanted. There are several well-reviewed books available from Microsoft Press that can further supplement the manuals if needed.

EDITING WITH MICROSOFT *WORD*

From the beginning, Microsoft *Word* has been different from every other word processing program on the market. *Word* Version 4.0 continues this tradition, although Microsoft has finally listened to many of the complaints about the earlier versions and has improved many areas of the program to make it easier (or at least more direct) to use.

Up until Version 4.0, the keyboard user suffered greatly with the product while the mouse user enjoyed easier editing. Microsoft has addressed this problem quite well. Many "short-cuts" have been provided that allow the user to escape from the time-consuming menu structure on which the product is based.

Microsoft *Word* is now more customizable than ever. The user can decide what level of formatting information to include on the screen, whether or not the menu should be on the screen at all times or hidden until called with the escape key, what the screen colors should be, whether or not to have the double line border around the editing area of the screen, and whether or not to have line numbers show on the screen. The cursor speed can now be controlled, thus ending the monospeed cursor (and backspace delete) blues. The fastest speed setting is too fast to control: this reviewer settled for speed 6 out of a possible 9. Vertical scrolling has been improved tremendously and is now 140% faster than it was in version 3.0.

The OPTIONS menu also includes choices for date and time formats, decimal character, bell, printer display, linedraw character set, summary sheet, type of display (text or graphics), and measurements for tab and margin settings.

With everything turned off, Microsoft *Word* presents the type of spartan exterior that is favored by several other word processors. It is a refreshing concept and I found this mode quickly adaptable for all my work. The text mode is also adaptable as the mode of choice in that the program responds much more quickly in this mode than it does in the graphic mode. Unlike earlier versions which, once loaded, remained in the loaded mode, Microsoft *Word* Version 4.0 allows the user to switch back and forth between the two modes using the ALT-F9 key combination. This feature is useful for highly formatted text work when a WYSIWYG representation is necessary.

While on the subject of WYSIWYG, *Word* has an annoying habit of showing double-spaced text on the screen. The effect of this is to reduce by half the number of lines of text that can be seen at any one time. It should be enough to know that text will be printed out double spaced, but it is normally not necessary to see it on the screen. Microsoft opted for output realism rather than ease of editing. This is a step in the wrong direction.

It seems to take a long time to get used to working with *Word*. Even the basic terminology is different and, although Microsoft now includes a prompt line on line 24 of the screen, giving the user some information about the selection currently highlighted (although it quickly became tiresome to have this line simply state "Select Option" instead of telling more about the function selected). More conventional terminology would have been preferable. For instance, scrap is actually a text buffer, select means define, extended select means define, and best of all, transfer load means load. The naming conventions and menu structure predate *Word*. A similar structure was recalled with Microsoft's Multiplan; it was hoped that they would finally give this up, and do things in a more direct and conventional fashion.

Once the user is familiar with the terminology and the sometimes nonintuitive keystroke combinations for the menus and finally, the new and improved shortcut key combinations, *Word* works much better than the previous versions. The program, as advertised, is much faster in all respects tested than its predecessors, and feels crisp even when being used on an old PC-1, something that could never have been said of the earlier versions. Text searching capability is 50% faster and replacing text is a whopping 230% faster than it was with Version 3.0. The program is finally in the same ballpark as other top-of-the-line programs on these standard measurements of performance.

Word still runs into memory problems which require that a file be saved before continuing when performing repeated search and replace operations with many replaces. This should not have happened and is a flaw that has not been eliminated from the program.

If used all the time one would get used to the program's "cursor." *Word* has a "text select block" that, in normal operation, is only one character wide. It is a block and does not blink; another example of a visible difference in this product compared with other word processors.

Once users learn to feel at ease with the method(s) of text selection in *Word*, block operations become simple; just delete to a buffer (scrap) using the Delete key and then insert the deleted text using the Insert key (the Insert key does not toggle back and forth between insert and overtype, the F5 key does that) in as many places as wanted. Different again, but not difficult.

Word really shines in its use of windows. It is one of the few products that allows a single copy of a file to open in two or more windows at the same time. In certain circumstances, this is a real advantage over the more conventional method of having two or more copies of the same document open in different windows. Changes made in one window are shown when that text scrolls through the second (or third) window.

The delete key in *Word* Version 4.0 still writes even a single character to the scrap (buffer) and the user loses keystrokes when the key is hit several times in rapid succession. This is unacceptable and represents a serious flaw in the program. It would be preferable for Microsoft to put in a keyboard buffer that would trap these keystrokes to let the proper number of deletions take place.

Word has finally added line numbers to its abilities, a feature missing from previous versions. With this addition, it is hoped that Microsoft will speed up the counter. It takes ten seconds for the line counter to move after the cursor is moved up a line, while at the end of a 4000 word single-spaced document. The cursor takes 25 seconds to move when the file is double spaced. Obviously, the program goes back to the beginning of the file and recalculates the current line number. This is much too long and needs to be adjusted.

TEXT ENHANCEMENTS WITH *WORD*

Text enhancements are included in the <F>ormat <C>haracter submenu and are applied to the text that has been selected (defined) before entering the menu. Text enhancements include the normal enhancements such as bold underline, superscript, and subscript, but also small caps, strike-through, double underline, and something called "hidden" text, which is text (or codes) that do not show or print unless specified.

For some reason, font and pitch are specified in this menu. This can create problems when the user decides that the document will finally be printed in 10 point Times Roman, even though it was originally set in 12 point Courier. The user must "select" the entire document, change the font and point settings in the Format character submenu, and apply this change to the whole file. Unfortunately, when this is done, all other character formatting will be overwritten and lost. All underlining, bold-facing, superscripts, etc., will be wiped out. While this is not a fatal flaw in the program, it is a truly annoying limitation that should not exist in a program of this caliber.

FORMATTING WITH *WORD*

Microsoft *Word's* forte is formatting. You can specify your document layout in inches, centimeters, points, or with either a 10 or 12 pitch (character per line) measurement. Once you have decided on your measuring standard, you are faced with a minimum of two format menus to address. The first of these is the <F>ormat <P>aragraph submenu that formats left/right/center/ justified, left and right indents, first line indent, line spacing, lines before and after the paragraph, and whether or not the paragraph should be kept together with the one preceding or following it, as well as something called "side by side," which allows you to set up such things as dramatic scripts in *Word*.

The second requisite format is the Format division submenu which itself has four submenus to deal with margins, page numbers, layout, and line numbers. A "Division" to *Word* is a discrete portion of a document that has a specific format. Any number of divisions can be included in a document each with completely different formats.

There are other format menus as well for such things as tabs, borders, running heads, and footnotes. It all allows for exquisitely intricate formats to be designed and applied to text.

Formats can be named and saved to the Gallery and can be applied against selected text. While all of this seems cumbersome, once defined and saved, the division formats stand ready to be applied to any text in any file. In this fashion, document formatting becomes easy. Microsoft also supplies a wealth of predefined styles from which to choose. In the end, there is not too much that cannot be done with *Word* when it comes to formatting.

One major improvement in *Word* 4.0 is that formats can now be searched and replaced. The user can actually go through a file and change formatting information globally. This feature, new in 4.0, will save much time and heartache for users who have to change document formats often.

If text is "justified" (one of the four options in the Format Paragraph submenu: left, centered, right, justified) it will show up justified on the screen as well. This is more of an annoyance than a help, and it is hoped that there will be some way of turning this feature off. Care must also be taken when working with justified text: In one instance, a long, unhyphenated word in one test document was summarily split to accommodate the justification algorithm. This should never have happened, but "ringdingthing" (one word) ended up on two lines with "ringd" on the first line and "ingthing" on the next line.

Word, like other top-of-the-line word processing programs, places interword microspaces to perform text justification, but does not allow for any pad microspaces to be placed between characters as well when there is a lot of "white space." Consequently, the pad spacing between words is sometimes more noticeable than need be.

PRINTING WITH *WORD*

Word is one of the few programs that still carries a repagination function (hidden away in the <P>rint menu.) Why a program as up to date as Microsoft *Word* still does not paginate dynamically is something of a mystery. The only advantage is that it allows the user to confirm the page breaks

when it repaginates and to make corrections where needed. This is no
advantage at all. If a user wanted to do this he or she could simply place
forced page breaks wherever needed just prior to printing the file. With
Word the user must go in and place them at repagination and, if there is
need to change them later, the breaks must first be removed and the location of the new page break confirmed (or moved to the new line). This is
unnecessary work.

This reviewer wishes Microsoft would allow the user to print in the
background without having to go through the process of preparing a document for the print queue, and then print that disk file (separate from the
active file) using the DOS background printing function. Not only is this
a circuitous path, it also makes *Word* run slower while in effect.

EXTENDED *WORD*

Through the years, Microsoft has added more and more features to their
word processing product. *Word* is now top heavy with features, but Microsoft has done a good job of keeping most of them out of the way of the user
in normal operation. The author is not a fan of the multilevel menu structure that Microsoft uses to present all of these features to the operator,
but the company has finally provided keyboard shortcuts for the most common commands so my complaints are somewhat muted. Still, the program
gets in the way of my writing more than I would like it to. A first class
program should not do this.

Many new features have been added to the already impressive list of
Microsoft *Word* and, depending on users' needs, they may or may not be
useful. The new features for Version 4.0 include the following:

Document Summary Sheet. The user now has the option of attaching
a document summary sheet to each file created. The summary sheet lists
information about the document, such as the date of creation and revision,
the author and operator names, key words, and comments. This feature
will be welcomed by people who need to keep track of hundreds of documents
on their disk.

Macros. *Word* has finally included keyboard and command macros with
their product. Users can now record keystrokes and commands, assign
them to a special key combination, and execute them inside of documents.
This single improvement makes a world of difference in any repetitive typing
situation.

Spreadsheet Linking. It is now much easier to move information from
most popular spreadsheet programs into word documents.

Lines and Boxes. Microsoft *Word* Version 4.0 has the best line and
box drawing ability of any word processing program currently available.
Boxes, once defined, are continually resized when words are inserted to or
deleted from the text that is boxed. Boxes can even be drawn properly
around proportionally spaced text. Line drawing can make a significant
difference in the readability of certain types of text, and this is a welcome
addition to the product.

Redlining. *Word* now supports redlining and revision marking. For
lawyers working on contracts and briefs, and for documents that make the
round to a group of people for review and comments, this feature is a
welcome additon. *Word* will also put line numbers in your document at print
time, excellent for certain types of legal briefs and computer program listings.

In addition to these new features, Microsoft has included many improvements to the latest releases. Improvements have been made in outlining, indexing, table of contents generation, and math capabilities.

Microsoft *Word* comes with its own 130,000 word-spelling checker and a 220,000 word thesaurus. Although users can now check the spelling of less than a full document, most people will use the spelling checker for complete documents, not just a single word. Even though *Word* has been speeded up in other areas, the spelling checker still pokes along at its own pace. Spell checking is slow, with most word searches for unrecognized words in a file taking from three to five seconds each. Corrections are not shown in the small text box in the spelling checker, and line breaks in this text box have nothing to do with word breaks. Words are split between lines. Something this elementary should not happen in a spelling checker of this level of sophistication. There is no way of editing text while users are in the spelling checker; they must first quit the checker, wait for the corrections made to date to take effect [45 seconds for a 3500-word document (hard disk system)], then find their place in the newly corrected document, make the editing changes, and then go back through the whole process of getting back to the spelling checker. When a word correction is not in the dictionary, a prompt signals for a "Y" to make a new change or an "N" to accept the change made that is not in the dictionary. This is a backward process. One surprise for the user when using the spell checker: page breaks are lost when the corrections are made to the document. If a user has laboriously put in special page breaks, he or she will have to go back and do it all over again. Any product that eliminates someone's hard work is really not going to bring raves. A change should be made in this "feature."

When Microsoft *Word* is measured against some of the desktop publishing packages on the market, it makes a favorable impression. There are only a few things that a desktop publishing package such as Aldus Pagemaker or Xerox Ventura can do that *Word* cannot. Automatic leading and kerning and on-screen insertion and manipulation of graphics and art are probably the most important advantages of desktop publishing packages. A new product from Microsoft, Pageview, has eliminated most of these advantages. With *Word* and Pageview, the user now has the ability to show a representation of what the finished page will look like on the screen. With this new product, operating independently from *Word*, but using *Word* files, users have virtually all of the capabilities of some of the best desktop publishing packages. In addition, they have the ability to do all document creation and editing inside of a word processor (*Word*) instead of inside a desktop publishing program. Anyone who has tried to edit text in a desktop publisher will appreciate this fact. Both Ventura and Pagemaker have import utilities, but they change the file formats and make further editing difficult inside of the original word processing program. When you exit Pageview, you are left with a modified but still perfectly good *Word* file that retains all formatting information in *Word* format.

MICROSOFT *WORD* AND THE MOUSE

Word was designed with the Microsoft Mouse in mind and, when using *Word* with a mouse, activities such as selecting (defining) text become much easier. The author has a personal dislike for the mouse, even though it is essential for some of my own activities but, even with this personal bias, *Word* really does make excellent use of the device. If I were ever to decide to use Microsoft *Word* extensively, I would finally succumb to the mouse.

SUMMARY *WORD*

Before summarizing *Word* it is important to state that I have also written reviews of Microsoft *Word* versions 1.0, 1.1, 2.0, and 3.0. My reviews have never been enthusiastic. In fact, I have severely criticized many aspects of the different versions of the program. I still do not like *Word*, but I must say that many of the shortcomings of earlier versions of the program have been addressed, and *Word* Version 4.0 is a much better product for it. Still, I am uncomfortable with the basic approach that Microsoft takes to word processing, finding *Word Perfect's* and *XyWrite's* approaches much more direct and natural for the user. *Word* just seems to get too much in the way when I am writing. I do not like the menu structure, nor for that matter, the way that certain functions are laid out. If I were a new user, and knew no other program, I am certain that I would grow to love *Word* and find that the approach was totally natural. However, I do not believe that you should have to "work" at loving a program. You should be able to appreciate it from the beginning, even when it is different from other programs. I do not feel that way about *Word*, even with all the changes and improvements that have been made in the program.

MALCOLM C. RUBEL

Printed and bound by CPI Group (UK) Ltd, Croydon, CR0 4YY

24/10/2024

01778291-0020